Jennie

JENNIE

The Life of Lady Randolph Churchill

Anita Leslie

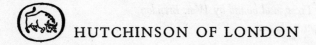 HUTCHINSON OF LONDON

Hutchinson & Co (Publishers) Ltd
178–202 Great Portland Street, London W1

London Melbourne, Sydney, Auckland,
Bombay, Toronto, Johannesburg, New York

First published June 1969

Second impression before publication

Third impression July 1969

DA
565
C6
L43
1969
cop.2

This book has been set in Bembo,
printed in Great Britain on Antique Wove paper
by Anchor Press, and bound by Wm. Brendon,
both of Tiptree, Essex

09 097220 1

✻ ILLUSTRATIONS

ACKNOWLEDGEMENTS

The author acknowledges the gracious permission of Her Majesty the Queen to publish extracts from letters written by Albert Edward, Prince of Wales. Acknowledgement is also made to King Michael of Roumania for permission to publish letters written by Marie, Duchess of Edinburgh.

The author wishes to express sincere gratitude to the late Randolph S. Churchill for his immense help in the writing of this book. Thanks are also due to Lady Randolph Churchill's nephews, the late Hugh Frewen, Sir Shane Leslie and especially Mr Seymour Leslie, who all took pains to hand on their memories in clear and delightful form.

For other reminiscences the author is indebted to Baroness Spencer-Churchill, Mr Peregrine S. Churchill, The Duchess of Abercorn, Lady Betty Cartwright, Prince de Ceary, Mrs George Cornwallis-West, the late Adlai Stevenson, the late Lady Violet Bonham Carter (Baroness Asquith), Mrs Sherman Haight, Mrs J. Spooner (Megan Foster), Mr and Mrs Oliver Goldsmith of Salisbury Hall and the late Colonel Paul Rodzianko.

The author is also indebted to the following for permission to quote letters of which they hold the copyright: Baroness Spencer-Churchill (Lady Blanche Hozier), Winston S. Churchill (Lady Randolph Churchill) and Roger Frewen (Moreton Frewen). For permission to quote their own letters the author thanks Prince de Clary, Sir Archibald James, Mrs Clare Sheridan, Sir Shane Leslie and the late Dame Ethel Smyth.

The copyright of all letters by Winston S. Churchill is held by C. & T. Publications Ltd and the author acknowledges permission to quote extracts from letters published in *Winston S. Churchill*, Volumes I & II, by Randolph S. Churchill, and in the *Companion Volumes* (Heinemann). Acknowledgements are also due to the authors, trustees and publishers of the following books for permission to quote: Edwin Arnold (*Reminiscences of Lady Randolph Churchill*, 1908); Odhams Press (*My Early Life* by Winston S. Churchill, 1908); Humphrys (*Lord Randolph Churchill* by Lord Rosebery, 1906); Hodder & Stoughton (*An Ambassador of Peace* by Viscount d'Abernon and *Politicians and their War* by Lord Beaverbrook, and *Memoirs of Lloyd George*); Weidenfeld & Nicolson (*Lord Randolph Churchill* by Robert Rhodes James, 1959); John Murray (*The Jerome Connexion* by Seymour Leslie, 1960, *The Life of Edward VIII* by Sir Philip Magnus, 1967, *Long Shadows* by Sir Shane Leslie, 1960, *From My Private Diaries* by Daisy, Princess of Pless, 1931); Putnams (*Edwardian Heydays* by George Cornwallis-West, 1930); Collins (*Winston Churchill as I Knew Him*, 1966); Martin Secker & Warburg (*My Diaries*, Wilfred Scawen-Blunt); Evelyn Nash (*Things I Can Tell*, Lord Rossmore, 1922); Cassell & Co. (*Memories and Reflections*, Lord Oxford and Asquith); Ivor Nicholson & Watson (*Lord Riddell's War Diary*); Hutchinson (*The Uncensored Dardanelles*, E. Ashmead Bartlett, 1928, *Lady Cynthia Asquith's Diaries*, 1968); W. H. Lucy (*Speeches of Lord Randolph Churchill, with a Sketch of his Life*, 1885).

The author apologises to any copyright holders it has not been possible to trace, and thanks them for any quotations.

For Randolph,
the bravest of friends

FOREWORD

As the plaintive bagpipe lament faded, the barge carrying the flag-covered coffin passed the saluting cranes of London's docks to disappear from view up the river Thames. England's Queen and the fighting men and the resistance leaders of countries whose hearts he had kept alive turned for home. The funeral had become private.

Winston wished to lie beside his parents in a quiet little church-yard called Bladon. Long ago he had written to his mother of the peace he felt there when visiting his father's grave. It was the place he chose above all others.

Lord Randolph Churchill, Winston's father, had made his mark in Victorian England, but of Jennie Jerome, the American girl who made a love match with him in the early 'seventies, not so much was remembered. 'What was she really like?' voices murmured that day. I knew a little. I could find out more. The idea of writing this book was born.

Jennie entered my life when I was six years old. We were spending a year in Ireland with her sister Leonie—our adored grandmother. It was a stimulating time for children (with a civil war on) and at night we would peep out at the dark dripping woods where 'men were secretly drilling'. We had no idea what the dangers were about but felt half thrilled, half terrified by stories richly related by the Irish servants.

Great-Aunt Jennie and our grandmother may have realised that we lived in a dramatic world of our own on the edge of the grown-ups' fear. They had us into the drawing room every evening to play the piano and delight us with stories of the operas. Sometimes they would both sit at the keyboard and play together, casting us the most expressive glances. They were a delight; but we had to be dragged back to the nursery.

When Aunt Jennie departed she seemed to have left her mark in every room; not only her favourite initialled music books remained, but ball gowns from the distant past—too good to throw away, and impossible to give to the poor—were left hanging in the big attic cupboards—white brocade, pink brocade and one in stiff orange ribbed silk. We were shown the white Alençon lace parasol made to match her wedding gown and a multitude of things in almost every room, objects of amber or tortoiseshell with Jennie's name in gold, lorgnettes, hat pins, mirrors. She loved presents— she received and she gave continuously.

After Jennie departed my grandmother would sit alone at the piano saying, perhaps: 'Here is a duet we used to play so well together. . . . She liked Debussy, I preferred Schumann . . . now listen to this . . .'

Here it was that we learned the stories of the operas. My younger brother was extremely musical and soon could pick out the melody of arias with his little finger, and he sang in a tiny treble absolutely true. With delight my grandmother would encourage him, and then recount the complicated story of *The Ring* which ended with a crescendo 'Ride of the Valkeries'—'Faster and faster—they're riding through the sky—look at the clouds outside tearing over the trees . . .' And then crash, she would stand up and play the final chord by sitting down on the keys!

From this enchanted kingdom, from the woods and the lake and firelit music hours, we were suddenly taken to London, a dismal transition. We longed for Ireland, where one could be excited and afraid.

My mother owned a house in Talbot Square, just round the corner from Jennie's, and it was some compensation when, on returning from an odious walk in Kensington Gardens, we would hear that our gorgeous great-aunt was coming to tea. Washed and brushed we would be hurried into the drawing room, and then, as I overheard the servants gossip about Lady Randolph Churchill's famed beauty, I looked at her with new eyes. Yes; I could see that her face was different—the deep-set shadowy eyes, the black brows lifted in amusement as she said, 'What are *you* thinking about?': the chiselled features—all this created an indelible impression. But how could 'the most beautiful lady in the world' have silver hair?

Did they look old? Did my grandmother look old? I don't know. I only know I adored them as they were. We hated the daily march (with a brute of a governess) to look at Peter Pan's statue. We rejoiced in the warmth of these two women in their sixties; we longed to get back quickly if they were coming to tea. Impossible to define how they altered a room by their presence, making one feel that life must be full of unknown treasures; their tread gilded the nursery stair like sunlight.

Then in the blazing hot June of 1921 we were banished to the top floor and told not to ask questions. We heard that Aunt Jennie had fallen and broken her leg. We could not know that our mother was awaiting a Caesarian operation. There came a dazing morning when the whistle-telephone in our nursery kept blowing and we learnt in the same hour that we had a little brother and that Aunt Jennie was dead—two events which astounded us equally.

Years later, during winters spent in Ireland with my grandmother, I came to know Aunt Jennie well, for she talked a great deal about that lively sister, and a hundred small stories carelessly garnered came my way.

'She could be a terror,' my grandmother would say, 'but for that fatherless youth she was just right. Never flattering or possessive, she tempered his steel. And though everyone called her selfish she cherished his ambition when better informed, more detached observers failed to discern greatness.'

Eventually I set out to discover all I could concerning a woman who must be called remarkable even if she had not been Winston's mother.

I

Jennie wove a fine puzzle for her future biographers by describing in her memoirs a babyhood spent in Trieste (where her father was American Consul from 1851 to 1853) and later claiming to have been eighteen when she married in 1874. The most elementary mathematician could work out a discrepancy.

Jennie was certainly sure of the house in Brooklyn where she was born, because she pointed it out, but there were no dated records of leases nor any birth registration. It was a teasing problem until her nephew Seymour Leslie discovered a letter written in 1888 from Moscow which made nonsense of her Trieste memories and firmly established the date on which she was born. This letter, written in Jennie's clear determined handwriting, begins:

Sliemenski Bazaar
Jan. 9th/88

Dearest Mama,

Do you know that it is my birthday today? 34!!! I think for the future that I will not proclaim my age. . . .

At the same time Jennie's grandson Randolph Churchill found an earlier letter, written on identical lines to her husband, which he published in volume I of *The Life of Winston Churchill*. These two letters, written on her birthdays, definitely confirm her birth date as 9th January 1854, after the Leonard Jeromes had returned from Trieste. She must have been twenty when she married Lord Randolph Churchill. The episode would not be worth recounting in detail were it not typical of Jennie's impulsive, ruthless nature. It is, of course, the prerogative of beautiful women to fib about age, but they seldom proceed to also publish a book which contradicts these fabrications! Of course, Jennie could not have expected that Mr Jerome's diplomatic career would be subjected to the searchlight of history, and her naughty trick revealed.

Having established that she never went to Italy as a baby, it is difficult to resist quoting from the pages she hoped would lend colour to her book: 'I remember how, as we crossed the Mont Cenis in a *vettura*, the deep snow filled my childish mind with awe and astonishment. . . .'

The true story, then, can begin.

Jennie was born at 426 Henry Street in Brooklyn, six months after her mother returned from Europe. Mr Jerome, a Republican, had resigned from the Trieste Consulate when (Democrat) President Pierce won the election. He had been happy to get back to Wall Street. Making money was his sport, while horses and music were his pleasures. Leonard Jerome had enjoyed Italy, but he was essentially an American. His wife on the other hand, had been completely captivated by Europe. Northern Italy lay at that time within the Austro-Hungarian Empire, and Trieste, its biggest port, presented a glittering social world, where the aristocracy entertained in their mountain castles during the summer months and the rich merchants built luxurious villas. Leonard had taken a liking to early Italian painting, and bought many pictures in what was then an un-fashionable style. Before leaving Trieste the Jeromes had their portraits painted by Schiavoni, and these were shipped back to America with the madonnas and a huge collection of furniture which got knocked to pieces in transit.

On reaching New York Mr Leonard Jerome had to face a financial crisis. His brother Addison, left in charge of the family stockbroking firm, announced that it had 'failed'. This frequently occurred in the Wall Street of the period, and only meant that Leonard must plunge back into the fray and recoup. For a time, however, Clara, who had bought splendid dresses on her way through Paris, had to face the fact that they were not very well off. Having produced her second daughter in unfashionable Brooklyn she unenthusiastically acquiesced in the name her husband desired (for she knew well of Leonard's past admiration for the great Jennie

2

Lind). 'Jennie?' she had exclaimed, 'just Jennie? It's an impossible name.' But Jennie it was; plain Jennie.

Soon after this baby's arrival the Jeromes moved to 8 Amity Street, a house with a garden, and it was here, not in the Italian Alps, that little Jennie Jerome must have gathered her first impressions. She and her sister Clara enjoyed a happy childhood. Although Mr Jerome was fond of the ladies, especially of ladies who sang, there were no disagreements in the home. If Leonard sent a message that he was 'unavoidably detained' his wife remained a well-bred sphinx. In all their lives the girls never heard an angry word between their parents, and whatever the strains might be in that Wall Street jungle, Mr Jerome remained a demonstratively affectionate papa. Their house was one in which small figures running with outstretched arms were caught and thrown into the air. Children were heard and seen and hugged at 8 Amity Street.

Each evening, when the South Ferry arrived with its load of top-hatted business gentlemen, Clara and Jennie would be walked out by the Italian nursemaid in the hope of meeting Papa—but if he was late no grumbles nor long faces were permitted. Mama might share their disappointment, but it was firmly understood that the hero would soon reappear, probably with gifts. The children slept confident in the knowledge that they had the dearest of all possible papas, splendidly making fortunes for them in the best of all possible worlds. Another little daughter was born and died young. This was the only sorrow they knew.

The Italian nursemaid of Jennie's memoirs really existed; she took them walking, taught them her language, pierced their ears for gold rings, and then is heard of no more.

A year or so rolled by and the little girls became aware, through servants' talk, as well as by noting the magnificent glass and silver which started to adorn the dining table, that they were becoming rich. The tall spare figure who strode off the evening ferry, carrying bracelets for Mama and dolls for them, had become a triumphant Railway King. He had the most generous nature and he gave with elegance. Later on they learned that Papa had thoughtfully settled a million dollars on their mother.

During the summer months the family moved to the fishing village of Newport for sea air and outdoor pleasures. Mr Jerome had to remain in touch with Wall Street, so he shared a yacht, but even in those days the cost of a professional crew could shock, and as Leonard set off shark-fishing in *Undine* he wrote to his wife: 'I wish I could always keep a yacht. I had rather have one than all the other luxuries that are indulged in by people of wealth. My dear little piccaninnies and you, my ever faithful and true wife . . . how happy I shall be to see you again. The boys are pulling me by the coat tail, so good night. *Dite Talla che Papa venga a casa subito . . . tre ò quatro giorni—addio—Leonard.'*

In 1856 Leonard and Addison Jerome formed a brokery firm with William Travers, the celebrated attorney and wit, who owned a stable of fast trotters. It was Leonard who took a tip from the secretary of the Cleveland and Toledo Company and bought up stock, which this man must have known to be false. When the railway failed, Leonard accepted the blame and paid up his entire personal fortune to save the Travers Jerome firm. Clara's 'million' had been invested separately, so she remained calm and approved her husband's decision to do a year's 'retreat' while studying Wall Street psychology. An American journal wrote: 'Leonard Jerome never flickered an eyelid in public but he was sore displeased that one he trusted had let him down.'

Within two years Leonard Jerome was back at the top, and if his daughters had heard rumours of 'ruin' it did not seem grievous. Their small world remained secure.

A third daughter was born, named Camille, who died in early childhood. After this domestic tragedy, when Clara was eight and Jennie four years old, Mr Jerome cheered his wife by taking her to Paris for a year. After installing her and the children at 63 Avenue des Champs-Élysées, he wrote to his brother:

September 13

Paris isn't yet as agreeable to me as New York except on a Sunday. The pleasure carriages that passed my window yesterday, 12 a.m. to 8 p.m., averaged about 50 a *minute*. I amuse myself with music in the morning, walking or riding in the afternoon and theatre visiting or billiards in the evening. . . I think I shall spend next summer at the Isle of Wight, a great place for yachting and horses . . . I advise you to teach languages to your sons young. Boys run to things they shine in. Whatever they *succeed* in, they are inclined to do well. . . .

I wrote Travers by the last mail to send me a wagon and a harness. If not already dispatched, cancel. I find horses here abominably dear. 2,000 francs is nothing for a pair you would not drive a second time. They do not admire speed. Showy, high stepping, short switch-tail and arching neck is the description that generally answers. I have been looking about only to find French horses so little to my fancy that I have ended by buying nothing. So if you happen to see a pair of horses you think would suit my driving, good size, good travellers, you may send them over.

The reference to music *in the mornings* seems curious but that was the time when rehearsals of operas or concerts were held and Leonard Jerome took great pleasure in launching young singers. He liked women for their voices. In a way this restricted the scope of flirtations, and Clara, who could not sing a note knew that she remained his dearest love. Whatever her feelings, she never scolded him. Knowing her Puritan views, her daughters were, years later, surprised to hear their mother's practical advice about how to hold a husband: 'Never scold a man, my dears. If you do he will only go where he is *not* scolded.' This piece of wisdom was passed on to three generations.

Gentle tactics won Mrs Jerome a magnificent diamond riviere, and in January 1859 Leonard wrote to his brother:

We have been to the grand ball at the Tuileries and were presented to the Emperor and Empress. It was universally conceded that Clit was the handsomest woman there. I never saw her look so well.

Now the little girls received a new image of their mother. They saw her radiant in diamonds sweeping off to court balls, and they listened with respect to her admonition, 'If *you* want to do this you *must* learn to speak French.'

Then suddenly they heard of war. War! The French Emperor, their Emperor, had attacked Austria. Victories came fast—Magenta and Solferino.

Louis Napoleon ordered a grand parade of the triumphant troops through Paris. Mr Jerome had moved his family for the summer to St Germain-en-Laye. He drove to the Place Vendôme on August

14th to watch the Emperor and the Prince Imperial take the march-past while Eugenie sat enthroned beneath a canopy of green velvet and golden bees. It was very impressive. When he returned late that night he described the regiments marching past with gaps in their ranks to show the places of the dead. On the next day, August 15th, Clara Jerome gave birth to another daughter. She had hoped for a son to name Leonard. Her husband tried to brush away her disappointment by choosing the French feminine version of his name—Leonie.

To comfort those who arrive as one girl too many I shall now skip eighty-five years to Leonie's departure from this world. This letter arrived unexpectedly as I was writing this page, and Sir Archibald James has allowed me to quote his letter uncorrected:

22/4/66

After 1931 Leonie often came down to the House and sent for me to find Winston for her. When she died Winston was at the Quebec Conference. At his behest the London memorial service was twice postponed so anxious was he to be at it but he was again delayed and he only got back a day or two after it was over. He came down to the House and proceedings started with his tremendous speech/report. You know what a tremendous amount of work and thought he put into his speeches, so that his mind would have been tremendously occupied in the preceding hours and days, Ordinarily punctilious over H. of C. practices, towards the end of the war he started to disregard one convention which is that after speaking one must not leave the Chamber until the following speech is concluded. This is because ordinarily it will have come from the other side of the floor. . . . As everything went flat after a Winston war-report speech, only a nonentity would ordinarily want to follow him, and this boredom Winston couldn't endure. On this Quebec occasion Winston rested about ten minutes in his place and then got up and went to the smoking room. I had gone there as soon as he had finished, and was sitting with some members in the middle of the room. Suddenly Winston was framed in the doorway, peering around. Spotting me, he walked across and, putting his hand on my shoulder, said, 'Come with me.' I followed him and sat down with him. He opened, 'I saw in the paper that you were at

6

Leonie's memorial service. I want you to tell me all about it', and he proceeded to cross examine me. Where did so-and-so sit? Was X or Y there? Was Olive there, and so on. And what hymns did they sing? All this he listened to with rapt attention. Then he started to talk. He put his hand on my shoulder. The tears streamed down his face. In wonderful phrases, pregnant with emotion, for some 10 minutes he delivered a sort of funeral oration, reducing me too to tears. 'The last link with my youth severed.' Then he fell silent for a minute or two, then rose, head bowed, patted me on the shoulder, and hunched with grief, strode away, suddenly straightening as he reached the door. It was an amazing performance when you think of his total detachment at such a moment. As he spoke to me the words that he had been delivering but a few minutes before were being hurried round the world, translated into every civilised language, affecting the lives of millions. And that sudden straightening by the door . . . back to the living from the grave.

2

After returning to New York in 1860 Mr Jerome bought a site on Madison Square where he proceeded to build a mansion in red brick trimmed with white marble—an enormous strawberry pie set amidst the chocolate rows of brownstone houses. The *New York Tribune* describes Leonard at this time: 'His passion for the theatre and opera was only surpassed by his love of horses. He built his stable before he built his house. It was of brick, faced with marble, three stories high, with a mansard roof. He filled it with horses and carriages of the finest makes. Except for the Emperor's Mews in Paris, it is doubtful if any stable in the world at that time surpassed Jerome's. Black walnut, plate glass, carpeted floors and other costly decorations ornamented the place. Above the stable he built a private theatre handsomely adorned. . . In front of his stable Mr Jerome built his house and for years it was the centre of fashion. From its doors one Sunday afternoon he drove the first four-in-hand ever seen in this city. . . .'

The seventeen-year-old Adeline Patti took New York by storm and Mr Jerome was able to offer her his little private opera house to rehearse in. When the children moved into their new town house they could listen to the young *prima donna* trying out roles and then run out to the stables to inspect their favourite horses. Mrs Jerome kept them in the country during Papa's fantastic house-warming ball, of which an eyewitness recorded:

Invitations were eagerly sought by the 400 of that day, and all the wealth and fashion and beauty of the metropolis took part in the dance. Two fountains were placed in the centre of the auditorium playing cologne and champagne and the floral decorations were marvellous. The front of the theatre was illuminated and the side-walls covered with crimson tapestry. The Supper must have cost thousands.

Lloyd Morris has written in *Incredible New York* that Leonard Jerome 'dazzled society with the glitter and novelty of his carriages, the costliness of his blooded horses. He excited its dubious admiration by his extravagance and assurance. Both were obvious in all his activities; his fantastic speculation, his scandalous love affairs, his incredible parties. . . . He made, lost and again made fortunes, he was reputed to be worth more than ten million dollars.'

The exaggerated description demonstrates the legend surrounding Leonard Jerome and rumours which reached the nursery lost nothing in the telling. Yet this enchanting papa always had time for his children. They saw him as the hero who must not be scolded, the gay horseman, the maker of millions, the intrepid gambler, the drier of tears.

When the Civil War broke out Leonard Jerome, as owner of America's only serious newspaper *The New York Times*, devoted himself to political issues and donated large sums to the War Wounded. No knowledge of war's horror reached the girls, but they were never to forget the solemn moment, when, from behind the half-drawn blinds, they peered out at the vast catafalque of Abraham Lincoln passing below.

During the fighting many owners of southern studs had brought them north for safety. No enmity existed between sportsmen, whichever side they were on. Leonard Jerome took much interest in these southern stables. When the war ended he bought his first race-horse for $40,000. This was the great-hearted Kentucky, who in August 1865 was to win the Inauguration Stakes, the first race ever run at Saratoga Springs. Jerome and William Travers, his business partner, announced they were going to raise the prestige of flat racing in America to English standards. They founded the Jockey Club and laid down its aims: 'To promote the improvement of horses, to elevate the public taste in sports of the turf, and to become an authority on racing matters in the country.' They laid out plans for a race-course close to New York City. Leonard purchased an

9

estate of 230 acres, with a hill where stands and club-house could be built, while the course curled in full view around it. He wrote: 'It will pass Saratoga in charm. We have the most picturesque scenery, hills, a hollow and a really good view and I am insisting on a competent engineer.'

The Jockey Club started in Leonard's office in April 1866, and in the following September, with tremendous fanfares, it held its first meeting at what was now called Jerome Park Racecourse. According to newspapers of the day this 'proved the social event of all time and started a new era in the horse-racing world'. General Grant, victor of the Appomatox, presided in the 'royal box' of a grandstand holding 8,000. Mrs Jerome, in puce silk, received numberless congratulations, while Clara and Jennie became wild with excitement. Their mother sternly resolved they should go to no more race meetings. Jennie describes her worldly début at the age of ten when she attended a fancy-dress party and her father found her in floods of tears because her costume did not make her look 'as I thought I was going to . . .'—a situation she said which was often to repeat itself.

A contemporary wrote of Leonard Jerome: 'He spent money as freely as he made it and never was happier than when contributing to the welfare and amusement of others. No matter how busy he might be he had always time to talk of racing, yachting and sport of any kind. . . . Any half-decent fellow who failed in Wall Street could borrow enough from Mr Jerome to start anew.'

His daughters, somewhat naturally, preferred his company to that of the serious mama who organised cold baths and the study of French grammar. Jennie has written of 'lessons and matinées at the opera "to improve our minds", sleighing and skating for pleasure, and on red-letter days a drive to Jerome Park on my father's coach, where I always occupied the seat of honour next him. Sometimes, from afar, I could see the blue and white of his racing colours come in first, which was a great excitement. On one occasion I was hoisted upon the back of his most famous race-horse, the celebrated Kentucky, whose sire Lexington and dam Magnolia by Glencoe, were of the best blood in England.' It seems unlikely that Leonard Jerome should have allowed Jennie to push her way over Clara, the meek elder sister, but whatever seat Jennie obtained she would always have *thought* it the best. The Jerome girls hardly realised how important the Jockey Club was to be to America. An old news-paper article reads: 'L.W.J. who was the master spirit of the club began collecting a stable of racers with characteristic dash. . . . But Jerome will be remembered more as a promoter than as an owner.'

A fellow broker wrote: 'He was a daring man in speculation, being guided implicitly by an almost blind confidence in his own destiny. And yet he was not reckless. He would risk $100,000 on a turn of the market with a cold calculating coolness which was not altered by either loss or gain.'

But it was his artistry with horses which won the applause of the mob. Snob chronicler of the time Ward McAllister records: 'He turned out daily with his dray or coach loaded with beautiful women, and drove to every desirable little country inn about the city, where one could dine at all well, crossing ferries and driving up Broadway with the ease and skill of a veteran whip which he was.' On Sundays Mr Jerome liked to drive up Fifth Avenue waving to friends strolling in the social church parades. 'Gay and laughing ladies in gorgeous costume filled the carriage. Lackeys, carefully gotten up, occupied the coupé behind; Jerome sat on the box and handled the reins. With a huge bouquet of flowers attached to his buttonhole, with white gloves, cracking his whip, and with the shouts of the party, the four horses would rush up Fifth Avenue, on toward the Park, while the populace said, one to the other, "That is Jerome".' Mrs Jerome, who had been brought up to spend Sunday indoors with blinds drawn, disapproved, and tried to keep the girls in the country.

Among the young singers rehearsing at the time on Mr Jerome's private stage was Minnie Hauk, reputed to be his daughter through an early romance. Mrs Jerome was very fond of Minnie and accepted her in the household. Minnie has also written memoirs; they are as nebulous as Jennie's and far more long-winded.

She arrived in New York, aged fifteen, and Mr Jerome took her out to sing at dinner parties with her hair still in pigtails. During her training she lived at Madison Square. She writes: 'During this period I was quite at home at Mr Leonard Jerome's home. His wife and three daughters welcomed me very warmly. Almost every Saturday Mr Jerome would take us girls in a dog-cart to his country seat near New York—later known as Jerome Park—and there we used to stay over Sunday, returning to New York the following morning.

'Mr Jerome possessed some beautiful saddle-horses and his daughters were in the habit of riding many miles before breakfast. They rode like Amazons and wished me also to mount a horse, which I had never attempted before. Desiring to avoid the appearance of fear I allowed myself one morning to be mounted on a horse which Mr Jerome himself had selected.' The pretty black pony terrifies her. On the next attempt the girls find a nice ploughed field for a gallop, but Minnie's pony lies down to roll. She never mounts a horse again!

More entertaining is her own description of her début in the private theatre. 'I had chosen for it *Linda di Chamounix*, and in addition to my studies I had to prepare my costumes. . . . Mr Jerome kindly presented me with a *rose moiré antique* for the second act, while Mrs Jerome lent me all the jewellery required to perfect my appearance as a grande dame. All the so-called "400" of New York were actually present. I remember that on either side of the stage there was a fountain of scented water—my appearance was a pronounced success and all New York rang with my name as "The Wonder Child".'

A few of Minnie Hauk's letters to Mr Jerome survive: 'New York, August 17 1866: Won't you come and take us out from the farm? You know I love to go out with you better than anyone else.'

'Philadelphia, October 24 1866: I should love to have those stockings worked with blue for *Sonnambula*. . . . Goodbye my dear Friend. Kiss Jennie and Clara for me and my regards to Mrs Jerome.'

On the back of a faded photograph of Minnie Hauk, the American *prima donna* who was to conquer Europe and to be the first Carmen, Mrs Jerome pencilled: 'So like Jennie—less good-looking!' Indeed, she was a darker, squarer version with a nightingale voice. Frank Griswold wrote, years later, to Leonie: 'I remember my first opera. I went in 1866 to the début of Minnie Hauk. Your father had educated her voice and morals I believe? Clara and Jennie were both in the box.'

Apart from the excitement of Minnie's début, the year 1866 held several events of interest to the Jerome schoolroom. Longshore racing had grown in popularity and their father spent much of his time racing his yacht *Undine* along the coast of Maine. He and his brother Lawrence were prominent members of the New York Yacht Club and in October they challenged three millionaires— Pierre Lorillard and the brothers Osgood—to a transatlantic race against *Henrietta*, the keel-schooner, 107 feet overall, owned by their young friend James Gordon Bennett.

The great December race between *Henrietta*, *Vesta* and *Fleetwing* has gone down in sailing history. Lawrence Jerome sailed with James Gordon Bennett in *Henrietta* and Leonard won considerably over $100,000 backing this yacht. Frank Griswold in *Clipper Ships* writes about Leonard Jerome: 'I well remember, when a boy, driving to Jerome Park with him during the winter of 1867, in a large blue and golden boat sleigh, which had been built for him to celebrate the event. It took six horses to pull the sleigh over the snow and what surprised me most was that he drove the ten miles in the cold without gloves.'

Frank Griswold also recounts the inside story of Mrs Ronalds' fancy-dress party (but not in *Clipper Ships*). Fanny Ronalds, a well-born, extraordinarily talented beauty with whom Leonard was deeply in love, is first described by Mr Grenville Moore in *Memories of an Old Etonian*: 'Her face was perfectly divine in its loveliness, her features small and exquisitely regular. Her hair was of a dark shade of brown and very abundant.' As she had a wonderful voice but, being in the very top drawer of *the* 400, could not demean herself by singing professionally, Mr Jerome's band-box theatre proved useful. She sang the lead in Italian operas in aid of wounded soldiers and Southern charities. When her voice grew exhausted Leonard Jerome and millionaire August Belmont devised 'Tableaux Vivantes', posed by society ladies. Fanny appeared modestly as an Italian Madonna while Mrs Belmont personified Winter, 'all hung with icicles made of *real* diamonds'. As Mr Belmont was courting Fanny as assiduously as Mr Jerome, this was a very thoughtful diversion.

A New Yorker wrote in his privately printed memoirs: 'There were two outstanding men at that time who were most prominent in all social and sporting matters. They both drove a coach-and-four, and had large racing stables; both were married and in the prime of life. These two men fell desperately in love with Mrs R—. L and A were rivals who kept the house of their lady filled with flowers and attempted to satisfy her every desire. She proved to

13

be an accomplished general, for she managed these two great men, as well as other aspirants, with much skill.'

When Mrs Ronalds sighed because she could not afford a fancy-dress ball, Leonard Jerome suggested that she deposit a few hundred dollars with his firm. A week later the investment was returned to her multiplied into thousands. The fancy-dress ball became 'the talk of the town. Invitations were sent out three months ahead to allow time for costumes to be obtained from Paris. Such hot-house fruit and flowers, such music, canvas-back ducks, terrapin and old wines had never before been seen on Manhattan Island. . . . Thousands of dollars had been spent on flowers alone and the ball lasted until six in the morning.'

Mrs Ronalds impersonated Music in a white satin gown embroidered with bars from Verdi's *Un Ballo in Maschera,* while her crown consisted of sparkling quavers and crochets lit up by tiny gas jets from a holder hidden in her hair.

Clara and Jennie were naturally allowed a preview of the costumes. What they never knew was what their mother guessed. Twenty years later Frank Griswold was present when Leonard Jerome and August Belmont were lunching together at Jerome Park. 'Do you remember Fanny's celebrated ball?' asked Mr Jerome.

'Indeed I ought to,' replied Belmont. 'I paid for it.'

'Why how very strange,' said Leonard. 'So did I.'

3

After this ball Mrs Jerome asked if she might move to Paris for her health's sake. Leonard was taken aback, for his wife had an excellent constitution; but the girls could be more intensively schooled in France, so he acquiesced and the whole family crossed the Atlantic. Mrs Jerome suffered from seasickness, but the three girls were excellent sailors like their father. Dobbie, the Negro nurse-companion, hated the sea and when they reached Paris, where she had to walk Leonie in the Avenue du Bois de Boulogne, she hated that city also. After settling his family in an apartment in Avenue Malsherbes, Mr Jerome returned sadly to the big house in Madison Square.

Having organised a brain-spinning course of study for the daughters, Mrs Jerome recovered her health with alacrity. 'My mother went out a great deal in French society, where her beauty attracted much attention, *la belle Americaine* having at that time all the charm of novelty,' wrote Jennie.

When Clara, the eldest, was eighteen she made her curtsey to the Emperor and Empress and attended her first ball at the Tuileries wearing a white crinoline. She suffered some confusion at having to walk up the grand staircase between the rows of gleaming *Cent-Guardes*, her dress felt so low cut and her skirts so enormous, but Louis Napoleon and Eugenie took pains to be kind to the American débutante.

Clara once drafted out her memories of the Imperial Court. When they stayed at Compiègne, sixty to a hundred people sat down each evening at a table laden with golden plate. Yet the atmosphere remained informal, for after the Emperor had led in Eugenie the guests could sit as they wished, 'the ladies choosing the gentlemen to take them in according to the custom of Compiègne.' Occasionally the Emperor organised a lottery of gifts and Clara received an inkstand shaped like a knotted handkerchief filled with gold napoleons. *'Mademoiselle, n'oubliez pas les Napoleons,'* he said. The most interesting salon in Paris was that of Louis Napoleon's cousin, the Princess Mathilde, and Mrs Jerome took her daughter there regularly.

Clara never produced a book, but she scribbled notes. On a certain evening in her mother's absence she was late meeting the friends who were to take her to the Tuileries.

They departed without me leaving a message they would wait at the top of the big palace staircase. I flew back to the carriage with Dobbie our devoted Negro nurse at my heels. She came from the old South and had very definite views on the importance of chaperoning young ladies. For nothing on earth would she allow me out of her sight until I could be handed over to my official duenna. We drove post haste to the Tuileries and there she descended beside me with an indomitable expression on her black face: 'A'm not going to leave you until ah sees you safe.' You can imagine the surprise of the palace guards who lined the great staircase as a young girl fluttered up the marble steps closely pursued by a large Negress wearing a green turban on her head and a red shawl around her shoulders.

Clara kept all her invitations embossed with the Imperial Crown. One of these, dated November 1869, summons her to a six-day hunting party at Compiègne. It was the first time she had travelled on the royal train without Mrs Jerome. Her mother read her letters aloud to the envious ten- and fourteen-year-olds in the schoolroom.

In the evening I put on my white with marguerites for the Prince Imperial was to have a Cotillion. We played *chats et souris*, so he ran after me and in and out, and I finally caught my foot in the Duchesse de Mouchy's dress and fell. . . . We have been asked to lengthen our stay until Tuesday—so I shall need another dress—something white trimmed with anything you think pretty. I think I must have it, in fact two if possible, for these ladies dress so much and never appear in the same. Dear Mamma, I love you and you are so sweet.

Addio,
Clarita

Jennie was still only sixteen when, to her chagrin, France went to war with Bismarck's Prussia. The spring of 1870 seemed particularly delightful. Mrs Ronalds and Minnie Hauk had both appeared in Paris and encouraged the girls with their piano study, and, more curiously, to 'walk with the toes pointed out'.

In May Papa took the older girls to the south of France. They drove down the coast from Nice to Genoa in open carriages, staying at small inns. After the first night Clara wrote not over-tactfully to her mother: 'Papa: looked so fresh and handsome that we told him the ladies would all be after him.' In June, when they returned to a new house in the Boulevard Haussman, Clara had a disquieting experience. Count Hatzfeld, a secretary at the German Embassy drew her into an alcove to whisper: 'I never saw their Majesties in better spirits than last night but God knows where they will be next year at this time.'

Despite rumours, Leonard Jerome departed for England, determined not to miss sailing in the great international yacht race between the English 108-foot *Cambria* and Gordon Bennett's 120-foot overall schooner *Dauntless*. *Cambria* sailed from Ireland to Sandy Hook in twenty-three days five hours and seventeen minutes, beating *Dauntless* by one hour forty-three minutes in a race of 3,000 miles! During these twenty-three days France attacked Germany and met serious reverses. Paris was in a state of ferment. Minnie Hauk, who had, at this of all moments, 'arrived to buy dresses', took the Jerome girls to the opera where they saw the bejewelled audience stand up to sing the Marseillaise. Next day Jennie watched *prima donna* Marie Sasse on an omnibus singing the National Anthem while cheering crowds followed. Lessons ceased. Governesses and maids disappeared. Mama sprained her ankle. Jennie and Leonie enjoyed the drama, but Clara fretted, for the old Duc de Persigny kept arriving with bad news from the Empress at St Cloud, and she sensed that the golden world which she had briefly tasted might disappear.

Usually the Jeromes followed the Empress to Biarritz for the summer, but now they remained in Paris, starry-eyed with excitement until one morning, before they had finished breakfast—this in itself seemed to constitute an enormity—the Duc de Persigny arrived crying: '*Tout est perdu; l'Armée n'est pas concentrée. Les Prussiens sont à nos portes.*'

The girls fled to their bedrooms to tie precious belongings in tablecloths. Clara was dissuaded from sorting out ball gowns and with Marie, the remaining maid, they set out on foot towards the station. As Mrs Jerome could hardly hobble, they hired men in the street to carry her. The girls' bundles proved too heavy for their strength and as they staggered panting towards the Gare du Nord, a very personal dislike of the Prussian Army filled them. Leonie often described departing troops lying on the platforms, while civilians tried to scramble on any train out of the capital. Having boarded one to Deauville, Mrs Jerome conferred with the maid, who was appalled at the thought of her ladies arriving in England without their hats. If allowed to return home she thought she could hire a cart to bring their trunks properly packed next day. So back she went and there she remained throughout the siege, for her ladies had caught the last train out of Paris.

Deauville was packed with stupefied refugees. Clara installed her sisters in the Palace Hotel before organising a wheelbarrow to transport her mother. Jennie clung to a bundle containing the famous diamond rivière entangled with her skating boots. They obtained a room and fell into exhausted sleep. Before dawn came a tap at the door. There stood Monsieur de Garonne, the Empress's Chamberlain, 'begging for concealment'. He hid with them all day, leaping behind the curtains when food arrived on trays. To Mrs Jerome's relief, for she was hardly up to chaperoning, that night he mysteriously departed. Two days later he reappeared to tell them that he had been arranging the Empress's escape to England.

Maidless and governessless, the Jerome ladies took the first available places on a cross-Channel boat. On arriving in Brighton they lodged at the Norfolk Hotel and, in a state of consternation, awaited Papa's reappearance. They hated the English grey stone beach, the English grey sky and the beastly bracing winds.

When Mr Jerome arrived he found his family behaving like real *émigrés*. Mrs Jerome affected all the airs of an Empress in exile. She did not want to return to New York; she could not desert French friends. So Leonard took his family to London and procured a suite of rooms in Brown's Hotel. Within a few days the Duc de Persigny came to call: 'Your last visitor in Paris. Your first in London I fear!' Mr Jerome thanked him for warnings and soon guessed that the former French Ambassador to London was in difficult financial straits but felt ashamed of letting English friends know of his plight, so Leonard took a room for him in Brown's Hotel and paid all the Duke's bills. De Persigny certainly cheered Mrs Jerome with his talk of a restoration—Bourbon if not Bonaparte. Nasty as the King of Prussia was, Mrs Jerome felt he could not prove such a cad as to make peace *with a republic*! Young Clara moped. She did not want anyone on the throne of France except her own dear Emperor and she was in love with the Marquis de Tamisier who could now only send her messages by balloon. She refused to enjoy herself, it would seem disloyal. Mr Jerome ordered the girls to recommence their studies, and he hired a special room in the hotel with two pianos where Clara and Jennie could practise duets. At least they had sufficient talent to enable them to pound out their feelings. Chopin's funeral march probably suited the mood of the moment. Jennie wrote: 'A winter spent in the gloom and fogs of London did not tend to dispel the melancholy which we felt.' Bitterly she resented the disappearance of the gay court into which she had planned to step. It was a very cross seventeen-year-old who had to walk across Hyde Park every day practising German conversation with an Austrian fräulein.

Having re-established his family Mr Jerome departed for France, to discuss the alleviation of the suffering in Paris—a precursor of Red Cross activity. With two American generals he was led through the enemy lines to meet an old friend, the American Minister, Mr Washbourne, who spoke with emotion of individual acts of courage and despair he had witnessed in Paris. On reaching his house in the Boulevard Haussman, Leonard found a shell had landed in the cellar, but his art collection remained intact and poor Marie was alive. He gave her a food parcel and next day Washbourne took him to see Bismarck on the city outskirts. No soap existed in Paris and Marie had not been able to wash his shirt. Bismarck's secretary noted 'the American gentleman dressed as if hurriedly in a flannel shirt with paper cuffs'. They discussed food supplies and next day Mr

Jerome and his party were led back. France then endured the bitterness of civil war. Fearing their house might be pillaged, Mr and Mrs Jerome returned to Boulevard Haussman to pack up the Italian pictures for shipment to New York.

On 24th May 1871 Mrs Jerome heard that the Tuileries had been set on fire. She set forth in bonnet and shawl to find a rough crowd throwing furniture out of the windows and holding auctions on the lawn. The Emperor's dinner service with a golden N surmounted by the Imperial Crown was being sold in lots. Without a moment's hesitation she joined the fray and bid for pile after pile of plates. Men with hand barrows were in much demand. She hired several and started for home, leaving the palace where she had known so many romantic evenings. Smouldering white bolsters and feather beds were being hurled from windows. Leonard Jerome expostulated when he saw the procession of barrows laden with china. 'A wonderful gift for the Emperor on his return. . . .'

But there would be no return for Louis Napoleon. The china went to Clara's grandson. When Winston lived at Chartwell he found the service very useful, and he enjoyed recounting the story of its acquisition.

When summer came Leonard took his family to the Isle of Wight, where he rented a cottage in West Cowes. He loved sailing, and the happy seaside life would be good for all of them. When Louis Napoleon and Eugenie visited the island on their yacht they invited the Jeromes for a day's sail. The Empress and Prince Imperial were never seasick, but, according to Jennie, Eugenie's Spanish nieces, the Mesdemoiselles d'Albe, lay green-faced in a coma. She records: 'I can see now the Emperor leaning against the mast, looking old, ill and sad. His thoughts could not have been other than sorrowful, and even to my young eyes, he seemed to have nothing to live for.'

In the winter of 1871 the Jeromes returned to Paris. Jennie found 'ruin everywhere; the sight of the Tuileries and the Hôtel de Ville made me cry. Some of our friends were killed, others ruined or in mourning, and all broken-hearted and miserable, hiding in their houses and refusing to be comforted.' The anticlimax of these years surrounded by lamenting French friends bit into Jennie's spirit. Her nature was not one to suffer disappointment gladly and she had ceased to feel American. The stage on which she had visualised herself had vanished. She stood in the Place de la Concorde staring at the statue of lost Strasbourg swathed in black and knew the infernal melancholy of baffled youth. Clara, moping over the Marquis de Tamisier, of whom her mother still disapproved, did not make particularly good company, and the unfortunate Leonie had been packed off to a boarding school in Wiesbaden.

Jennie, at eighteen, had become far more beautiful than Clara. The deep-set eyes and black brows and naturally red lips gave her an extraordinary radiance. The Jerome circulation must have been particularly good. Leonard preferred driving his horses without gloves even in mid winter and his daughters gave the impression of using rouge just because they were so healthy. They had enchanted Cowes society, and the agony of the after-dinner piano piece drummed into English girls by some unfortunate governess was transformed into a magic moment.

During the long days spent sailing or driving they learned to know their parents more intimately than they had before. It was in a way the last undisturbed time they had together before husbands came to break up the nest and the torments and complications of adult life began.

In rowboats and amidst picnic baskets they wheedled Mama into relating her girlhood in western New York. She and her sisters had known since childhood that Red Indian blood ran in their veins and this intrigued the new generation. 'Don't tell people,' Mrs Jerome would say. 'They might not think it chic but you ought to know because it will help you to understand yourselves.' Mama had been born Clara Hall of Palmyra and her mother had been half Iroquois, a beautiful creature who had died leaving three little girls to be brought up by rich, cross, non-Indian aunts. Perhaps it was because she had never known her own parents that Mrs Jerome lavished so much attention on her own children. 'And tell us how Papa proposed and why you married him,' they would ask, knowing that Mama loved to relate her story of that expedition to Niagara Falls when Papa had led her away from the others to dance perilously on the edge of the falls shouting, 'I won't come back till you've promised to marry me! Look! I'm falling—I'm falling!'

And against the roar of the water Clara Hall had finally shrieked, 'I will!'

4

Finally the Jeromes had to realise that *their* Emperor would never regain his throne. Philosophically they decided it might be possible to like Englishmen as well as Frenchmen. They did *not* know, for their father shielded them from business troubles, that 1873 had been a bad year, with the crash of the state-sponsored railway shaking Wall Street. Leonard Jerome, like many financiers, suffered huge losses and, having closed down his town house, he was personally economising while striving to pay for his expensive family in Europe. As co-founder of the Jockey Club and prime organiser of flat racing in America, he held the highest social status: but he now lived in two rooms instead of twenty. There is a story of him at this time:

> At last, one evening, while he was entertaining some friends at dinner, a telegram was brought to him, which he opened, read, and laid by the side of his plate. When the dinner was over he rose and asked pardon for the impoliteness of reading the telegram, 'but gentlemen,' he continued, 'it is a message in which you are all interested. The bottom has fallen out of stocks and shares and I am a ruined man. But your dinner is paid for and I did not want to disturb you while you were eating it.' There was a babble of questions; then a sudden scattering, and Mr Jerome was left with his telegram. He has chosen to remain alone ever since. Only a very few persons are now admitted to his companionship and fewer still to his intimacy. 'Ruined' as he called himself, Mr Jerome was still a fairly wealthy man. He had settled a

large fortune upon his wife; he recovered a fortune from the wreck of his speculations, he has made a fortune since by his investments. But in Wall Street he no longer ruled, and that to him meant ruin.

This then was the father who wrote that he could not join them for another carefree summer, but that they could rent the same gay little Villa Rosetta. From the heat of New York he wrote on August 7th, 1873, wistfully using the family pet names:

Mrs Clit, Miss Clarita and Miss Jennie,
Dearly beloved. It is nearly two weeks since I had a letter. You must be sure to write the particulars of all that is going on. I have no doubt you will see many nice people and will have Cowes all to yourselves as far as Americans are concerned. Did you get the tent from London? And do you make it lively and have you secured the Villa Rosetta for another year? etc. I rather like the idea of Cowes next summer and a yacht. Don't forget while sitting under your own vine and eating up your own fig tree that I am awfully disappointed if I don't get my weekly letters.

Within a fortnight there came an avalanche of news. Clara and Jennie, after being presented to the Prince and Princess of Wales, were invited to a dance given by the officers of the cruiser *Ariadne*, guardship in Cowes Roads for the Royal Regatta. They would wear tulle dresses adorned with fresh flowers for the occasion.

As the launch carried them to the gaily lit cruiser, Clara's and Jennie's animated faces looked up at the first naval ship they had visited. Their invitation card, sent by the captain and officers of HMS *Ariadne*, read:

To meet

Their Royal Highnesses the Prince and Princess of Wales

and

Their Imperial Highnesses

The Grand Duke Cesarevitch and Grand Duchess Cesarevitch

Under the words 'to meet' Jennie, who kept the card, later wrote 'Randolph'. The twenty-three-year-old second son of the Duke of

Marlborough attended the dance with none of the American girls' sense of anticipation. He disliked dancing, and merely cast a perfunctory glance around the ballroom: then he stood staring. A merry group surrounded the Jerome sisters, and the jolt of feeling Lord Randolph Churchill experienced drove him to find a friend who could arrange an introduction. This done, he had to ask one of the girls to dance. Jennie's grey eyes met his—the long lashes made them look 'as if put in with a sooty finger'. Randolph proved unsure of the steps of a formal quadrille, so it was a relief when he suggested they should sit out. Jennie soon discovered that Randolph talked better than he danced, and some quality in the man held her while waltzes were played away unheeded. For his part, Randolph Churchill was surprised to find a beautiful girl who had felt so much of life—for at nineteen Jennie had known the depths of dramatic despair over the fall of the Second Empire. At the evening's end she promised Randolph she would ask her mother to invite him to the Villa Rosetta.

When they reached home Jennie casually suggested to Mrs Jerome that it would be pleasant to invite Randolph and his friend Colonel Edgecombe to dinner. An invitation was sent next morning.

The dinner proved a great success. The Jeromes kept a French cook, and the company's gay spirits were heightened by Clara and Jennie's duets at the piano. These girls were quite different from anything that ever came out of the schoolroom of an English country house. That night, when Clara, who had glided in and out of love several times, told her sister that she did not care for Lord Randolph, Jennie cut her short, saying she had a presentiment this was the man she would marry. Clara laughed incredulously, for Jennie had never before spoken seriously of any man.

Meanwhile Randolph, discussing the sisters with his friend Colonel Edgecombe, confided that he meant if he could to make 'the dark one' his wife.

Next day Jennie and Randolph met 'by accident' on a walk. Mrs Jerome demurred when again asked to invite him to dinner but, as it was his last evening, she sent one of her calling cards engraved:

Mrs Leonard Jerome

The Misses Jerome

24

writing on the back: 'I shall be most happy to see you at dinner this evening, truly yours, C. H. Jerome.' This little card Randolph kept until the end of his days.

The evening again passed pleasantly at Villa Rosetta, where the unmusical Lord Randolph Churchill evinced an extraordinary enthusiasm for duets—and Colonel Edgecombe related later what a pretty sight the golden head and the dark head made side by side over the keyboard. When coffee had been served, Lord Randolph kept his wits sufficiently to inveigle 'the dark one' out into the tiny garden, where promptly he proposed and to his joy was accepted. Their son has written: 'That night, the third of their acquaintance, was a beautiful night, warm and still, with the lights of the yachts shining on the water and the sky bright with stars.' Neither of them had ever been in love before. They expected the world to stand still. When Jennie, flushed and defiant, was left to face Mama and explain why she had remained for so long in the garden, she announced that she had accepted a marriage proposal. Far from expressing pleasure at the news, Mama used deflating words such as 'precipitate' and 'over-hasty'. She insisted that her daughter must think it over. This, parried Jennie, was quite unnecessary. What has thought to do with love?

Meanwhile, Randolph returned to Blenheim Palace to break the news to his parents. The Duchess of Marlborough was anything but pleased to learn that her favourite son had proposed to an unknown American girl after three days' feverish courtship. Randolph's long incoherent letter to his father, who was away, pleads every excuse and reason that enters his head:

August 20th 1873

I do not think that if I were to write pages I could give you any idea of the strength of my feelings and affection and love for her; all I can say is that I love her better than life itself, and that my one hope and dream now is that matters may be so arranged that soon I may be united to her by ties that nothing but death itself could have the power to sever. . . . You won't feel any annoyance with me for not having consulted you before saying anything to her. I really meant to have done so; but on the night before I was leaving Cowes my feelings of sorrow at parting from her were more than I could restrain, and I told her all. I did not say anything to her mother, but I believe that she did after I was

25

gone, for she wrote to me just as I was starting—and she said in her letter that her mother would not hear of it. That I am at a loss to understand.

This was typical. How could the Duke of Marlborough's son understand that any foreign mother should not accept him without question. He went on to describe his own pitiable state of nervous misery and to get down to brass tacks:

I now write to tell you of it all, and to ask you whether you will be able to increase my allowance to some extent to put me in the position to ask Mrs Jerome to let me become her daughter's future husband. I enclose you her photograph, and will only say about her that she is as good as she is beautiful, and that by her education and bringing-up she is in every way qualified to fill any position.

This was exact. Her talent for carrying on conversation, her manners and quick perception would have fitted Jennie for any situation in Europe.

In this letter to his father Randolph did not quite threaten to refuse to stand for Parliament, but he dropped a strong hint:

In the last year or so I feel I have lost a great deal of what energy and ambition I possessed, and an idle and comparatively useless life has at times appeared to me to be the pleasantest; but if I were married to her whom I have told you about, if I had a companion, such as she would be, to take an interest in one's prospects and career, and to encourage me in my exertions and in doing something towards making a name for myself, I think that I might become, with the help of Providence, all and perhaps more than you ever wished and hoped for me.

This was extremely clear. If the Duke of Marlborough allowed him to marry Jennie then Randolph guaranteed a transformation into the ideal son—if on the other hand his 'fondest hopes' were blighted, they could expect the worst. The Duke's reply expressed strong disapproval. 'It is not likely,' he wrote on August 31, 'that at present you can look at anything except from your own point of view; but persons from the outside cannot but be struck with the unwisdom of your proceedings, and the uncontrolled state of your feelings which completely paralyses your judgement.' Even more infuriating were the verses penned by Lord Blandford to his younger brother:

An Elegy on Marriage

'Twas yours and not another's hand that built
The fun'ral pyre near which you tarry.
The dagger's plunged into its bleeding hilt,
Thy fate is sealed if thou doest marry . . .

Remorse shall seize upon thy stricken soul
When tinselled charms begin to pall.
Thy part is strife, a fractious grief thy whole
If thou doest thus in weakness fall . . .

Perambulators and the babies' rusks
Shall be among thy chiefest cares.
See thou to the bottle that it sucks,
Revolt? Thy spirit will not dare . . .

And when thy better half shall whine or fret
Because thou dinest not at home,
Perchance the scene will turn into a pet,
Then! Wilt thou at thy fortunes moan!

So go you forth on your appointed way
And treat my poor advice with slight,
Still will I for a golden future pray,
'May I be wrong' and 'You be right!'

Jennie wrote fully, but without giving names, to her father in New York. In a long prescient letter, presumably of September 8th, Mr Jerome replied:

Union Club
1 West 27th Street

My dear Jennie,

You quite startle me. I shall feel very anxious about you until I hear more. If it has come to that—that *he* only 'waits to consult his family', you are pretty far gone. You must like him well enough to accept for yourself which for you is a great deal. I fear if anything goes wrong you will make a dreadful shipwreck of your affections. I always thought if you ever did fall in love it would be a very dangerous affair. You were never born to love lightly. It must be *way down* or nothing. Something like your mother. Not so Clara—happily not so. Such natures if they happen to secure the right one are very happy but if disappointed they suffer untold misery.

You give no idea of who it is and but for a letter from Clara some week or two ago, I should be utterly in the dark. . . .

I am spending most of my time preparing for the races. The weather favourable we shall have a splendid meeting. The park is looking beautiful. . . .

From present appearances it is quite likely I may join you as early as November. Do you intend to hunt at Pau this winter. Now that you are engaged it may not be worth while to risk your precious neck. If I go to Pau I hunt; Mama may as well make up her mind to that. She thinks I am too old but I will show her to the contrary.

Do you apprehend any serious opposition from me supposing it comes to that? Hardly. Yet you know my views. I have great confidence in you & still greater in your mother and anyone you would accept and your mother approves I could not object to. Provided always he is not a Frenchman or any of those continental cusses. . . .

A week later, when given exact news, he wrote: 'I must say I have been very happy all day. I have thought of nothing else. . . . I am confident that all you say of him is true. Young, ambitious, uncorrupted. . . .'

But when Mr Jerome learnt that the Duke of Marlborough was making objections in London, anger filled the proud Yankee and he cabled a withdrawal of his consent. Jennie was forbidden to answer Lord Randolph's letters, but after a week's furious argument she set pen to paper. On September 23rd, 1873, her young man replied:

I cannot tell you what pleasure and happiness your letter has given me; it makes me feel quite a different being, so you really must not threaten me with a long silence. You certainly have great powers of perception, and I cannot but own that there is a good deal of truth in what you say about my being one moment very despairing and another moment very sanguine. I cannot help it; I was made so.

My father has been away for a few days, and yesterday I got a 'piece' from him on the subject of his consent. After a good deal of unnecessary rigmarole and verbosity he says:

'The great question is still unsolved, whether you and the young lady who has gained your affections are, or can be, after a few days' acquaintance, sufficiently aware of your own minds to venture on the step which is to bind you together for life. What I have now to say is that if I am to believe that your future is really bound up in your marriage with Miss Jerome you must show me the proof of it by bringing it to the test of time, I will say no more to you on this subject for the present, but if this time next year you come and tell me that you are both of the same mind we will receive Miss Jerome as a daughter, and I need not say, in the affection you could desire for your wife.'

Now these are his words but I do not mind telling you that it is all humbug about waiting a year. I could and would wait a good deal more than a year, but I do not mean to, as it is not the least necessary, for though we have only known each other a short time, I know we both know our own minds well enough, and I wrote a very long and diplomatic letter to my father yesterday, doing what I have done before, contradicting him and arguing with him, and I hope persuading him that he has got very wrong and foolish ideas in his head. You see, both he and my mother have set their hearts on my being member for Woodstock. It is a family borough, and for years and years a member of the family has sat for it. The present member is a stranger, although a Conservative, and is so unpopular that he is almost sure to be beaten if he were to stand; and the fact of a Radical sitting for Woodstock is perfectly insupportable to my family. It is for this that they have kept me idle ever since I left Oxford, waiting for a dissolution. Well, as I told you the other day, a dissolution is almost sure to come almost before the end of the year. I have two courses open to me; either to refuse to stand altogether unless they consent to my being married immediately afterwards; or else—and this is still more Machiavellian and deep—to stand, but at the last moment to threaten to withdraw and leave the Radical to walk over— all tricks are fair in love and war.

A favourite quotation for thwarted lovers! Randolph's father seems to have been kindly though chilling. It is difficult through the pompous Victorian style of his letters to perceive the human being. Randolph's mother, a daughter of the third Marquis of Londonderry, was a great heiress, a formidable duchess and although unable to show her feelings, a passionately loving mother. Of her two surviving boys, Randolph was the favourite. His elder brother, Lord Blandford, who had five years previously married the Duke of Abercorn's daughter, had already proved himself a worrying son and an appalling husband.

The five daughters had to be brought up and brought out. Then it was their duty to marry. Governesses taught them to read and grooms to ride but no one took pains to make plain girls less self-conscious and five husbands of desirable status were not easy to find. In that stratified Victorian aristocracy it was the boys who mattered. Randolph and his clever, difficult brother had been reared amidst this adoring flock of sisters. They went to Eton and then to Oxford and took their sip of pleasure in the wilful arrogant way permissible to sons of an English Duke. But despite packs of hounds and tours of Europe, happiness does not seem to have rested on either young man. And despite protestations of affection they were afraid of their parents. Randolph could speak glibly of 'earning his living' but no jobs existed for his class.

In the campaign of alternate threat and supplication which Randolph adopted, the enclosure of Miss Jerome's photograph was a wise move, for, however dismayed at the thought of an 'American alliance', the Duke and Duchess must have entertained a certain curiosity concerning the cause of so much emotion in this hitherto unsusceptible son. And the cameras of 1873 had not learnt to lie. Harsh lights and black shadows showed up coldly the lines of Jennie's beautiful face.

Stunned by the speed of Randolph's decision, both parents continued to urge caution. They had always believed that a considerable political career lay at his feet. Now, with a General Election imminent, it was the moment to launch him. He stood on the threshold. Serving England was the only career open to an intelligent young man born in his circle. He could be a Member of the House of Commons, a Master of Hounds, or loaf around in society. Yet Randolph had seemed only half anxious to step into the arena.

30

Self-analytical, he had often doubted if he had the temperament for public life, but now he vibrated with energy. In October, after the Duke had promised to give his consent to the marriage as soon as he got into Parliament, he wrote from Blenheim:

> The clouds have all passed away, and the sky is bluer than I have ever seen it since I first met you at Cowes. It is exactly six weeks tomorrow since we met on board the *Ariadne*, and I am sure I seem to have lived six years. How I do bless that day, in spite of all the worry and bother that has come about since. . . . Our early golden dreams of being married in December won't quite become realised, but still it won't be very long. . . .
>
> It is curious what an effect books have on me. I have two old favourites. When I feel very cross and angry I read Gibbon, whose profound philosophy and easy though majestic writing soon quiets me down, and in an hour I feel at peace with all the world. When I feel very low and desponding I read Horace, thorough Epicuranisms, quiet maxims and beautiful verse are most tranquilising. Of late I have had to have frequent recourse to my two friends and they have never failed me. . . .

He goes on to discuss the General Election which would almost certainly result in him being elected member for Woodstock:

> But, after all, public life has no great charms for me, as I am naturally very quiet, and hate bother and publicity, which, after all, is full of vanity and vexation of spirit. Still, it will all have greater attractions for me if I think it will please you and that you take an interest in it and will encourage me to keep up to the mark.
>
> I hope your sister is well, comforts you, and sticks up for me when you abuse me to her or doubt me.

For a man who was to prove the most dynamic parliamentarian of the age he sounds tepid. He does not particularly want to enter the House of Commons, he is going to stand merely because it has become a convenient way of pleasing his father and obtaining a bigger allowance.

No one thought of writing the news to the fourteen-year-old 'kid-sister' Leonie at her Wiesbaden boarding school. She heard of Jennie's engagement from a stranger and wrote in the diary which she kept in three languages, under the date of September 27th, 1873: 'Last night at the circus someone told me that Jennie would marry the second son of the Duke of Marlborough—a Good Thing tho' he *is* a younger son!'

Jennie's letters to Randolph were interesting. With Clara she attended the trial of Marshal Bazaine, former Commander of the defeated armies.

All eyes turned on him, and some of the women jumped on their chairs, levelling their opera-glasses at the unfortunate man. This was promptly put a stop to by the gendarmes present, who pulled the offenders down unceremoniously by their skirts. '*Fi donc*' I heard a gendarme say, '*C'est pas gentil*', nor was it.

Bazaine's advocate in defending cried out: '*Mais, regardez-le donc! Ce n'est pas un traitre, c'est un imbecile!*' The Marshal was found guilty, sentenced to death and then allowed to escape.

A more personal note creeps into her letters when Jennie assures Randolph that she is not jealous: 'My dear, I am not afraid of anyone in England, even that dreadful clever charming Miss Harris. I hope she is married by this time & won't have an opportunity of making herself agreeable to a certain susceptible young man of my acquaintance for whom I have *un petit faible* . . . My dearest Randolph, tell me what you are thinking of? . . .'

During their months of engagement both Randolph and Jennie could write tartly enough. Hunting, electioneering and the long drawn out illness of an aunt supplied the material for Randolph's letters but he handled his pen well and scolded Jennie for using the verb 'to prorogue' incorrectly. She argued impenitently that the young Count de Fénelon took her side.

'Hang *le petit Fénelon*,' wrote Randolph. '. . . little idiot. What do I care for him? He may be a very good authority about his own beastly language, but I cannot for a moment submit to him about English. . . .'

In January 1874 Gladstone announced the dissolution of Parliament and England hummed with political activities. 'My darling Jennie,' wrote the candidate for Woodstock, 'You heap coals of fire on my head by your dear loving letter received this morning. I remember now I did write rather a cross letter last Tuesday but you must make allowances for me as I have been awfully hustled and worried . . . My dearest what a nice letter you wrote to my mother, she was so pleased with it. You have the happiest and nicest way of expressing yourself of anyone I know. You will be happy to hear that my father is very much struck with your handwriting which he assured me had a deal of character. . . .'

Lord Randolph was popular with the farmers around Blenheim who had seen him since boyhood tearing over the countryside on horseback but he was completely inexperienced on the platform and he had in the past months concentrated on courtship rather than speechmaking. On the first day of the campaign all went well, for the annual coursing meeting took place and he could write to Jennie:

Blenheim, Monday.

. . . all the farmers were there, and as they had a day's sport were all in great spirits. I took the chair at their dinner at the Bear Hotel and you have no idea how enthusiastic they were for me.

But as the hour of public meetings approached he grew ill with nerves. If a first-class speaker, one Mr Edward Clarke, had not been summoned from London to help, he might well have lost the seat. Mr Clarke was appalled at Randolph's awkwardness and lack of knowledge of political affairs. Although gifted with an excellent memory Randolph couldn't even learn his speech by heart. He wrote it out on bits of paper which he hid in the bottom of his top hat. The audience soon noticed this juvenile stratagem and began to shout: 'Take the things out of your hat.' Mr Clarke had organised friendly questioners throughout the Hall and rehearsed Randolph in the answers, but disorder broke out. Finally Mr Clarke came to the rescue with a skilful professional speech while poor Randolph looked around for the men who were supposed to ask him the questions whose answers he knew! After all he was only doing all this in order to please his father and get Jennie. In his letters to her he described each episode but not exactly. The predicament from which Mr Clarke rescued him was skimmed over.

We had a great meeting last night which was very successful; we had a good speaker down from London, and I made a speech. How I have been longing for you to have been with me. If we had only been married before this! I think the reception you would have got, would have astonished you. . . .

33

But he hated it all. Excitement disagreed with him. He could not eat nor sleep.

At last it was over. 'I have won a great victory,' he telegraphed to Jennie. 'Great enthusiasm. Expect me Saturday.' Congratulations arrived from Mr Jerome in New York:

> You do not tell me how much you were pelted with eggs and stones etc. That I suppose you leave to my imagination. . . It opens to you a magnificent field . . . a field wherein with half an effort you are bound to play no ignoble part.

Randolph hoped to travel to Paris immediately after the Election, but the news that his aunt Lady Portarlington was dying at her Irish home turned him from Dover to Dublin. He waited with the family for three weeks. After the funeral he hurried to Paris for the few days before he had to take the Oath in London. This visit, according to the fifteen-year-old Leonie, was fairly tense.

The marriage settlements were proving very tricky and Jennie and Randolph were never allowed to see each other alone. My grandmother told me how exasperating it was to have Mama 'always just within earshot pretending to write letters.' This constant chaperonage led of course to a technique of flirtatious glances and fluttering eye-lashes which said a great deal, but no mother in her senses, especially a socially ambitious mother, allowed a girl to risk her reputation—and this necessitated a twenty-four hour alibi. The Jerome girls were never allowed out alone, and my grandmother related with wry humour that although it was considered improper for a lady to travel alone in a carriage with a man she could go out riding 'with Tom, Dick and Harry', as long as she never got off her horse. Victorian realism.

As mother could not talk frankly about sex it must have been difficult to warn efficiently. The final facts had to be learnt in the marriage bed—until then ceaseless vigilance.

In a way these formidable conventions made for harmony. At least everyone knew the rules and the mother-daughter arguments of today did not exist.

Now that his son was in the House of Commons and Disraeli again Prime Minister, the Duke of Marlborough felt all might be right with the world. He travelled over to Paris with the Duchess in a benign mood and they found themselves charmed by the Jerome ladies. Jennie's good looks exceeded expectation; the photograph had not suggested her colouring—the deep grey eyes and red lips. When Mr Jerome arrived in April from America he found all marriage details settled except for the dowry, which he was expected to provide with a flourish. It was not the American habit for girls to support their husbands, whereas in England it had since medieval times been considered right and natural for an heiress to devote her fortune to sustaining a man's career or estates. Leonard Jerome put his views clearly and the Duke of Marlborough felt embarrassed because he himself suffered financial difficulties in the upkeep of magnificent Blenheim. An English Duke could not be parsimonious. Marlborough had been forced to sell off many family treasures already and his own daughters would need dowries. During a period of negotiations in which Mrs Jerome proved even more American in her views than Leonard and according to Randolph 'twists him round her little finger', there was some strong disagreement. Randolph wrote to his father:

Mr and Mrs Jerome and myself are barely on speaking terms, and I don't quite see what is to be the end of it. I think both his conduct and Mrs J.'s perfectly disgraceful and I am bound to say that Jennie entirely agrees with me.

Poor Leonard Jerome had experienced severe financial reverses in the last year but he could not resist Jennie's pleading. Eventually he settled £3,000 a year on the pair, and the Duke paid off Randolph's debts of £2,000 and increased his allowance to £1,100 a year. When all had been arranged, Mr Jerome wrote in a friendly tone:

Dear Duke,
. . . I have every confidence in Randolph and while I would entrust my daughter to his sole care alone in the world, still I can but feel reassured of her happiness when I am told that in entering your family she will be met at once with 'new and affectionate friends and relatives'.
I am very sorry you are not able to come over to the wedding. We had all hoped to have had the pleasure of seeing both yourself and the Duchess. Under the circumstances, however, we must

of course excuse you—and we do this the more readily as we know the occasion has your best wishes and the young people your blessing.

In regard to the settlement—as it has finally, I am happy so say, been definitely arranged—little more need be said. In explanation of my own action in respect to it I beg to assure you that I have been governed purely by what I conceived to be for the best interests of both parties. It is quite wrong to suppose I entertain any distrust of Randolph. On the contrary, I firmly hope and believe there is no young man in the world safer, still I can but think your English custom of making the wife so utterly dependent upon the husband most unwise.

In the settlement as finally arranged I have ignored American customs and waived all my American prejudices and have conceded to your views and English custom on every point—save one. That is simply— a somewhat unusual allowance of her money to the wife. Possibly this principle may be wrong but you may be very certain my action upon it in this instance by no means arises from any distrust of Randolph.

With kind regards,
Believe me dear Duke,
Yours most sincerely,
Leonard Jerome

Having obtained sufficient income, the young lovers were free to arrange the wedding. Hundreds of magnificent presents arrived and Leonie made detailed lists in her meticulous script. She started with the gold Russian *coffre* and a locket of pearls and turquoises from the Prince and Princess of Wales and carried on down through the Peerage mingling in well-known names from New York. The objects sound enchanting. They must be spread around the world in antique shops and museums, their story forgotten.

April 15th, the Duchess of Marlborough's birthday, was chosen for the wedding. Randolph's eldest three sisters, his brother Lord Blandford, and his aunt Lady Camden arrived in Paris with the best man Francis Knollys, private secretary to the Prince of Wales. Leonie wrote an account of the large family dinner in a letter which she never posted. It was found in her desk some eighty years later. Dear kind Papa must have sold quite a few shares in Wall Street, for the inspection of Jennie's trousseau revealed 'twenty-three very pretty dresses, six or seven bonnets and some very fine linen'.

On the following morning the three Jerome sisters were up early. Leonie looked out of her window to see the sun shining on the budding chestnut trees. She and Clara wore dresses of pale blue silk with white embroidery, their bridesmaids' presents (crystal lockets) hung around their necks. While Mama wept a bevy of maids hooked and laced Jennie into her gown of white satin with a long train and flounces of Alençon lace. Over this shimmering cascade a long tulle veil was finally placed 'covering her entirely' and Mr Jerome came to kiss his daughter and place a necklace of pearls around her neck. Then he led her down to his carriage and drove her to the British Embassy where the ceremony was to take place. The bridesmaids and Mrs Jerome, who wore 'a grey silk dress with street trimmings', followed in another carriage. As was the custom of the time, while the guests enjoyed a sumptuous wedding breakfast, bride and groom ate in a little drawing room by themselves. After a few words with the guests Jennie moved upstairs to change into her going-away outfit, 'a very pretty dark blue and white striped dress for travelling and a white hat with a white feather'.

In her hand she carried her father's wedding present, an exquisite parasol of white Alençon lace with a gold and tortoiseshell handle. There were no tears in Jennie's eyes as she embraced her family. Flushed and elated, she climbed into the open carriage drawn by four grey horses with two postillions. Clara and Leonie threw slippers as the carriage moved away towards some secret country destination, while Mama collapsed weeping.

Jennie and Randolph seemed to have everything—youth, brains, charm, situation, high spirits and real love. Yet sadness filled Leonard Jerome. Jennie had been his favourite child, a replica of himself; he had always wished she had been born a boy and even then, on the brink of a new life so full of promise, he wondered how she would settle down.

5

In early May the young pair arrived at Woodstock, where cheering tenants unharnessed their horses and dragged the carriage from the station to Blenheim Palace. As they passed the entrance archway, Randolph, with the enthusiasm which all landed Englishmen feel for their homes, cried out: 'This is the finest view in England.' Jennie says she was able to ripost by quoting Pope's lines on Blenheim:

> 'See, sir, here's the grand approach;
> This way is for his grace's coach;
> There lies the bridge, and here's the clock,
> Observe the lion and the cock,
> The spacious court, the colonnade,
> And mark how wide the hall is made!
> The chimneys are so well designed,
> They never smoke in any wind.
> This gallery's contrived for walking,
> The windows to retire and talk in;
> The council chamber for debate,
> And all the rest are rooms of state.'
> 'Thanks, sir,' cried I, ' 'tis very fine,
> But where d'ye sleep, or where d'ye dine?
> I find by all you have been telling,
> That 'tis a house but not a dwelling.'

The Duke and Duchess were waiting on the steps to greet them. Jennie felt the gimlet eyes of Randolph's mother and sisters.

During the following days the atmosphere of constraint remained. Jennie had no small opinion of herself, and if the Duchess wanted to know how Miss Jennie Jerome had been educated she would give a display. She had, of course, worked far harder at her music than the Churchill sisters; for Jennie, taught by Stephen Heller, four or five hours' piano practice a day had become a habit. And the gruelling days spent with French and German governesses had left her fluent in both languages. She was well read, because in France girls were *made* to read. Knowing her achievements, the young bride showed off. And this diminished still more her popularity with the feminine members of her new family.

When they took her riding, expecting at least to have an advantage in this domain, she capped their prowess and made sure they noticed she was a skilful horsewoman, one trained by her father to keep light sensitive hands. A sister-in-law could hardly have been more irritating.

Despite her arrogance they were proud of Jennie's astonishing beauty. No family of the English horse-breeding caste could fail to admire the bone structure of the new mare who had entered their stable. The priceless gift of health which Jennie brought to a delicate overbred race passed entirely unnoticed.

Perhaps Jennie was determined not to be overawed by her stuck-up in-laws. None of them dreamt she was writing naughty letters to Mrs Jerome laughing at their frumpy clothes and at the water jugs on the dinner table with thick ordinary tumblers, 'the kind we use in bedrooms'. They knew nothing of Paris fashion and their table-mats were the wrong shape—so were their shoes! Long after she reminisced: 'How strange life in a big country house seemed to one who, until then, had been accustomed only to towns!' Every day followed a routine, and although Jennie enjoyed appearing in her twenty-three Paris dresses which were so much smarter than anyone else's, she resented formality. The ceremonious breakfast when the ladies appeared in long velvet or silk trains and the gentlemen in morning coats could be curtailed when the family were alone, but at lunch the Duke and Duchess always followed the eighteenth-century custom of themselves carving up the joints for the entire family, the tutors and governesses. Then the remains would be carried off by the children to the deserving poor, for children always existed in these big houses, grandchildren, nephews and nieces creeping in before the youngest of each generation left the schoolroom.

Jennie describes it: 'When the family were alone at Blenheim everything went on with the regularity of clockwork. So assiduously did I practise my piano, read or paint, that I began to imagine myself back in the schoolroom. In the morning an hour was devoted to the reading of newspapers, which was a necessity if one wanted to show an intelligent interest in the questions of the day, for at dinner conversation invariably turned on politics. In the afternoon a drive to pay a visit to some neighbour or a walk in the gardens would help to while away some part of the day. After dinner, which was rather a solemn full-dress affair, we all repaired to the Vandyck room. There one might read one's book or play for love a mild game of whist. . . . No one dared suggest bed until the sacred hour of eleven had struck. Then we would all troop out into a small ante-room, and lighting our candles, each in turn would kiss the Duke and Duchess and depart to our own rooms.'

It was a relief for the newly married couple to move off to their own house in Curzon Street, where Jennie could enjoy her first London season. The few hundred families constituting society opened up their town houses to give dinner parties at which conversation was deliberately kept political or abstract. So small was the circle of diplomats, politicians and aristocratic landowners that all the guests at the magnificent nightly balls knew each other.

It was Disraeli's Belgravia which Jennie described when 'dinners, balls and parties succeeded one another without intermission till the end of July, the only respite being the Whitsun recess. A few of the racing people might go to Newmarket for a week, but the fashionable world flocked only to the classic races, the Derby, Ascot and Goodwood. . . . We used to drive down in coaches in Ascot frocks and feathered hats, and stay to dinner, driving back by moonlight.'

At Ascot Races in 1874 Jennie wore, according to the mode, her wedding dress of white satin slightly transformed, a bonnet of nodding pink roses and she carried Papa's present, the parasol of exquisite lace, held like a cobweb behind her head, Lord Randolph's bride was the cynosure of all eyes.

The warm days of June and July rolled by. Jennie was formally presented to Queen Victoria at a drawing room, and the Prince and

Princess of Wales, to whom she had curtseyed the previous summer, proved most kind. Young married couples, according to the conventions of the 'seventies, did not appear in public for several months after marriage—they were supposed to feel shy. But this was a state of mind difficult for either Randolph or Jennie to assume. They accepted the more amusing invitations. At a ball in honour of the Czar Alexander II at Stafford House, His Imperial Majesty dashed a little cold water. When Jennie was presented and he learned she was a bride of only a few weeks, he remarked coldly, '*Et ici déjà!*' A Czar of all the Russias could spare the energy for such trivial criticism.

On May 22nd, 1874, Randolph delivered his maiden speech in the House of Commons. It concerned a proposal to make a new military centre near Oxford. Randolph spoke hotly and thoughtlessly in defence of the peace of his former university, stating he did not wish it to suffer 'roystering soldiers and licentious camp-followers'. This tirade brought biting comment from Sir William Harcourt, who professed himself shocked that one who bore a name so inseparably associated with the glories of the British Army should have used the term 'roystering soldiers' or that having been elected by a majority all of whom did not belong to the upper class he should have spoken of 'railway roughs'. Disraeli, who had known Randolph since he was a boy, took the pains to write a note to the Duchess of Marlborough:

> You will be pleased to hear that Lord R. last night made a very successful début in the House of Commons. He said some imprudent things, which was of no consequence in the maiden speech of a young man but he spoke with fire and fluency; and showed energy of thought and character, with evidence of resource.

Disraeli wanted to soothe the Duchess. It had not been a successful début but it had shown the consternation which a lively young man could arouse.

Lord Randolph cared little for politics as yet; the taste of excitement, of being able to arouse the House, was new to him.

In June, Clara came to stay, and her letters, written from a house where Disraeli, Sir Charles Dilke and Lord Rosebery were frequent guests, reveal an astonishing frivolity. There is never a word concerning the conversation at Jennie's political dinner parties but 'Darling Mama' got pages about quadrilles for the Prince of Wales' 'Pack of Cards' fancy-dress dance to which he only invited twenty-four ladies outside the royal family. Jennie is attired as the Queen of Spades, is to dance with the Duke of Atholl as King of Diamonds, and Clara as the Seven of Hearts is to dance with Lord Macduff as Seven of Spades. The costumes cost £15 a piece and Randolph is furious.

The frequent visits to Blenheim were not an unqualified success. Although she could no longer ride and had to spend every afternoon with the Duchess, Jennie did not try to endear herself, while Clara provoked the unmarried girls by obviously preening her own good looks. And instead of admiring Blenheim she would talk about the Château de Compiègne! For all their French education the Jerome girls had not as yet learnt tact. They thought life at Blenheim boring and they showed it.

A letter from Jennie to her mother written on October 21st and sent with insufficient postage stamps reveals a basic difference between French and English social habits: '. . . on our return found the drawing room full of lots of people having tea. I escaped as soon as I could. You cannot imagine how stiff & uncomfortable the first hour of their arrivals are. No one knows each other & so content themselves with staring. Tonight I suppose will be like last night, some playing whist or billiards or working. You can't imagine what gossip & slander people talk, really to my discreet ears it seems quite incredible—everyone is pulled to pieces . . . & it is not only the women who back bite—but the men I assure you are quite as bad. . . .'

Randolph's letters to Mrs Jerome during this month were full of praise for the Parisian baby clothes she sent and he described Jennie's London bedroom as 'too lovely, quite a pleasure to be confined in it'.

In November, when shooting starts, Jennie enjoys the splendid picnic lunches laid out in some lodge, after which she follows the shooters in a pony carriage, but the Duchess walks five miles through turnip fields!

On November 28th there was a shoot at Blenheim, and the imprudent Jennie went out with the guns, over-exerted herself, and a rattling drive home in a pony trap augmented her pains, which the local doctor tried in vain to stop through Sunday. At one-thirty on the morning of Monday November 30th a premature baby son was born.

The church bells around Blenheim rang joyously, and Randolph and the Duchess of Marlborough wrote detailed letters to Mrs Jerome in Paris.

> We had neither cradle nor baby linen nor anything ready, but fortunately everything went well & all difficulties were over-come.

Thus wrote the Duchess, whilst Randolph's postscript stressed urgency: 'We hope the baby things will come with all speed. We have to borrow some from the Woodstock Solicitor's wife.'

Jennie's baby was christened Winston Leonard Spencer Churchill. A wet nurse arrived and when her strength allowed Jennie returned to London. She was only twenty and her interests did not centre in the nursery. She wrote:

> After the comparatively quiet life of Paris, we seemed to live in a whirl of gaieties and excitement. Many were the delightful balls I went to which, unlike those of the present day, invariably lasted until five in the morning. Masked balls were much the vogue. Holland House, with its wonderful historical associations and beautiful gardens, was a fitting frame for such entertainments, and I remember enjoying myself immensely at one given there. Disguised in a painted mask and in a yellow wig, I mystified everyone. My sister [Clara] who was staying with us, had been walking in the garden with young Lord ——, who was a *parti*, and much run after by designing mothers with marriageable daughters. Introducing him to me, she pretended I was her mother. Later in the evening I attacked him, saying that my daughter had just confided to me that he had proposed to her, and that she had accepted him. To this day I can see his face of horror and bewilderment.

In London Jennie tried mixing interesting literary people into her formal parties for the Prime Minister and the Prince and Princess of Wales. One evening after Disraeli had monopolised her the Prince chaffed: 'And tell me, my dear, what office did you get for Randolph?' She laughed, for she was sure her husband would obtain what office he chose. Dizzy concealed his abstemiousness with flowery compliments. When Randolph offered a liqueur the old man would gaily refuse: 'My dear Randolph, I have sipped your excellent champagne, I have drunk your good claret, I have tasted your delicious port, I will have no more.'

Jennie, who had never dealt with cooks and thought that, as in France, delicious food automatically rolled out of all kitchens, suffered anxious moments when her hazy suggestions resulted in the meat course being dumped into the soup, but the notoriously gourmet Prince of Wales preferred the ready wit of her table to larks' tongues served in a stodgier atmosphere. Lord Blandford, Randolph's curious, outrageous, clever, elder brother began to hold her in healthy respect. One day he gave her a ring, which Jennie proudly showed to her mother-in-law. To her mortification the Duchess declared the ring properly belonged to Blandford's wife and that he had no right to give it. A family row ensued, conducted with a virulence that Jennie did not know could exist. Blandford's immediate letter to his mother began:

My dear Mama,
    Well acquainted as I am with the intense jealousy that you often display in your actions and the mischief which you so often make . . . etc.

The Duke sent on the correspondence to Randolph, covered by an epistle starting:

Randolph,
    Your mother has received today the enclosed correspondence. I have only three words to say to you upon it . . . etc.

In vain Jennie begged to return the ring, but the brothers were now well launched on a kind of correspondence they appeared to enjoy. The Duke received an uncontrite note.

My dearest Papa,
    I most respectfully remark with regard to yr letter of this afternoon that I think I have formed a hasty judgement of the enclosed correspondence. I venture to think that expressions such as *'dishonourable'*, *'treacherous'* and *'liar'* are hardly applicable

44

to me. As long as these expressions remain in force further communications between us are not only as you remark useless but impossible.

Yrs affectionately
Randolph

Jennie always felt stunned by these outbursts. She had hardly been able to credit the story which Randolph had told her of the Duke of Marlborough's quarrel with his brother Lord Alfred Churchill over a Bill dealing with Church Rates. So enraged had the Duke been by Lord Alfred's liberal approach to this matter that he had literally forced his brother to resign from Parliament and had even refused to attend the final dinner given by the constituents of Woodstock. Randolph, then a boy of fifteen, had been sent to recite the necessary speeches. Jennie had to realise how different family relationships could be from her own. Emotional and hot-tempered as the Jerome girls were, their every disagreement resulted in tears of self-reproach. Tantrums were followed by pleas for pardon, the angry word by the goodnight kiss.

A sheaf of undated letters written by Jennie on one of her numerous visits to Mama in Paris was preserved by Randolph. They describe outings into French society and already express anxiety concerning his health. 'It seemed so lonely not to find you dearest. I took particular pains to shut the door of yr room. I cld not bear the desolate look it had ... I hope yr cold is not worse and remember only 6 cigarettes. . . . Please take care of yourself darling boy and come back soon to your lonely Jennie.' Then we hear: 'The Baby is such a darling, he is growing so fat and he nearly walks alone.' She writes sleepily one evening after three hours of skating lessons ('edges both back and forward'): 'Tell me really how you are . . . please dearest get well and come back. . . . The Baby is most flourishing, but he never will kiss me unless I say "For Papa".'

Clara again came to stay in Randolph's house for the season. Various letters to her mother in heavy monogrammed envelopes survive. For an educated girl of twenty-five, the tone seems idiotic, yet a vivid picture emerges. These letters were not written for posterity, and the reader who gets tired of tulle and bonnets must visualise a world in which dressing mattered very much indeed. Lord Randolph Churchill himself was much absorbed by the cut of his frock coats and was sometimes criticised for over-dressing. He liked delicately tinted shirts and wore as much jewellery as taste could permit, including Jennie's first gift, a diamond ring shaped like a Maltese cross. Emerging from his reading of Gibbon or Horace, he would spend quite a time surveying his reflection in the mirror while a valet added last touches.

In this context Clara's letters to Mrs Jerome who purchased all her daughter's clothes in Paris seem less curious:

[p.d.   Monday morning
 1875]   48 Charles St

My darling Mama,

I never had such a nasty drizzling odious crossing!

Jennie and R. just going off to a charming little dinner at Lady Dufferin's which had been arranged for *me*, but I was so tired that, after having a little something to eat, I went straight to bed. I just got your letter this minute and am so sorry about the bonnets but I can get on with some old ones until they come. R. has got my invitation for this Court ball next Thursday at Buckingham Palace through Francis Knollys which will be very jolly; and also one, he thinks, for the Dudleys for Wednesday. Tomorrow Jennie thinks I ought to wear the white crepe with sequins as it will be my very first appearance, and it is everything to look well. . . . Poor Rosamond in bed today with a feverish cold—

Love to Leonie,
Clara

At this period Rosamond, Randolph's younger sister, must have disliked Jennie and Clara with their French gowns and rosy lips. Clara rattles on about herself in pale cream lace with rosebuds, or white satin with blue bows and forget-me-nots, while Rosamond looks 'rather pasty' and the Duchess frowns.

It would have been wiser to assume humbler airs and be liked. The whispers that Jennie and Clara rouged recommenced. As all make-up was taboo, to have naturally red mouths and easily flushed cheeks seemed an unfair advantage. Fifty years later I heard Clara indignantly refuting the charge! 'We never did use rouge. It was our circulation. Other girls used to slap their cheeks before entering a ball room. We were always pink.'

On she goes. A letter dated June 16th, 1875, continues the usual refrain to:

Darling Mama. . . . We had a most charming dinner last night. I wore the blue chosen by Leonie and Jennie her black gauze and Mrs Standish her black. Vogüè[1] gave me a most charming bouquet. Blount gave one to Jennie and then we went to the play where Vogüè *would* sit next to me. And then dressed and went to the Marjoribanks' Ball. Jennie wants me so much to be nice to Sir William Gordon-Cumming and wants him to make up to me. I think *entre-nous* that it wd take very little to make him devoted to me, although he is a man who never speaks to a young girl and only flirts with married ladies. He began *très sérieusement à faire la cour* to Jennie but last night he would not leave me in the hall. But I could not think of him at all as he is very poor and awfully conceited and not *sympathique*. I don't think I could really like a man like that.

Clara was wise. Sir William Gordon-Cumming, Bt., a rich Scottish landowner and Guards officer, was unkind and had an odious habit of waylaying young married women. He ended badly in the Tranby Croft scandal.

Clara continued:

Tonight there is this dreadful dinner at the Square, [the Marlboroughs] which will be such a bore. Rosamond has been a week at Brighton and is looking very well so perhaps they will ask some 'choice young man' for her. I can't tell you how jealous Randolph says the Duchess is of Jennie and I. She is always very kind and amiable but *une certaine aigreur* in the way she talks. Poor Jennie doesn't know what to do while we are at Ems as she thinks it very expensive to come with us and it would be considered very fast for her to stay here by herself without Randolph. What a pity it is she has not more money. . . .

The Duchess of Marlborough had by now married three of her five daughters, the eldest, Cornelia, to the seventh Lord Wimborne, Fanny to Randolph's friend Edward Marjoribanks, (later Lord Tweedmouth), and Ann to the seventh Duke of Roxburghe. It was now Rosamond's turn, and the poor girl could hardly have

[1] Compte de Vogüè, racing friend of the Prince of Wales.

enjoyed her first season while suffering a liver complaint culminating in jaundice. For another two years, until she married Lord de Ramsey, Rosamond would be dragged around by her mother and scolded for looking poorly.

A long-awaited letter from Curzon Street is perhaps worth recording in its entirety for the picture it gives of Ascot Races in 1875. The importance of correct attire for each event is stressed. There were special gowns with long sleeves for breakfast. A lady could only attend a play in black or dark blue, although evening dress and diamonds were *de rigueur* for the opera, so that after the theatre they had to drive home and re-dress for a ball.

Saturday, June 12th 1875

My darling Mama,

We have just come home and I sit down immediately to write you *with my hat on*. I wrote you from Ascot a tremendously long account of all we were doing but I found out afterwards the servant preferred going to the races and never posted it at all. We were a cheery party . . . I never saw such wonderful *toilettes* and the Royal Enclosure was very swell and select. Lord Harrington took me to lunch in a private room with the royalties, the Prince himself giving his arm to Jennie and altogether the day was *très réussi*! Vogüè and Halley Blount were a great addition as of course they were all devoted to us and as Halley and Castlereagh etc. were stopping with the Prince they were considered big swells. I can't tell you how much I like Vogüè. I always thought I would if I ever knew him and I think he likes me. All the Frenchmen came home with us piled up on the coach and had tea on the lawn . . .

Everyone dragged in one after the other for breakfast, then we dressed for the races. I wore Leonie's blue silk which was thought very pretty. The Princess was not there, but the Prince flourished and won a lot of money and did like the other day. I walked about with all the men and then took lunch with Mr Delane, editor of *The Times*. He has a charming house on the other side of the course and we only had chic people. . . . Vogüè and Hardwicke came to dine. I wore my white muslin and pink roses and Jennie wore her dark blue low dress. Lady Dudley kept seats for us every day at the races and was most kind so handsome too. Lord B. walked a little with me but he was very distrait throughout the meeting as he had horses running every day. . . . The Prince is very kind to us and takes us for a little walk every day. Thursday was Gold Cup Day. Jennie wore her wedding dress with new crêpe de Chine trimmings and I my pale blue with marguerites *au corsage* and my new marguerite bonnet which is very pretty. We managed to have lots of fun after the races as Oliver Montagu invited us to take tea at the 'barracks of the Blues' at Windsor. So we all crowded on top of the coach and Oliver and Col. Williams (Col. of the regiment) received us in grand state with tea on the lawn, the band playing. . . We got home tired after a long dusty drive and gay although some of the men who lost were rather cross. *Friday*. A bad day but I never enjoyed myself so much. I wore my pink foulard and Jennie her dark blue and the men were all *very* nice to us. After the Races Hardwicke took us all with the coach to see the Queen's hounds in their Kennels (which I don't know how to spell!), and then we went home and as more of the men have won back their money the dinner was more cheerful. Jennie wore her pale blue tulle with silver and I my white tulle with jet and then went to the Ball at Chiswick (the Prince and Princess's place) which was a great success. Carrington and Vogüè were there and looked particularly dashing. I never enjoyed a dance so much although I think Lord E[ssex] a humbug. The Princess had on a brown tulle and looked very well and we did not get home till 5 o'c. Old Lord Westmoreland (that is he is about 45) took a great fancy to me, but he is a bore I think although he is considering something wonderful this evening. . . . I ran up to see Baby Winston a minute and here I am writing you my journal. . . .

Your loving,
Clara

A letter she forwarded to Papa in New York read:

Saturday 19th June 1875

My darling Mama,

I slept to-day until 1 o'c and found Sydney and Col. Edgecombe in the Salon waiting for Jennie and R. to come to lunch and to talk of the Ball last night. It was a great success and I enjoyed myself immensely. . . . The Prince gave me his bouquet in the flower figure and I saw Rosamond and Miss Stephens *green* with jealousy. He (the Pce) was very civil to Jennie and I talked to the Princess so taking it all in all it was most satisfactory. . . . Kiss Leonie.

Your loving,
Clara

The Prince of Wales liked Jennie from the start. She enjoyed showing off her own beauty in the ballroom; the magnetic drawing of every man's eyes as she entered gave her conscious pleasure, but she had more than her looks to offer. She was fun, and the Prince needed this commodity. Clara's last letter of the 1875 season burbles on:

My darling Mama,

Jennie's last night!

Dined out and then went to the Duchess of Wellington's, a very small party and then came home, dressed again and we went off to the Duchess of Westminster's. It was a beautiful ball. . . . The Prince was very good to me and asked me for a dance and I think it was because I looked well. Everyone told me my dress was the prettiest. The Duchess and Rosamond looked so jealous when Jennie and I appeared in our new dresses. . .

Count Schovaloff the Russian Ambassador has invited us for *Dimanche la nuit* to dine with him and meet the Russian Grand Duke and the Prince and Princess. I don't know why but people seem to always ask us whenever H.R.H. goes to them. I suppose it is because Jennie is so pretty and you have no idea how charming Randolph can be when *il fait des frais*! And I don't want to be conceited but I think I make myself agreeable too as they could easily ask them without me. If you could only see what sticks English women are and how badly most of them dress. . .

She had noticed Randolph's gleaming charm which he could turn on and off at will and that hostesses eagerly sought for Jennie when the Prince would be present. How easy life was for the clever and beautiful. But an unexpected storm was about to drive the Churchill family out of English society.

6

The summer of 1876 passed pleasantly enough with a visit to Blenheim, where Jennie was now accustomed to the two-hour breakfasts in formal attire and the dignified rhythm of existence. She would wander around the rooms looking at the wonderful pictures which the Churchill's took for granted. Indeed, none of Randolph's sisters had even looked at Sir Joshua Reynolds' portraits of the family or Raphael Madonna given to the Great Duke by the King of Prussia. It was like living in a museum. Jennie noted with amusement the action taking place in Rubens' *Progress of Silenus* and *Lot and His Daughters* which hung in the dining room. 'If familiarity breeds contempt, it also engenders indifference, and the most prudish of governesses, sitting primly between her charges, never seemed to notice these pictures, nor did any members of the family.'

She grew a little closer to the Duchess, whose affectionate qualities had broken through when Jennie's baby had been born. Little Winston was now learning to creep in the top-floor nurseries, watched and cosseted by his nurse Mrs Everest.

In the following autumn the Prince of Wales departed on a spectacular tour through India. Among the personal guests in his suite was Lord Aylesford, 'Sporting Joe', a jolly, English gentleman, hard-riding and not over-imaginative. For several months the royal party moved around shooting elephants and tigers, and attending gorgeous state banquets. It was on February 20th, 1876, when they were all encamped in magnificent tents, that Lord Aylesford received a letter from the wife he had left in England announcing her immediate elopement with Lord Blandford, who was ready, for her sake, to desert wife and children. In his diary that day H.R.H. wrote: 'Letters!!' and the Prince sincerely commiserated with the miserable husband. On February 28th Lord Aylesford gloomily departed on an elephant's back on the first stage of his return journey to England, where he intended to shoot the naughty Marquis, now referred to by H.R.H. as 'the greatest blackguard alive'.

Lord Aylesford, though a great sportsman and what other Englishmen called a good fellow, proved somewhat unsubtle in attack. The hornets' nest he stirred up during the week he reached London was to ruin his own life as well as that of his wife.

He could not immediately find his target, so he stamped around quoting the Prince's uncomplimentary opinion of Blandford, and announced that he was going to sue for divorce. It was the fashion for the society revolving around the Prince of Wales to conduct constant but private love affairs without disturbing dignified appearances. The servants, the children, the Press must never know.

During the month of March, while the Prince was travelling homeward, London society buzzed with nervous excitement and closed their ranks. The big families were determined to prevent public scandal.

The facts, which, of course, Jennie knew in detail, were as follows. Since he had been expelled from Eton for over-accurate work with a catapult, Lord Blandford had given his parents cause for worry on many occasions. During seven years of marriage to the charming daughter of the Duke of Abercorn he had remained an incorrigible lady-killer and only his wife (nicknamed 'Goosey' by her own family) failed to notice these liaisons. When her husband admired 'dear Edith Aylesford's pretty dresses' she annoyed him by innocently copying them, and when Blandford took lodging for himself and his horses in a hunting inn adjacent to the Aylesford home she never thought it the least odd. All that winter, during Joe Aylesford's absence in India, there were tracks through the snow and nightly openings of a certain window which left grooms, maids and other staff in no doubt as to how the nobility spent their nights. Lady Blandford tried to amuse her husband, whom she saw seldom and in ever more lugubrious mood. Practical jokes were her forte, and on a certain morning in February, after guilelessly remarking on rumours that Edith Aylesford might be expecting an heir, she devised a joke which, by coincidence, excelled all others and drove her husband from the house. Under the large metal cover of his breakfast dish she replaced the poached egg by a small pink baby. Such a surprise! Lord Blandford lifted the cover, choked and fled. A week later poor 'Goosey' knew why.

Meanwhile Randolph rushed to his brother's aid, or so he thought. He telegraphed the Prince of Wales to try to stop Aylesford's divorce proceedings and begged the guilty couple to drop all notion of running away. Lady Aylesford, who suddenly realised that her own position in society was imperilled, went into hysterics and Lord Blandford backed out of whatever promises he had made. 'Sporting Joe', who thought he'd been damn badly treated and had left India, according to Lord Carrington, 'heartbroken at the disgrace', was determined to shoot *and* divorce—in that order. Colonel Williams, his brother-in-law, thought it right to call out Blandford for a duel, while Lord Hartington and Lord Hardwicke begged him not to.

Meanwhile the Prince very fairly maintained that Aylesford should be left free to make his own painful decisions. The usual rite of producing a son or two before embarking on other amours had not in Lady Aylesford's case taken place. She had given her husband three daughters. He naturally wished for an heir to his name and an heir of his own blood, not the baby his wife now carried.

Somewhat late in the day Lord Blandford and Lady Aylesford decided that they did not want a scandal and now their one idea was to stop 'Sporting Joe' from proceeding with the divorce. It was impossible, however, to call a halt at this stage.

It is difficult to perceive where logical thinking began. If they did not want a scandal why did Lord Blandford make no effort to hide his tracks and why did Lady Aylesford write they were eloping? How could they have been so stupid? What did they expect? The oft-concussed 'Sporting Joe' seems more clear-headed. Even his desire for a duel remains humanly comprehensible.

In her 'flap' Lady Aylesford now made an appalling move. She gave Blandford a packet of admiring letters she had once received from the Prince. Blandford handed these to Randolph, who said he would use them to force H.R.H. to force Aylesford to drop the divorce. Randolph obviously enjoyed the situation; he even boasted to his friends that he held the Crown of England in his pocket. With Lord Alington, an older man who should have known better, he called upon the Princess of Wales at Marlborough House and told her that 'being aware of peculiar and most grave matters affecting the case, he was anxious that His Royal Highness should give such advice to Lord Aylesford as to induce him not to proceed against his wife'.

Randolph bluntly told the Princess that 'he was determined by every means in his power to prevent the case coming before the public, and that he had those means at his disposal'. He referred to the letters as of 'the most compromising character and warned that he had legal assurance that the Prince would be subpoenaed to give evidence if the divorce case continued and that if published, the letters would ensure that His Royal Highness would never sit upon the Throne of England'. What can this be called but blackmail? The Princess suffered much distress, and when the Prince, exhausted after five months' travelling, received the news in Cairo, he quite naturally fell into a rage and dispatched Lord Charles Beresford post-haste to London with orders to request Randolph to name his seconds and arrange a place on the north coast of France for a duel with pistols.

The Prince was tired, cross and hot. This unwise challenge relieved his feelings, but gave Randolph the chance to taunt him with what Lord Carrington called a 'dreadful letter', sneering at H.R.H. for suggesting a duel he knew to be impossible.

Queen Victoria stood by her son and on April 14th her Private Secretary, Ponsonby, wrote: 'The Queen has such perfect confidence in the Prince of Wales, that His Royal Highness's disclaimer of any evil intentions is sufficient to convince Her Majesty that the letters are perfectly innocent. But the publication of any letter of this nature would be very undesirable, as a colouring might be easily given and injurious inferences deduced from hasty expression. The Queen, therefore, regrets that such a correspondence, harmless as it is, should be in existence; but her Majesty thinks it quite right that His Royal Highness should not interfere in Lord Aylesford's affair in consequence of this threat. . . .

'The Queen feels very deeply the pain this matter has caused the Prince of Wales, and had there been any probability of a public scandal into which his name could be dragged by these villains she would have agreed to thinking it advisable that he should not return until a frank explanation had been publicly made.'

The Duke and Duchess of Marlborough were close friends of the Queen and this appalling drama, of a type which they expected from Blandford but not from Randolph, reduced them to deep depression. Nervous breakdowns had not become the fashion, but by the time the Prince arrived back in England a number of people were showing the symptoms. The injured Lady Blandford separated from her husband, Lady Aylesford surrounded by a gaggle of scolding sisters retreated to tragic hiding in the country, Lord Blandford cast his eyes elsewhere and in a way Randolph won his personal battle because on May 12th Lord Aylesford let the Prince know that 'in order to avoid great public mischief' he would renounce his divorce plans.

It was not a hilarious prelude to Jennie's third London season. She had been an appalled spectator of the entire débâcle and she had done her utmost to restrain Randolph, writing: [Undated] Dearest Randolph: . . . I was so distressed hearing of yr new quarrel that I was on the point of writing you a very cross letter, when, luckily for me (as you no doubt would have been furious) I received yr other letter telling me that it was all over. Really darling forgive me for saying it—but if you want to end the discussions and quarrels on *that* disagreeable subject, why don't you drop it—why talk about or occupy yourself with it?'

She was not surprised when the Prince announced he would enter no house in England which remained open to Blandford or to Randolph Churchill. Wisely Jennie begged for a trip to America 'for a breath of fresh air' and the Marlboroughs supported her.

After despatching a letter of apology to the Prince which received no acknowledgement, Randolph agreed, and they sailed to Canada, unfortunately hitting high temperatures—the last thing needed in the circumstances—'We seemed to spend most of the time eating melons and having cold baths, so overpowering was the heat.'

But Randolph, who now became morose because the Prince had taken umbrage at his behaviour, cheered up in the new continent. They poured out the tale to Mr Jerome, who took it calmly: 'Forget it. Let us go off to Newport to sail and drive and see what I have got left of a racing stable.'

At Newport, once discovered by Mrs Leonard Jerome as a little fishing village, Jennie saw a 'plague' of millionaire palazzi and châteaux had replaced the country cottages of her childhood. But they were splendidly entertained driving out to August Belmont's ten-course dinners along the road where she had once whipped up her donkey team.

Mr Jerome was still eminent on the Turf, and the party moved gaily on to Saratoga for the races. Here it was that Randolph received the formal form of apology to the Prince which had finally been drawn up by the Lord Chancellor and approved by Disraeli and Lord Hartington. It took all Mr Jerome's tact to cool him down after reading it.

Queen Victoria was among the few people who appear to have showed any heart in this heartless affair, and she had personally asked the Prime Minister to try to effect a settlement for the sake of her old friends the Duke and Duchess of Marlborough 'who were looking dreadfully ill and wretched'.

The Duchess wrote soothingly concerning the 'Interviews' which had taken place and a PS. in the Duke's hand read:

'Dearest Randolph: Your letter should be to the Prince, & I will look over & consider it well for you before sending it. Remember "a soft answer turneth away wrath".'

Randolph writhed at being forced to sign an apology, but with a twinkle in his eye Leonard Jerome reminded him that it was at Saratoga that General Burgoyne had surrendered his army to the Americans, insisting it was a convention not a capitulation. So on 26th August, ironically stressing his address, Randolph signed the formal apology, but he added a postscript with a sting in it:

. . . Lord R. Churchill having already tendered an Apology to H.R.H. the Pr. of W. for the part taken by him in recent events, feels that, as a Gentleman, he is bound to accept the words of the Lord Chancellor for that Apology.

Randolph S. Churchill

This provoked H.R.H. to further anger. He and his friends protested that Churchill had forfeited for ever the right to describe himself as a gentleman.

Nevertheless, Lord Randolph remained a Member of Parliament and his parents dear friends of the Queen, and after further correspondence on the subject, which Disraeli described as 'almost as troublesome as the great crisis which had arisen in the Balkans', the Prince of Wales indicated that his formal acknowledgement could be construed to imply acceptance of Lord Randolph Churchill's apology.

Old Mr Jerome could not take these goings-on as seriously as English society did, and after some soothing advice he sent Randolph and Jennie off with his brother Lawrence Jerome, to the Centennial Fair at Philadelphia. As they left the Saratoga hotel, a huge bill was handed to Randolph. When Mr Jerome remonstrated, the proprietor explained: 'The Lord and his wife *would* have two rooms, hence the expense.' Lawrence Jerome, famous for his quips, kept them 'in transports of laughter', and they returned to England 'invigorated and refreshed'.

Meanwhile the old Duke and Duchess had passed a summer that was anything but refreshing. Despite Queen Victoria's kindness, the tension increased until Disraeli thought it wise to press the Duke to become Viceroy of Ireland, and, despite the colossal expense which this post demanded and which the Duke could ill-afford, he felt obliged to accept. To carry out the duties in a becoming manner cost £40,000 a year and the salary was only £20,000. The Duke would have to sell many art treasures from Blenheim to pay for his years as Viceroy. The Prince laughingly suggested that some desert island would offer more suitable banishment for Randolph and Blandford, but he was not in jest when he announced the continued boycott of any house that received a Churchill. This amounted to complete social ostracism. Two people only ignored the Prince's decree; the Duchess of Manchester says she told the Prince to his face: 'I hold friendship higher than snobbery', and John Delacour, a close friend of Randolph, when reprimanded by the Prince answered, 'I allow no man to choose my friends.' Queen Victoria remained aloof from this battle, but then *she* gave no amusing parties. When Her Majesty informed the Prince that Lord Randolph Churchill could not be entirely excluded from court festivities he replied that on such occasions he would bow without speaking.

The Marlboroughs were lucky, despite the outlay, to have the Irish Viceroyalty. Blenheim Palace was closed, save for caretakers, and the entire household moved to Dublin. Blandford, original cause of the trouble, wandered away, conducting experiments scientific and otherwise. Lady Blandford retired quietly with her children and her hurt. Lady Aylesford suffered silently and ignominiously in the country. Randolph prepared to accompany the Duke to Dublin, where he could accept the post of unpaid Private Secretary without disturbing his status as an M.P.

Before moving to Dublin, Jennie took one of her little holidays to Paris, whence she wrote loving notes to her husband about looking after Baby, going to church and reading *Macbeth*—as if each was a tremendous feat. She was lonely without Randolph, and reserved the evening letter as *la bonne bouche* with which to end her day.

Another undated letter from Paris anxiously asks if Randolph has been dangerously ill, as Oliver Montagu had told her: 'Darling, I shall never forgive you if this is true—ill & never let me know anything about it & me amusing myself all this time—instead of being with you. . . .'

On December 11th 1876 the new Viceroy made his State Entry riding through Dublin in uniform with his glittering staff while the rest of the family followed in carriages surrounded by postillions and outriders. Randolph and Jennie carried their two-year-old son on the seat beside them.

If the Duke of Marlborough was groaning at the enforced expenses of a Viceroy his impenitent son was prepared to enjoy himself. Mr Justice Fitzgibbon, describing the immediate friendship he struck up with Randolph, writes: 'How it grew so fast I can hardly tell. I suppose electricity came in somewhere. . . .'

Randolph was given the official 'Secretary's House' in Phoenix Park, a short walk from the Viceregal Lodge, and this charming rambling white building with its green garden and the park beyond formed the background for Winston's first conscious memories. He went there aged two, and left no longer a baby but a stout-hearted little boy of five.

For the next three years Jennie delighted in all that Ireland had to offer, the hunting, the country life, the Dublin entertainments. Lord d'Abernon describes her:

. . . I have the clearest recollection of seeing her for the first time. It was at the Viceregal Lodge at Dublin. She stood on one side

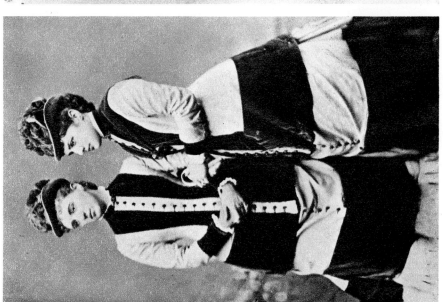

Far left Clara and Jennie,
dressed by Worth
Left Leonard Jerome

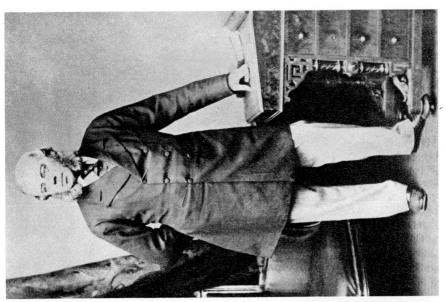

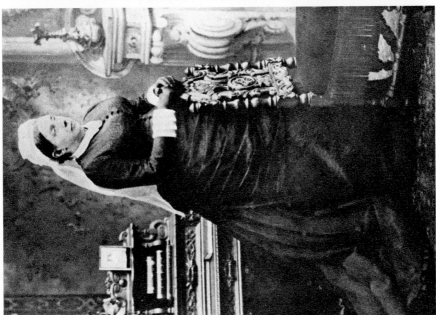

'The in-laws'—the Duke and Duchess of Marlborough

My dear mama bathe in the
I am so glad sea to day.
you are coming love to papa
to see us I had your loving
such a nice winston

Above Jennie, Jack and Winston
Below A letter from Winston

to the left of the entrance. The Viceroy was on a dais at the farther end of the room surrounded by a brilliant staff, but eyes were not turned on him or on his consort, but on a dark, lithe figure, standing somewhat apart and appearing to be of another texture to those around her, radiant, translucent, intense. A diamond star in her hair, her favourite ornament—its lustre dimmed by the flashing glory of her eyes. More of the panther than of the woman in her look, but with a cultivation unknown to the jungle. Her courage not less than that of her husband—fit mother for descendants of the great Duke. With all these attributes of brilliancy, such kindliness and high spirits that she was universally popular. Her desire to please, her delight in life, and the genuine wish that all should share her joyous faith in it, made her the centre of a devoted circle. . . .

Years later, Winston in *My Early Life* added to this quotation: 'My mother made the same brilliant impression upon my childhood's eyes—I loved her dearly; but at a distance.' His reminiscence continued: 'My picture of her in Ireland is in a riding habit fitted like a skin, and often beautifully spotted with mud. She and my father hunted continually on their large horses; and sometimes there were great scares because one or the other did not come back for many hours after they were expected.'

The numerous letters which Jennie wrote to her husband when he departed on visits are full of references to the obstreperous 'W' as well as to the hunters. She describes balls and racing and trips to Dublin shops. 'I bought Winston an elephant this afternoon which he has been asking me for for some time. I was on the point of saying to the saleswoman "an elephant", I just stopped myself in time. . . . I am delighted you are going to get me a saddle. Don't you find your way too often to the Candy's, for I know your foible in that quarter. I shall immediately become jealous. . . . I rode the bay the first time. He went perfectly with me tho he kicked and jumped about before I got on. . . .'

'Dearest Randolph . . . I rode the chestnut who went very well. Colonel F. said he thought she was well worth £200. I rode without the martingale & found she held her head perfectly. . . .'

Another undated letter probably written in early 1877 contains a squiggled 'W', which is Winston's first signature.

'Winston is here making such a noise I can hardly think of what I'm writing. I hope you are enjoying yourself. The house does pretty well with only Kate, her style of waiting on the table is peculiar—but as long as one gets something to eat what does it matter. Clara & Winston send their love. Your, J.

W's signature. [Here follows a firmly scrawled W.]

There was something very moving about discovering this letter in the Chartwell Trust Archives ninety years later. The thought of that chubby hand eagerly making its first mark for some reason made my eyes fill with tears.

One more contented letter rounds off the picture of life in the lodge in Phoenix Park: 'Winston has just been with me—such a darling he is—"I can't have my Mama go—and if she does I will run after the train & jump in" he said to me. I have told Everest to take him out for a drive tomorrow if it is fine—as it's better the stables should have a little more work. . . Goodbye darling. I love you ever so much. Your J.'

These years in Ireland were probably the happiest of Jennie's life.

Who could have expected that exile would change Randolph into a steel-hard, ruthless politician. The blow dealt him by the Prince of Wales consolidated his talents, and he learned to despise the vapid society revealed by Clara's pen. As his son would write, had this family trouble not arisen he might have 'wasted a dozen years in the frivolous and expensive pursuits of the silly world of fashion'. The Irish genius for talk sharpened his own natural powers, and while he shot snipe or sailed in the sixteen-foot boat he kept at Howth or attended Fitzgibbon's parties where 'the nights were consumed with whist, chaff and tobacco' he was training himself to become the most telling speaker in the House and the most fascinating character of the Victorian era.

Meanwhile Ireland simmered. The terrible famines of 1846–7 would not be repeated, but the peasants lived on the edge of starvation in their beautiful fertile land. They had been taught no agriculture since the Union of 1800; they lived on potatoes, and when wet years brought blight they saw death stand waiting in the door.

Jennie, who had scarcely heard of Ireland before she went there, saw for herself the edge of misery in the cabins and yet she wrote:

'I found the Irish life very pleasant with its various occupations and amusements, and I delighted in the genial character and ready wit of the people. During the three years we lived there I cannot remember meeting one really dull man. . . . Hunting became our ruling passion. Whenever I could "beg, borrow or steal" a horse I did so. We had a few horses of our own which we rode indiscriminately, both of us being light weights. Many were the "tosses" I took, as the Irish papers used to call them, but it was glorious sport, and to my mind, even hunting in Leicestershire later could not compare with it.' Her father had always maintained that the greatest sins for a woman were to sing a false note or to jerk a good horse in the mouth. 'Hands, hands! Light hands and a horse is yours!' She remembered Papa's words as the hounds went away and the big banks and ditches of Meath loomed before her.

Jennie's letters to New York and Paris were full of incidents more entertaining perhaps to undergo than to read of, how her favourite mare had finished a fourteen-mile run with the boldest spirits, kicking back as she should at narrow banks, changing legs on the wide ones, soaring over an old iron bedstead used as a gate, waiting for her to crawl from a ditch to be hoisted by farm boys back in the saddle. She was young and strong and full of laughter.

The Viceroy did not spend the whole year in Dublin. One winter he rented Knockdrin Castle in County Meath 'where the foxes were wild as the people', and another season he took Lord Sligo's superb eighteenth-century house at Westport in County Mayo. Lord Sligo had been one of the best landlords during the Great Famine, staying with his people and struggling valiantly to help them, yet Jennie could record, thirty years after that disaster: 'In our walks we had many opportunities of seeing the heart-rending poverty of the peasantry, who lived in their wretched mud hovels more like animals than human beings.'

Back in Dublin Randolph made friends with the Nationalists. Jennie said that Isaac Butt could recount stories well, but she thought him too serious, constantly dwelling on the miseries and oppression of his countrymen. 'He would appeal to me as an American to agree with him and when in rash moments I did, would then declare I was a Home Ruler. The words "Home Rule" were the invention of Butt. He thought the old cry of "Repeal" would frighten the

English, while the phrase Home Rule had a cosy, innocent sound.'
When Jennie's and Randolph's conversations reached the ears of the
Viceroy he thought them great heresy.

Would the unfortunate Duke's worries never cease? He had
suffered monstrous shame, inconvenience and expense on account
of his sons; now Randolph and his wife thought fit to entertain the
leader of the Irish Party!

In 1877 Rosamond, aged twenty-five, became engaged to
William Fellowes, son and heir of Lord de Ramsey, whom the
Duchess did not think good enough for her. Jennie wrote (undated):
'Dearest Randolph; It is all settled about Rosamond & Captain
Fellowes. . . . I must say I don't think Rosamond is making a mistake,
he is so nice & improves greatly on acquaintance. I am afraid your
mother worries herself about what people will say. She seems to
think it a great comedown tho she likes him—we were the only
ladies last night at dinner. The Duke of Connaught was in a most
villainous temper & I think I was the cause for it, of course at the
ball there wasn't a soul to speak to or to dance with & I am sure
he would have given anything to have spoken to me. He kept
staring at me with his goggle eyes & when he went away with what
I suppose he thought was a charming smile & said "Good night" in a
loud voice, I made him a most ceremonious curtsey.'

Poor shy royal duke! The person who would enliven his later
years had only just appeared on the scene. The eighteen-year-old
Leonie, emerging from her gloomy Wiesbaden finishing school,
had just completed an intensive year of piano lessons in Paris.
She came to enjoy a Dublin season before returning to Papa in
New York. Among the Irish landowners who visited the Viceregal
Lodge was one Sir John Leslie whose home lay surrounded by
forests and bog in County Monaghan. His son, a shy lieutenant
in the Grenadiers, danced with Leonie and then proposed to her
behind a pillar. Miss Jerome fluttered in the approved fashion and
turned him down. Jennie found them looking slightly flushed,
and remarked sharply, 'What are you two talking about?' and hurried
them off to other partners. But the conversation was resumed at
intervals over the next five years, until eventually Leonie became
John Leslie's wife.

The Marlborough Irish excursion nearly killed the Duke. Not
only did he have to pay £20,000 a year out of his pocket for the

glories of office, but serious political troubles blew up. Disraeli had written to him concerning Ireland: 'A portion of its population is attempting to sever the constitutional tie which unites it to Britain in that bond which has favoured the power and prosperity of both.' This was an untrue statement. Ireland's prosperity ended in 1800, when George III forced her Union with England by bribery and by creating peers. Disraeli had throughout his life ignored every plea for improved Irish legislation and thrown out every important Irish Bill. Lord Randolph Churchill seems to have been the only Tory who showed some sympathy for the Irish point of view. In 1877 he made a speech at Woodstock attacking his own party's failure to grapple with Irish problems. This aroused fury in the Tory Press: 'It is no exaggeration to say that neither Mr Parnell nor Mr Butt could have used stronger language in support of their respective lines of action', wrote Hicks-Beach, Chief Secretary for Ireland, to the Viceroy, asking for an explanation of his son's opinions. The rigid old Duke felt once again he'd had the breath knocked out of him. His answer began.

Guisachan, September 25 1877

My dear Beach,
The only excuse I can find for Randolph is that he must either be mad or have been singularly affected with local champagne or claret. I can only say that the sentiments he has indulged in are purely his own. . . .

Randolph remained impenitent, writing to the *Morning Post* about the misgovernment of Ireland since the Act of Union.

Jennie received a good scolding in her husband's absence, but she refused to take sides. Husbands should not be nagged about politics—what was it Mama had always said—if you scold a man he will only go elsewhere? And she embarked on a new rose garden. 'The French,' she told the Duchess, 'are the only people who have invented a rose without a thorn, I doubt if it could stand up to this climate.' To her sisters she wrote: 'Now I suppose I mustn't even laugh at Mr Butt's good stories. . . .'

Randolph's letters while on London visits were generally, but not always, full of politics. After a journeying over to see Sir Charles Dilke concerning a vote of censure upon the Government's Middle East policy, he wrote:

I missed the afternoon post because the discussion lasted till
eight o'clock. I am sure the debate will be very stormy. I am in
great doubt what to do. I think I could make a telling speech
against the Government but old Bentinck got hold of me today
and gave me tremendous lecture. Of course I have my future
to think of, and I also have strong opinions against the Government policy. It is very difficult. I shan't decide till the last night
of debate which won't be till next Monday or Tuesday, so my
departure for Ireland will be postponed.

Northcote made a very feeble speech to-night and the country
every day gets more and more against the Government. Russia's
terms of peace are monstrous, but after all it concerns Austria
so much more than us, and if she won't move we are practically
powerless.

I had a pleasant evening last night at Dilke's. . . You need not
be afraid of these Radicals, they have no influence on me further
than I like to go but I hate the Government. . . .

A casual note of the time said: 'I dined with Lord Wharncliffe
last night, and took in to dinner a Mrs Langtry, a most beautiful
creature quite unknown, very poor, and they say has but one
black dress.'

Curiously enough Jennie's two future brothers-in-law, Moreton
Frewen and John Leslie, were vying over her favours but the one-
black-dress stage did not last long, for the Prince of Wales was about
to sweep the Jersey Lily into his own orbit. She would become the
first 'professional beauty'—that is, her photograph would be sold
in shops and the English public allowed to enjoy vicariously the
Prince's love affair.

That summer Jennie slipped over to London, and attended the
'Peace with Honour' banquet given for Disraeli on his return from
Berlin. She enjoyed the old Prime Minister's description of Mr
Gladstone being 'inebriated with the exuberance of his own ver-
bosity'.

On March 7th Randolph made a derisory speech in the House,
which attracted much attention and must have made the President

of the Local Government Board, against whom it was aimed, hate him for life. Even now the prick of his phrases can be felt.

The House may have been aghast at Lord Randolph's rudeness, but it shook with inward laughter. Mr Chaplin snapped that if such were Randolph's opinions he should 'lose not a moment in going over to the other side of the House', but the Bill was dropped and Randolph wrote to his father: 'I do not think the Government is at all ill-disposed for my attack on them.'

In 1879 a wet summer resulted in another Irish potato blight, and hunger again crept over the land. The Government took precautionary measures and the Duchess of Marlborough raised a private fund which reached £117,000. Lord Randolph spent the entire winter organising distribution of seed, food and clothing. He travelled through every Irish county before his father's term as Viceroy expired.

On March 8th, 1880, Disraeli, now Lord Beaconsfield, dissolved Parliament and in an open letter to the Duke of Marlborough made the election a vote of confidence in the Government's foreign policy and the need to stamp out Home Rule.

To the amazement of Queen Victoria the Liberal Party won a colossal victory, and old Mr Gladstone, whom she so disliked, came back as Prime Minister. Randolph held on to his family seat but with a reduced majority.

Disraeli then resigned from politics and a new era started in which the names of Parnell, Chamberlain and Lord Salisbury began to emerge. Randolph was still a backbencher with a flair for biting words. He could wake up the House of Commons, and he could make it laugh unkindly. The rapier wit and sarcasm had not yet caused his friends to suspect that he was seriously interested in politics. The Prince's friends wondered uneasily if he was practising clever invective just so that he could ask unpleasant questions in the House concerning the heir to the throne.

7

Jennie's second son was born in Dublin on 4th February, 1880 (a premature baby like Winston), and named John Strange after an elderly friend of the Duke of Marlborough—John Strange Jocylyn (later 5th Earl of Roden) who was a pompous but kindly sportsman and often lent his best horses to Randolph. The Duke had retired from office, and was returning to Blenheim, where neglected tenants complained and solicitors were totting up the cost of four years' Viceroyalty. Randolph procured a small London house, 29 St James Place, which lay next door to that of Sir Stafford Northcote, the Tory Leader. While awaiting the vast horse drays which were to unload what Randolph called 'the props'—those tons of unfashionable eighteenth-century furniture which she had bought cheaply in Ireland, Jennie stayed at a nearby hotel with her children and their dear Mrs Everest.

A letter written to her sisters who had departed to New York reveals Jennie's hopes that the Prince of Wales might relinquish his social ban:

29 St James Place S.W.
May 30th 1880

Dearest Leonie,

I was so glad to see the arrival of the *Bothnia* last week and to know that you are all safe. I have been very dissapated [*sic*] of late, there seems to be so many things going on. . . .

Last Sunday R. and I dined with Philip C— at his little house on Clapham Common. He made himself so agreeable and gave us such a capital dinner, his house was full of pretty things, and he had *violet* silk curtains and yellow walls in his living room! He talked a great deal about Clara and kept asking me 50 times when she was coming over. Tell her, that if Papa agrees, she had much better take him. He is as goodlooking as ever—and *so* agreeable and clever. R— swears by him.

Randolph made a speech the other night about 'Bradlaugh' [the atheist member who refused to take the oath] which was a tremendous success. Everyone was full of it and rushed up and congratulated me to such an extent that I felt as tho' I had made it. I'm told that Tumtum expresses himself highly pleased and the result is that we have been asked to meet both him and the Princess tomorrow, at a dance Lord Fife is to give. I suppose he must have been told to do it as he is about the Court officially. Friday I went to two balls both very good.

Such an absurd thing happened yesterday. The Star man [Thomas Boscowen, later seventh Viscount Falmouth] was here having tea when a very smart carriage drove up, powdered footmen, wigs, silk stockings and inside a very fat old trump. 'Who on earth is this old demon?' I said. 'Why, it's my mother!' the Star confessed. *Tableau!*

There are 2 such pretty girls going out now, the Duchess of Newcastle's daughters, they dress so well. The other night they had mauve satin ball dresses, the skirts tulle with little plisses.

Winston and I went yesterday to the Horse Guards for the Queen's birthday and nearly came to grief in the crowd, had it not been for Lord Valentia who came to the rescue and pulled us out. I've seen nothing of Johnny Kaye of late. I'm told that Mrs Candy is in love with him and much to his ennui rushed about after him. The other day she heard him asking me if he might come to tea—and to my astonishment *she* appeared! I'm glad to say he did not turn up so she was sold! Consuelo [the American Duchess of Manchester] proposed herself to dinner the other night. We had old Chancellor Ball and Lord Portarlington and she being *en veine*, insisted on telling 'roguey poguey' stories, which I think astonished them—they did me! Quite between ourselves I think it *du plus mauvais goût* to talk like that before men.

Best love *et à bientot*.

Yr loving, Jennie

'Star' Falmouth's name occurs often in the notes and diaries of the Jerome girls. He was twenty-eight when first introduced to Jennie at Ascot Races soon after her marriage, and until he married twelve years later he remained a steady admirer—indeed his devotion did not end then. Soldier, sportsman and gallant, he was an old friend of Randolph's and had been asked to be his second during the brainstorm weeks when the Prince was issuing challenges to a duel. 'The Star' was a right man for dawn meetings with cloak and pistol. Jennie's first description of him gushes: '. . . and Mama he has such a lovely moustache.' This amazing moustache, bigger and better than other men's, is also recalled by my father, who was often taken out by him with his own sons from prep school. The only other eyewitness account I have of the seventh Viscount Falmouth comes from a rather harsh great-aunt. 'Handsome and stupid!' But not too stupid to become Military Secretary to the C.-in-C. in Ireland and Colonel in the Coldstream Guards and to receive the K.C.M.G. Not too stupid to keep Jennie Churchill's affection all through life.

For some curious reason Victorian convention, which never allowed a lady to be alone with a man except when riding, permitted admirers to be invited to afternoon tea. Perhaps the constant re-entering of footmen, with little jugs of milk or replenishments of sandwiches, was considered sufficient to preserve the proprieties. On this particular afternoon 'Star' was probably not particularly anxious for his mother's company, and Jennie must have greeted the old dragon with that guilty expression which a *faux pas* pastes over the countenance. Reared by a Puritan mama, the Jerome sisters did not easily yield to the peculiar and limited brand of amorality practised by 'the Prince's set' in the wings of Queen Victoria's austere court, but there is something beguiling about the swain who is always there, always watching and quite determined that time is on his side.

The excitement of watching Randolph plunge into politics after four years' absence now absorbed all Jennie's attention. She had married a fascinating young man who was violently in love with her. She had thought him the most engaging man in the world, and in a light-hearted way she had looked forward to being his helpmate in whatever activities he undertook. She had not expected him to become the most brilliant and controversial politician in England, nor had she expected him to be unkind.

There was none of the brutality of the all-powerful Victorian male in Randolph; he merely seemed a febrile being without heart. In all the records of his boyhood pranks, in the baiting of schoolmasters and university dons and political opponents, there is never a shaft of human gentleness. Ready to leap into any row, he obviously enjoyed wielding cudgels. Fiercely egocentric, and arrogant as only a Duke's son in Victorian England could be, he stalked elegantly through London of the 'eighties. His wit and liveliness and charm, and his sharp original mind, made people love him and wish to be loved, or at least noticed. But Randolph Churchill was incapable of loving or noticing any human being as such. He admired clever men: and he certainly admired his wife, but neither she nor his sons would ever hear the warm word for which they yearned. Perhaps it can toughen boys to revere a father who never notices their existence? But it drove Jennie to a hardness unnatural to her.

Randolph was adroit at calling attention to himself. On May 24th of this summer, when he made his melodramatic attack on Bradlaugh, the free-thinker who had published a rude broadside about the House of Brunswick, Randolph threw the pamphlet on the floor of the House of Commons and stamped on it.

The Prince of Wales should have been delighted at this defence of his family, but, despite a smile at Jennie during Lord Fife's ball, he did not relent, as Sir Stafford Northcote's diary for July 12th 1880 reveals:

. . . I asked him [Lord Beaconsfield] whether Randolph Churchill was forgiven yet in high quarters. He said alright as far as the Queen was concerned, but that the Prince of Wales had not yet made it up with him, which Lord B. thought very unfair, as he and Hartington had been called in as umpires and had decided that Randolph should make an apology . . . under the impression that the matter was to end there, but the Prince having got the apology, still kept up the grievance, but nothing, said the Chief, will help Randolph into favour again so much as success in Parliament. The Prince of Wales is always taken by success.

And a letter from Jennie to Mrs Jerome, who was having hysterics over Leonie's current beau, a younger son of Earl Fitzwilliam, shows that most great houses still remained barred.

Dearest Mama,

I owe you all letters but the time flies and life here in London is such a 'hurry scurry' that even when I have a quiet moment it is with difficulty that I settle down. Old Everest got a cold and I had to give her a holiday—and she is still away. Luckily I found a very good monthly nurse who looks after the Baby. Winston is a very nice boy, and is getting on with his lessons, but he is a most difficult child to manage—so much for the infants.

You will be glad to hear that R. has been covering himself with glory, and I am told he has made himself a wonderfully good position in the House. Last Monday he spoke on an Irish Question which interests all the landlords at the moment, and he has made a *really* splendid speech—everyone says so—and Gladstone got up and answered him for an hour. I am sending you *Vanity Fair*. It is a capital caricature I think. When this Govt. goes out (which they say will be soon) I fancy R. and his boon companion Sir Henry Drummond Wolff must be given something. I am only so afraid of R. getting spoilt—he wd lose half his talent if he did. I keep reminding him of it. London is very gay just now. I haven't been to many balls; as I simply can't afford to get dresses and one can't always wear the same thing. Besides I am not bidden to the ones I want to go to [on account of the Prince] and I do not care about the others. This week I am going out every night, tomorrow to the opera; I was sent a box so I called Nautica and Johnny Kaye. We were thinking of going to Dinard for August but they say Parliament will not be up till September. I shall send Winston and John to Ventnor for a month. Money is such a hateful subject for me just now don't let us talk about it.

So glad to hear the Races had come off so successfully but I agree with you in everything you say about Fitzwilliam. I never thought it was a good match in money point of view but if they had as much to live on as we have they wd do well enough. As far as position goes nothing cd be better, and last but not *least* Leonie could never find a *nicer* man. At the same time I clearly see all the objections and no-one feels more than I do all you say of her being worthy of something better from the worldly point of view—but when I look around here it seems to me the chances of *any* girl are very small—there are so few *partis*, and when I see a girl like Georgie,[1] with everything that money, dress and position can do for her, hanging on for year after year! and she is not the only one—there is one of the Duchess of Newcastle's daughters, Lady Beatrix Clinton a nice looking girl, very well educated and with a large fortune, they say £12,000 a year. Well this is her first season, and she insists on marrying Johnny Kaye's brother Mr Cecil Kaye, a sick tiresome youth. I'm only telling you this to show you what nonsense it is trying to arrange marriages and how difficult it is to marry at all.

Of course if you ask me not to encourage Fitzwilliam I won't At the same time I am *dreadfully* prejudiced in his favour. . . . Give my best love to Papa and Randolph's who wants me to say that he is delighted at the success of the Races. He takes the greatest interest in it all. Ever yr loving,

Jennie

The Jerome girls all married Englishmen and revered the 'Establishment', but they never quite adjusted to certain sides of Victorian England. The brief glimpse they had been given of the delightful theatrical Second Empire court (waltzing in crinolines towards the disaster of Sedan), twisted their views regarding that stiff London society, which nevertheless they determined to charm.

It was some time before the Prince or the Duke of Marlborough or the party leaders were made to realise what the cold water of exile had done to Randolph Churchill. He had learned to think independently, to live without approbation. Politics were no longer a duty, they had become a sport. In the summer of his return to London he invented the 'Fourth Party', the most feared and merciless Opposition ever known in the House of Commons.

Rumours of his father's fame must have reached the nursery regions of 29 St James Street, where five-year-old Winston was learning, none too willingly, to read and write. He saw less of his mother for Jennie had 'caught the fever' and spent evenings in the House of Commons listening to the debates. It had not yet become the fashion for society ladies to crush into the Speaker's Gallery, so night

[1] Lady Georgina Churchill married the Viscount Curzon later Earl Howe after three more years 'hanging on'.

after night she found herself in the company of a few serious-minded women, with Mrs Gladstone queening it in her reserved seat.

Randolph worked hard at his speeches, writing them out and learning them by heart. Jennie wrote: 'Next to speaking in public oneself, there is nothing which produces such feelings of nervousness and apprehension as to hear one's husband or son make a speech . . . Randolph, even after years of practice and experience, was always nervous before a speech until he actually stood up. . . . Those years [1880-4] of political activity when the Fourth Party was at its zenith were full of excitement and interest for me. Our house became the rendez-vous of all shades of politicians.'

The story of the Fourth Party has been too well told to attempt a summary, but we can imagine the plotting and planning that took place in Jennie's small house and her jubilation as she saw her husband 'abandon his perch on the back-benches' and come forward to sit with Sir Henry Wolff, Mr Gorst and Mr Arthur Balfour on the front bench below the gangway, the occupant of this particular seat departing to 'serener quarters, saying to Sir Henry Wolff, "This is getting too hot for me."' Lord Randolph thenceforward was regarded as the rightful owner of that coveted place.

The dinners which Jennie gave in her little house next to Sir Stafford Northcote's were 'the greatest fun'—'fun' in fact was the word which Randolph brought into English politics. He nicknamed his Party Leader 'the old Goat' and one hot afternoon he said to Edward Clarke in the Lobby, 'Sitting up there behind the old Goat, you will never have any fun at all.' Jennie delighted in the plans for outrageous skirmishes and it seemed all the more amusing to reflect on the consternation that would be caused if the conventional Sir Stafford could hear through the wall.

In *The Life of Lord Randolph Churchill* his son has written: 'The compact which bound the "Fourth Party", as they were soon called by general consent, was simple and elastic. No questions of policy or leadership arose. Each was free to act in perfect independence: but it was agreed that, whenever one of them was attacked, the others should defend him. Upon these conditions was created a Parliamentary group which proved, in proportion to the numbers, the most formidable and effective force for the purposes of Opposition in the history of the House of Commons.'

Friends should be given no quarter. Even when Bertie Mitford asked him while strolling in the Park, 'My dear Randolph, for good-ness' sake leave my unhappy estimates alone', he replied: 'Very sorry for you, my dear fellow, but we must harass the Government.'

John Gorst and Arthur Balfour were music-lovers and Jennie often accompanied them to concerts. 'My fashionable friends, spying the three of us walking together, often teased me about my "weird companions"—one solemn with beard and eye-glass, the other aesthetic with long hair and huge spats. Mr Balfour's knowledge of music was remarkable, considering the little time he was able to devote to it, and he was no mean performer at the piano, reading and playing classical music. We often played Beethoven or Schumann together. But it was not without difficulty that he could get away from his parliamentary duties, which increased yearly, and often I was disappointed of his company as shown by the following letter:

1883   House of Commons
My dear Lady Randolph,
    I am groaning and swearing on this beastly bench. While you are listening to Wagnerian discords, I am listening to Irish grumblings—there is a great deal of brass in both of them; otherwise there is not much resemblance! I *am* sitting next to ——, I *might* be sitting next to you! ...
                                        Your miserable servant
                                        Arthur James Balfour'

Arthur Balfour, nephew of Lord Salisbury, remained the meekest member of the Fourth Party. Gorst was a distinguished lawyer quick to perceive the flaw in an argument and his alliance with Randolph was described by Sir Henry James as 'a poacher's combina-tion—a pointer to find game and a greyhound to run it down'. The other member, Sir Henry Wolff, was 'a ready speaker and industrious politician; old enough to compel respectful treatment from the House, young enough to love fighting and manœuvres for their own sake'.

The Duke of Marlborough, dazed and yet impressed by his son's renown, did not cease to remonstrate when Jennie invited the wrong people to dine—Sir Charles Dilke, Mr Joseph Chamberlain and Sir William Harcourt were considered dangerous radicals. The true-Tory desire to never change anything, not even thought, was terrifyingly shown up in this stiff, well-meaning old aristocrat.

All through the spring and summer of 1880 the incorrigible

Fourth Party harried the Government. When Bills were launched 'there was not a single sitting from which they were absent, or a single clause which they did not amend, or seek to amend'. Their firework attempts caused irritation and amusement. In August the Fourth Party was accused (amidst laughter) of having made 247 speeches and asked seventy-three questions, yet 'all the time the House as a whole was kept in subjection and often in good humour, by the excellent quality of the speeches, the wit by which they were adorned, the fertility of resource which distinguished them and the reality of the arguments advanced'.

Sir Stafford Northcote, the Conservative Leader, was a charming old gentleman without vigour. 'His speeches were tame and ineffective . . . the mild expostulations with which Sir Stafford was accustomed to conclude the debates disappointed his followers.' The four gentlemen sitting below the gangway sustained by their own gaiety and wicked humour had no patience with him and Sir Stafford in turn found them annoying. 'There are two great parties in the State,' said a member one night:

Mr Parnell: 'Three.'

Lord Randolph Churchill: 'FOUR!' (Laughter).

And so amidst, it always seems, the laughter of the House the Fourth Party whose members could be contained on one good-sized sofa, launched forth on an independent career which the old Tories, as much as the Liberals, viewed with apprehension.

Much of Randolph's wit seems venomous and spiteful, and he obviously revelled in rudeness to worthy middle-class bores in particular, but he had the spark of genius. He could create atmosphere. The House of Commons came alive at his touch. Gladstone, the greatest orator of his century, he provoked and angered in party debate. Lord Randolph Churchill, in his grey frock-coat and dandy turn-out, knew how to taunt, and the benches would fill when the whisper went around 'Randy's drawing him!' The naughty members of the Fourth Party would take up an entire evening, each in turn baiting the splendid old man. Jennie assessed Mr Gladstone and Lord Salisbury as the pleasantest dinner companions she ever sat next to, but Gladstone must have hated Randolph's barbs and Salisbury would deliberately break him. She wrote of Gladstone's attractive old-world manner and his way of turning sharply round with his hand to his ear, the gesture so well known in the

House of Commons. 'On one occasion I had been at the House hearing Randolph make a fiery attack on him, which he answered with equal heat and indignation. The hour was late, and Randolph and I had just time to rush home and dress to dine with Lord and Lady Spencer. The first person I met as I went in was Mr Gladstone, who at once came up and said: "I hope Lord Randolph is not *too* tired after his magnificent effort".'

Apart from their concerted attack on the Liberals, the Fourth Party were determined to dislodge their own leader. Towards the end of August—and a particularly hot August it was—Lord Harting-ton rebuked the Fourth Party for being a nuisance. He read out his figures. During four months Mr Gorst had spoken 105 times and asked eighteen questions; Sir Henry Wolff had spoken sixty-eight times and asked thirty-four questions; Lord Randolph Churchill had delivered seventy-four speeches and asked twenty-one questions.

The House was exhausted, but the four members of the Fourth Party, having harassed and teased and drawn attention to themselves, departed to their various country pursuits in the best of spirits.

8

Jennie's role would be to applaud, not to advise. She had fallen in love with a young man who abhorred politics and only stood for Parliament to gain an allowance from his father. Six years later his name was the most discussed in England. She observed the metamorphosis with pride and astonishment. Lord Rosebery described Randolph: 'He was brilliant and courageous, resourceful and unembarrassed by scruples, he had fascination, audacity, tact; great and solid ability wedded with the priceless gift of concentration; marvellous readiness in debate, and an almost unrivalled skill and attraction on the platform; for he united in an eminent degree both the parliamentary and the popular gifts, a combination which is rarer than is usually supposed.

'He had also the vital mainspring of zest. To whatever he applied himself he gave for the time his whole eager heart.'

Jennie wrote: 'As we could not yet enter the same house as the Prince of Wales, much of the vain & foolish excitement of London society was closed to us & politics became our entire & all absorbing interest.'

Disraeli, who had known him since he was a schoolboy, remarked the emergence of this extraordinary butterfly from the dusty cocoon of the ducal palace. Although he disapproved when Randolph fraternised with the Irish members, Dizzy could write frankly: 'I am glad he is going to speak about Ireland. He will speak on such a subject not only with ability but with authority. . . .'

Jenny spent the autumn of 1880 at Blenheim with her children.

After a week or so in the Palace she always started to grumble. This year, while Randolph devised what he called 'political dynamite' for the next session Jennie realised how much she missed her sisters. The Jeromes always formed a mutual admiration society and what she called *le cafard* beset her as the evenings grew darker and the corridors colder. A letter to Mrs Jerome reveals the longing for her own clan:

Blenheim Palace,
Woodstock.
Nov. 21st.

Dearest Mama,

I was so pleased to get your letter. You know you don't treat me very often to one! I'm so delighted to think that you are coming over in March. It will be great fun going to Paris together. It is such ages since I've seen you. It is really too long. I quite forget what it is like to be with people who love me. I do so long sometimes to have someone to whom I could go & talk to. Of course Randolph is awfully good to me and always takes my part in everything, but how can I always be abusing his mother to him, when she is devoted to him & wd do anything for him—The fact is I *loathe* living here. It is not on account of its dullness, *that* I don't mind, but it is gall & wormwood to me to accept anything or to be living on anyone I hate. It is no use disguising it, the Duchess hates me simply for what I am—perhaps a little prettier & more attractive than her daughters. Everything I do or say or wear is found fault with. We are always studiously polite to each other, but it is rather like a volcano, ready to burst out at any moment. Clara & Leonie both know what her ways are like. So it is no use describing *les petites misères* that make up the total of one's existence here. What one can laugh at in the abstract is most bitter when one is living with a person or accepting their hospitality. We've been here more than a month. The children have got charming nurseries & are well looked after. I've got a very nice room & sitting room on the ground floor; I paint and do pretty much what I like. Well! You can believe me when I say that I wd be happier living quite alone in our little house without seeing a soul. However it is not for long, only a fortnight more. I know I am very foolish to mind what can't be changed but it is trying! Now to talk of something cheerier you will be glad to hear R. made a capital speech at Portsmouth. I wish I cd send you the *Morning Post* but I couldn't get it. Of course the Liberal press is furious at his attacks on the Govt. but their spiteful articles are rather flattering than otherwise. How I wish the Conservatives might come in. We could then have a chance. Meanwhile our money affairs are pretty much like everyone else's it seems to me, hard up notwithstanding Papa's generous 'tips'.

Randolph is obliged to spend so much in a political way, going to those meetings etc. and this big public dinner in Woodstock will cost a lot . . . the building alone costing £120. . . . But his demonstration is of great importance to R. & the thing must be well done with Ld Salisbury & a lot of big swells coming. You don't know how economical we try to be. I've not bought but one winter dress, and that was bought in Woodstock for twenty-five shillings and made by my maid—dark red thin flannel. Clara and Leonie would cry Fi! of my wardrobe. There is no one here but Ld Portarlington & Lady Londonderry—the Dowager, the Duchess's mother. They both asked after Clara & said nice things. I've heard no amusing gossip, only a few letters from sporting friends. Best love to all dear Mama.

Ever

Yr loving

Jennie

PS. R. sends his best love—Bye the bye couldn't you send a barrel of American eating apples to St James Place? I'm so fond of them.

Randolph persuaded Lord Salisbury to speak at Woodstock on November 30th. This was Winston's sixth birthday and the little boy had a first glimpse of the man who would be swept to the Premiership by his father's brilliance.

Piano practice took up hours each day wherever she might be, and now Jennie started painting in the grand manner with large canvasses and extravagant tubes of paint. An undated note reads: 'Dearest Randolph, You must not be unhappy about me, for I shall soon get used to my solitude, particularly now that I have taken up my music & painting.'

In the spring of 1881 Disraeli remarked about Randolph: When they come in they will have to give him anything he chooses to ask for & in a very short time they will have to take anything he chooses to give them.'

Randolph showed his nerve. In January 1881, alone and against Disraeli's advice, he attacked the Coercion Bill which he believed would further embitter Ireland. After a forty-one-hour sitting he made his final speech amidst an ominous silence. Gladstone and half his Liberal Party believed Home Rule was the right answer to Ireland's woes, but the entire Tory Party stood angrily against a return to Government in Dublin. On account of the Protestant North, Lord Randolph Churchill thought Home Rule impossible, but he maintained that if England ruled Ireland from Westminster she should make the Irish love her! These are his words which in 1881 met a chilling silence in the House of Commons: '. . . I wish the Chief Secretary joy of these beautiful Bills, but I may tell the Right Honourable Gentleman that he has acquired by them the undying dislike and distrust of the Irish people. . . .'

Jennie, who had been horrified by the poverty of Irish peasants, felt herself more moved by this speech of Randolph's than by any other of his career. She pressed forward against the grille of the Speaker's Gallery to watch her husband 'glaring at the carpet and moodily twisting his moustache', while Sir William Harcourt rose with the whole Tory Party behind him to suggest contemptuously that Randolph devote his energies in future to advising the Irish.

Throughout that summer of 1881 the distress of Ireland increased and Gladstone's Land Bill did nothing to alleviate hunger or anger.

The diary of the Liberal Leader's private secretary reveals:

'November 2 1881: R. Churchill continues to "star" in the Provinces and there is no denying that he is making a position for himself.

'It is sickening to think that a man of such unscrupulousness & with such utter want of seriousness should be coming to the front in politics & would on the formation of a Tory Govt. be trusted with governing the country. The Tories are bad enough as regards measures but they are worse as regards men, commencing with Ld Salisbury & the weak-kneed Northcote down to such men as R. Churchill and J. Lowther with whom politics is a burlesque. . . .'

But the Fourth Party was in deadly earnest: from this time all Lord Randolph Churchill's speeches were reported verbatim in *The Times*.

At Christmas Randolph and Gorst spent a week in Dublin with Mr Justice Fitzgibbon discussing starvation and evictions. Randolph's next speech on the troubles of Ireland greatly angered Gladstone, who called it 'hotter in tone and weaker in argument than usual'.

It was this winter, when his father's fame was rising in crescendo, that the sensitive little seven-year-old son was sent to that horrific boarding school which he described in *My Early Life*. It was not Jennie's fault. As an American unused to the basically barbaric practice of packing small boys off into unknown preparatory schools, she disliked losing sight of Winston at this tender age, but Randolph assured her he had enjoyed his own preparatory school, and Ascot seemed healthier than London. The heartbreaking loneliness of the little boy he has himself narrated. How poignant is that description of the journey towards a place where he innocently imagined he was going to enjoy himself with other boys!

> The fateful day arrived. My mother took me to the station in a hansom cab. She gave me three half-crowns, which I dropped on the floor of the cab, and we had to scramble about in the straw to find them again. We only just caught the train. If we had missed it, it would have been the end of the world. . .
>
> The school my parents had selected for my education was one of the most fashionable and expensive in the country. . .
>
> It was a dark November afternoon when we arrived at this establishment. We had tea with the Headmaster, with whom my mother conversed in the most easy manner. . .
>
> When the last sound of my mother's departing wheels had died away, the Headmaster invited me to hand over any money. . .
> How I hated this school and what a life of anxiety I lived there for more than two years.

Mentally, and physically, the children suffered from masters who had selected the correct career for sadists. The odious Rev. H. W. Sneyd-Kynnersley has been vividly described by Winston's son in Volume I of the full life: his name and cruelty deserves to be fully revealed.

While hideous months were dragging out for Winston, his father could write jubilantly to Wolff: 'I had a most warm welcome at Oldham. The meeting numbered some six hundred—all working men. I spoke for fifty-five minutes—quite entrancing (my speech).

What you would have given to have heard it! ! !' And a few weeks later: 'Well! Hull was a triumph. I never had such a success with a large audience. Every point told surprisingly.'

Then, in the spring of 1882, at the height of the Irish crisis, Randolph became seriously ill and for five months unable to go to the House of Commons he lay fulminating on a sofa. Leonie came to London, hoping for a gay season with her married sisters, but on her first walk in Hyde Park Sir W. Gordon-Cumming, whom Clara had scorned, came up to her and remarked rudely: 'Over here husband-hunting?' On the next day a more comic episode deflated poor Leonie completely. Her father had asked her in Jennie's absence to be kind to an American friend of his, Mr Pierre Lorillard. This 'old gentleman', as Leonie regarded him, was a very cultured millionaire who had been in love with Clara. Leonie thought of him merely as one of Papa's old racing cronies and owner of a famous stud. Accompanying him to a large luncheon party she held forth somewhat patronisingly on the interesting sights of England, ending with a description of the classic races. He listened humbly until she announced, 'And you really *must* see the Derby.' 'Yes,' said Mr Lorillard, 'I hope to. I won it last year.'

When Mr Jerome sent her American racing annals she wrote him: 'Jennie has carried off Vol. II to Blenheim. I am getting to see Winston tomorrow at Ascot—am I not becoming a model aunt?' She noticed the child looked peaked, but thought the news would be unwelcome.

In April Jennie persuaded Randolph to take a trip to America, where they always 'felt alive'. They were staying with Mr Jerome when they heard that Lord Frederick Cavendish, and their friend the Permanent Under-Secretary Mr Burke, had been murdered in Phoenix Park. Randolph immediately wanted to sail home and join in the uproar created by these assassinations—so unfortunate for Ireland; but Jennie begged him to remain. Leonard Jerome wrote to his wife. 'I think Jennie is wonderful for him, he draws on her strength. I love having them here. I believe completely in R.'

When they returned to England Jennie found herself inundated by distressed letters from Mama. Clara, now twenty-eight, was scorning the peer of Mrs Jerome's choice, to marry a good-looking penniless Englishman named Moreton Frewen. Jennie was asked to find out about him in England. Enquiries throughout Leicestershire revealed amusing but unreassuring information. Mr Frewen was a famous horseman, every sportsman in England knew and liked him, but he was a stone who had started off with a little financial moss and rolled it all off in Wyoming. Lord Lonsdale said he was a wonderful shot. Lord Charles Beresford said no one rode better to hounds. Men would choose him above others for a hunting expedition, less enthusiastically as a son-in-law.

It was a turbulent summer for England. After Colonel Arabi's *coup d'etat* in Egypt, Gladstone dispatched a naval force to shell Alexandria. During this engagement Randolph's friend Lord Charles Beresford, who commanded the gunboat *Condor,* played a spirited part ashore and became a popular hero, which aroused jealousy in other gentlemen. Bullets whistling past the ear were rare and any action had to be snatched as a precious chance to exhibit courage. The conquest of Eygpt offered a golden opportunity for the danger-starved exhibitionists. As his rivals had to admit to Lord Charles's personal courage, they clamoured against the entire expedition. When he returned to convalescence at Wimbledon, Lord Randolph joined in, calling the expedition 'a wicked war, an unjust war, a "bondholder's war".'

Jennie had more personal worries. She found an outraged Mrs Everest waiting for her with a pale little Winston. The child had now suffered nearly two years at this expensive boarding school where the small boys were ill-fed and beaten till they bled. When the good nurse showed the birch marks, Jennie determined to take her son away immediately, to build up his health at the seaside.

The other little wretches lingered on at St George's until the perverted sadist who ran it died of a heart attack—none too soon. It was typical of English snobbery in the 'eighties that aristocratic parents thought this a nice school because the headmaster's coat-of-arms hung outside the front door.

Many years later, when I took my eight-year-old son to spend a day with Winston, he described afresh the horror of that school. 'If my mother hadn't listened to Mrs Everest and taken me away I would have broken down completely. Can you imagine a child being *broken down?*' When looking at my boy he said: 'Well, he looks happy and mischievous too—that is how children should be— I can never forget that school. It was *horrible.*'

Lord Randolph agreed that he must be moved and a pleasant

school run by two ladies was discovered at Brighton but Winston would long after complain that the boys had only one *half* sausage for breakfast. Lord Randolph, so original in expression himself, remained unamused by the quaint phrases of the young. His letters to Wolff at this time show varied moods: 'Your letters are to me like a glass of the best champagne—exhilarating & stimulating.' And from Monte Carlo in January 1882: 'All your news about my conversation with various distinguished people concerning myself is very pleasant reading, but my disinclination to return to England for the meeting of Parliament grows stronger every day & I seem to have lost all interest in things political.' And again in 1883: 'They do not know how easy it would be to be rid of me. I am sick of politics which only play the dickens with one's health & are a dreadful tie.'

Jennie, being exceptionally robust, was at first puzzled by Randolph's lapses of energy for she came of splendidly healthy stock. Gradually her distress deepened. She realised that Randolph was basically delicate, and lived entirely on his nerves; but she did not know that a cruel disease was creeping through his system to blunt the perspicacity of that razor-sharp mind.

He always rallied to excitement, and in the spring of 1883 he launched forth a daring campaign, demanding a new leader for the Tory Party. He published a letter in *The Times* urging the replacement of Sir Stafford Northcote by Lord Salisbury. His friends had warned him against the fury they knew this letter would cause. When Lord Randolph went to the House scarcely a member would speak to him. He sat hunched up in his corner seat, abandoned even by the three members of his Fourth Party. But the indignation shown in Westminster produced no echo in the country. With extraordinary acumen Lord Randolph Churchill was turning the old-fashioned Tory Party into the working man's delight: and the great industrial cities, including Manchester, acclaimed his demand for a pugnacious party leader. 'Randy is right', became the common cry.

Lord Salisbury remained silent during this fray. He was a friend of Sir Stafford Northcote, and he was too gentlemanly to be rude, though not too gentlemanly to take the old man's place when the time came.

Randolph glowered for a week in his corner seat. Then he wrote an even stronger letter calling for 'a statesman who knows how to meet & who knows how to sway immense masses of the working classes & who either by his genius or his eloquence, or by all the varied influences of an ancient name can "move the hearts of households".'

Lord Salisbury remained yet more silent, for these attributes could be applied to Randolph as neatly as to himself.

Soon after Northcote had unveiled Disraeli's statue, Randolph wrote the most pungent article of his career, entitled 'Elijah's Mantle'. In it he expounded his view of 'Tory Democracy' and called on Lord Salisbury to come forward as the new leader of a revived party, intimating frankly that if Salisbury declined he was himself ready to do so.

A roar against this 'impudence' rose up, and then faded. Lord Randolph Churchill found himself listened to with new respect. His nightly battles with Gladstone caused someone to remark: 'You will kill Mr Gladstone.' 'Oh, no!' answered Randolph, 'he will long survive me. I often tell my wife what a beautiful letter he will write her, proposing my burial in Westminster Abbey.

He must have understood his own illness by now but excitement led him on. And what good company he could be—when the company pleased him. How easily the despondency lifted! Charades and after-dinner games were not his form, and he usually retired when these were suggested; but if forced to take part he raised more laughs than anyone.

In politics Randolph's appeal was that of the natural leader. The cheers of rough crowds delighted him. He could have led a rabble to battle. His own party were shocked by certain proclamations: 'I hope before long to see Tory working men in Parliament. . . . If you want to gain the confidence of the working classes, let them have a share, and a large share, a real share, and not a sham share in your party Councils.'

He had the magic. An Irish opponent, T. P. O'Connor, wrote at this time: 'Everybody now recognises that all the spirit and go which exist in the Conservative Party have been infused into it by this dashing, irrepressible and, at first sight, frivolous youth.'

Lord Rosebery has striven to recapture the effect of his speeches: 'For Randolph was, I suppose, at his best on the platforms before a great audience. I infer this from the vast popularity that his platform speeches obtained for him, from their immense vogue, and the extraordinary anxiety to hear him. In liveliness, in vigour, in sureness of touch, in the power of holding an audience, he transcended, I suspect, not merely Disraeli, but every one in living memory except Mr Gladstone, Mr Bright, and Mr Chamberlain. His secret would have been worth knowing, but I never had the good fortune to hear him on the platform. . . . A political opponent at a meeting would not have been appreciated or welcome. . . . My own surmise would be that the attraction of Randolph's speaking was due as much to the speaker as to the speech. The speech itself was always excellent of its kind, often exaggerated, with passages of admirable humour, irony and rhetorical power. But had these speeches been delivered by any middle-aged gentleman on the front bench, they would have been much less successful. It was Randolph's personality that was so winning: his audacity, his extravagance, his reckless party spirit, his physical qualities, his slight form, his modulated but penetrating voice, even his perpetually twisted moustache; and above all, perhaps, the fact that this stripling had come to stir the dry bones of party and to divert the jaded attention of the audience from actors, however eminent, of whom they were rather tired, to a fresh young character. He was, in a word, supremely interesting.'

During the spring of 1883 Sir Henry Drummond Wolff had the idea of creating a Conservative Party Association. The idea struck him during the unveiling of Disraeli's statue, when many members wore primroses which had been Dizzy's favourite flower. Wolff mentioned his idea to Randolph who impetuously exclaimed, 'Let's go off and do it at once!' The Primrose League was launched at Blenheim to 'embrace all classes and all creeds except atheists and enemies of the British Empire'. The Duchess of Marlborough was made President of the Ladies Council, while her daughters and daughter-in-law were enrolled as Dames with numbered diplomas. This led to fun for the energetic. Wearing her badge, Jennie travelled the country, organising village sing-songs and recitations to make converts. She was ready to do anything for the Tory Party, she said, except speak in public and her piano-playing and acting talent came in very useful. It sounds amateurish, but the power of the Primrose League spread fast. To both middle classes and hungry classes this extrovert effort had appeal. The Liberals mocked, and Lord Salisbury

85

gave only cautious approval, until the Primrose League swept the country. It was perhaps gall to the Liberals to see a branch of the stuffy old Tory Party crashing the class-barriers and using pretty ladies to attract votes; fraternising with the working class had been *their* prerogative.

In July 1883 the old Duke of Marlborough suddenly died. He had dined with Randolph the night before, triumphant at having tottered to the House of Lords to oppose a Bill which would permit a man to marry his deceased wife's sister. The Duke's impassioned speech secured its defeat by a narrow margin, and for another generation unfortunate widowers yearned in vain for attractive sisters-in-law. But the Duke joined his forbears with a sense of duty done.

Perhaps His Grace's feelings had been intensified by his son and heir: Blandford caddishly complained that when sent to Northern Ireland to choose a wife among the Duke of Abercorn's daughters he had had the least attractive foisted on him. Now, while that unfortunate lady was in the process of divorcing him, the curious, clever, mysterious scientist became eighth Duke. His unhappy wife declined to take the title of Duchess and remained Lady Bland-ford. Their eldest son, three years older than Winston, was put in his father's care and led a wretched existence. In his own words he was 'given no kindness and entirely crushed'. This callousness to a boy who must have already suffered deeply during his parents' estrangement is perhaps the final verdict on that 'wicked Duke', so often castigated by the American Press. Blandford charmed many people, his qualities were unusual ones of near-genius and brilliant conversational power, but callousness remains his hall-mark. How did the heart get bred out of the Churchill brothers? For Jennie, who always knew herself to be the most beautiful woman in a room, held Randolph by pride rather than affection. She knew by now he was incapable of loving. He remained intoxicated by her physical attributes, but love, as she had seen it in her own home, did not exist. It was a slow realisation. Randolph would stand up for her against the Duchess; he would delight in her company, but there were none of the warm gestures needed by her emotional impulsive nature. This coldness did not improve her. She grew to rely too much on outer triumphs, on the effect she could make in her expensive dresses, in the power of her own face.

After the Duke's funeral at Blenheim, Randolph took her and Winston to Gastein for the rest of the summer. Winston was still in poor health, but they took him for mountain walks, frequently meeting Bismarck out with his boar-hound and two detectives. The round blue eyes of the nine-year-old English boy widened as his parents explained *who* Bismarck was—a powerful but disagreeable personage who had caused Mama to flee from Paris without her bonnets.

Lord Randolph's letters to Wolff describe, in the usual light-hearted vein, a tea party with the Emperor Wilhelm I: 'You will be glad to hear that the Emperor of Germany had the honour of being introduced to me on Saturday last at a tea party at Count Lehndorff's. This Count, I must tell you, is a Prussian who owns the *bicogne* which I am inhabiting with my suite. He waited on us Saturday afternoon, and with almost Oriental deference begged that we would honour the Emperor by meeting him. I write all this, lest you should see garbled accounts in the newspapers. The Emperor, I must admit, was very guarded in his conversation, which was confined to asking me how long I had been here and whether I had come for my health. I imitated his reserve. My wife, however, sat by him at tea, and had much conversation, which, I have ascertained, was confined to the most frivolous topics. I have reason to believe, though it is humiliating to confess it, that the fame of the Fourth Party has not yet reached the ears of this despot. I must say he is a very fine old fellow, and the Germans seem really to love him.'

Jennie commented on the Emperor's diet while on a cure: 'He began with poached eggs and went on to potted meats, and various strange German dishes, adding many cups of strong tea, and ended with strawberries and sweetened champagne.'

The new Duke of Marlborough asked Randolph and Jennie to spend the winter with him at Blenheim. This proved a happy time for Jennie, who found her naughty, clever brother-in-law most congenial, and she enjoyed hunting. Randolph revived his Harriers and taught her to whip-in, but she never could remember the hounds of the pack by name or character. He, a true hound man, knew each member with proper intimacy.

Meanwhile Parliament missed him.

9

The new master of Blenheim Palace spent his days conducting scientific experiments in the laboratory he had built on the top floor. His electrical inventions terrified the twenty-odd housemaids, and he obtained the reputation of being a sorcerer as well as a lady-killer. The private telephone system which he invented independently of Edison provoked more annoyance than fear. Wires lay along the corridors, entangling the feet of guests, but the staff smiled at what they called 'the Duke's toy'. Randolph begged him not to sell off family pictures and the famous Sunderland library, but Marlborough was determined to clear out old books and works of art and to put the money into farming. He spent thousands on hot-houses and started a vast collection of orchids. Although Randolph deplored these agricultural schemes they remained a friendly pair of brothers, strange men both for the grim old Marlboroughs to have bred. Each night when Jennie and Randolph came in happy and tired from the chase, the Duke charmed them through dinner, and the conversation was eclectic. Jennie had never enjoyed the Palace so well.

Randolph now needed a larger but cheaper London house, so they moved out of Mayfair to 2 Connaught Place and there, on the top floor overlooking Marble Arch, Mrs Everest established her nursery for the last time. Jack was three and Winston getting on for nine. Their lives still revolved around that dear nurse. She remained the centre of the universe, while they got only fleeting glimpses of their mother, and their father, the unattainable hero, never spoke to little boys.

88

2 Connaught Place stands near the site of Tyburn gallows, and although Jennie scoffed at ghosts there were strange sounds at night on the staircase. Alterations to the cellars revealed old mass graves. The new Duke pressed them to instal electric light of his design, and the vibrating dynamo in the cellar may well have driven spirits upstairs to seek peace in the nursery!

Jennie continued to meet Gladstone at dinner parties and he retained the most gracious manner towards his tormentor's wife. It may be relevant here to insert the assessment of the Grand Old Man, eventually made by the tormentor's son: 'So long as his light lasted the House of Commons lived, and amid the fiercest passions and even scenes of violence, preserved its hold upon the sympathies and imagination of the whole world; and at his death it sank at once, perhaps for ever, in public esteem.'

Pity for the poor became a virtue in Victorian England, but any serious attempt to alter poverty was considered Radical and dangerous. The Liberal Party talked much of industrial reform, but with increasing prosperity it grew too often pompous. It was Lord Randolph, the sporting aristocrat with the none-too-pious turn of wit, who caught the imagination of the working classes and drew them to his own party, or to the section of his party he named Tory Democracy.

Lord Charles Beresford made this point in a letter: 'You are the only man in the House who can hit Gladstone in the head and bowl him over like a rabbit so hit. Everyone else, if they hit him at all, hit him in the ——! This looks vulgar, but it is true—organise and guide the masses and not treat them as scum as the Tories have so often done.'

Randolph could draw a laugh from the street crowds as well as from the House, and he warmed to the rough acclaim of that cry 'Give it to 'em hot, Randy!' At the other end of the social scale a different interest flickered up. The Prince of Wales, relieved to know that he need not fear Randolph's enmity in Parliament, became increasingly intrigued by the rebel's success. For some time Jennie had been using smiles and glances to fish for Royal forgiveness. She knew the Prince had always liked her personally, and this made it easier. It seems curious that the Prince could ever forgive Randolph's threat to reveal his personal letters, but eight years after the Aylesford case, His Royal Highness intimated to Sir Henry James, the

Attorney General, that he would be prepared to dine in his house when the Randolph Churchills as well as Mr and Mrs Gladstone would be guests.

The date was 9th March 1884. Jennie had worked long for this evening and she carried it off perfectly. She took pains to charm old Mr Gladstone and she conversed naturally and humorously with the Prince. Due to her no one felt awkward or constrained. Randolph had an eye for a dazzling performance. While remaining edgy he appreciated the fact that no woman in Europe could have handled the situation more adroitly.

H.R.H. informed Queen Victoria that all had gone well, and on June 2nd, at the Café Anglais in Paris, he again dined with Sir Henry James when Randolph and Jennie and the American sportsman J. Gordon Bennett were present. The Prince did not actually enter the Churchill house for another two years but Jennie's candour had won him.

In Sir Philip Magnus's revealing *Life of King Edward the Seventh* the boredom and frustration which afflicted English society at that time are well described: 'A combination of unlimited leisure with unprecedented wealth fostered a restless pursuit of pleasure which failed to procure contentment. The Prince of Wales displayed many symptoms of that malaise which afflicted most members of the society over which he reigned, and the task of keeping him amused was regarded as a major social problem throughout the last decades of the nineteenth century. A variety of frivolous stratagems were devised in an effort to charm away the tedium of assembling again and again in the same great country houses, and some hostesses were prepared always to divert their guests, including the Prince, by a discreet allocation of bedrooms in accordance with their known but unexpressed wishes.'

Jennie had been forbidden access to this world for a long time. She re-entered it in glory, but the years of Randolph's banishment taught the value of caution. She herself was never bored, either in town or country, except when the old Marlboroughs kept her disciplined at Blenheim. She had vitality to impart to suffocating house parties, and the pleasure of knowing herself important kept her naturally good spirits bubbling. She was nearly thirty, and the hard years had given her a sense of timing. She possessed an emotional artistic passionate nature unsuited to mere social rounds, and to help the audacious Randolph balance on his tightrope was exactly her métier. She set herself out to be the most sought-after woman in London and the Prince's buddy rather than his lady love. Daisy, the fascinating Countess of Warwick, was about to start her reign in that capacity. Who padded up which corridors during the house parties given for the Prince of Wales has in some cases been kept discreetly indefinite. His Royal Highness certainly loved Jennie's company by day (and may have sought it by night), but the hundred-odd notes which he wrote to her—at least the surviving ones—give no inkling of the ultimate relationship. These letters are nearly all undated, and, although very personal and full of compliments, they never border on the terms which he used to 'Darling Daisy'. Jennie amused the Prince and Randolph fascinated him. It was really too cruel that H.R.H. had been forced to years of angry separation from the couple whose company he enjoyed most. Jennie used tact, not the fireworks of her sex-appeal, to give the Prince the chance to reassert his friendship. After the terrible things that Randolph had done to him and the violence of the Prince's remarks in the ensuing years, it seems miraculous that they discovered how much they liked each other after all. Eventually, on 16th May 1886, His Royal Highness dined with Lord and Lady Randolph Churchill at 2 Connaught Place and Marlborough, who had precipitated the whole Aylesford scandal, was a fellow guest! This was one of the numerous occasions when the electric light went out and the wicked Duke had to work importantly with fuses.

Before this particular dinner party, however, great political changes were to take place. In these upheavals the Fourth Party played an important part. It is not often that a genius, whether ballet dancer or politician, has to be forced on to the stage. This had happened in Randolph's case, but once he grew accustomed to the footlights, once he discovered his own power, nothing could hold him. He still hated speaking; he suffered terribly from nerves, and yet the test of his talent delighted him. Jennie sustained him prior to each carefully rehearsed speech, and suffered the agonies a wife should when her husband went too far. It was Lord Randolph Churchill who invented the Tory Democracy, a party with human feeling despite Labouchere's gibe 'you might as well talk of black-white men'. It is curious that one so hot and human on the political platform should be so cold and inhuman in the home. But so it was and the small boys in Connaught Place never received a nod from this scintillating father. Only the Prince of Wales looked on them with a kindly smile and brought each a gift when he came to a meal.

The Prince, emotionally, was a very kind man. He liked people to be happy, he hated them to be unhappy, but he did not know quite what to do about it. During this last year he had, in disguise, accompanied the Chief Medical Officer to some terrible hovels in London slums, and been so overcome by the sight of a starving woman, lying on a heap of rags with two half-naked children clinging to her for warmth, that he attempted to pull a handful of gold from his workman's trousers. In order to prevent a riot he had to be restrained but at least the right impulse was there.

Since the days of Queen Elizabeth the English aristocracy had developed a social sense in advance of any in Europe, but the Industrial Revolution produced untold misery in the towns, and Lord Randolph Churchill made several of the best speeches of his career on the necessity of breaking class barriers. He started by smacking his own Party, in the *Fortnightly Review*: 'Unfortunately for Conservatism, its leaders belong solely to one class; they are a clique composed of members of the aristocracy, landowners and adherents whose chief merit is subserviency. The party chiefs live in an atmosphere in which a sense of their own importance and the importance of their class interests and privileges is exaggerated, and which the opinions of the common people can scarcely penetrate. . . .'

Later, in a speech attacking the Central Committee of his Party, he hit harder: 'Some of our friends in the party have a lesson to learn which they do not seem disposed to learn. The Conservative Party will never exercise power until it has gained the confidence of the working classes; and the working classes are quite determined to govern themselves; and will not be either driven or hoodwinked by any class or class interests.'

Throughout the spring and summer of 1884 Lord Randolph made audacious speeches and his wife travelled serenely around England, begged to attend every great house party by those who wished to keep the Prince of Wales 'amused'.

Leonie stayed for two months in Connaught Place, and her letters to Mama were full of Lady Blanche Hozier, the gay and unorthodox daughter of Lord Airlie. Letters of 1884 read: 'We had a very pleasant evening at Blanche's last night and I only wished you had been there. Tosti was so amiable, sat and played till one o'clock! Such talent he has. He improvised and sang quaint little Italian songs. . . .' On June 18th she wrote to Clara: 'We sat a little while in the House of Lords. Lord Dorchester made such vigorous signs to me that we had to retreat! But it amused me to see half of the members sound asleep. Hopie yawning! Lord Ribblesdale with his mouth wide open! not at all pretty. . . . Jennie and Kinsky came in after.'

This is the first mention in Jerome letters of Count Charles Kinsky, the Austrian nobleman who had won the Grand National on Zoedone in 1883. He was already devoted to Jennie.

During her sojourn in Jennie's house Leonie noticed with pain Randolph's habit of shooing his sons away with his newspaper when they were brought to the dining room to say Good morning— 'the two pairs of round eyes, peeping around the screen, longed for a kind word.'

When Leonie sailed back to New York she was hotly pursued by John Leslie, now a winner of a medal at the battle of Tel el Kebir. She finally accepted the proposal he had started making six years before. They were married in Grace Church, New York, that September, and returned to London just before Randolph set sail for a holiday in India.

Mama wrote to Jennie: 'Dear Randolph, I think he well deserved it & I hope he will come back well & strong to enjoy life for many long years. He has made himself such a good name so early in life, he ought to reap a rich harvest later. I suppose the dear children are both with you for the holidays. Clara writes me that Winston has grown to be such a nice charming boy. I am so pleased. Will you give him my best love, and my little Jack. I hope he is the same darling boy as ever. I am dying to see them again. What a delightful surprise it must have been for Jack and Leonie to be with you at Connaught Place instead of going to Clarges Street, I can't get over it, such a nice house, & such a lot of jolly little people living together. I do hope you will all keep well and try to be *good* & enjoy yourselves. . . .'

Jennie was perhaps more adept at enjoying herself than being good, but this was a very happy family party for her with Winston and Jack and Clara's baby son Hugh grouped around the Christmas tree.

Mr Jerome wrote to Jennie on 26 February: '. . . I have watched with wonder Randolph's rise in the political world . . . I confess I am amazed, so young! so reckless, inexperienced & impulsive. That he should have fought his way up through the fiery elements without as the trotters say a 'skip or a break' is indeed wonderful. I hope he will come home soon & that he will find himself in accord with Lord Salisbury touching Egyptian affairs.'

Randolph's letters to Jennie during the three months he spent travelling through India are full of tigers. He shot one, 'a magnificent specimen, nine feet seven inches in length, a splendid skin— which will, I think, look very well in Grosvenor Square. . . . Tigers in the Zoo give one very little impression of what the wild animal is like.'

Randolph had returned home when, on 5th April 1885, Winston, who was learning to canter, to dance and to collect stamps, at his Brighton school, wrote to him: '. . . I have been out riding with a gentleman who thinks that Gladstone is a brute and thinks that "the one with the curly moustache ought to be Prime Minister".'

On April 19th Lord Randolph Churchill attended a big Primrose League Banquet. When he rose to propose the toast he spoke briefly of his visit to India, and the seven hundred guests, surfeited with party politics as with food and wine, suddenly felt the cool breeze of genius blow through St James's Hall: 'My Lords and gentlemen, our task of governing India, which we have been carrying on now for more than a hundred years, is a task of great difficulty and danger, the difficulties and danger of which do not diminish as time goes on. Our rule in India is, as it were, a sheet of oil spread over a surface of, and keeping calm and quiet and unruffled by storms, an immense and profound ocean of humanity. Underneath that rule lie hidden all the memories of fallen dynasties, all the traditions of vanquished races, all the pride of insulted creeds; and it is our task, our most difficult business, to give peace, individual security, and general prosperity to the two hundred and fifty millions of people who are affected by those powerful forces, to bind them and to weld them by the influence of our knowledge, our law and our higher civilisations, in process of time, into one great, united people; and to offer to all the nations of the West the advantages of

94

tranquillity and progress in the East. That is our task for India. That is our *raison d'être* in India. That is our title to India. . . .'

During the eventful summer of 1885 Churchill led his 'ginger group' in harassing Gladstone's Government. Never relying entirely on his excellent memory, Randolph would lock himself up in his study at 2 Connaught Place, preparing and revising until he could emerge with a speech, in his own words 'red hot'. The atmosphere of secrecy and tension increased on the two occasions when Mr Parnell called to ask his views on coercion in Ireland. He answered that if he ever became a member of the Government he would oppose renewal of the Crimes Act. Parnell answered: 'In that case, you will have the Irish vote at the elections.'

Small boys were to be neither seen nor heard in a house where such momentous meetings took place. Winston and John had to content themselves with the pride of watching people in the street recognise and cheer their father as he drove by.

At the end of May, Randolph journeyed to France with Sir Henry James, who described the crossing:

My dear Lady Randolph,

A word of our journey. At Charing Cross station, Friday morning, the Inspector informed us it was blowing roughly from the S.E. in the channel. R. C. derided the idea: 'Nonsense, what a weak creature you are; beautiful day.' At Folkestone, Captain's cabin reserved for two; Randolph spurned it, 'beastly place, I shall go on the bridge.' I reclined and read and saw no more of my companion until we arrived at Boulogne. At first I could not find him, at last a sailor came to me and said, 'The gentleman is very ill, but he is trying to come upstairs now.' Then I saw a figure crawling out of the forecastle. He had been on the bridge, literally washed off it, lay on the deck for a time, over the deck the sea poured. . . . To my altered friend I rushed. He really was very ill, and placed a fixed gaze on the ground, still thinking of and feeling the horrors of that voyage. A stout red-faced man approached him, 'Let me as one of your most ardent admirers shake hands with you.' I much doubt if that man will ever make that request again. Propping himself up by means of my umbrella, and tottering notwithstanding, sea-water running away in great quantities from his great coat, a new hat quite spoilt, Lord Randolph slightly inclined a fixed eye embedded in a ghastly countenance of a leaden yellow colour upon that admirer who fled. . . . Before Amiens he awoke, quite sprightly and with a good colour, smoked two cigarettes, and abused Granville so I knew he was quite well. . . .'

A month later Gladstone's Government was defeated by a late night vote. Great excitement prevailed. Lucy describes the House that night:

There is a great deal more in Lord Randolph Churchill than meets the eye. His reckless manners cover a deep and serious purpose, and his natural abilities will enable him to gain it. Let us cherish this picture of the noble lord standing on the bench below the gangway waving his hat over his head with one hand, whilst the other is held to his mouth in order the better to direct his triumphant shout towards the Treasury bench, where Mr Gladstone sits quietly writing his letter. [The nightly letter to the Queen.]

Lord Rosebery likened Randolph's shout to the 'who-whoop of fox-hunters at the death'. Hastening to Lord Salisbury to discuss the crisis, Hicks-Beach asked how a government could be formed without Churchill whom he described as 'far and away the most popular Conservative in the House of Commons'.

When on June 12th Salisbury was asked by the Queen to form an Administration he had to face a difficult decision, for Randolph Churchill obstinately refused to serve in the cabinet if Sir Stafford Northcote remained Leader of the House of Commons. After a week of nerve-racking correspondence it was decided to give Northcote an earldom and make him First Lord of the Treasury. Northcote's diary on June 20th says of Lord Randolph: 'He has practically got rid of me and now he will prove a thorn in the side of Salisbury and Beach.'

The Fourth Party, which had spent many hilarious hours on Jennie's big sofa, moved *en masse* into the new cabinet. Balfour became President of the Local Government Board, Gorst was Solicitor General, Wolff departed on an important mission to Egypt and Lord Randolph became Secretary for India. Queen Victoria did not approve of this appointment but she thought 'the India Council would be a check on him'.

Randolph was curiously nervous when he crossed the Solent with the other ministers to kiss the Queen's hand at Osborne, and Her Majesty noted this fact with approval. But Lord Rosebery wrote: 'Never was the House of Commons led more acceptably than in that short summer session. The secret of his success lay apparently in personal example, discipline, and courtesy, but he was, besides, a favourite of the House.' And again: 'His demeanour, his unexpectedness, his fits of caressing humility, his impulsiveness, his tinge of violent eccentricity, his apparent daredevilry, made him a fascinating companion: while his wit, his sarcasm, his piercing personality, his elaborate irony, and his effective delivery, gave astonishing popularity to his speeches. Nor were his physical attributes without their attraction. His slim and boyish figure, his moustache which had an emotion of its own, his round protruding eye, gave a compound interest to his speeches and his conversation. His laugh, which has been described as "jay-like", was indeed not melodious, but in its very weirdness and discordance it was merriment itself.'

This was Jennie's husband in July 1885. Jennie's only reference to him in this vital month exists in a letter to her sister: 'The Prince told Randolph he *must* take me to Mme L—— for a new dress for the Chiswick Ball.' What Jennie did not tell her sisters until much later was that some four years previously Randolph had separated himself from her physically. She was hurt, puzzled and suspected other women, but for a long time she kept her mortification to herself.

In September 1885 her sister Leonie had a son (Shane Leslie) ... my father... and her sister Clara a daughter (Clare Sheridan), and Winston was sent to the east coast for his holiday, whence a letter to his mother written on September 2nd pleaded: 'The governess is very unkind, so strict and stiff. I can't enjoy myself at all.'

10

On entering the cabinet Lord Randolph Churchill had to seek re-election. He was overwhelmed with work. His wife and his sister Lady Georgina Curzon—the one he usually referred to as 'my sister the stud groom'—undertook the canvassing at Woodstock. Jennie has described her own methods: 'I felt like a general holding a council-of-war with his staff in the heat of a battle. . . . Sometimes with these simple country folk a pleading look, and an imploring "Oh please vote for my husband, I shall be so unhappy if he does not get in," or, "If you want to be on the winning side, vote for us, as of course we are going to win," would be as effective as the election agent's longest speeches. . . . The distance to cover was great, and motors were not in existence. Luckily, Lady Georgina Curzon, who was a beautiful driver, brought down her well-known tandem, and we scoured the country with our smart turn-out, the horses gaily decorated with ribbons of pink and brown, Randolph's racing colours. Sometimes we would drive into the fields and getting down, climb the hayricks, falling upon our unwary prey at his work. There was no escaping us. . . .

'Party feeling ran high and in outlying districts we would frequently be pursued by our opponents, jeering and shouting at us; but this we rather enjoyed.'

She quotes a jingle of the time to appreciate which the photograph of the tandem must be studied:

But just as I was talking
With Neighbour Brown and walking

To take a mug of beer at the Unicorn & Lion,
(For there's somehow a connection
Between free beer and election)
Who should come but Lady Churchill, with a turnout that was
                      fine.
And before we stopped her horses,
As she marshalled all her forces,
And before I knew what happened I had promised her my vote;
And before I quite recovered
From the vision that had hovered,
I was much too late to rally, and I had changed my coat.

And over Woodstock darted
On their mission brave, wholehearted,
The tandem and their driver and the ribbons pink and brown.
And a smile that twinkled over,
And that made a man most love her
Took the hearts and votes of all Liberals in the town.

Bless my soul! that Yankee lady,
Whether day was bright or shady,
Dashed about the district like an oriflamme of war.
When the voters saw her bonnet,
With the bright pink roses on it,
They followed as the soldiers did the Helmet of Navarre.

Copying these tactics, the Liberals produced two ladies of their
own to cajole the countryside. But as a farmer was heard declaring
when Randolph's large majority was announced—'It was the tandem
wot done it.' Jennie returned triumphantly to London after making
a little speech thanking the voters 'from the bottom of my heart'.

Sir Henry James, the Liberal Attorney General, whose letters
Jennie kept, wrote her:

New Court Temple
1885

My dear Lady Randolph,

You must let me very sincerely & heartily congratulate you
on the result of the election, especially as that result proceeded so
very much from your personal exertions. Everybody is praising
you very much.

J.—H

But my gratification is slightly impaired by feeling I must introduce a new Corrupt Practices Act. Tandems must be put down, and certainly some alteration—a correspondent informs me—must be made in the means of ascent and descent therefrom; then arch looks have to be scheduled, and nothing must be said 'from my heart'. The graceful wave of a pocket handkerchief will have to be dealt with in committee.

Still, I am very glad.
Yours most truly,
Henry James

The Jerome sisters knew they had pretty ankles and were not averse to others knowing it—in a good cause. With a certain humour the Prince of Wales congratulated Randolph on Jennie's speeches. Lord Randolph replied in the grand style, adding: 'It is a further source of infinite satisfaction to Lady Randolph to know that possibly by action on her part she may have been fortunate enough to influence in any degree Your Royal Highness's views on a subject of large political importance.' It would have been *lèse-majesté* in this instance to ask if it was the ankles or the tandem 'wot did it'.

Leonie was now enjoying the London season while her Grenadier husband was engaged in not-too-onerous guard duties at the Tower of London. Years of martial discipline did not alter dear Jack's vagueness, and his wife had to keep his social diary. One morning she realised with horror that within the hour Jacksy was due to act as a godfather at the christening of Lady Blanche Hozier's new baby daughter. In her own diary Leonie scribbled a description of how she had to borrow Jennie's barouche to chase after her husband and bring him to the font in full uniform, there being no time to change. Jacksy did not hold the baby firmly and Leonie leant forward to save little Clementine from a ducking. She did not guess this mite would marry her nephew Winston.

The post of Secretary of State for India held enormous, even despotic power; Randolph could deal direct with the Viceroy, and most of the India Office officials had regarded the advent of so young a man with foreboding. They soon learned to respect him. Godley, the permanent Under-Secretary, wrote: 'Few high officials can ever have been his superior, or indeed his equal, in the magical art of *getting things done*.' And Lord Dufferin, the Viceroy, has written that what struck him most about Lord Randolph was 'to use a horrid word, "the receptivity" of his mind'.

When the Finance Committee held a meeting to discuss bi-metallism, a subject on which his brother-in-law, Moreton Frewen, was exceedingly voluble, Lord Randolph asked Godley to help him, artlessly announcing, 'I'm as ignorant about these things as a calf.' Frewen, who had lost several millions for his friends, thought he knew the solution to all financial problems, but his turbulent ideas were more than governments could grasp.

In early July, Lord and Lady Randolph Churchill stayed at Windsor with the Queen. The atmosphere remained pleasant, although Jennie was uncomfortably aware that her husband's behaviour in the Aylesford affair had not been forgotten. A month later, annoyed by the Queen's interference in Indian affairs, Randolph protested to Lord Salisbury against the appointment of Arthur, Duke of Connaught, to the Bombay Command. 'Egyptian experience would lead you to the conclusion I think that in actual hostilities Royal Dukes are a source of great embarrassment, discontent and danger.

'The giving of lucrative public appointments to members of the Royal Family is not only heart-breaking to the Military and Naval professions but in this present day is undoubtedly attended by great electoral disadvantages at home.'

The Queen was greatly incensed by these views. Her Majesty's journal for August 17th states: '. . . Startled by Lord Salisbury telegraphing absurd behaviour of Lord Randolph, who wished to resign because I had asked privately of Lord Dufferin, through Lord Salisbury, as to Arthur's fitness for Bombay. . . . However, he has since returned to reason, "having taken calomel" as Lord Salisbury amusingly words it, and is not going to resign. . . .'

After zealously working for Lady Dufferin's Medical Fund for Indian Women, Jennie was hoping to be given the Order of the Star of India, a decoration with 'a pretty pearl and turquoise cipher attached to a pale blue ribbon edged with white', but her husband did not think it proper to recommend his own wife. Perhaps the Prince of Wales dropped a hint for, in December, after the General Election, Jennie received with delight a summons to Windsor.

Lady Randolph Churchill:

Bonnet and morning dress, grey gloves. To kiss the Queen's hand after receiving the decoration, like the gentlemen today. A room will be prepared for her.

Queen Victoria received her in a small room, back to the window, wearing a long white veil which made an aureole round her against the light. After a few kind words she pinned the order on Jennie's left shoulder. 'I remember that my black velvet dress was thickly embroidered with jet, so much so that the pin could find no hold and unwittingly the Queen stuck it straight into me. Although like the Spartan boy I tried to hide what I felt, I suppose I gave a start, and the Queen realising what she had done was much concerned.'

After a few words Jennie was curtseying herself back to the door when the little Queen stepped forward with a smile.

'Oh! you have forgotten the case.' This natural touch relieved the terrifying formality of an interview with Queen Victoria. Mr Worth designed a pale blue dress in the exact shade of the ribbon and her Star of India remained a source of real pride.

During the late summer of that politically heated year the problem of Upper Burma came to the fore. When the old King of Burma had died seven years previously he left thirty sons intriguing for the throne, and at the end of a palace shambles Prince Theebaw had managed to massacre twenty-seven of his brothers and their families and to instal himself as King. Eight cart-loads of butchered princes of the blood were thrown into the river while less important dependants were dumped into the gaol pit. Only two of the princes escaped, and these took refuge with the British Resident, who stoutly refused to give them up when the Burmese Minister for Foreign Affairs argued that the massacre was 'in accordance to precedent' and that England ought to respect the customs of other countries.

Queen Victoria indignantly refused to send the telegram of congratulations usual to a monarch mounting the throne, and relationships deteriorated, until by 1885 England considered it imperative to put a full stop to intrigues which endangered the Indian Empire. When Lord Randolph considered the case for action complete he made clear the maxim that if force is used it must be immediate and overwhelming. To this end he telegraphed to the Viceroy

Lord Dufferin: 'The terms of your ultimatum are approved. But I am strongly of opinion that its despatch should be concurrent with movement of troops and ships on Rangoon. If ultimatum is rejected, the advance on Mandalay ought to be immediate.'

The ultimatum expired on November 10th. It took only seven days to rout the Burmese Army and occupy Mandalay. King Theebaw was taken prisoner and Upper Burma annexed by the last day of December. The campaign cost the British one officer and three men.

Randolph arranged for the proclamation to be made on January 1st, 1886, as a New Year present to the Queen, but Her Majesty did not seem very grateful, writing on December 30th: 'The youngest member of the Cabinet must *not* be allowed to dictate to the others. It will *not* do and Ld Salisbury really must put his foot down.'

Yet Her Majesty kept a soft spot for her young minister. On one occasion, when she enquired why the India Office box had reached Balmoral full of grey substance and this was discovered to be ash from the innumerable cigarettes which the highly-strung Lord Randolph had smoked in London, the old Queen laughed heartily.

At the General Election of November 1885, with two million new voters at the polls, Randolph flung himself violently into the campaign, speaking in the industrial midlands and taking his chance of winning a seat from the Radicals in their citadel of Birmingham. He had long ago boasted, 'The Whigs can no longer call us the party of the classes. If they do I'll chuck big cities at their heads.'

He alone could fill the halls with boisterous working men who loved his fiery wit and matchless oratory. His invention of Tory Democracy he called the 'most simple and most easily understood denomination ever assumed'. Roars of laughter met his castigation of the Liberals, whom he described as 'careering about the country calling themselves the "people of England".' His own party smugly realised they had the greatest draw in the country.

Meanwhile, the Duchess of Marlborough, who had suffered a miserable quarrel with her elder son over his sales of Blenheim treasures, joined Jennie in house-to-house canvassing. It was very different from Woodstock. On one occasion Jennie entered a butcher's shop and the wife called down to her husband, 'Lady Churchill is here.'

'Well you can tell Mrs Churchill to go to hell,' came the reply.

But she made some headway with grumbling factory workers who resented being asked for votes. 'But you have something I want. How am I to get it if I do not ask for it?' she cajoled.

They laughed at this womanly logic and a little cheer followed her out.

Randolph reduced the majority of the great John Bright, but as one old man put it to Jennie, 'I like your husband and I like that he says. But I can't throw off John Bright like an old coat.' Bright won, according to expectations, and Randolph returned to the House as Member for South Paddington, a seat which had been reserved for him.

The final results proved a deadlock. The Liberals held 335 seats, the Tories 249 and the Irish (who through Parnell had promised Randolph to vote with his party) got 96.

Lord Salisbury did not wish for a coalition. Both parties were divided on the supreme issue of the century—Home Rule for Ireland —and during the first months of 1886 little else was discussed.

Robert Rhodes James, in his book *Lord Randolph Churchill*, devotes a masterly chapter to this period of Home Rule: 'The struggle over the first Home Rule Bill lasted for barely six months. That brief period saw ancient alliances crumble and disintegrate almost over night. . . . From this extraordinary political interlude hardly a single major career emerged unaltered and unscathed. . . . Many of the Liberal leaders had been soured by events since 1880 in Ireland. They had seen the hand of friendship contemptuously rejected; they had suffered the assassination of one of their colleagues, they had been forced to adopt repressive measures to maintain the bare semblance of law and order in Ireland.'

Briefly, the 'soured' section of the Liberal Party was against Gladstone's determination to give Ireland Home Rule (and ignore the protests of Protestant Ulster). The Tories decried repressive measures but were appalled at the thought of Home Rule.

Parliament reassembled on 21st January, 1886, and Lord Salisbury's Government fell five days later. On the night the Tories were turned out of office Randolph, walking along the lobby with Lord Rosebery said: 'Well, it's over, but it has not been bad fun.'

'Just what Fleury said of the Second Empire.'

Gladstone formed his third ministry at the end of January. Lord Randolph Churchill travelled to Ulster on February 22nd for an Anti-Home-Rule Rally of his own devising. He invented the unfortunate slogan, 'Ulster will fight and Ulster will be right'. Angry talk resulted, and Churchill was accused of an irresponsible incitement to revolt. The Irish members booed him in the House of Commons.

In a long political letter to his chief, Lord Salisbury, written on March 24th, Randolph mentioned: 'My boy at school at Brighton nearly died of inflammation of the lungs last week, but is now out of danger and recovering well.' Winston had never been robust since his terrible two years at St George's School. Jennie kept a closer eye on him now and took him around with her during the holidays. Sometimes he could play with the son of her good friends the Duke and Duchess of Edinburgh (he was a son of Queen Victoria, she a Russian Grand Duchess). Jennie kept many of the Duchess's charming letters. One says: 'I thought as you are fond of skating you might like to try it at Buckingham Palace where the ice is excellent and quite safe.' Others ask Jennie to bring her elder boy to play with their son of the same age; a letter written on February 24th, 1886, amusingly deplores the necessity of a lady-in-waiting. 'I am afraid my very stiff Lady Emma Ashbourne will not contribute much to the cheerfulness of the party. She is the most genuine type of a British old maid, quite ready to be shocked at everything. But she is a truly infuriated "Conservative" and always talks about liking to murder or to blow up the Grand Old Man with her own hands. This is not shocking I suppose as it is only *party feeling*. Alas why can't I come without a lady and enjoy a gay little dinner without the feeling of a governess watching your movements.'

In the following summer at Cowes the Duchess wrote: 'Dear Lady Randolph, You are so surrounded by admirers, nautical pleasures and royal favours that I hardly venture to approach you with an invitation to dinner. . . . Would you and Winny come tomorrow to luncheon at 1.30 & to have an afternoon at the seaside. Would he put on very simple clothes. . . .'

The friendship continued after Edinburgh became Duke of Coburg and left England.

On April 14th, 1886, Randolph did not deign to attend a great

105

Unionist Rally held at Her Majesty's Theatre, calling it 'a piece of premature gush', but Jennie and his mother invited grand parties to their private boxes and were delighted by the enthusiastic roars for Randolph.

In the House of Commons a month of brilliant oratory over the unhappy subject of Ireland continued. Randolph showed up like a trained boxer, accurate in attack, cruel in taunts.

On June 7th the Home Rule Bill broke the Liberal Party in two. Gladstone made the greatest speech of his life: 'Ireland stands at your bar, expectant, hopeful, almost suppliant. Her words are the words of truth and soberness. She asked a blessed oblivion of the past, and in that oblivion our interest is deeper even than hers. . . .'

White-faced and exhausted by the gigantic struggle of the last months the old Prime Minister ended with the words: 'Think, I beseech you, think well, think wisely, think not for a moment but for the years that are to come, before you reject this Bill.'

Then amidst scenes of unparalleled excitement the Bill was defeated by 341 to 311. Some thirty English Members of Parliament could not steel themselves to think for the years to come. During two terrible wars sons and grandsons of the men who threw out Gladstone's Bill for Home Rule would die because Ireland was England's enemy.

The second General Election of 1886 then had to be fought. Again Randolph's wife and mother set forth like hardened warriors. Jennie, who had sworn she could never bring herself to speak in public, opened a branch of the Primrose League in Manchester. Dressed to kill, and cleverly hiding her notes behind a fan, she got through a good clear speech, catching the intonations of her husband. The local Press, overcome with admiration, concluded its account with 'Lady Randolph was ably supported by Lord Salisbury's nephew Mr Balfour, M.P.' With delight she forwarded this cutting to Arthur Balfour.

Lord Randolph spoke only twice, but forcibly, during the Election, and on one of these occasions, while attacking the Liberal Party's humbug in general, he mentioned the Foreign Secretary Lord Rosebery who owned 23,000 acres and drew an income of £24,000 per annum.

Rosebery reproached him graciously.

My dear Randolph,

Never in the annals of civilised warfare has so inhuman an outrage been perpetrated as you committed last night.

I do not complain of your speaking of my 'enormous & unlimited wealth' though as a matter of fact it is not enormous, & I have never had any difficulty in finding its limits. But what is monstrous is this, that in consequence of what you said thousands of mendicant pens are being sharpened. The parson's widow, the bedridden Scot born at Dalmeny, the author who has long watched my career, the industrious grocer who has been ruined by backing my horses, the poet who has composed a sonnet to the G.O.M., the family that wishes to emigrate—all these and a myriad others, are preparing for action. Not to speak of the hospital that wants a wing, the roofless church, the club of hearty Liberals in an impoverished district, the football club that wants a patron, the village band that wants instruments, all of which are preparing for the warpath. . . .

Randolph, who was exhausted (and would hear the Election results while salmon-fishing) wrote back:

2 Connaught Place, W. July 1st, 1886.

Dear Rosebery,

Your letter is most affecting, but what can I do? You will support that old monster, and therefore you must be fleeced and fined in the world. And in the future world, well. . . ! ! !

I am off tomorrow to Norway, post only twice a week, telegraph station 100 miles off. So I shall be well out of the way of news of these damned elections. Don't punish me by repeating this bit of news, as I have concealed it from my colleagues.

Yours ever, Randolph S. C.

The Tories won. Gladstone resigned. Salisbury was again Prime Minister. On July 25th the Queen wrote in her Journal: 'Lord Salisbury came to me again at four and we talked over everything . . . He feared Lord Randolph Churchill must be Chancellor of the Exchequer & Leader which I did not like. He is so mad & odd & has also bad health. . . .'

It would have been better for Randolph had he retained the India Office where he had the work in hand. A splendid dictator, he could be a maddening colleague. On August 3rd, 1886, he accompanied Lord Salisbury and the rest of the cabinet to Osborne to kiss hands. Lord Cranbrook notices that the new Leader of the House of Commons incessantly smoked cigarettes and seemed strangely nervous. Jennie had qualms concerning his health, but she thought she could organise his life more calmly now that he was settled on top of the mountain—of two mountains! For a man of thirty-seven to find himself Chancellor of the Exchequer and Leader of the House of Commons, with an almost certain four years of office in view, must, she thought, quieten him. There would be hard work but not the strain of electioneering or of creating an opposition. In the end he couldn't *not* be Prime Minister.

Randolph's idiosyncrasies when speaking seemed no handicap. He had a curious guttural pronunciation, almost a lisp, which increased when he was nervous: but this weakness endeared him, if anything, to his friends. On August 21st, at the start of his first speech as Leader of the House, he spoke haltingly until, sensing his party's approval and inhaling confidence, he suddenly felt his superb mastery of language return.

This was Lord Randolph Churchill in his heyday, when his 'wit, his irony and his invective delighted his audiences'. This was the man Rosebery called half aristocrat, half Bohemian. But when he had the world at his feet he still needed to be petted and an undated letter from Leonie at about this time begs Jennie 'not to worry about any other woman's influence—he will always be alright when you are with him'.

It is from a voluminous correspondence with the Duchess that we learn that in March a serious quarrel had taken place and that Jennie did not yet know that her husband had syphillis. Pathetically she was trying to get him back. Randolph had always suffered from ill-health, and there is no evidence to show exactly when he became infected. Of the several conflicting stories the least credible seems to be that given by Frank Harris in his memoirs. What *is* certain is that all through the summer of 1886 Jennie was appealing to her mother-in-law for advice, and the old lady wrote her kind, sensible letters urging patience, saying men were like that and arguing against the likelihood of another woman. In October there was a sudden reconciliation. Obviously Randolph had told her the reason for his coldness. It must have caused her anguish, but now she understood. Once again their mutual letters begin 'Dearest ——'.

𝔘 11

As Chancellor of the Exchequer Lord Randolph delighted his subordinates as he had in the India Office. 'He ruled as well as reigned,' remarked the Secretary of the Treasury. 'He had a mind and made it up, a policy and enforced it.'

The civil servants felt that Churchill understood basic finance and enjoyed his remark to a clerk ordered to simplify some decimal figures, 'I never could make out what those damned dots meant.'

Sir Stafford Northcote, Lord Iddesleigh, was now Foreign Secretary. As Leader of the House of Commons Randolph had a great deal to say on foreign affairs: he fretted at Iddesleigh's indefinite policies and teased Salisbury with complaints. Randolph had long been friendly with the German Ambassador, Count Hatzfeldt, who thus assessed him to Bismarck: '. . . I was especially struck by my interview with Randolph Churchill because, of all those whom I have seen, he alone sees into the future, possesses genuine ideas, correct or incorrect, and seems to pursue a settled policy.' Then a crisis blew up, over the Dardanelles, covetously eyed by Russia.

On September 30th, 1866, Randolph wrote to the Prime Minister: 'We shall never get joint action while Iddesleigh keeps rushing in where Bismarck fears to tread. . . . I feel sure that our present niggling meddling intriguing fussy policy is gaining for us the contempt and dislike of Bismarck every day.

'I do pray you to consider these matters. How can you expect Hatzfeldt to communicate with such an old muff as Iddesleigh.

'The only reason I accepted Iddesleigh was because it was supposed that he would act under your directions. . . . Really if it was not for not wishing to cause you any annoyance I would put such a spoke in old Iddesleigh's wheel when I speak on Saturday as would jolt him out of the F.O. . . .'

Unappreciative of this cheeky tone, the Prime Minister replied coldly. Then on October 2nd, before 14,000 people at Dartford, Lord Randolph made an inflammatory speech on foreign affairs which seriously discomfited the Government and caused Lord Rosebery to conjure: 'Randolph will be out or the cabinet smashed up before Christmas.'

Having upset all applecarts, not only in England but on the Continent, Randolph darted off to enjoy a holiday in France. For some extraordinary reason, perhaps to catch attention, he travelled under the name of Mr Spencer—this semi-disguise aroused immense curiosity and a throng of reporters followed at his heels to see what the noble lord was up to.

On his return he showed his lack of admiration for the alarmed cabinet and to the Minister for War he wrote: 'I am awfully worried and anxious about our legislation. . . . Anything more rotten than the Ld Chancellor's Land Bill I never saw. . . . I cannot get my ideas on foreign politics attended to. Iddesleigh is conducting himself like a child—no settled purpose or plan but fussy suggestions from day to day which make me cry with vexation when I read them. Ah! What an ass he is!'

To the Prime Minister he wrote: 'I am afraid it is an idle schoolboy's dream to suppose that Tories can legislate, as I did stupidly. They can govern and make war and increase taxation and expenditure à merveille, but legislation is not their province in a democratic constitution.'

This was plainer speaking than the Prime Minister could stomach. At the end of November Lord Salisbury replied to a colleague who had pleaded that he should stand firm with Randolph: '. . . what you call my self-renunciation is merely an effort to deal with an abnormal and very difficult state of things. It arises from the peculiarities of Churchill. Beach having absolutely refused to lead, Churchill is the only possible Leader in the House of Commons—and his ability is unquestionable. But he is wholly out of sympathy with the rest of the Cabinet. . . . As his offices of Leader of the House gives him a claim to be heard on every question, the machine is moving along with the utmost friction both in home and foreign affairs. My self-renunciation is only an attempt—a vain attempt—to pour oil upon the creaking and groaning machinery. Like you I am penetrated with a sense of the danger which the collapse of the Government would bring about: otherwise I should not have undertaken—or should have quickly abandoned—the task of leading an orchestra in which the first fiddle plays one tune and everybody else, including myself, wish to play another.'

On November 22nd, Randolph and Jennie were invited to dine at Windsor and the Queen noted: 'Lady Randolph (an American) is very handsome and very dark. She said some strange things to me. . . .'

Far more entertaining than Windsor Castle, where Jennie found the habit of conversing in whispers and answering the Queen's questions against silence 'conducive to shyness', were frequent visits to Sandringham, where the Prince and Princess of Wales entertained merrily. Jennie wrote: 'One felt at home at once; indeed, the life was the same as at any pleasant country house. Breakfast, which began at nine o'clock, was served at small round tables in a dining room decorated with Spanish tapestries given by the late King of Spain. The men wore shooting get-up and the ladies in any dress they chose to affect—short skirts and thick boots or elaborate day gowns. No one cared or noticed. . . .

'The amount of scribbling which goes on in a country house, and in which Englishwomen in particular indulge, is always a source of astonishment and amusement to foreigners. I have heard them exclaim: "*Mais qu'est-ce qu'elles écrivent toute la journée?*" No foreigner indeed can understand the Englishwoman's busy life, full as it is of multitudinous occupations, varying from household duties to political meetings.'

The ladies would walk or drive pony-carts to the huge delicious picnic lunch in a tent. There was hardly time to digest lunch before it was time to face another meal. At five o'clock all had to be back at Sandringham for the great feature of five o'clock tea. 'The simplicity of day attire was discarded in favour of elaborate tea-gowns. After tea, Signor Tosti, a great favourite with the royal family, would be made to sing. He would ramble on in his delightful impromptu manner for hours. Besides his musical gifts, he was a most amusing man, and kept us all laughing at his stories and witty sallies. Sometimes I played duets with the Princess who was particularly fond of Brahms's Hungarian dances, which were just then in vogue. Or it might be that we would go to Princess Victoria's sitting room, where there were two pianos, and struggle with a concerto of Schumann. The pace set was terrific, and I was rather glad there was no audience.

'Then came that sound unheard for many years now—the dressing gong and off came the tea-gowns and on came the low-necked, tightly-laced evening dresses. The gentlemen wore full dress with decorations though never uniform, and the assembly was well organised, the Prince taking each lady in turn to dinner. After a game of whist or an hour's conversation the Princess of Wales would lead the ladies laughing and chattering to bed. Occasionally the Princess might ask one into her dressing room which was crowded with objects and souvenirs of all kinds. . . . On a perch in the centre of the room was an old and somewhat ferocious white parrot. . . . At other times the Princess might surprise you by coming in to your room, ostensibly "to see if you have everything you want" but in reality to give a few words of advice, or to offer her sympathy if she thought you needed any.'

Jennie expected Christmas 1886 to be particularly felicitous. The boys, now twelve and seven, came home for the holidays which they intended to spend chiefly in London. On December 20th Lord Randolph travelled by train to Windsor to stay the night. After dinner he had an audience with the Queen and having discussed business she noted he looked gloomy and graciously condoled with him on the approaching Parliament 'as you had been so tired in the last'.

Randolph answered evasively and that night, on Windsor Castle notepaper, he wrote a letter to Lord Salisbury strongly protesting against the intended Army and Navy estimates which he found 'very greatly in excess of what I can consent to. . . . I do not want to be wrangling and quarrelling in the cabinet and therefore must request to give up my office and retire from the Government.'

Randolph had often threatened to resign on slight pretexts, and he did not intend Lord Salisbury to accept his resignation this time —maybe he thought his move might bring down the Government and force him to the premiership or more likely that he would be begged to remain on with increased power. Whatever he thought he said nothing to his Queen or to his wife.

On December 22nd, while Randolph lunched with Mr Smith, Minister for War, at the Carlton Club, the Prince of Wales was lunching alone with Jennie at Connaught Place. They discussed pleasant prospects for the new year—parties, scandals, amusing people, and, as always, Jennie was able to make the Prince laugh. It was a casual light-hearted meal.

That night, again at the Carlton Club, Randolph and Sir Henry Wolff dined together early, and Randolph spoke of the step he had taken. Before they reached coffee a letter from Lord Salisbury arrived accepting Randolph's resignation. The Prime Minister did not even suggest he should think over his impetuous move, stating starkly: 'In this unfortunate state of things I have no choice but to express my full concurrence with the view of Hamilton and Smith and my dissent from you—though I say it, both on personal & public grounds with very deep regret. The outlook on the Continent is very black. . . .

'The issue is so serious that it thrusts aside all personal & party considerations. But I regret more than I can say the view you take of it, for no one knows better than you how injurious to the public interests at this juncture your withdrawal from the Government may be.'

Randolph immediately dispatched a special messenger acknowledging receipt of his Chief's letter to Hatfield where Lord and Lady Salisbury were giving a ball. Then he and Sir Henry Wolff returned to Connaught Place where Jennie was waiting for them to accompany her to the theatre. As they left the house she asked Randolph some question concerning the list of guests for a future reception at the Foreign Office. She felt puzzled when he answered: 'Oh! I shouldn't worry about it if I were you; it probably will never take place.'

That night Jennie enjoyed The School for Scandal, but she and Wolff noticed that Randolph seemed preoccupied, and after the interval he left their box ostensibly to go to his club. In reality he went to hand in to The Times office a copy of the letter he had written to Lord Salisbury from Windsor Castle, so that it could appear a few hours later.

Jennie came home and went to bed without concern. Next morning her tea tray was accompanied by *The Times* containing Randolph's letter of resignation. She could not believe it. She has described that morning when, coming down to breakfast white and shaking, the paper in her hand, she found her husband calmly smiling. 'Quite a surprise for you,' he said. 'He went into no explanation and I felt too utterly crushed and miserable to ask for any, or even to remonstrate. Mr Moore, Permanent Under-Secretary at the Treasury who hero-worshipped Randolph, rushed in and with a faltering voice said to me, "He has thrown himself from the top of the ladder and will never reach it again." '

Lord Randolph's bombshell irritated everyone. It was the day before Christmas. Members of Parliament were scattered in their country homes attending to the wrapping of presents and decorating of trees. No member of the cabinet had even suspected that a serious dispute might be brewing.

Lord Salisbury had received Randolph's final letter while discoursing with the Duchess of Teck (Queen Mary's mother) at his ball. Randolph's mother and younger sister were guests in his house and it must have been with mixed feelings that he bade them good night.

Next morning he was woken early by Lady Salisbury to say goodbye to the Duchess of Marlborough. 'Send for *The Times* first,' said the weary Prime Minister. 'Randolph resigned in the middle of the night and if I know my man, it will be in *The Times* this morning.'

The Duchess of Marlborough and her daughter left Hatfield in some indignation at not having been seen off by their host. The Duchess's immediate letter to Lady Salisbury was returned unopened, for that lady held very strong political views, and henceforth refused to be civil to Randolph's mother, even at her husband's request.

The Queen was naturally furious at learning the news of a minister's resignation from her newspaper, and the consensus of opinion grew that Churchill had behaved outrageously.

His friends were cut to the quick, while enemies rejoiced. Most men thought him insufferably conceited and that a real spill might teach him a lesson. Others said nothing could ever chasten Randolph's spirit.

What really bit him? No one could understand. Only Jennie, still reeling from the shock of his revelation, guessed that he was feeling the increased malaise of his disease. He must have reckoned the time was due for a bid for immediate power. He had in the past said that politics were the most exciting form of gambling. Perhaps he was just throwing the dice.

Jennie bore her anguish in secret. It was years before she confided in Leonie, and she never told Clara the whole truth.

For a few days it was not possible to assess how disastrous the throw might be. Jennie and Randolph together laughed at a misprint in the *Irish Times*: 'Lord Randolph has burnt his boots.' But the announcement was, alas, to prove absolutely accurate.

12

Jennie struggled through Christmas week in a daze, while her husband lay moodily smoking cigarettes on the big sofa in his private room. A few friends called to plead or remonstrate. Maybe the Government would be forced to resign? Maybe they would beg him to reconsider?

Randolph's attempt to put things right with the Queen met short shrift. Her Majesty had been outraged; and was determined to secure as Chancellor of the Exchequer the shrewd old financier Goschen, to whom she wrote personally: 'Lord Randolph dined at my table on Monday evening, and talked with me about the Session about to commence, and about the *procedure*, offering to *send me* the proposed rules for me to see. And *that very night at the Castle,* he wrote to Lord Salisbury resigning his office! It is unprecedented! ...'

In what now seemed the distant past, in the June of six months before, Randolph's good friend Lord Justice Fitzgibbon had written from Ireland: 'Can Goschen by no means be induced to take the Exchequer? ... Age and financial experience have immense weight in that post out of doors. ... The English are your sheet-anchor and finance is their pole-star, and a middle aged commercial Chancellor would make them easy in their minds, when you could not. ...'

Goschen himself had penned a most unflattering opinion of Randolph: 'Churchill's selection, or self-election for the Commons Leadership is, to me, a staggerer. I regret it deeply; for it is a pre-

116

mium on the arts by which he has risen into notoriety. I dare say he will steady down; but as he imitated Dizzy at a distance, so men of even lower *moral* (sic) may imitate Churchill.'

The name of Goschen as his possible successor was broached at Mrs Jeune's political luncheon on Boxing Day. Randolph, having ingenuously confessed that he had never expected his resignation to be accepted, seemed startled at the suggestion of this elderly economist who was not even an M.P. at the time. Then he made his famous remark: 'I had forgotten Goschen!' The wits have had it since that Goschen is remembered in history as 'the man whom Lord Randolph forgot'.

The Prince of Wales stood loyally on the Churchill side. Apart from real affection for Jennie he found her husband's company more entertaining than that of any other man. When Lord Randolph sent H.R.H. a sheaf of correspondence and sought to explain that he had merely endeavoured to pare the Service estimates, the Prince forwarded the file to Queen Victoria, who became yet more incensed at a 'most objectionable and even dangerous correspondence' and ordered the Prince to break off all communication with Lord Randolph. Edward always stuck to his friends, and he pleaded again with his mother: 'January 22nd (1887): You are, if you will allow me to say so rather hard on Lord R. Churchill. I do not enter into the question whether he was right or wrong in resigning on the point at issue between him and his colleagues, but he has at any rate the courage of his opinions. . . .

'Ld Randolph is a poor man and a very ambitious one, but he gave up £5,000 a year in ceasing to be Chancellor of the Exchequer. Now that he has left office I am not likely to see much of him as he goes but little in society. Though I certainly do not agree in all his public views (and I have often told him so) still, I cannot help admiring many of his great qualities. Should his life be spared (and he has not a good life) he is bound to play sooner or later a prominent part in the politics and destinies of the country.'

In vain the Prince tried to comfort Jennie. She was too down to earth to share his optimism. In her own words: 'When I looked back at the preceding months which seemed so triumphant and full of promise, the débâcle appeared all the greater. I had made sure that Randolph would enjoy the fruits of office for years to come, and apart from the honour and glory, I regretted these same "fruits".

But on the subject he was adamant. "Politics and money do not go together" he would often say to me, "so put the thought away."

'How dark those days seemed! In vain I tried to console myself with the thought that happiness doesn't depend so much on circumstances as on one's inner self—but I have always found in practice that theories are of little comfort.'

For a week or so it appeared as if the Government might dissolve and the Liberal Lord Hartington be asked to head a Coalition. Lord Salisbury said to Wolff: 'More astonishing things have occurred than that in a government formed by Lord Hartington, Lord Randolph Churchill and I should have office.'

But surmise ended when, after much wavering, Goschen accepted the office of Chancellor of the Exchequer and good, dull, reliable Mr Smith became Leader of the Commons.

The Duchess of Marlborough, believing fanatically in her younger son's genius, made one pathetic appeal to Lord Salisbury who answered not unkindly: '. . . he is very amiable, very fascinating, very agreeable to work with as long as his mind is not poisoned by any suspicion. Nothing has happened seriously to injure or damage a career of which you are so justly proud or to deprive the country of the value of his services in the future. . . . ' Nothing, except a gamble for leadership which had failed.

Jennie tried to show high spirits, but inner fear assailed her. Watching Randolph closely she guessed he had not the physical strength to make a come-back, unless lucky winds blew him quickly to power. She had to resign herself to waiting on fate.

In mid-January Lord Iddesleigh died tragically at 10 Downing Street. He had been bitterly wounded because at Goschen's insistence the Foreign Office was to be taken from him. In a way, this noble-minded and patriotic statesman who had been so hounded by Randolph in the past was killed by the shuffle resulting from the resignation. The Press played up this point cruelly and it was Lady Iddesleigh who first wrote to Randolph urging him not to blame himself. Randolph was immensely grateful for the 'gentle unselfishness' of a great lady in her time of sorrow.

Lord Salisbury answered Randolph's sympathetic note sadly:

My dear Randolph,

I am very grateful for the kind sympathy expressed in your letter of yesterday, and very much touched by it. Your testimony to my bearing towards our old friend in the past is thoughtful and generous.

It was a very painful scene that I witnessed on Wednesday in Downing Street. I had never happened to see any one die before—and therefore, even quite apart from the circumstances, the suddenness of this unexpected death would have been shocking. But here was, in addition, the thought of our thirty years companionship in political life, and the reflection that now, just before this sudden parting, by some strange misunderstanding which it is hopeless to explain, I had I believe for the first time in my life, seriously wounded his feelings. As I looked upon the dead body stretched before me I felt that politics was a cursed profession.

Lord Salisbury must have been a devious man, for there was no 'strange misunderstanding'. Lord Iddesleigh had been thrown out of the cabinet because he had unwarily offered to resign whenever convenient.

As February arrived and the Government started to waddle along without him, Lord Randolph and a friend, Mr Tyrwhitt, departed for a holiday in North Africa and Sicily. For two months Lord Salisbury could not, as the Queen demanded, 'get at this impertinent and not reliable or loyal ex-minister'. Lord Randolph was enjoying a variety of adventure. Wife and mother had to share his letters:

Messina, March 9, 1887.
Here we are caught like rats in a trap. Just as we were packing up yesterday to leave for Naples it was announced that on account of cholera at Catania, quarantine had been imposed on Sicily, and that we could not leave. This is a great blow, for we do not know how long we may be detained here. There is nothing to see or do, and the hotel is dirty and uncomfortable. . . . We are in despair. . . .

But three days later Randolph met 'a man who knew a man who

knew some Sicilian fishermen who for a consideration would get us across the Straits. . . . We embarked in an open boat at eight o'clock on Wednesday evening in Messina Harbour, with nothing but a tiny bag and a rug, with a dissolute sort of half-bred Englishman and a Sicilian to act as interpreter and guide, and six wild singing, chattering Sicilian fishermen.' They reached the mainland in two hours. 'At last we found a little fishing village where all was quiet. In we ran, out we jumped and off went the boat like lightning. After climbing up some precipitous rocks, fortunately without waking anyone or breaking our necks, we found temporary shelter in a miserable inn, where we represented ourselves as having come by boat from Reggio and being unable to get back on account of the strong Sirocco wind. . . .' When their guide returned with a hired cart they set off in the dark, eventually reaching the house of an Englishman where they slept before taking the train for Naples. After this lark Randolph reached Rome in high spirits and there he met Lord Rosebery who was returning from India. During their long and hilarious dinners reminiscing about their university days together, Randolph remarked: 'There is only one place. That is Prime Minister. I like to be boss. I like to hold the reins.'

Rosebery replied: 'I think it is an odious place, a sort of dung hill. Moreover a P.M. in the House of Lords is a nobody.'

'Perhaps that is so on the Liberal side but not with us,' said Randolph. 'After your success as Foreign Minister you should never enter the cabinet again except as Prime Minister.'

'I would sooner be a lord-in-waiting,' replied Rosebery. (When the time came, however, he served as Liberal Prime Minister graciously enough.)

Meanwhile Jennie had to run Connaught Place without that useful £5,000 a year. To Randolph's intense annoyance Mr Goschen refused to buy his expensive official Chancellor's robes. 'I should have thought Goschen would be the last man to refuse to buy "old clothes",' he remarked tartly.

Devoted Mr Moore never recovered from the blow of his hero's resignation. He died in the next few months, but Jennie held her head high and went out on that famous Jerome 'cure for the dumps'—frequent trips to Mr Worth to buy new gowns.

The three sisters were now living within a stone's throw of each other. By crossing Oxford Street into Seymour Street and

Connaught Place they kept a few yards out of Mayfair. This economy all three considered heroic. It was hard on them, brought up as millionaire's daughters, to be reduced to modest allowances from Mr Jerome in their prime of life. Clara, who had married her splendid, handsome Englishman—the bi-metallist Moreton Frewen —suffered a side-line blow when Randolph resigned, for her husband had lately become Secretary to Mr Goschen, and it was a chance for him to get his foot into the world of high finance when his chief unexpectedly became Chancellor of the Exchequer. But by ill-luck he could not honourably retain the post, because Goschen replaced his brother-in-law. So poor Clara had to be more parsimonious than ever. It was something to be able to trot across the road each morning to borrow a fiver off Jennie. Leonie, who had married John Leslie, the only son of an Irish baronet, with an income of £23,000 a year, should have been well-off, but her in-laws determined to be strict because they were still resentful that their son had married an American!

Naturally, all his daughters were for ever wailing to Leonard Jerome for larger allowances, but the old giant was growing weary. He had made three fortunes and lost two and a half. At seventy he retired from Wall Street to organise American flat racing, where his abilities were much needed. Generous as he was to the girls, he could no longer earn on the big scale.

The Prince of Wales always took pains to be gracious to Mr Jerome when he met him in the south of France, complimenting him on his progeny and his sailing and racing prowess, He liked to talk about horses with the old man, who was raising the standards of American flat racing to those of the English turf.

While Mama and Papa were resting in Cannes and Randolph jaunting through Italy, Leonie wrote to Jennie begging her to enjoy a Dublin season with her. There is apprehension in Jennie's reply:

2 Connaught Place, W.

Dearest Sniffy,

I confess I have been a brute not to have written but what with letters to R. and the Duchess besides others, and my painting & music, I haven't had a moment. I shall be *so* glad to see you dear— but I do not think that I shall be over until the 6th or 7th of March as I want to go to the Drawing Room on the 3rd on account of the Queen [being offended by Randolph's resignation]. The Duchess writes that you are considered the 'Belle of Dublin!' You must not be low dear. I shall soon be over & intend staying the whole month. I feel rather in the dumps myself today. I dined last night with the Salisburys where they had a dance afterwards. I had a long talk with Lord S. after dinner but I did not get much out of him. He is very shy and nervous and I had the greatest difficulty to get him to speak of Randolph.

It is too long to repeat but I rather had the impression that they could never come together again. Don't repeat this, of course it is impossible to say what may happen in the House. As Arthur Balfour said—their difficulties haven't commenced yet and when they do—they may have to go to Randolph.

But Sniffy I feel very sick at heart sometimes. It was such a splendid position he threw away. In the bottom of my heart I sometimes think his head was quite turned at the moment & that he thought he cd do *anything*. However, 'it is an ill wind that blows *no* good' and R. had been so much easier and nicer since that I ought not to regret the crisis. He writes most affectionately & very often & I hope all will be righted when he returns. . . .

Yr loving
Jennie

In her memoirs Jennie recorded: 'Our relations with Lord and Lady Salisbury became gradually more and more strained. . . . Mutual friends tried indeed to bring about a *rapprochement* and eventually we were asked to dine. The dinner, which was a large one, was a fiasco so far as the object of our being there was concerned, and beyond a bare greeting, neither Lord nor Lady Salisbury exchanged a word with Randolph. This he resented very much and regretted having gone.'

Probably the Salisburys were insensitive to Randolph's tense state, for when, later on, it became useful to invite him for a political garden party, Lady Salisbury asked him and Jennie to spend the night at Hatfield. 'Mr Chamberlain and Randolph were being advertised as the principal speakers. Great was to be the gathering of Unionists and a solid front was much desired. At the last moment, however, Randolph flatly refused to go. No arguments moved him; he insisted that I should keep the engagement alone. As I drove up to the historic Elizabethan house my feelings were anything but enviable. I shall never forget the look of blank dismay and the ominous silence with which my feeble excuses for Randolph's absence were greeted. That night at dinner in the splendid banqueting hall, I sat next to Lord Salisbury; courteous as ever he talked pleasantly to me, but made no allusion to the subject uppermost in his mind.'

Jennie spent a miserable night hoping that thunderstorms would keep everyone away, but next morning the sun shone and 'masses of people brought by special trains from London filled the beautiful gardens crowding round at the various speeches. Cries for Randolph were heard on every side, many had come expressly to hear him, and bitter was the disappointment when they realised that he was not there.'

Jennie crept back to London and wrote to her sister: 'Who would be the wife of a politician?' The speeches Randolph did make were as good as ever, and he still had the ear of the House of Commons. He might, as his son Winston would write, have been wise to retire for a time, '. . . leaving his party to the place of power to which he had raised them with all the glamour of three years of cumulative and unexampled success still untarnished: he might well have been content to stand for the season apart from the floundering progress of the Administrative, leaving to others to muddle away the majority he had made. And he could have counted, not without reason, upon the continued affection of the Conservative working classes. . . . As the years passed by and the discredit of the Government increased, the Tory Democracy would have turned again to the lost leader by whom the victories of the past had been won.' But Randolph knew that time was not on his side.

Now the London season of Jubilee year was upon them, and a hundred interesting events gave Jennie no time to brood. 'Strangers came to London in numbers that season, attracted by the unwonted sights and festivities. I met many at Lady de Gray's, she having always been one of the most cosmopolitan of hostesses.' All the big hostesses slaved to entertain important foreigners and potentates. 'Blue skies, flags, processions made London unusually attractive.' At the great thanksgiving service in Westminster Abbey Jennie occupied one of the best places—the Prince had seen to that. She describes the gorgeous uniforms and beautiful dresses enhanced by

123

the 'dim religious light pierced here and there by the rays of the summer sun as it streamed through the ancient stained glass windows'. She saw tears dropping from the Queen's eyes.

Great amusement was caused by the Shah of Persia, who had travelled to London with every intention of enjoying himself. At a banquet at Buckingham Palace he had been asked to give his arm to Queen Victoria when a younger and more fleshy lady caught his eye. Lords-in-waiting diverted him with difficulty towards Her Majesty. 'With reluctance and a cross face he dragged the Queen along as he strode into the dining room.' Then at a court ball the Shah's eye travelled with purpose around the room and somewhat naturally alighted on Jennie. The Shah had heard of Lord Randolph Churchill and, to the Lord Chamberlain's horror, against all etiquette, he demanded that the couple should be presented to him immediately. Jennie, much embarrassed, found herself being ushered up on to the royal dais where the Shah wrung her hand with force and then waved her away to make room for Randolph. It was the Prince of Wales who hurried to their rescue, helping Jennie down from the dais and whispering with amusement, 'I see you are getting black looks from the Duchess's bench.'

A yet more comical episode occurred when Jennie had to present the ladies of an Indian maharaja's household to the Queen at a drawing room. When the day arrived she felt ill and asked sister Clara if she would take her place. Moreton Frewen was away in Constantinople, on an official assignment with the Nizam of Hyderabad's deposed Prime Minister, who was for various reasons to be kept out of London, so Clara had less to do than her sisters and was ready to oblige. Always sweet-natured and vague, but well versed in court etiquette, she accepted without carefully studying the detail of the procedure. As she presented the Indian ladies, Queen Victoria, now very close-sighted, mistook her for the Vicereine and, as she rose from curtseying, Her Majesty kissed her. Clara, amazed but anxious to be polite, returned the kiss. It was now Her Majesty's turn to be surprised, for although the Queen kisses her Vicereine, only Queens kiss Queens. Clara looked around discomfited, to see the Prince of Wales shaking with laughter. She retreated blushing in a series of low curtsies.

During these summer junketings Randolph kept apart. He was seeking to form another nucleus of sharp wits on the lines of his

Fourth Party. He visualised a Centre Party with Lord Hartington and Mr Chamberlain. But although Jennie launched Chamberlain in London society and handled Hartington's friendship carefully, she failed to make the men like each other.

In June the Churchills with Hartington, Chamberlain and other politicians were invited by the White Star Company to cruise about the Solent, watching the Naval Review. Chamberlain had left the Liberal Home Rule Party and Lord Salisbury was making overtures to him. Jennie knew of Randolph's hope of a new arrangement and she played her line carefully, but without success. She was sitting out on the deck with Hartington when Chamberlain drew up a chair and he brusquely started to discuss a possible new party. 'Lord Hartington, taken *au dépourvu*, looked uncomfortable and answered very shortly. Mr Chamberlain, full of his scheme, pressed the points home, taking no notice of the monosyllables he got in answer.'

Jennie judged the case hopeless, and this was a blow for Randolph, who considered Hartington's judgement infallible—'slow but sure'.

When the London season ended, Clara received orders from her husband to rent a large country house for Goodwood Races and to throw a splendid house party for Sir Salah Jung, the Indian he had been trotting around the Bosphorus. Randolph praised the dexterity with which Moreton had kept this exiled noble away from England during the official Jubilee festivities. It was important not to offend either the Nizam of Hyderabad or his exiled Prime Minister, whose father had brought in Hyderabad on the British side during the Mutiny. Mr Frewen had performed his task admirably, negotiating for wives and chiming clocks all through the Balkans. Now Sir Salah expressed the blameless desire to see a big English race meeting and, as official ceremonies were ended (Her Majesty gone to Balmoral and London emptying), it was decided there could be no harm in allowing this Indian noble a fling. His state of exile in no way curtailed his vast expense account, so Moreton cabled Clara— herself sorely beset by creditors—to organise a slap-up show and to spare no expense. Despite such short notice she managed to rent Lavington Park, a large house a few miles from Goodwood Race- course, and to hire a staff, including a famous chef. Footmen were impossible to find for temporary jobs, so, having only one small specimen of her own, she borrowed Leonie's medium-sized and

Jennie's large ones. The insufferable Moreton then cabled her that all were to wear Frewen livery. She could not alter the uniforms, but her maid had to change the buttons to those bearing the Frewen crest. Jennie and Leonie thought it all a huge joke, and were delighted to help their sister collect the 'cheerful party' which Moreton's cable also ordered. 'I think husbands had better be left out of this,' said Leonie, 'they haven't always got our sense of humour.'

In the end the house party consisted of the Arthur Pagets, the Ernest Becketts, the Duke of Marlborough and Count Charles Kinsky. Entering into the spirit of the thing, the Duke brought his private coach and Kinsky his private Hungarian band. A more successful entertainment for Sir Salah could not have been devised. The Duke was expert with a four-in-hand, and each day he drove his coach to the races in style, with the Indians in their bejewelled turbans raising cheers throughout the Sussex countryside.

Everyone enjoyed Goodwood Races except the house staff. Clara received tales of woe from the hired chef, a most important person much in demand at the best houses. He had graciously agreed to allow Sir Salah's Mohammedan cooks to prepare the proper meat dishes for the Muslim contingent, but now they were falling over each other in the kitchen and the gardener raged as he spied Indians (who considered European lavatories unhygienic) using the rose garden. The climax to this house party came when a dance was given and Kinsky's Hungarian band enthralled Sussex with their renderings of Strauss waltzes. The Jerome sisters, who so loved dancing, found expert partners and were blissfully revolving to the strains of the 'Blue Danube', when Moreton Frewen noticed turbaned figures slinking from the house. He asked the Indian nobles if the music did not please them. Sir Salah knew him well enough to answer that such discord was more than they could bear. After the party ended Moreton wrote to Leonie: 'I hope Jennie has written to thank Sir Salak for that silver work, if not please remind her and ask her to write an exceptionally friendly letter.'

Clara deemed it all 'a great success in trying circumstances'. Jennie and Leonie loved every minute of the three days, and Sussex talked of nothing else all summer.

13

Jennie tried for a time to laugh about Randolph's resignation and Queen Victoria's indignation. A letter from Marie, Duchess of Edinburgh, written that summer from Osborne Cottage, East Cowes, shows how lightly she could recount the recent drama, and Queen Victoria's daughter-in-law evidently enjoyed the joke.

Dear Lady Randolph,

Can I come this afternoon about five and bring the boys to play with your very amusing eldest son. They might be perhaps sent off in a rowing boat if too troublesome in the grounds. I am dying to hear some more of Lord Randolph's Windsor stories, but without the accompaniment of several pairs of eager royal household ears! Fancy if it was all reported to her. . . . And that I was encouraging a minister 'in disgrace'. But the ex-minister is really too amusing and makes me die with laughter. Au revoir then I hope, and without disturbing any nautical projects.

Marie

It seemed impossible that Randolph should have fallen from power for ever. All would be forgiven: the House of Commons could not do without him. He gave it so much laughter. Jennie refused to countenance her own grim wondering.

Now that Randolph was out of office and had time to spare he reverted to that love of his youth—the Turf. In partnership with Lord Dunraven, a sportsman who had ranched in Wyoming with Moreton Frewen, he bought a string of race-horses. Jennie shared

127

his enthusiasm. She had enjoyed flat racing since the old days in America when her father's great horse Kentucky carried his blue and white colours to victory and she as a little girl would be thrown up into the saddle. Now it was Randolph's brown and pink that caused her heart to flutter as the field moved off.

'We took a small house, Banstead Manor, about three miles from the town of Newmarket, where I passed many a pleasant week', she wrote. 'We would ride out in the early morning from six to seven to see the horses do their gallops. It was a most healthy and invigorating life.'

Just before Christmas, having arranged for Leonie and Clara to entertain their boys in London, Lord and Lady Randolph travelled to Russia, a trip which aroused suspicion and consternation in Government circles.

Queen Victoria warned Lord Salisbury: 'December 27th 1887: Think of great importance that the Foreign Governments and the country should know that Lord Randolph is going simply on a private journey in no way charged with any messages or mission from the Government. . . .'

Meanwhile poor Winston and Jack missed their parents sorely. From Connaught Place Winston wrote on Boxing Day:

Dearest Mother,

I did not know your address or how to send it [the letter]. I have got two prizes one for English subjects & one for Scripture.

I must tell you all about Christmas Day.

Aunt Clara was too ill to come so Aunt Leonie & Uncle Jack were our only visitors. We drank the Queen's health Your health & Papa's. Then Everest's and Auntie Clara and Uncle Moreton. In the evening I went to Stratford Place [Sir John Leslie's house] and played games till 6.30.

I get on all right with Mademoiselle.

Aunt Leonie & Auntie Clara both gave me 10/- which I was to spend on a theatre. . .

Grandmama wrote me from Blenheim and wanted me to go to Blenheim but I told Auntie Leonie and she is arranging it. I don't want to go at all. . . .

Leonie obviously used her discretion on Winston's behalf and an angry letter from the Duchess survives.

128

My dear Leonie,

I must say I am very much disappointed at Winston not being allowed to come here for a few days. I had made every arrangement to take great care of him knowing he is susceptible to colds, and I do not think there could have been as much danger as there is in going to Pantomimes in London. Besides I feel it's all an excuse of that horrid old Everest to prevent my having him & his being happy with his cousins without her.

I feel that Randolph & Jennie would not have objected to me seeing a little of him as really I hardly ever see him, & must say I am very much vexed. He is not fit to go to Harrow if he is not fit for a visit here. The house is quite warm. But it cannot be helped. I have heard nothing from R. & Jennie, but the newspapers are full of them. I hope you are well & enjoying a happy Xmas. With much love,

Yours,
F. Marlborough

Winston enjoyed the holiday more with his cosy 'confidante' Mrs Everest and his affectionate young aunt than at Blenheim, where his cousin 'Sunny', now the nineteen-year-old Marquess of Blandford, lived unhappily with his overpowering grandmother and snubbing father.

In addition to pantomimes, and being taken around like an important grown-up person, Winston had inveigled Leonie's mother-in-law Lady Constance Leslie into arranging a meeting with his favourite author, Rider Haggard. Lady Constance wrote to him: 'The little boy Winston came here yesterday morning, beseeching me to take him to see you before he returns to school at the end of the month. I don't wish to bore so busy a man as yourself, but will you, when you have time, please tell me, shall I bring him on Wednesday next, when Mrs Haggard said she would be at home? Or do you prefer settling to come here some afternoon when I could have the boy to meet you? He is really a very interesting being, though temporarily *uppish* from the restraining parental hand being in Russia.'

By New Year's Day Mrs Everest had come down with diphtheria and Dr Roose moved the boys to his own house. Winston

wrote plaintively: 'It is very hard to bear . . . we feel so destitute . . .
I feel very dull, worse than school. . . .' Two days later they had been
sent to Blenheim and the Duchess was mollified. She sent them back
to her own town house, 46 Grosvenor Square, whence Winston
wrote on 12th January 1887:

> Dearest Mother,
> Grandmama has kindly allowed us to sleep here until you come
> back. I do long to kiss you, my darling Mummy. I got your kind
> letter yesterday. How I wish I was with you, in the land of the
> 'Pink, green & blue roofs' . . .
> My holidays have been chopped about a good deal but as I
> expect an exeat in the term I do not wish to complain. It might
> have been so much worse if Woomany had died. . . .
> I am going to a play called 'Pinafore' tonight (Thursday) with
> Olive Leslie.
> Tomorrow I am going to Dr. Godson's party. Sat. Sir G. Wom-
> well is going to take me to Drury Lane so I am making up for
> other inconveniences. Auntie Leonie and Auntie Clara gave me
> together a beautiful theatre which is a source of unparalleled
> amusement.
> I must perform before you when you come back. . . .

The Duchess reported to Randolph:

> I fear Winston thinks me very strict, but I really think he goes
> out too much & I do object to late parties for him. He is so
> excitable. But he goes back to school on Monday. Meantime
> he is affectionate & not naughty & Jack is not a bit of trouble.

On January 23rd she wrote again: '. . . Winston is going back
to school today. *Entre nous* I do not feel very sorry, for he is certainly a handful. Not that he does anything seriously naughty except
to use bad language which is bad for Jack.'

During the forthcoming term Winston, sick with nervous apprehension, was to scrape through his examination into Harrow and
then to get mumps. His letters to his mother beg for pocket money,
and 'Sperm Oil', and 'Spirits of Camphor' for the footlights of
Aunt Leonie's theatre.

Winston saw a little of his American grandfather this year. When
the old man sailed back to America, Lady Constance Leslie wrote

sarcastically to the Duchess of Marlborough: 'Old Mr Jerome starts on Saturday for America to make a new fortune for Clara and Leonie.' These two daughters had not been as heavily endowed on marriage as Jennie. Although their husbands appeared to be rich or on the verge of riches, they could only afford small-size butlers and footmen whereas Jennie managed to pay the wages demanded by the tall species and keep a carriage.

Meanwhile the newspapers bubbled on about Lord Randolph Churchill and 'the object of this merry chatter was enjoying himself'. So was his wife.

The Princess of Wales had given Randolph a personal letter of introduction to her sister the Czarina, and when Queen Victoria remonstrated the Prince argued: 'I know that Lord Randolph's visit has no political object of any kind as I saw him the day before he started at Ashbridge.'

The Queen replied on January 3rd, 1888: 'I cannot I own, quite understand *your* high opinion of a man who is clever undoubtedly, but who is devoid of all principle, who holds the most insular and dangerous doctrines on foreign affairs, who is very impulsive and utterly unreliable. . . .

'*Pray don't* correspond with him, for he really is not to be trusted and is very indiscreet.'

Despite the Queen's protests the Prince could not bear to give up his invigorating correspondence with Randolph.

The Randolph Churchills were lionised by Russian society. Jennie found herself captivated by the brightly lit snow-covered streets of St Petersburg and the lavish entertaining. It was all so well done; masses of flowers, notwithstanding their rarity in such a rigorous climate, decorated every interior, and the staircases were lined with footmen in gorgeous liveries. 'I was prepared to suffer a great deal from the cold, but found, as in most Northern countries, that the houses were heated to suffocation, and the windows were rarely opened. On the other hand I thoroughly enjoyed the outdoor life of sleighing and skating. Comfortably seated in a sleigh, behind a good, fat coachman to help keep the wind off, I never wearied of driving about. The rapidity with which one dashes noiselessly along is most exhilarating, notwithstanding a biting wind or blinding snow.'

The Russian sleighs were smaller than American ones, and well-fastened fur rugs prevented the passengers falling out; a net held back snow from their faces. The coachmen wore fur-lined coats, bright red or blue caps with gold braid: and drove arms extended, to preserve circulation. Jennie, brought up by a great expert, noted the talent used in driving these small sleighs.

'The horses are so beautifully broken that a word will stop them. The whole time I was in Russia I never saw a horse ill-used.'

Randolph had an hour's talk with the Czar Alexander III at Gatchinka, while Jennie chatted about England with the Czarina, whom she had met long before at Cowes. She noticed how simply the imperial family lived in the great rambling palace, preferring to use only a few small rooms, furnished in English country house style.

Every day of the two months' visit was spent sightseeing or tearing over snow in sleighs, tobogganing or skating: 'I was able to indulge to my heart's content in my favourite pastime of skating. . . . But great was my disappointment to find that the Russians did not care for figure-skating, and, in fact, did not skate well . . . they much preferred tobogganing down the ice hills, half a dozen or more persons in a sleigh.'

Jennie, who had learnt to dance on skates in childhood, had the pleasure of showing off her skill and finally of skating down the ice hills at terrifying speed. Forgotten were gloomy English politics!

In the evenings came opera, ballet and balls, ending with drives across the frozen Neva to hear the Tziganes. They were also invited by the Czar to Gatchinka, driving out with a hundred other guests in carriages. Royal etiquette seemed much easier than in England. Peter the Great had disliked formality, and as he cut off the head of anyone who did not share his views, Russian court rules became and stayed deliberately easy.

The Churchills attended the New Year reception in the Winter Palace, where they saw the great ladies of St Petersburg in their splendid national costumes covered with Siberian sapphires and emeralds, all wearing the Russian head-dress called the 'Kakoshnitz'. The royal choir sang the mass splendidly; the deep male voices had been selected from throughout Russia.

Having no sumptuous national dress, Jennie draped herself in a blue and gold tea-gown—and well she knew her power to excel in that snow-glittering land of beautiful women. Many, many years later old Russian princes who had escaped the Revolution were to tell me—'Dark Jennie we called her—no other woman could so deliberately impose her beauty. When she entered a ballroom there was always a moment's hush.' It must have been a great pleasure to her—this finding of a new world to dazzle.

To his mother, Randolph wrote: 'I am sure in England it would bore me dreadfully to go to all these dinners and parties and things, but here it amuses me. I wonder why it is. . . .'

And to *her* mother, who was keeping an eye on Papa at Monte Carlo, Jennie wrote the letter which would give away her age to future biographers.

Jan. 9th/88   Sliemenski Bazaar
                                                           Moscow
Dearest Mama,

Do you know that it is my birthday today? *34* ! ! ! I think for the future that I will not proclaim my age, as I have done heretofore. Well I hope Clara has sent you the letters that I have written to her—as really what with sight-seeing & visits, one has little time for correspondence. I daresay you have seen in the Times the different notices & articles in reference to R. & our visit to Russia. There is no doubt that we have been treated with the greatest consideration—quite like royalty—We have been here a week. I have enjoyed it immensely. We have visited everything worth seeing—dined with Prince Dolgorovki the Gov. General of Moscow, went last night to the 'Bal de la Noblesse', have been to all the shops & several theatres & tomorrow we go by seven o'clock train to a celebrated convent about 2 hrs by rail from here. Get back at 5 & go off to St Petersburg at 9. I suppose that we shall stay another week. . . . You have heard no doubt of poor Everest's illness—but Roose gives a fairly good account of her now—& I hope by the time we get back that she will be alright. The children are at Blenheim. We have not had a single letter since our departure. We were only to receive them through the courier to the Embassy. However we shall find our bundle at St Petersburg —I mean to have lots of skating if possible there, as there is a splendid place & all Society goes—a band & etc. I wonder how Clara & Leonie are getting on, I am longing to hear from you all —Give my very best love to Papa & tell him I hope the 'system' is satisfactory. Have you been having the same cold as everywhere —Fancy if Randolph had gone to Madrid—he wd have suffered tremendously as they cannot keep the cold out—Here one is really too warm in the house like America. Well goodbye dearest Mama. I hope this will find you both well—Tell Papa that politically I think it was not a bad move of R.'s—to come to Russia. I think a few enemies will rage at the fuss made over him—

With best love

Yr loving

Jennie

PS. R. has given me a muff for my birthday which will put yours quite in the shade.

Travelling on to Moscow, they attended the 'Bal de la Noblesse' with the city's Governor. This was Jennie's, but not Randolph's idea of entertainment. The music was inspiring and there was a Marshal of the Ceremonies 'strutting about, full of airs and graces, introducing people, arranging and ruling with great precision the intricacies of the various dances. Officers would be brought up to me, clicking their spurs together and saluting; then they would seize my waist without a word, and whisk me around the enormous room at a furious pace, my feet scarcely touching the ground. Before I had recovered, breathless and bewildered, I would be handed over to the next. . . .'

So the Churchills departed for Berlin, exhausted but enchanted, and happily with no bones broken on snow, ice or dance floor. Their memory lingered on in Russia—the mysterious Lord Randolph whom the Czar insisted on treating as envoy, and his wife, 'the beautiful black-haired woman who danced light as a moth on skates'.

Jennie's comparisons of the Russian and German courts, written without bias before the First War, are interesting enough: 'After ultra-fashionable and brilliant St Petersburg, Berlin society seemed a little quiet. There is no doubt it would be difficult to find a greater contrast than the Russian and German courts presented at that time; the one brilliant, imposing, lavish in its extravagance, barbaric in its splendour; the other, unpretentious and, perhaps, a little dull but full of tradition and etiquette. In Berlin, and particularly at the court, signs of the all conquering and victorious army were everywhere apparent; everything military was in the ascendant. I remember Prince William [the Kaiser] visiting me at the Embassy and our having a great discussion on German and Russian uniforms.'

Perhaps the most pertinent observation Jennie made concerning the well-read, highly educated Russian and German *grandes dames* was that they played no part in politics, whereas the English upper classes scarcely educated their girls at all, one old governess being considered good enough in the grandest country house, but, once they were grown up, English women stepped boldly into the political scene and imposed their views on Westminster.

Charles Kinsky had been posted to the Berlin Embassy, so Jennie had the joy of his company for morning drives and rides and whenever he could escort her in the evening. After ten days spent visiting museums and galleries, in one of which Randolph was none too pleased to see the Rubens sold by his brother, they returned through Paris to London to face another busy season. The House of Commons admitted it had been dull without Randolph, for, as Rosebery wrote: 'He had also the vital mainspring of zest. To what ever he applied himself he gave for the time his whole eager heart.'

Would the Tories take him back? Did they hunger for this zest? Could they forgive the fireworks?

14

During the summer season of 1888 Jennie plunged into the grand social world. Winston's letters from school hit this point: 'I also hope that you are enjoying *yourself* at *Ascot* as much as *I* am *enjoying* myself at Harrow. . . .' He ranks as 'one of the most prominent trebles' in the school choir and seems very pleased with himself: but on July 12 a long letter from a master speaks of 'phenomenal slovenliness'. Jennie often seemed too busy to respond to pleas for visits, but Mrs Everest came regularly, and Winston had no qualms about parading his dear nurse in her funny bonnet around the school in front of the other boys. Although 'idle' and 'constantly late' he stood firm—indeed immovable—on what were to him important issues.

The summer holidays were spent blissfully with Mrs Everest's sister at 2 Verona Cottages, Ventnor, and the boys looked so well that Randolph sent them there again after Christmas, when he actually noticed his children were 'seedy and looked pale'.

Blandford, as the family still called the eighth Duke, departed to America. Despite his appalling way of treating women Jennie liked him and many people fell to that 'diabolical charm'. Moreton Frewen describes him from a man's point of view: 'I have known one or two first-class minds whose achievements have been nil. Take George, eighth Duke of Marlborough, an almost incomparable mind, indeed in receptivity, range and versatility, hardly to be matched. . . .'

The Puritan American Press cared nought for his inventions. At

136

the time of Leonie's wedding a New York paper harped unctuously: 'It will be remembered that the bride's sister married Lord Randolph Churchill, a brother of the Duke of Marlborough, but an abler and better man than the Duke who is badness personified.'

The Duke, like Moreton Frewen, was seeking gold. Frewen tried to extract it by a machine from the refuse of gold mines while Marlborough experimented in the transmutation of metals. Both were convinced bi-metallists, and thrust their views on whatever governments they could persuade to listen.

After Mr Jerome had introduced Marlborough to New York's sporting set he wrote to his wife: 'The Duke has gone off this morning with Lawrence [Jerome] and a party to the Adirondacks trout fishing, to be gone a week. I rather think he will marry the Hammersley. Don't you fear any responsibility on my part. Mrs H. is quite capable of deciding for herself. Besides I have never laid eyes on the lady but once. At the same time I hope the marriage will come off as there is no doubt that she has lots of tin.' To Mrs Jerome, now settled in London to fuss over her daughters' morals and debts, he wrote endearingly of his own easy requirements: 'When in town I have a small room in the rear of the Brunswick's sixth story where I sleep and dress. It gives square to the sun and is warm enough without a fire. I am as comfortable in it as if I had the whole house. I spend my time mostly at the Jockey Club and its office. At the office, horse-talk and business, at the Club, meals, library, whist, billiards, talk with friends. When it gets a little warmer I shall be off racing, yachting, visiting & knocking about generally. If you had any go in you like either of the girls & could mount your horse & keep up, we might knock about together & enjoy it. But you haven't a bit of taste that way & never had. And you couldn't stand that sort of life now even if you liked it once upon a time.

'And you say you should be in duty bound *to take care of me*! What stuff! I don't want to be taken care of & what's more I won't be. . . .

'Randolph is doing magnificent work. Every move he makes strengthens his record. . . . Hope you are not pinching too closely. No necessity of it. Love to all.'

Another letter affirms: 'Don't want a valet. Shouldn't know what to do with him. I made two gold pieces yesterday. Don't think I

137

can do better than send them to Leonie. In fact I have dedicated all such findings to her. She must spend them *without accounting to Mama*!

'Last Sat. I went down to Willie K. Vanderbilt's with the Coaching Club, a very delightful party. We had perfect weather coming & going. When I tell you I rode 54 miles each way over a good deal of bad road & felt no inconvenience whatever then or thereafter you will conclude that a certain supposed ailment of a fundamental and fatal nature has existence only in the brain of Dr Pratt. We are racing daily at Jerome Park & working with many men and teams at the "new Jerome Park" (that is what Morris insists on calling the new course). . . .

'Union Club (later). Well, Blandford is married! I went with him to the Mayor's office in the City Hall at one o'clock today & witnessed the ceremony. The bride was looking very well & all passed off quietly. I took charge of his cable to the Duchess, also sent one of my own to Jennie. I dine with them at Delmonico's this evening: a dinner given by Mr & Mrs Clews to his bride. I shall go down to the *Aurania* in the morning to see them off. They had great difficulty in arranging the religious marriage. The clergy refused, he being a divorced man. However they found a parson of the Methodist persuasion who consented to perform the service. An hour ago it was all done.'

Mrs Hammersley was a kindly widow famous for decorating the *salon* behind her opera box with festoons of expensive orchids. On account of lampoons she had changed her name from Lilian, which rhymed too easily with million. Reaching England, the Duchess Lily found with chagrin that owing to the Duke's divorce Queen Victoria would not receive her at court and, worse still, that her husband topped the list of lovers of a well-known houri, Lady Colin Campbell. Blandford had given her a palazzo in Venice on condition that he pay her an annual visit, and Whistler's picture of Lady Colin in the nude adorned his bedroom. Photographs of her were hidden—but not too well—in many cupboards.

Despite this the new Duchess strove to play her part handsomely. She furnished Blenheim with acres of lead roof, a superb organ and a fine boathouse. And she was particularly interested in, and kind to, her husband's nephew Winston.

This year—the third since his resignation—brought Randolph a

Jennie

Above Clara, Jennie and Leonie, with their mother and children
Opposite above The Royal Yacht at Cowes: Jennie on left and Kitty
Mott on right
Opposite below Leonie, Hugh Warrender, Jack, Jenny and a
convalescent Winston

The brothers: Jack and Winston

final chance to return to power. The vital moment arrived when the splendid old Birmingham Radical Mr John Bright died in March, 1889. It was just the right time for a fresh start. Long, long ago, Randolph had cried that if enemies denouncing the Tory Party as upper class only he would 'throw big cities at them'. He had hankered for Birmingham, an active centre of political thought instead of safe, dull, old Paddington. Now that his famous opponent had died, a delegation of Birmingham Tories arrived in London to beg him to stand. Sure that he could fight a rousing election battle they offered every support. Eager friends in the House offered him their seats if by ill chance he did not get in. Jennie was elated; she knew that Randolph would be in his element in the great democratic industrial city and she steeled herself once more for door-to-door canvassing. She had made great headway in the previous contest, and knew she would be cooler and more experienced this time. In fact she could not wait for the fight.

On April 2nd a delegation of eminent Birmingham Tories arrived at the House of Commons to ask Lord Randolph officially to stand for their city. He must have been delighted, for he asked Louis Jennings, the staunchest friend he had left, to draft his farewell to Paddington and a new address to Birmingham. Jennings retreated to the library to work on the draft when the deputation arrived. He left the library for a moment to chat with them and saw they were 'radiant' at the prospect of getting Randolph as their candidate.

Meanwhile Randolph was discussing the matter with Beech. Lord Hartington suddenly entered to say that Chamberlain was 'furious' at Randolph's intention to stand for Birmingham, which he regarded as his province.

Randolph then made an unbelievable, an unwise and uncharacteristic move. He weakly agreed to allow the Liberal-Unionists Hartington and Chamberlain to decide whether or not he should accept the Birmingham delegation. Naturally, they snatched at the opportunity to make this decision for him. They said 'No'. Jennings was horror-stricken when he heard what his hero had done, and Rosebery later wrote: 'The Randolph of 1884 would not have hesitated, or left the decision to a Committee. But the Randolph of 1889 had no longer the nerve of his prime.'

Yet none could call Lord Randolph Churchill a cowardly man.

He himself walked to the room where the delegation was waiting and told them of the decision. For a moment they could not believe their ears. Then, as the truth seeped in, this last-minute dashing of their hopes aroused a bitter rage which nothing could allay. They left the House cursing not only Churchill but the whole Tory Party.

H. W. Lucy, the Parliamentary reporter, saw Randolph leaving the room where he had spoken to the Birmingham delegation. 'He was so altered in personal appearance that for a moment I did not know him. Instead of his usual alert swinging pace, with head erect and swiftly glancing eyes, he walked with slow weary tread, his head hanging down, and a look on his face as if tears had been coursing down it.'

Jennie was waiting for him at home. She had set much store on this new opening, and eagerly she ran to her husband to hear the news. She has written a mild account of her disillusionment: 'On the day when Randolph returned from the House of Commons and informed me of the pressure brought to bear on him, and how he had given in, I accused him of showing the white feather for the first time in his life. He had, he said, "made up his mind to abide by the opinion of the leaders of the 'Party' ". "But not when those leaders are your political enemies," I cried. Arguments, however, were useless.'

Lord Randolph Churchill, most audacious and independent of parliamentarians, had reached a stage when he could still speak brilliantly: but he could not bear to make a decision: his judgement had gone before his power of oratory. The sudden blackouts, which none recognised as mortal illness, must have caused torment to that sensitive spirit. Jennie could not yet realise that he was finished—nor indeed could the House of Commons. The old Tories still feared him. At times he would delight them with his wit, and deliver an hour-long speech which held the members in fits of laughter, but no sooner had he enchanted than he would enrage with some plan of his own for better housing or legislation which might anger the brewers. This rich and important section of Tory supporters felt outraged by a speech in the Midlands in which he dared to say: 'The great obstacle to temperance reform undoubtedly is the wholesale manufacture of alcoholic drink. . . . Do imagine what a prodigious social reform, what a bound in advance we should have made if we

140

could curb and control the destructive and devilish liquor traffic, if we could manage to remove from amongst us what I have called on former occasions the fatal facility of recourse to the beerhouse which besets every man and woman, and really one may almost say every child, of the working classes in England.'

Randolph blithely went on: 'I tell you my frank opinion—the time has already arrived when we must try our strength with that party. . . .' The Tories did not want to hear this 'frank opinion'. They completely disassociated themselves from Randolph's crusade which had been partly inspired by Jennie's horror at the appalling drunkenness she saw in London streets. A few minutes from her lovely house lay the poorer streets of Paddington where, on Saturday nights, men could be seen lying in the gutters and drunken women fighting.

On the day after he had advocated curtailing the freedom of brewers, Randolph spoke, for the first time since his resignation on Ireland. In this speech, advocating Local government and Land Purchase Randolph stated that he found the Irish 'a very pleasant people and a very amiable people and very easy to get on with if you take them the right way' and that 'something like one hundred millions ought to be pledged to buy out big landowners and create small peasant holdings'. His far-sighted plans caused even more rage.

A fellow M.P. who had been pressing Randolph to address his constituency wrote that it would now be undesirable. All the Tories shouted that they 'could not afford to offend brewers and publicans, who have done so much for us in the past, and that any scheme proposing a loan of money to Ireland to buy out Irish landlords was most unpopular and regarded as Gladstonianism pure and simple'.

Part of this offending speech, which most wittily invented arguments between himself and a kind of Dickensian Mr Podsnap, contained statements such as—'I am certain that intolerance and contempt of Irish opinion and prejudice, hopeless prejudice against Irish ideas, produce a corresponding rancour and hatred among the Irish people against us, and terribly envenom the feelings and relationships between the two countries.'

As Lord Randolph Churchill felt a fundamental attraction to the Irish people, and jeopardised his own position with the Tory Party by appealing for money as well as for 'liberality, generosity and above all sympathy' in the Irish policy, it may well be asked why he disagreed with Home Rule. His concise answer lies in a letter written to a Mr Ogilvie who was about to address Longford: 'The Irish people in respect of their material interests have always been bright and quick-witted; they will with their ready imagination quickly discern that though it may be pleasant and profitable to be represented in the Imperial Parliament . . . it will be a widely different state of affairs when they—the Irish agricultural population—are handed over, body and soul, tied and bound and without appeal, to the uncontrolled dominion of that "separate and independent" party.

'I have always been opposed to what is called "Home Rule" more upon the grounds that to the Irish people themselves it must bring distress, poverty, misery and ruin, than on account of the dangers it will entail upon the British Empire, though these dangers are exceedingly great.'

History has proved Gladstone was right and Churchill was wrong: but it was Randolph who attacked, to his own detriment, England's constant misgovernment of Ireland since the fatal Union of 1800.

Jennie's letters to her sons during these years always built up the image of a wonderful father. A note to Jack at preparatory school is typical: 'Chatsworth. My dearest Jack. . . . It is very pleasant here and there are many beautiful things to see in the house, pictures, china, books etc. Also wonderful gardenias—gardens and fountains. . . . Papa is here enjoying himself after all his speeches. . . .'

The sombre reality she would hide as long as she could. Winston has written: 'The speeches of Lord Randolph Churchill in Parliament during the years from 1887 to 1890 were the best in manner and command he ever made.' But, at the time, Winston was a disregarded schoolboy writing wistfully to his father in July 1889, when he had been over a year at Harrow, and Speech Day was approaching 'You have never been to see me & so everything will be new to you. . . . I shall be awfully disappointed if you don't come.' Before the summer term ended measles spread through Harrow and most of the boys went home. Winston pleaded with his mother: 'There is really no danger whatever, but I should have imagined that as 300 Mamas & 300 Papas like to have their "offsprings" home you would like to have me. Please, please do!' And he made clear his feelings: 'When you come I like to have you all to myself. Please do do do do. . . .'

As Jennie realised the finality of her husband's sentence she tried to augment his non-political pleasures: and the first of these was the Turf. He still enjoyed fishing, but horses had been the love of his youth, as of Jennie's.

Success in a classic race came unexpectedly when his splendid little mare Abbesse de Jouarre (by Trappist out of Festive, named by Jennie after reading Renan's book) won the Oaks in 1889. Randolph was away after salmon in Norway and Jennie was spending a hot afternoon on the Thames. 'Who won the Oaks?' she called to a lock-helper. 'Abscess on the Jaw' he shouted back, and Jennie nearly fell into the water, knowing she had missed that moment which no money can buy—of leading in a classic winner.

The pleasures of their racing stable atoned for much, and Randolph revealed his feelings at the end of a letter to Arthur Balfour regarding his pet 'Eight Hours for Miners Bill.' 'You can realise how much importance I attach to the question when I tell you that I am actually coming up from Lincoln and missing three important races in which our horses run, to vote for the Bill: I do not think I would do this for the Monarchy, the Church, the House of Lords or the Union!'

It was easier for Jennie to divert Randolph in the stables than the drawing room. No bore was allowed over the threshold of 2 Connaught Place, and she thought that her unusual parties distracted him; but she had to amuse unobtrusively, for any obvious effort to treat Randolph as an invalid grated on his nerves, and he often snapped at her or complained extravagantly of Winston's non-perfection.

During these difficult years Jennie came to rely increasingly on Charles Kinsky, whom she had first met when he was an attaché at the Austria-Hungarian Embassy in London. Kinsky was gay and attractive and a beautiful dancer. English society had been enchanted by the young officer, and he made his mark by winning the Grand National of 1883 on his own horse Zoedone. The London clubs had laughed at a foreigner for daring to make the attempt, but he laughed back after galloping to victory over the Aintree Course. An elderly Colonel stamped up to congratulate him. 'And do you know what?, Kinsky said, "Don't congratulate me, I've nothing left to live for." '

It took the great jumps of Aintree to elicit the accolade of approval which a typical Englishman, the Duke of Portland, thought fit to bestow: 'Most of us regarded him as one of ourselves.' Slim and alert, a lightweight who could take any type of horse over stiff hunting country, and an all-round charmer, Kinsky made the most of the years he spent in England.

Court life was far less formal than in Vienna; and soon after Kinsky met the Jerome sisters, who fêted him as the best dancer they knew, he had realised who would be the love of his life.

Very little has been written about Charles Kinsky and in correspondence he was discreet. Perhaps the most vivid picture of him emerges in a letter written by the sixteen-year-old Winston to his brother Jack after Count Kinsky had taken him to see the fireworks at the Crystal Palace in 1891.

Winston was in London for the Eton and Harrow match and the German Emperor and Empress were visiting London—'. . . the whole town is in a ferment', Jennie had written to Randolph, 'the Emperor begins his day at eight in the Park riding with half a dozen A.D.C.s in uniform and he changes his clothes about five times a day. Margot Tennant sallied forth yesterday on a prancing steed determined to make his acquaintance and she did. . . .'

Winston's letter to Jack, who was suffering from mumps, gave his day in detail:

'Breakfasted with Mama at 18 Aldford Street. Arranged with Count Kinsky that he should take me to the Crystal Palace, where the German Emperor was going (he drove me in his phaeton).

'The programme of what we saw (everything of course was awfully well done on account of the Emperor) is as follows.

'Wild Beasts (wonderful never seen anything like them.)

'*Fire Brigade Drill before the Emperor.*

'This was perfectly splendid. There were nearly 2000 firemen & 100 Engines. They all marched past and finally all the lot galloped past as fast as they could go. Then we went & had dinner.

'The head man said he could not possibly give us a table but Count K. spoke German to him & it had a wonderful effect. Very tolerable dinner. Lots of Champagne which pleased your loving brother very much.

'Then ensued a most exciting incident.

' "Row with Kaffir".

'We went to see Panorama but it was closed so we went to the Switch Back Railway. On the way however we came across a new thing called the "Ariel Car" which rushed across a wire rope

144

nearly 300 yards in length & awfully high. We waited about 10 minutes for our turn & then the thing went wrong & the Gun summoning people to the fireworks went off, so Count K. & I clambered over the rails in anger & wished to go. However a half bred sort of Kaffir who was in charge attempted to stop Count K., caught him by the coat tail. The Count whom you know is immensely strong grew furious and caught hold of the blackguard's hand, crushing the fingers in his grasp; the Mulatto dropped the coat & took to swearing telling Count K. that he should think himself "d – – d lucky" that he did not pitch him over the bannisters. "By – – –", said Count Kinsky, "I should like to see you touch me." "You go and learn manners", retorted the cad. "But not from you", said Count K.

'Then the audience & the other people outside made the scoundrel be quiet & we went our way angry but triumphant.

'The Fireworks were wonderful & I wished you had been there to see them.

'They began with a perfect volley, rockets, etc.

'Then there were two great set pieces of Cornflowers & Roses (the Emperor's Favourite Flowers) which afterwards changed to the heads of the Emperor & Empress.

'Then we went & got our coat & each had an American drink & then we went to our carriage. Count K. drives beautifully & we passed with our fast pair of horses everything on the road.'

All through my childhood the side-saddle that Kinsky gave to Jennie as a sort of thank-you gift for her encouragement before the National hung on a rack in our Irish stables. It was a beautifully constructed little saddle with high pommels, impossible for modern riders. My grandmother kept it for sentimental reasons, until she died during the Second World War. Then it must have been sent as a White Elephant to some bazaar.

A coloured print of Zoedone, signed 'Charles Kinsky', hung in the cloakroom, but only a groom, not Kinsky, held the horse.

When transferred to Paris, and then to Brussels and Dresden, Kinsky did not give up his string of hunters in Leicestershire, or his London flat, which an English butler kept 'at the ready'.

Kinsky's frequent changes of post made it all the easier for his romantic devotion to Jennie to continue unobserved. No one quite knew if the gay count was on semi-official business or visiting his horses, when he appeared in London. And many of Jennie's friends were indebted to him for a diversity of reasons. He was kind, thoughtful and cultivated. The young musician Ethel Smyth, who broke away with difficulty from the conventional social life forced on girls of her class, was helped by Jennie in London and then by Charles Kinsky in Vienna. It is really the tributes written by this serious, masculine woman of talent which show up the side of Kinsky's character which was not merely frivolous and delightful.

Jennie's sisters were constantly in her home. Leonie never could bring herself to like Randolph; she had always felt a little afraid of him and she flinched at his heartlessness, but he enjoyed her quick wit and he probably talked to her more openly than to any other woman. Randolph had always taken a certain sardonic pleasure in shocking. Once, at a fashionable race meeting, he teased his sister-in-law for her artless enjoyment of *le monde snob*. 'I care nothing for those haughty dames all dressed up and giving themselves airs—Lady X, and Lady Y,' he announced none too softly. 'In fact I don't like ladies at all—I like rough women who dance and sing and drink—the rougher the better!' Leonie's embarrassment delighted him. 'That's the truth,' he insisted. 'Great ladies bore me!'

Clara's husband amused Randolph with his bi-metallic ideas, though he was careful never to invest in Frewen schemes, apart from one invention designed to crush gold out of mine refuse. With the Prince of Wales he had visited Clara's Mayfair house where the entire dining room table was covered by a model of this wonderful gold-crusher.

When Clara fell on evil days she moved to Seymour Street, where, being only a minute's walk from either sister, she could hasten for help when bills became pressing. Over the three sisters presided their Red-Indian-faced puritan Mama. Mrs Jerome stayed in each daughter's house in turn and then retreated to Hastings, whence she could deliver tirades against extravagant living and loose morals. Clara, Jennie and Leonie received these lectures with secret titters. Yet Mama could still make them feel guilty, and they still adored this immovable granite boulder standing firm against the tides of loose social fashion.

Perhaps as an after-effect from her husband losing great fortunes, Mrs Jerome was extraordinarily stingy. In order to *teach* her girls that one must *suffer* when in debt, she allowed no fires when they

146

came to stay. They continued to pay Mama frequent visits and to endure her scoldings, but the sons-in-law kept well away.

Leonie often brought her little sons to stay at Banstead, and then the nursery overflowed. Mrs Everest was hard pressed, keeping Winston and Jack tidy for meals and the small boys washed. My father writes that he must be the last living person to have stood in a bath to be scrubbed by Mrs Everest! Once he was brought down to meet Uncle Randolph and the gaunt bearded figure unsmilingly handed him a golden sovereign. Clutching his treasure, the little boy retreated to the cosy realms upstairs where Mrs Everest presided.

This was the period in which Winston was gleefully riding his first bicycle and breeding his own bantams at Banstead and piteously begging the uninterested Lord Randolph to visit him at school. During the Christmas holidays of 1890 he came down with measles, and gave it to Count Kinsky, who wrote him nicely in man-to-man fashion after the unwanted gift:

25 January 1890   Paris
My dear old Winny,
    Well, I caught it off you no doubt but I don't mind. I am really quite right again. . . . You know the measles are nothing when one is a child but it's much worse with grown up people. . . . Write to me sometimes. I shall always answer. . . .

Winston had suffered the complaint gladly enough, as he did not have to do his holiday task and thus had time for other more personal interests.

And far away in Austria, in a humble house on the river Inn, it had been the first Christmas on earth for a baby called Adolf Hitler. His father was a drunken bully, his mother an amiable peasant girl. No records of his childhood remain, whereas almost every note that Winston penned was kept by Jennie—even when they are bitterly protesting at her failure to visit him. 'Darling Mummy,' he would write, 'I am getting on capitally in my new form. . . . I want to go on fencing & as you will perceive am very anxious to have my Bicycle cleaned. . . .' All through the next months his blithe enquiries concern his pony Gem, the beautiful hampers sent him by Mrs Everest and the chickens whom he hopes are 'joyful'. As Winston sleeps happily at Banstead Manor or at Harrow School, he does not dream his enemy has been born.

15

Meanwhile in the rushing, gushing America of the 'nineties Mr Jerome worked gallantly. He transferred the old Jerome Park Jockey Club to a vast new course: 'We have 292 acres . . . the work of surveying and laying out the tracks has commenced. . . .' Any money he made was offered to 'the girls' and they all planned to winter together in Paris at his expense. Papa wrote bravely: 'The plan strikes me as very sensible, very possible and very jolly. Clara should take her children by all means. I have proposed to let Jerome Park for ten years—I think I will get it. . . . The three courses will then work in perfect harmony, Jerome Park, Sheepshead and the New Course. We will make Jerome P. the *Auteuil* of New York not altogether steeplechasing but principally. It is admirably adapted for steeplechasing and too cramped for modern flat-racing. The New Course will open May 30. Jennie and Randolph have promised to come over for the occasion. You may be sure it will be a great event.'

He has four horses in training, yet lives simply in a hotel room and writes to Mrs Jerome: 'I have no use whatever for a servant. When one has been in the habit of putting on one's own shoes and stockings for sixty to seventy years it would become rather awkward to have another do it. Randolph has come out of the *Temperance* affair very nicely. I hope to live to see the day when he will be the great leader in the richest of all rich fields *Free Trade*.'

In the early spring he took Jennie and Leonie to Monte Carlo, whence they sent oranges to Winston. Then he had to return to

148

New York. In December 1890 the old man returned to England for the last time. He scolded his wife for her uncomfortable economies and taking a house in London he ordered fires to be lit in *every* room. After Christmas he grew seriously ill and moved to Clara's house where he sat in a high backed red velvet chair to receive his grandchildren. Winston Leonard Spencer Churchill was now sixteen and Jack was eleven; after them came Hugh Frewen and golden-headed Clare, in white lace with blue shoulder ribbons, and the three Leslie boys. They would always remember the splendid old man. Jennie fought back her tears when he talked of Randolph's come-back. Clara's beau, King Milan of Servia, called daily and left crested cards, many of which survive: '*Quelques boutailles de vieux cognac que j'ai procuré a Paris pour votre cher malade,*' etc.

In the New Year, when his cough grew worse, Mrs Jerome moved him to Brighton for sea air: and there he died, leaving his daughters dazed with grief. Until Leonard Jerome left them his daughters did not realise how much they had always relied on him.

During the past year Randolph had spoken often and well in the House of Commons but his eccentricities had lost him every friend. The last of these, the interesting Mr Jennings, fell out with him over an amendment concerning the Government Commission appointed to investigate charges of complicity made against Parnell concerning the Phoenix Park murders. Randolph had previously drawn up a Memorandum attacking this abnormal tribunal in a paper on which his son has commented: 'If it were necessary to base his reputation for political wisdom on a single document I should select this.' Randolph was right in maintaining that Parnell was monstrously treated: but when the accusations were proved forgeries, and the forger committed suicide in a Madrid hotel, he shocked the House with a tirade in violent and questionable taste. Worse than this, he compromised the loyal Jennings, who was waiting to speak. Jennings never forgave him. Soon after this, when Parnell had been ruined by Captain O'Shea's divorce action, Mr Lucy wrote: 'The Conservatives hate Lord Randolph for divers reasons. One is that his defection from their ordered ranks deprives them of a powerful force. If he would only run in harness, giving up to party what he now wastes in action, he would be an immense accession of power. If he could only be depended upon he would be welcome to take the place that has never been filled since Disraeli died. But the dream is hopeless. . . .'

There lay the bitterness for Jennie—the dream was indeed hopeless. Mr Lucy wrote on: 'He is an interesting personality. Whatever we, in varying mood or from different points of view, think of him as a statesman, we are all interested in him, read what he has to say, watch what he does, and talk about him. . . .'

But his wife could hardly bear to watch. She wrote to Winston: 'I am still arguing to get Papa to sacrifice that terrible beard, but up to now without success.' She had worse anxieties. Personal economy had never been among Lord Randolph's assets and now that his judgement was growing shaky he allowed huge debts to accumulate. Jennie, completely untrained in money matters, could only worry, add up bills wrongly, fling them aside and dash to the dressmaker for moral restorative. A request for an ambassadorship to help Churchill's financial situation was refused by Lord Salisbury.

As his health deteriorated Lord Randolph took to incessant travelling accompanied by his devoted manservant Walden. Jennie always kept him well posted with political news. In December 1890, when he was in Rome, she wrote: 'Really I admire Parnell. I was sure he wd get his own way.' She had heard that if he was turned out on account of adultery the Irish Party would 'never leave a stone unturned until they had "shown up Morley and Hartington".'

During the winter of 1891 Randolph traversed Mashonaland, and his letters sound lively enough, especially when he manages to purchase shares in a Rand mine which soared in value.

Now he wrote long, almost affectionate letters to Winston and received carefully penned missives back, describing the lovely pony which had been given to Jack to make up for mumps. But when speech day came at Harrow School poor Winston had no parent to visit him. Jennie for some reason did not get down, and yet she carefully kept his piteous letter. '. . . My darling Mummy, I am sure you have not been very much troubled about me this term. I have asked for no visits & I forfeited the pleasure of seeing you on Speech Day therefore I do hope you will endeavour not to disappoint me utterly with regard to July 11th & 12th.' This referred to the Lord's Cricket Match in London, and Jennie wrote back from Banstead: 'Oh! dear oh! dear what an ado! You silly old boy I did not mean that you would have to remain at Harrow only that I cd not have you here, as I am *really* obliged to go to Stowe on Saturday. . . .' She was young and worldly, and put a grand invitation before her son's holiday, but she had sat with him at Lord's all the Friday and on the Saturday arranged for Charles Kinsky to give him a whacking good time.

All Winston's letters to his younger brother are full of affection and encouragement during the school years. He tries to fight off possible unhappiness or disappointment and writes cheerfully about the holidays: 'I hear your pony is a regular beauty & the fastest on Newmarket heath but I don't believe he will beat the "Gem" . . .'

A surprising PS. to one of Winston's letters to his mother reads, 'Really I feel less keen about the Army every day. I think the church would suit me much better. Am well, safe & happy. About Fireworks ask Count K.'

Maybe this sudden lack of enthusiasm for a soldier's career was engendered by the difficulty he found in passing examinations. In two undated letters of about this time Jennie reveals her anxiety. 'I have much to say to you, I'm afraid not of a pleasant nature, you know darling how I hate to find fault with you, but I can't help myself this time. In the first place your father is very angry with you for not acknowledging the gift of the £5 for a whole week—& then writing an offhand careless letter—Your Report which I enclose is as you will see a very bad one. You work in such a fitful unbusiness [*sic*] way, that you are bound to come out last—look at your place in the form! Your father and I are both more disappointed than we can say, that you are not able to go up for yr preliminary exam: I daresay you have 1000 excuses for not doing so—but there the fact remains! If only you had a better place in your form & were a little more methodical—I would try to find an excuse for you. Dearest Winston, you make me very unhappy. I had built up such hopes around you—& now all is gone. My only consolation is that your conduct is good, & that you are an affectionate son— but your work is an insult to your intelligence; if you would only trace out a plan of action & take a good pull before it is too late— You know dearest boy that I wd always help you all I can. Your loving but distressed Mother. J. S. C.' Another letter sent from Scotland— '. . . I tried to catch some fish in the loch yesterday but only succeeded in getting 2 rises. Darling Winston—I hope you will try & *not smoke*. If you only knew how foolish it is & how silly you look doing it you would give it up and work hard this term to pass yr preliminary. I will get Papa to get you a pony & perhaps next summer there will be something to shoot at Banstead. Anyhow dear—I will do my best to get you some sport & make you enjoy yourself—but you must do something for me in return. Now mind you write a nice long letter & tell me all you do—I want you *so* much to get on. Don't forget to brush yr teeth! & think often of Your loving Mother J. S. C.'

Perhaps Winston thought it smart to copy his father, who was seldom seen without a cigar. Jennie and her sisters all puffed cigarettes in private, sometimes up their bedroom chimneys, so as not to set a bad example to their sons!

That summer Charles Kinsky stayed at Banstead. Leonie and eagle-eyed Mama were also there.

The boys built a secret den in a tangle of undergrowth, and held feasts surrounded by high grass and wild rabbits. Kinsky helped them erect a target, and Jennie wrote her husband: 'I am going to try and borrow a gun for Winston, he must learn to shoot.' The gun was produced by Kinsky, who dispatched it to Winston from Vienna as he left for 'manœuvres'.

Two Connaught Place was closed during Randolph's absence, and Jennie stayed with her sisters when in London. Jennie describes one 'frantic summons to dine and sleep' she received from a friend Mary Gerard, whose husband the Lord Gerard had embarked on an affair below stairs. Jennie was forced to hear both sides of the story: 'I went over and found Mary in a dreadful state of mind and Billy too. It appears that it is quite true about his cook and that the night before he had discovered her with a valet whereupon she bolted and Billy was like a madman. The moment I arrived he took me off and burst into tears and told me the whole story how he could "worship" this woman, how he had offered her ten thousand pounds a year if she would live with him, and how she wouldn't—which I don't believe is true. Well to make a long story short I can't get out of it for he swore he would shoot himself if he did not find her—and I passed the rest of the night with Mary who was going to leave at once. . . . I feel so sorry for poor Mary. She was in such a rage and Billy fancies she knows nothing. She said, "fancy, he came and lived with me a fortnight ago fresh from the cook who was probably fresh from the valet". She swore she *never* would have anything to say to him again—and would have Hugh T. about as much as she liked.' Servant problems existed even in the eighteen-nineties!

On September 25th, when the boys had returned to school after a summer 'as happy as kings riding and shooting', Jennie wrote: 'Dearest R. At last I have seen the boys safely off. Winston conveniently worked himself into a bilious attack and had to stay on a couple of days. On the whole he has been a very good boy—but honestly he is getting a bit old for a woman to manage. After all he will be 17 in 2 months and he really requires to be with a man. . . . Winston will be alright the moment he gets into Sandhurst. He is just at the "ugly" stage—slouchy and tiresome. . . .'

But her account of the bilious attack was not very exact. She had, perhaps against her will, deceived Headmaster Welldon, and Winston wrote her cockily.

[19 September 1891]   [Harrow]
Darling Mummy,

Welldon wants you to write to him & 'explain' why I did not come back Thursday. 'The Doctors Certificate' says he 'accounts for Wed.' I told the animal I understood that you telegraphed, it was sufficient. 'Nay' saith he. . . . So he proposes that you should write him a letter saying that I was unable to 'favour him with my presence' on account of ———— anything. Twiggez-vous?

Don't say anything about the Theatre or that would make him rampant. Merely say I looked tired & pale from the journey (as indeed I did. . . .)

'Have you found a Gold Mine? What beautiful diamonds those were you sent Mama', wrote Winston as his father sailed for home. Later in the term he announced his intention to exchange his bicycle for a bulldog bitch, a transaction which caused Mrs Everest much consternation. She said it showed his lack of 'money sense'. Then he wished for church confirmation. 'Perhaps it will steady him' wrote Jennie, but added her suspicion that he expressed this desire 'only because it will get him off other work'.

Winston's letters become less tender as he grows older. Now he demands money and pheasants as well as kisses, and his mother has to write every detail of her activities to her 'Old Puss'. At thirty-seven she still takes a day's hunting when she can get it—'. . . great fun . . . but at first I was so blown that at the 3rd fence, I cut a lovely somersault—I shan't be able to chaff you any more about yrs.'

Mrs Everest's letters remain exactly the same—she exhorts him to avoid wet feet and pours out a stream of loving advice: 'I hope you will try & work well dearest this term to please his Lordship on his return & your Mamma has given you every pleasure & indulgence she could these holidays so I am sure you will try & do your best to please them & disappoint some of your relations who prophecy a future of profligacy for you. I trust you will be kept from all evil & temptation. I will pray for you & don't forget to pray hourly to be kept my sweet precious dear Boy.'

He would think twice before letting Mrs Everest down.

16

In November 1891 Lord Salisbury's nephew, Arthur Balfour, the most charming (if the most spineless) of Randolph's Fourth Party friends, was appointed Leader of the House of Commons, and Randolph, travelling back from Africa, wrote to Jennie: 'So Arthur Balfour is really leader—and Tory Democracy, the genuine article is at an end. Well, I have had quite enough of it all. I have waited with great patience for the tide to turn, but it has not turned, and will not now turn in time. In truth, I am now altogether *déconsideré*. . . . All confirms me in my decision to have done with politics and try to make a little money for the boys and for ourselves. I hope you do not all intend to worry me on this matter and dispute with me and contradict me. More than two-thirds, in all probability, of my life is over, and I will not spend the remainder of my years in beating my head against a stone wall. I expect I have made great mistakes, but there has been no consideration, no indulgence, no memory or gratitude—nothing but spite, malice and abuse. I am quite tired and dead sick of it all, and will not continue political life any longer. I have not Parnell's dogged, but at the same time sinister, resolution, and have many things and many friends to make me happy without that horrid House of Commons work and strife. After all, A. B. cannot beat my record; and it was I who got him first into the government and then into the Cabinet. . . . It is so pleasant getting home again. I have had a good time, but now reproach myself for having left you all for so long, and am dying to be again at Connaught Place.'

His sons also were dying to see their father. Winston's eager letters, asking if he had shot a lion or begging for an antelope's head, had followed him all through Mashonaland. Jennie described her elder son: 'Winston has improved in looks and is quite sensible now.' The boy was indeed turning into a young man with an apt pen who could pin-point his mother: 'You say I never write for love but always for money. I think you are right but remember that you are my banker and who else have I to write to? Please send me *"un peu"*.' The little French phrase was that so often used by the Jerome sisters when writing to dear Papa. Jennie had always hoped that Winston would speak fluent French. She had employed a 'nice young man from Cambridge who speaks 12 languages' but he seemed unable to aid Winston's progress in even one. When Winston's headmaster stressed the importance of French for the Army examinations she wrote to Randolph: 'Welldon says Winston should have special help for the French. I am going to try and find a little governess (ugly) who wants a holiday. Just to talk and read with him. . . .'

Despite these efforts her son never learned to speak even passable French. Maybe the little governess was *too* ugly! Now, in December 1891, when told he must spend a month of his Christmas holidays in a French family, Winston bombarded his mother with protests: 'I should like to know if Papa was asked to "give up his holidays" when he was at Eton.' But Mr Welldon insisted it was absolutely essential if he was to pass into Sandhurst. Jennie stood firm and Mrs Everest prepared 'some Fine Flannell Sheets' in case French sheets were damp.

On Christmas Eve Winston wrote from Versailles in a frenzy of self-pity: 'Write to Baron Hirsch. Do! I have not heard a word from all those "friends" you spoke about.'

Jack's babyish pen described Lord Randolph's return in January, 'with a horrid beard so raged' [*sic*], 'and the *Globe* newspaper said "Lady R. Churchill nimbly ran across the dock".'

Hating every moment of his exile Winston argued that a lunar, not a calendar, month had been agreed on. Peppering his epistles with French words he pleaded for an extra week with his father in England, but Randolph refused: 'The loss of a week may mean your not passing. . . . After you have got into the Army you will have many weeks for idleness and distraction.' As a Christmas treat

Winston had to content himself with an outing to Baron Hirsch, the Prince's millionaire financial adviser—who treated him to a visit to the Morgue to view corpses.

In July 1892 came the General Election, which returned 255 Home Rulers under Gladstone against 315 Unionists (Conservative and Liberal). Once more Lord Randolph Churchill found himself in the Opposition, and memories of his past brilliance—for none had ever excelled him in attack—aroused cautious hopes. 'No one cherished these hopes more ardently than I', wrote his son in *My Early Life*. 'Although in the past little had been said in my hearing, one could not grow up in my father's house and still less among his mother and sisters without understanding that there had been a great political disaster.'

The Churchill boys started to burn with hope, just as their mother secretly relinquished it. She knew of his constant giddy attacks and now, while he toyed with political rearrangements, she hoped that he would not be lured once again into the arena.

In August Randolph dining with Chamberlain admitted that he had 'always been a Liberal at heart'. It was only Home Rule which had kept him from changing party. In his diary, Chamberlain wrote: 'He can hardly expect now to supplant Balfour and he is too proud to care for any but the first place.'

That October, when Jack had just gone to Harrow and Winston was slaving for a second try at the Army examination, Jennie's letters full of such exhortations as, 'It will be all right if you put your shoulder to the wheel this time' suddenly ceased. She was dangerously ill with pelvic peritonitis. Randolph kept his sons posted and they came up to see her from Harrow in some trepidation. Winston's letters, his last from Harrow, were concerned and rather endearing. 'Enclosed are 4 kisses. Please return.'

In January 1893, when Winston had just scraped into Sandhurst and was staying with the Dowager Duchess near Bournemouth, he got concussion falling out of a tree, which seriously upset his convalescent mother.

Randolph, meanwhile, was toying with new political ideas, and the Tory Party wondered if, having grown more amenable, he could once more be useful to them. During a meeting at the Carlton Club there were loud cries for 'Churchill' after the parliamentary leaders had spoken. Amidst acclaim Lord Randolph rose,

157

to promise his utmost support for his 'old friend Mr Balfour'—he who had been called the outrigger of that frail craft the Fourth Party.

When Randolph sat on a back bench in the House of Commons Arthur Balfour speedily scribbled: 'If it had ever occurred to me that you could sit anywhere but on our bench, I would have spoken about it to you last night. *Everyone* desires you should do so and *most of all* yours ever A.J.B.'

Not for six months did Lord Randolph Churchill rise to speak in the House of Commons. It was February 17th, 1893, when, against his wife's advice, he left 2 Connaught Place to make a speech on the second Home Rule Bill. Jennie no longer sat eagerly in the gallery. She waited at home, nervously wondering which kind friend would tell her how Randolph's enunciation sounded. With pity she had watched him taking endless pains with this speech on his favourite subject, while suffering from palpitations and vertigo. She had noticed his suddenly increased deafness and numbed fumbling fingers. She had to bear the agony of watching him depart, grey-faced and with a strange distraught expression, on this afternoon when the House hoped for a 'come-back'. It was a terrible strain for her.

Owing to technical formality, Lord Randolph had to wait for an hour, trembling with nervous tension, before rising to address an expectant House. What Jennie had long known then became apparent to the House of Commons. There were brilliant passages in Lord Randolph Churchill's speech but most of it was inaudible. A dying man was trying to beat his own infirmity. Lord Rosebery has written: 'Randolph's was a generous nature in the largest and strictest sense of the word; generous and profuse both with money and praise. His lack of jealousy and his personal charm arose from the same quality—that there was no perfection or claim of perfection about him. He was human, eminently human; full of faults, as he himself well knew, but not base or unpardonable faults, pugnacious, outrageous, fitful, petulant but eminently lovable and winning'—and of his speeches: '. . . one is chiefly struck by their audacity and their extravagance . . . these dead speeches of his, though they now lack the vivid quality which made them when delivered so interesting and diverting, have a lingering charm of their own: if only from a delectable acidity which keeps them cool and fresh. . . . And even with his unfulfilled promise he must be remembered as one of the most meteoric of Parliamentary figures, as the shooting star of politics and as one who, when in office, strove for a broad and enlightened policy to which he pledged his faith and his career. He will be pathetically memorable too, for the dark cloud which gradually enveloped him, and in which he passed away. He was the chief mourner at his own protracted funeral, a public pageant of gloomy years. Will he not be remembered as much for the anguish as for the fleeting triumphs of his life? It is a black moment when the heralds proclaim the passing of the dead, and the great officers break their staves. But it is sadder still when it is the victim's own voice that announces his decadence, when it is the victim's own hands that break the staff in public.'

At the end of February, on one of his better days, Lord Randolph did make a vigorous speech which excited the House and as he felt the atmosphere change he grew more audible and for a few hours his ashen cheeks were flushed with triumph.

Then the Duchess of Marlborough, heartbroken at seeing the terrible determination of her beloved son 'to die by inches in public', conferred with Jennie, and the two women who loved him most called upon the doctors to examine him afresh. He ignored their order for complete rest and to give up smoking.

Now Jennie's friends implored her to prevent her husband from returning to the House of Commons. She refused to risk hurting Randolph by telling him how terrible he looked, how inaudible his words. For Jennie the joy of the day and the pain of the day were what mattered. All through the spring she let the gaunt trembling figure shuffle to the door, clutching his sheaves of notes. With a frozen heart she watched him climb into the barouche and drive to Westminster. But she would not seek to restrain him.

To Winston, who was now eighteen, she continued to write breezily: 'You *are* a lazy little wretch. I thought of course I would hear from you this morning. *Write.* I hear your new hat is a terror. Aunt Clara said you looked too funny in it. Please send it back.'

And later: 'I hope you are "comporting" yourself properly. I feel a little nervous at your visiting alone. I don't want to preach dear boy but mind you are quiet and don't talk too much and don't drink too much. One is easily carried away at yr age. . . . Papa seems to have had a great reception at Liverpool & his speech is most stirring—Bless you, hold yourself up & behave like the little gentleman you are.'

Randolph continued his correspondence with Lord Rosebery in handwriting ever more shaky, and all through the spring of 1893 he attended one political meeting after another. Jennie was well enough for Ascot races and wrote to Winston: 'I have had a delightful week & won my money—Shall make you a present of £2. It *is* hot! I hope you are careful not to get in the sun. One might get a sunstroke. Papa is busy preparing his speech for Leicester.'

That summer the boys were sent to Switzerland with a tutor while Jennie took Randolph for 'health's sake' to Kissingen. They spent an evening with old Bismarck whom she had so hated as a girl in 1870. On August 9th she wrote to Jack:

Aug. 9th: Hotel Victoria, Kissingen

Dearest Jack,

I envy you being in Switzerland—I have never been there. . . . We went & dined with the 'Great Bismarck' last night. It was very interesting & I got on very well with him. He smoked a pipe a yard long! Papa is much better I think the place suits him. Give my love to Winney.

Your loving
Mother
J.S.C.

To Winston she later wrote: 'We have just received your letters and are very pleased to think you are enjoying yrself—I am glad of course that you have got into Sandhurst but Papa is not very pleased at yr getting in by the skin of yr teeth & missing the Infantry by 18 marks. We are not as pleased over your exploits as you seem to be! Prince Bismarck is here & came to see us yesterday. It was very interesting meeting him. I had forgotten that he is 78. . . .'

Later, when Winston got into trouble for breaking a watch his father had given him, she wrote: 'Of course Papa is angry after giving you such a valuable thing. . . . Oh, Winny what a harum scarum fellow you are! You really must give up being so childish. I am sending you £2 with my blessing & love.'

From now on poor Winston received letters of sarcastic rebuke from Lord Randolph. He was chided for forgetting to write 'Dear

160

Father' instead of 'Dear Papa', and angrily harangued for bad English as well as for hinting for a bigger allowance.

Jennie feared that she spoilt her son; there were many tart reminders about the value of money, such as: 'I really think that Papa gives you a very fair allowance & you ought to make it do—he would be very X if he knew that I gave you money. It is yr own fault if you spend all yr money on food & then have nothing for other wants. . . .'

In the vast accumulation of letters concerning the Churchill family in these years the gems are really those of Mrs Everest to Winston at Sandhurst, 'Take care of yourself & don't tamper yourself with physic & take plenty of open air exercise & you will not require Medecine [sic]. It will ruin your constitution also your interior, such a mistake. Be a good Gentleman upright just kind & altogether lovely.' When he gets a weekend in London she exhorts him 'not to have bad companions, go to the Empire or stay out late at night'.

We rage with Winston when the Dowager Duchess wants to send beloved Everest packing and are glad that Jennie stands by the old nurse. Sometimes the cadet feels lonely in the barracks and wishes his mother could 'come & scold'.

Randolph also misses her when she goes to Paris: 'My dearest. When are you coming back? It is lonely in this house—breakfasting alone & lunching alone.'

In 1892 Randolph's brother, the 'wicked Duke', was found dead in his laboratory on the top floor at Blenheim, 'with a terrible expression on his face' the housekeeper told my father. He was conducting experiments to the last. His widow Lily assuaged her feelings by tearing up the photographs of Lady Colin Campbell and posted the fragments to that lady in Venice. The Whistler nude portrait was never seen again.

The Duchess Lily left Blenheim, and whenever Winston needed good sea air she invited him to her house, 26 Brunswick Terrace at Brighton.

Meanwhile Jennie suffered a fearful scene with Randolph after he discovered that she had paid a secret visit to his doctor. To the last he would insist that he was not mortally ill.

The months dragged miserably by, and on one heart-rending afternoon when Randolph was having one of his worst days and his faltering incoherent sentences trickled slowly out before a half-empty House, Arthur Balfour sat with his hands over his face. Lord Randolph Churchill spoke for the last time in June 1894. It was agony. He lost the trend of his arguments and Balfour and Hicks Beach had to prompt him. They drove to see Jennie afterwards and with tears in their eyes begged her to keep him away from the House.

At last she steeled herself to suggest a world trip. To her surprise Randolph philosophically accepted, and himself ordered 'an agreeable and clever doctor for the trip'. They had, for economy's sake, given up 2 Connaught Place and were staying with the old Duchess in Grosvenor Square. Wilfred Scawen Blunt paid Randolph a visit, and wrote: 'He is terribly altered, poor fellow, having some disease, paralysis, I suppose, which affects his speech, so that it is painful to listen to him.'

But alone with Jennie he spoke more easily and she planned the world tour with a bitter zest. With her Jerome staying power, she was able to keep a brave face to the world. Although the doctors were reticent with her she had long guessed the issue. Randolph was sliding towards paralysis and death. Her job must be to enliven the last years. She tried to pour her own strength into this caricature of the dynamic young minister of only eight years before. She was glad he did not register the effect he made on other people. She lied to her sons, saying she would bring him back well after the long voyage, and she comforted the distracted Duchess who had hardly recovered from the death of Marlborough. She held her head high in public and before Clara, who had troubles of her own. Only with Leonie did she unburden herself: 'The cruelty of it!' she said. 'He was so nearly Prime Minister. There wasn't time.'

Count Charles Kinsky, having loved Jennie for many years, wrote comfortingly and promised he would wait.

A letter to her younger son at Harrow written at this time shows the usual maternal concern.

50 Grosvenor Square

Dearest Jack,

. . . I gave Winston a lecture for not writing to you. He is a lazy boy—& such a foolish one! Fancy he went to Brighton for the Sunday & must needs go & take a Turkish bath. The result is a sore throat & palpitations so that today he can't go to his work. He is really too silly and childish. I feel very X, & don't see how he is to pass his exam if he goes on like this.

Bless you,

Yr loving mother

I.S.C.

There was a big farewell dinner party in Grosvenor Square which many of Randolph's old political acquaintances attended, and for a few hours he spoke lucidly and indeed wittily about his forthcoming trip to Japan and India and the 'Burma which I annexed'.

The real farewell had come on the previous evening when Lord Rosebery (now Liberal Prime Minister) and Lord Tweedmouth came to dine. Rosebery wrote years later: 'I cannot even make up my mind whether I had dined or stayed away. It was all pain and yet one would not like to have missed his goodbye. I still cannot think of it without distress.'

On June 27th, 1894, Lord and Lady Randolph Churchill departed for Canada. Winston obtained leave from Sandhurst to see them off. As they drove to the station his father patted him on the knee 'in a gesture which however simple was perfectly informing'. It was the last, almost the only, affectionate gesture that Lord Randolph Churchill had ever shown his son.

17

They sailed against doctors' orders: Jennie received a last-minute warning from the doctors 'to earnestly counsel your Ladyship to insist upon an immediate return to England in case Lord Randolph should show any fresh symptoms', but she felt that it was her duty to keep Randolph contented while trying to hide his affliction from the world.

The sailing from Southampton with the nervous young Dr Keith, the faithful valet Walden, and Gentry, her prim lady's maid, could hardly have been grimmer, but once out in the Atlantic Jennie tried to cheer up. She walked the decks and played in the ship's concert and found small happenings to laugh at. Friends who met her during this trip were amazed at her courage during this terrible task of shielding her haggard, semi-articulate husband from public gaze while encouraging him to enjoy a last glimpse of the world. When they reached Bar Harbour she met some of her father's old friends. 'It was a real joy to dance the "Boston", which only Americans know properly.' At this time she wrote to Jack at Harrow:

July 10th.   Bar Harbour
Dearest Jack,
    I wonder how you are getting on? I hope Winston sent you my letter from New York. It was so hot and noisy there we were very glad to come away. But all the places are so far from each other in America. This is eighteen hours by rail from N.Y. It is a most lovely spot right on the Atlantic and yet high mountains.

The air is wonderful and might do Papa a great deal of good. I think we shall stay 3 weeks. Of course it is very dull, not a soul one knows. We take long drives, read a great deal and Mr Keith and I walk. I miss you and Winston and feel very far away. Send this to Winston and give him my love. I hope to be able to tell you that Papa is much better in my next. Anyhow this will give him a good chance. Mind you write and think of me often.

Your loving mother,
J.S.C.

And in August, after crossing Canada by train, she unburdened to Leonie, 'I feel doubly low when I think how delightful this trip might be—if things were different.' She longed to ride over the prairies as her sister Clara had with Moreton Frewen, and the beauties of the Rocky Mountains even excited Randolph; but real excursions were out of the question. She wrote to Leonie from Banff Springs Hotel, Banff, Alberta:

Aug. 7—1897

Dearest Sniffy,

I write to you although I owe a letter to Mama but this must do for the family and I know no address but yours. . . . We left Bar Harbour last Fri & arrived at Montreal next morning . . . stopped the day there—& then came straight through to this place 22 hrs from Vancouver—5 days & nights in the train was tiring, so we agreed to stop 2 days here. We are off again tonight. We have got a Pullman private car of our own—which is as comfortable as such things can be but very expensive. R. had a letter to Sir W. Van Moren the Chairman of the C.P. Railway & he thought all he had to do was to ask for a car—and be sent free. . . . After a gt many excuses & telegrams it ended in our having to get one ourselves & pay something like $300 but the journey cd not be done otherwise. R. is not as well as he was at Bar Harbour. Of course the journey has told on him—but I feel it is always going to be so. As soon as he gets a little better from having a rest & being quiet he will be put back by this travelling—& *nothing* will deter him from doing what he likes. He is very kind & considerate when he feels well—but absolutely *impossible* when he gets X & excited—& as he gets like that 20 times a day —you may imagine my life is not a very easy one. Then Keith gets '*enervé*' and worried. Our plans as far as we can make them are to go from Vancouver to San Francisco & to sail for Yokohama the 24th August. R. won't take any thought or consideration of the war because it does not suit him & 'poohpoohs' any danger or inconvenience. I confess I think it will all be settled before we get there.

Meanwhile her sons travelling in Europe sent letters that were all affection. Winston's, beginning, 'My own darling sweet Mamma', sought to comfort her—'it is a horrid bore not to have my own one love to talk to. . . . I think of you always and long to kiss you again.'

On this journey in America Jennie saw for the first time women swimming in a private pool. They wore voluminous costumes and stockings but she commented tartly on 'both sexes disporting themselves, bobbing up and down, diving and swimming, without shyness—and, I must say, without vanity: for it must be owned that women do not look their best in such circumstances.'

They inspected San Francisco's Chinatown with a detective and witnessed a delicious fight among seals at Monterey. Reporters besieged them and Jennie was furious when a remark she made to a nearby stranger appeared under the headline: 'Lady Randolph tells Good Stories on the Porch of Del Monte!' While watching a ball in the hotel she had happened to describe a Frenchman with whom she had once danced: '*C'est terrible*.' He had panted, 'Why do you dance if you hate it?' '*C'est*' *pour l'hygiène—mon médecin me le recommande*.'

But, being Jennie, she felt so sorry for a woman reporter who burst into tears when pushed out of her bedroom that she granted an interview later in the day. Jeromes wept easily and always weakened at the sight of others' tears. 'Poor thing! I daresay if the truth were known she hated the interview as much as I did.'

After crossing the Pacific they reached Yokohama just after a Japanese victory over the Chinese. Jennie describes her visit to a theatre. 'We sat on the floor of our so-called box, and had tea like the crowd. And such a crowd! It was an endless source of interest and amusement to watch them.' And in the famous nursery gardens she bought tiny, stunted trees including a ten-inch-high century-old maple which she knew would make 'an unusual present for the Prince of Wales—so hard to give him anything different!'

A happy three weeks followed at Hyanashita, three thousand feet up in the mountains. They climbed to the resort by rickshaw. 'Once we stopped at a tea-house, where the landlady, with much in-drawing of breath, gave us Japanese tea.' The staid Walden and poker-faced Miss Gentry raised their eyebrows when the jinrickshaw men 'the perspiration pouring from their brown bodies, took off their white jackets (the one garment) and proceeded to wash and dash water over themselves from the pump nearby. . . . The face of my maid (a prim highly respectable person) was a study as the men resumed their mushroom hats and girded up their loins afresh.'

Jennie felt herself revive when away from prying eyes: 'Everything was so reposeful, from the quiet Japanese landscape with its soft greys and greens, to the bevy of little musmés who waited upon us, moving silently and swiftly about in their stockinged feet, always smiling and gentle.'

On returning to Yokohama they found great excitement in the harbour over the arrival of four German battleships on their way to Korea to observe the progress of the Japanese-Chinese war. Jennie and Dr Keith went to see a play representing the recent battle of Pyong-Yang. 'It was densely crowded and with difficulty we got places in the gallery. In the last act the Chinese troops represented by three Chinamen were perpetually being killed by twenty Japs, who rushed about bugling incessantly, brandishing swords, letting off rifles, and enjoying it madly.'

After travelling on to Tokio, Jennie obtained an invitation to visit an old-fashioned Japanese house: 'I wish I could describe its fascinations; but where there were no ornaments, no furniture, no pictures save a kakemono here and there, no curtains, no colour anywhere, it is difficult to say wherein lay the charm. And yet it was charming. The fineness of the matting, the beauty and workmanship of the woodwork, the lacquer frames of the screens, which were so adjusted that they parted at a touch without a sound, the extraordinary cleanness everywhere, and, above all, the different little courts on which the rooms looked, were delightful. The bathroom particularly pleased me. Made of some light-coloured wood, it shone like satin and felt like it.'

An episode which Jennie recounted to nephew Hugh Frewen, but naturally omitted from her memoirs, occurred in this house.

To her great content Jennie had lowered herself into a marble bath tub of delicious hot water. She was blissfully relaxing when the door opened and in walked the Japanese postman to deliver her mail. He looked completely baffled at the screams and splashes which ensued.

Before leaving Tokio Jennie went for an evening walk escorted by Matsuda their guide: 'The open screens of the private houses permitted us to look through them; at one the sound of a samisen attracted me, and I could not resist stopping and looking in. Beyond two rooms, by a not over-bright light, I saw a little Japanese woman sitting on a mat singing softly in a minor key, accompanying herself on the samisen. I asked Matsuda if the woman minded publicity. Looking very shy and uncomfortable he said, "Oh, Japanese no look in—not good manners." I felt fearfully crushed.'

Travelling on to Nikko, in a dream world of beautiful bridges and temples, they reached Kyoto, the ancient capital. There is pathos in the difference between Jennie's gay published memoirs and her personal letters. It was from Japan that she ended a long letter to Winston, on 11th October: '. . . Bless you darling. I can't tell you how miserable I am often, so far away from you all—but I shall feel nearer when I am in India and perhaps things will look brighter. Tell Jack I will bring him something nice from India.'

Winston's September letters grow ecstatic over the joys of riding cross-country. After two falls off hirelings he writes: 'I do love this kind of riding. You know how little I have hunted. I don't think that anything would stop me if I had a good horse. . . . I am pinching & scraping to try and hire a better animal for a month and any contributions you may feel inclined to send will be thankfully received.'

Meanwhile Dr Keith began to wilt. To Dr Roose he wrote from Yokohama: 'I have lost all control over your patient. He intends to take a journey tomorrow that I distinctly disapprove of, and all I have said has been to no avail.'

Randolph's 'numbness and irritability' were increasing. In October Keith laments that Lord Randolph will not hear of giving up India. 'One hour he is quiet and good-tempered, the next hour violent and cross. He has taken a violent dislike to one of his valets and is sending him home.'

Winston naively suggested that Dr Keith ought to restrain his gloom. 'Poor old Grandmama is very low. It seems to me to be unnecessary to send her anything but good reports. . . . If you only knew what importance she attaches to every cheering good word about Papa—I am sure you would persuade Dr Keith to tell only what is pleasant to hear.' A more sombre note crept in after he visited his father's doctor in November but he still felt *unnecessary* alarms should be avoided. On November 2nd he wrote: 'I persuaded Dr Roose to tell exactly how Papa was—you see I only hear through Grandmama Jerome who does not take a very sanguine view of things—or through the Duchess who is at the one extreme one moment and at the other the next. . . . I had never realised how ill Papa had been and had never until now believed that there was anything serious the matter. I would advise—if I might, that you and Keith write nothing but good news to the Duchess. . . . She lives, thinks and cares for nothing else in the world but to see Papa again —and has a week of misery after anything like an unsatisfactory report. She was delighted with your letter which cheered her up immensely. Well, goodbye my darling dearest Mama.'

Jennie had been grateful for the soft enchantments of Japan. At a time of horrible strain the quiet soothed her torn nerves. 'For months my ears still listened for the two most characteristic sounds in Japan—the tap-tap of the little pipe as it is emptied before being refilled, and the mournful notes of the reed lute which the blind *masseur* plays as he walks through the village street.'

From Hong Kong they paid a visit to Canton where Randolph bought Jennie a last gift, a jade bracelet to keep the devil away. When the guide proudly led them to the execution ground to see the pickled heads of eight men newly decapitated, Jennie and Keith decided to cut short the sightseeing.

At Singapore, while staying at Government House, Randolph's condition deteriorated still further and Keith, at his wits' end, wrote to Dr Roose: 'This has been the worst week since leaving home by a great deal. Lord Randolph has been violent and apathetic by turn. . . . I have warned him again in the most solemn manner that I entirely disapprove of Burma, but with no effect. . . .'

On they journeyed, Jennie trying to enjoy a vast feast in the palace of the Sultan of Johore and applauding the fat Circassian wife sent from Turkey. At Rangoon, Government House was placed at their disposal. To everyone's relief the Governor was away so there could be no question of entertaining. Official parties with people anxious to meet Randolph were her worst torture. She visited pagodas by moonlight, but Randolph could not accompany her. She tried to elicit his interest, telling him how three princesses, relatives of the late King Theebaw, had called on her. 'They presented me with some artificial flowers made by themselves, also some cheroots they hoped I would smoke and departed in a cart drawn by bullocks.' But Randolph was hardly able to smile now, hardly able to get the words out: 'Hope you forbore to tell them your husband annexed Burma?' She laughed at his little joke, then hid herself away to weep at the telegram which had arrived from Charles Kinsky. Capitulating to his family's demand, he was engaged to a young Austrian countess.

18

On 18th November, 1894, from the Bay of Bengal, she wrote to sister Clara: '. . . You must not be very angry with me for not having written to you. My letters to Leonie are intended for you & Mama too. . . . I assure you I am always thinking of you darling and I would give anything to be with you all now. . . . We are on our way to Madras from Rangoon. We get there on 21 & stay with the Wenlocks. We stayed a week at Rangoon intending to go up to Mandalay & Behar 150 miles further North but the steamer did not fit in & we heard there was a lot of cholera & so R was willing to give it up. Keith and I did all we could to prevent his going to Burma as we feared the heat for him but it was useless. He would have gone alone if we had insisted. After leaving Japan we had 3 days in China seeing Hong Kong and Canton, the latter an extraordinary place. We went there by steamer up the "Pearl River" 12 hours each way & spent the day in Canton. The "Heathen Chinee" were very nasty glaring at us. They hit Walden & spat at Dr Keith so we did not tarry but whisked through the streets in palanquins only getting out to go into shops. From Hong Kong we went to Singapore 5 days by sea—every place is 5 days by sea. . . . I have met very few people one cd talk to since we left England. I can't tell you how I pine for a little society. It is so hard to get away from one's thoughts when one is always alone. And yet the worst of it is I dread the chance even of seeing people for his sake. He is quite unfit for society & I hate going to the Wenlocks. One never knows what he may do. At Govt House Singapore he was very bad for 2 days and it was dreadful being with strangers. Since then he has become much quieter & sometimes is quite apathetic but Keith thinks it is a bad sign. I am going to try to get the opinion of another doctor at Madras & I want if possible to get him home or at least near home. I am sure it is quite impossible for us to go travelling about in India. It means staying with people all the time & R is too unfit for it. Of course he does not realise there is anything the matter with him as he feels well physically. Dearest Clarinette I cannot go into all the details of his illness but you cannot imagine anything *more* distracting & desperate than to watch it & to see him as he is & to think of him as he was. You will not be surprised that I haven't the heart to write to you about the places & things we see. I try to keep a diary for your sakes but when I write to you I cannot get away from my troubles. I know my letters are dull when they might be interesting. I had a telegram from Charles at Rangoon telling me of his engagement. I *hate* it. I shall return without a friend in the world & too old to make any more now. Well there! enough about myself. I wish I cd have some good news of you & Moreton poor dear. Your life is not all *couleur de rose*. Whose is? It is so easy to tell people to be philozophical (I can't spell any more) how can one be. . . .'

It was a terrible blow, this telegram from Charles Kinsky who had promised to wait for her. But the dice were too heavily loaded and the old Prince, his father, had threatened to cut off funds if he married Jennie. Charles was an immense spender, and always allowed big debts to accumulate. No one could know *how* long Lord Randolph would live, but old Prince Kinsky was not ready to take chances. Under great pressure Charles had allowed himself to become engaged to the Countess Elizabeth Wolff-Metternich. Jennie sent Leonie one heartrending plea to try to stop the marriage. Fearless as she was, Leonie did her utmost and Charles Kinsky sent her a message to say he was trying against heavy odds to remain a free man.

'Keep your strength and pluck up', wrote Winston, but now, in the damp heat, for the first time Jennie began to droop, and she felt that further peregrinations through India would be beyond bearing. It was almost a relief when Dr Keith said they had *got* to get home. He had wired to Dr Roose on 23rd November from Madras:

'Consultants confirm diagnosis, time about six months. Tell Lady Wimborne.'

But still Randolph wanted to see the sights. Jennie brought him to Cairo for a few days and wrote to Leonie: 'We have had a good passage and Randolph is very quiet. I think he will be easily managed henceforth. His will is very feeble. I had to give in about Monte Carlo as he set his heart on going there instead of Cannes. We shall go to the Metropole at first and make plans later. I don't know if the Duchess will come. It may be too long a journey for her in which case we should return to England. If she comes, perhaps Winston will bring her out.'

But Randolph was too weak to leave the ship again. They reached 50 Grosvenor Square on the day before Christmas. The Duchess was waiting to help nurse her son, and Winston, now twenty years old, had been alerted to the truth.

To Leonie, who was in Ireland, Jennie wrote:

3 January   50 Grosvenor Square
 . . . Don't dream of coming over at present & until it suits you. There is little to do here & I am really in a much better frame of mind than you can possibly imagine as regards the wedding. The bitterness if there was any, has absolutely left me. He and I have parted the best of friends, and in a truly *fin de siècle* manner. So darling don't worry about me on that score. I am not *quite* the meek creature I may seem to you. Pity or sympathy even from you is wasted on me. No one can do me any good. He has not behaved particularly well & I can't find much to admire in him but I care for him as some people like opium or drink although they wd like not to, *n'en parlons plus*. Randolph's condition and my precarious future worries me much more. Physically he is better but mentally he is 1000 times worse. Even his mother wishes now that he had died the other day. What is going to happen I can't think or what we are to do if he gets better. Up to now the General Public and even Society does not know the real truth & after *all* my sacrifice and the misery of these 6 months it would be hard if it got out. It would do incalculable harm to his political reputation & memory & be a dreadful thing for all of us. We can't make any plans for the next few days. My life is dreadful here, so disorganised & un-

173

comfortable, no place to sit, everything in confusion. I've got a cold which makes me feel 'like mud'.

Yrs loving

J.

On January 9th Charles Kinsky acceded to his father's demands and married the young countess. It was no shock, for Jennie had discarded hope. Suffering from headaches and fatigue, she seldom left Randolph's room. Clara Frewen wrote to Leonie describing the following days: 'I knew the collapse would come for she hasn't eaten or slept since she arrived & wd scarcely move out of his room till today. I am playing watchdog and won't let a soul come near her room & am happy to say she is sound asleep. . . . Everything here is *lugubre*, masses of Churchills who sit with the old Duchess and go one by one into Randolph's room.'

Day after grim day rolled by. Occasionally for a few minutes Randolph's brain might clear, but his wife and mother had to pray that he would not last long.

In the early morning of January 24th Winston was summoned. He ran across snow-covered, deserted Grosvenor Square, to stand by his mother and grandmother while this father he had yearned to know passed quietly away.

The grandeur of the funeral destroyed thought. Numbly Jennie sat through the service at Westminster Abbey, and numbly drove through streets crowded with silent mourners to Paddington and thence by train to Bladon churchyard. She recognised the genuine sorrow of those who had known Randolph in the past and the poignancy of his fate stabbed her afresh, but she was too tired and dazed to suffer. It was difficult to comfort the Duchess. She had set such store by this brilliant younger son, and now, when hundreds of letters of condolence poured in, she broke down completely. Could she ever forget Lady Salisbury's refusal to see her after Randolph's resignation? The cruelly, insultingly returned letter? To Lord Salisbury, who she believed—not without justification—had snatched at the opportunity of sliding Randolph out of office, she answered hastily:

Private   Jany 26 '95

Dear Lord Salisbury

I thank you for your sympathy with this terrible sorrow.

174

But oh it is too late too late. There was a day years ago when in my dire distress I went to you & asked you as a father to help me—for my Darling had no father. He had but *me* & I could do nothing though I would have given my life for him. I went to you—I would have fallen at your feet if you could have helped me & sympathised with me. He knew not what I did but I was desperate & I knew he had been misled & made a fatal mistake & yet I knew all his cleverness & real goodness & what he had been & could be to his Party. He never knew what I did & I felt I had failed because I could not explain myself. Your heart was hardened agst. him. I suppose he had tried you & worry & anxiety beset you or it was Fate.

But from that hour the iron entered into his soul. He never said so. He never gave a sign even to me of disappointment but for Days & Days & Months & Years even it told on him & he sat in Connaught Place brooding & eating his heart out & the Tory Press reviled him, the Tory Party whom he had saved, abused & misrepresented him & he was never the same. The illness which has killed him is due they tell me to overwork & acute mental strain & now he is gone & I am left alone to mourn him . . . it is bitter anguish to feel what I do. He had the greatest admiration for you & you might have done anything with him. But he was young & I sorrowfully admit —he was wrong—He has suffered for it & as for me my heart is broken. . . .

It's all over now. My Darling has come Home to die & oh it seems such bitter mockery that *now* it is too late he seems to be understood & appreciated.

Believe me, Yrs sorrowfully,
F. Marlborough

It was natural that Woodstock should mourn for the Churchill who had grown up there and natural that his political friends and enemies should together join in tribute. But there was a real sadness in the land—England sighed for this wild bird who had bewitched her with the unexpected phrase. What won't a country forgive the man who destroys dullness! He would best be assessed by a young historian, Robert Rhodes James, seventy years later: '. . . it was the impact of his personality which was the great factor. He was the child of the morning. He brought a gust of fresh air into the dusty confines of English public life.'

When the funeral was over Jennie retreated into her room to wonder how she would build up a new life. She could not remain in Grosvenor Square trying to comfort the Duchess. There were aspects she found too painful to discuss with a distracted mother, who insisted it was overwork which had killed Randolph. The correct term was *paralytica dementica*. As far as she knew there had never been a time when Randolph could have been cured of his terrible illness.

Among the hundreds of letters she must answer was one from the Prince of Wales written on the very evening of her husband's death:

My dear Lady Randolph,
 The sad news reached me this morning that all was over . . . & I felt that for his and your sakes it was best so. . . .
 There was a cloud in our friendship but I am glad to think that it is long been forgotten by both of us. . . .

He went on to mention Randolph's 'extraordinary vitality' and to say it was good of her to write 'when worn out in mind and body'. A few days later he wrote again. 'On returning to town today I found the lovely little Japanese box. You may be sure that I will always greatly value it as Randolph's last gift. I hope you are none the worse for all you have gone through. Should you wish to see me I could call at 5 tomorrow. . . . The gift for the Princess I will keep till her return.'

How distant seemed the tiffs of yesteryear! Jennie turned to the future.

On February 20th Winston received his commission and settled happily into barracks at Aldershot. Stiff from hours of riding, he wrote to his mother, 'Everything goes on satisfactorily . . . Lord Falmouth's gloomy predictions notwithstanding.' 'Star' Falmouth was an infantryman! To Jack he wrote: 'I should like that picture of Charles Kinsky on Zoedone very much—it would just go over my mantelpiece and is exceedingly appropriate.'

Meanwhile Jennie had to face hard facts. She found herself without a home and exceedingly short of money. Randolph had always lived extravagantly and now she learnt that his debts totalled £70,000 which, as luck would have it, could just be paid off by the booming Rand Mine Shares he had bought in South Africa. Henceforth she must exist on her father's settlement, and her sons must live carefully. Winston's pay as a lieutenant hardly covered his mess bill; Jack, still at Harrow, must be lectured on the virtues of economy in the tuck shop and elsewhere. Already their cousin, the twenty-two-year-old Duke of Marlborough, was being forced to consider a loveless marriage with one of America's greatest heiresses. After a crushed, unhappy boyhood he now heard the family chant that he was disastrously poor for a duke. His duty lay towards Blenheim and its fourteen acres of decaying roofs, and to marry the young lady of his heart's desire would be letting the side down. Reluctantly this intelligent, high-strung, sensitive, bullied human being was steeling himself to cross the Atlantic to marry Consuelo Vanderbilt, whose mother had more or less proposed to him, a story that has been painfully recounted from the bride's angle in *The Glitter and the Gold*. Within the snowy, dark-skied month of January 1895 Jennie had lost the two men of her youth and she felt inwardly frozen. No one could pretend that the prospect looked lively for a woman of forty-one.

By how narrow a margin had Charles Kinsky eluded her? At this stage the story should, I think, be told by a living member of the Kinsky family. Prince Clary, whose mother was born a Kinsky, has written out for me his memories of this elder cousin, whom he knew well and hero-worshipped in his youth. Charles Kinsky belonged to that strait-laced Austrian nobility which accorded extreme importance to lineage and quarterings. It was indeed their habit, on the rare occasions when a daughter of the English nobility married into their ranks, to request a pedigree from dazed peers and country gentlemen who might have owned their lands since the Norman Conquest but took little interest in the coats-of-arms of great-great-grandmothers. All through the years when the Kinskys knew Charles was in love with Lady Randolph Churchill they had worried only slightly because they knew he could not marry her. Randolph's fatal illness put a new complexion on the matter. They were absolutely determined to shackle him to a young girl of his own rank.

Anecdotes concerning Kinsky's exploits lingered on in London clubs for a generation. Few can now remember him, but his cousin Prince Clary writes 'My grandmother, Countess Sophie Kinsky, used to say that Charles became engaged to the young Countess Elizabeth Wolff-Metternich only because he had given up every hope of being able to marry Lady Randolph. His bride was pretty and eminently suitable. My grandmother told me that when Charles Kinsky heard that Lord Randolph was a dying man he wanted to break off his engagement and that it was only under heaviest pressure from his family that he gave in. The old Prince Kinsky was one of the great Austrian landowners with vast and perfectly run estates. As long as he remained alive Charles was entirely dependent on the allowance his father chose to give him. As far as I know this allowance was very large indeed, but he spent money lavishly and his father had several times paid considerable debts which had worried the family.'

The old Prince's fear that his extravagant son might marry a yet more extravagant older woman is understandable. And indeed there were other reasons why Jennie could not be welcomed. At forty-one she was unlikely to produce an heir, she had *no* quarterings and she was not a Catholic. The latter obstacle might well have been overcome, for the Roman faith could have suited Jennie's fervent temperament, but quarterings are not to be invented and her age was an insuperable drawback.

So Charles Kinsky had let himself be driven into marriage with a suitable girl. Three weeks later his honeymoon was not enhanced by the news that Jennie was free. Apparently Kinsky took it very hard. There were no children of the marriage and relations have recounted that he often appeared to be *'agacé'* with his young wife.

After the jolt Jennie speedily pulled herself together. The Jerome sisters shared a sense that it was *wrong* to bow the head to disaster. At the end of February Jennie decided to leave to others the task of sorting out Randolph's tangle of debts. Clad in deep mourning and attended only by her maid Gentry, she departed for Paris, where the code of the time allowed English widows to entertain quietly instead of undergoing six months' purdah in London. To Jack she wrote; 'We had a capital crossing—great crowds but we accomplished it all right. We have found an apartment 34 Avenue Kléber....'

Leonie and John Leslie agreed to join her with two small boys and the faithful Walden took charge of the apartment, and the 'foreign staff'.

On March 1st she wrote to fifteen-year-old Jack giving permission to buy a morning coat for his Easter holiday and adding, 'Mind you bring a knicker-bocker suit for you will want to bicycle—and get yourself a pair of low-heeled shoes with not *too* thin soles. . . . It is bright and sunny here although the ice has not quite gone. They skated in the Bois yesterday. I fancy Walden & Gentry will become quite French scholars with so many French servants around. We are comfortable here and you will like it.' On March 8th she wrote him again. 'It has been snowing here and it is very cold. Aunt Leonie sends you her love. Norman and little 'Chou-chou' [Leonie's sons] have arrived, the latter [Seymour] a little darling. I feel very sorry for him. Winston writes often. He is very happy.'

On March 8th Winston wrote: 'I do hope my dearest Mama that you will keep well and not give way to depression. I am sure that Aunt Leonie will look after you and make the time pass pleasantly.'

This was the right way to face adversity. Jennie could not guess that the angel of destiny had guided her away from that delightful Austrian to meet a man who above all others possessed the means of teaching her son the art which in the end he would most need.

19

'Paris was such a contrast to London even to a child. It was so clean and brightly lit', writes my uncle Seymour Leslie seventy-two years after the time he was carried into the apartment in Avenue Kléber. The little boy lying on a sofa, unable to walk or to go to school, studied the grown-ups who came and went. His large brown eyes hungrily watched mother and aunt in their stiff, silk dresses proceeding to the salon where he could not follow, and he avidly lapped up their casual remarks. Important guests brought him presents—some so valuable they were taken away immediately and never seen again! But his favourite toy, a tiny phonograph with a small wax cylinder which hummed *'Nous n'irons plus au bois, les lauriers sont coupés'*, remained with him for a long time. Kind Walden would carry him down for carriage outings or run up the stairs crying: 'Hold tight, Master Seymour, we will race the lift'.

Jennie and Leonie had always loved Paris, the city of their youth, and Seymour watched his mother and aunt regaining their natural good spirits. The Marquis de Brèteuil, the Prince of Wales's great friend, issued invitations to what was considered the most interesting house in Paris. The Marquis was very fond of Jennie and his beautiful country place, Brèteuil, filled with works of art and rather frightening tapestry-hung beds, was open to her. Lord Dufferin, the British Ambassador, often visited Jennie and a letter he wrote about Randolph gave her much satisfaction. 'I found him more courteous, more considerate, more full of sympathy, than any of those with whom I had previously worked.' Head held high, Jennie felt her way back to life. When the weather grew warmer, bicycles were purchased, for it was quite *comme-il-faut* for a recently bereaved widow to pedal through the Bois de Boulogne in black bloomers.

Seymour is the only living person who can give us an eye-witness account of Jennie's four months of 'heavy mourning' in Paris. In his *The Jerome Connexion* he describes his mother and aunt, the two sisters, 'so different, so complementary'. They both had quick tempers, but the subtle Leonie, unlike Jennie, 'listened and ultimately became a sort of universal confidante, of absolute discretion, to whom the famous and distinguished turned for sympathy . . . I see Jennie as in a throng but Leonie alone with one other'.

He also relates that, like most children of that class and era, he was completely ignored by his father. Having remarked that it was indeed a pity that a third boy had arrived instead of a daughter, John Leslie forgot about him, and Seymour actually noticed his father for the first time in this Paris apartment. Carried into his mother's bedroom on the first morning in Paris, he saw with surprise a man with a moustache beside her in bed. '*Qui est ce Monsieur, maman?*' he asked. Jennie related this story with relish at her dinner parties.

When Winston had an accident trying out a horse on a steeplechase course, his mother wrote admonishing him, but he argued: 'I think—if you will let me say so—that you take rather an extreme view of steeplechasing—when you call it at once "idiotic" and "fatal". Everyone here rides one or other of their chargers in the different Military Races.' On March 28th he rode in his first steeplechase and came in third. 'They thought it very sporting, I thought so too.'

Before this information could be assimilated, a telegram arrived to say that old Mrs Jerome was seriously ill at Tunbridge Wells. Her daughters hurried back to England, and the letter to Winston written on April 1st by Mrs Everest to thank him for adding to her small allowance ends: 'Jackie this morning tells me Grandmama Jerome is very ill. . . . Her Ladyship is at Tunbridge Wells & Mrs Leslie too. They are both with her, poor Mama she has had a lot of trouble lately. . . . The Duchess has let 50 Gr. Square & goes away on the 11th. . . . I hope you will take care of yourself my darling. I hear of your exploits at steeplechasing. I do so dread to hear of it.

Remember Count Kinsky broke his nose once at that. It is a dangerous pastime but I suppose you are expected to do it. Only don't be too venturesome. Goodbye darling with much love to you. . . .'

Mrs Jerome died on April 2nd after Winston had paid a last visit. It was with heavy hearts that her daughters, all three now in heavy mourning, returned to Paris. Mama had been a rock in time of trouble and they would miss her scoldings. But life was there to be lived and soon the invitations, handwritten on paper with inch-thick black borders, issued forth to their 'intimate friends'. Now they were nursing bruised feelings in unison, trying to cheer each other up, above all trying to distract Jennie. They all found solace in concerts and operas and sometimes they would climb up to the organ loft of St Sulpice to sit beside their friend, the great Widor, as he practised.

The Jerome spirits began to rise. Troubles were forgotten. But the sisters, so musical and artistic by nature, ignored the great artistic movements of this period. This was already the Paris of the Post-Impressionists. They had heard of Renoir but, surrounded by *meubles du dixhuitième* and brain-washed by Mrs Jerome into respect for the conventional, they never appreciated the exciting trend of contemporary art. And the over-educated French aristocracy, so witty at their dinner tables, revered the dull *Salon*!

Meanwhile young Winston, intoxicated by the joys of polo, wrote his mother: 'It is the finest game in the world and I should almost be content to give up any ambition to play it well and often.'

Jack came over for his Easter holiday and joined in the bicycling, which had become the smartest of sports. My grandmother told me that the charm of cycling through the Bois in the early summer morning, when birds were singing and before dust rose up from the carriages, was something the next generation could not imagine. Occasionally there were spills. When Jack returned to school Jennie wrote him: 'I hope you arrived safely. You promised to wire—but did not! . . . I am contemplating starting off on a bicycle this morning—altho' my leg is stiff but it's no use giving in. I hope you will work hard this term. Mr Weller will expect to hear wonderful French after 3 weeks of Paris. . . .'

Then, as the chestnut trees blossomed and bright parasols enhanced the boulevards, Mr Bourke Cockran came to dinner. It was Clara who brought him to the Avenue Kléber, vaguely describing 'a friend of Moreton's from Washington who knows something about bi-metallism'. Thus she described the Democrat Irish-American orator who three years previously delivered what one American paper called 'the greatest speech ever made at a political convention'. The *Toledo Sunday Journal* wrote up that scene: 'Consider for a moment. An audience of twenty thousand men and women. A hot stuffy hall, close, leaky and uncomfortable. Hard wooden-seated chairs. . . . An audience weary, hungry and thirsty, that had sat from 4.30 p.m. to 2 a.m. . . . Merge all these conditions before you and think what it meant for one man to hold the crowd spell-bound for nearly an hour and then decide that never before has there been in this land so dramatic a moment as when the imposing, heavy-browed lawyer from New York, bearing most evident signs of the terrific mental and physical strain he had been under-going, faced the throng. Group all these factors before you and then see the army there gathered, breathless and bewitched. . . .' No microphones existed. And the New York *Herald* commented on the aftermath. 'Cockran's walk back to his seat was attended by an ovation such as few men could draw from a friendly audience and none probably has ever before forced from one so large and hostile.'

But American politics meant nothing to the Jerome sisters. Jennie expected some old bore of a Congressman, hipped on financial theory. She felt a tremor of surprise when Mr Cockran entered her drawing room—for he *was* extraordinary-looking, a heavy-boned bull of a man, wide-shouldered, with a huge head and the long Irish upper lip. His features looked hewn rather than chiselled and bright blue eyes shone incongruous as forget-me-nots stuck in a mask of granite. He was ugly—but in a magnificent way. No man looked like Bourke Cockran, and no man could speak like him. The perfection of his French and the musical intonation of his English, his memory for poetry and his flair for extemporising, the whole style of the man astonished. When taken to Seymour's room the child laughed at his big head and asked to try on his hat. He spoke French with the little boy and gave him as a present 'Les Veilles Chansons de Boutet de Monvel'.

Sitting beside Jennie at dinner, Bourke delighted her with droll stories, the first of which concerned an Irishman he had overheard

183

at her father's race-course, Jerome Park. Surveying the fashionable throng in the grandstands, this 'Mick' swaggered away snorting in a vein which Bourke could well reproduce, 'And what's yon to Mallow races!'

The Jerome sisters worked hard at their parties; guests were expected to invigorate each other. And here was a man who could charm in two languages—and several dialects! A man who could make you laugh and cry in the same instant.

He was a great character. I knew him well for the first nine years of my life, but my own biased childish memories are based on his kindness and indulgence. I have had to discover since his early makings.

Born in County Sligo in the same year as Jennie (so at this meeting he would be forty-one) Bourke came of a line of hard-riding Irish squireens. His father had been Catholic, his mother an intensely pious convert from a grander Protestant family. His father broke his neck in a steeplechase before Bourke was five years old—but not before he had taught the little boy to hate him by unjust thrashings.

The Cockran boys were shipped off to France at an early age to be educated according to the standards deemed necessary by their devout and socially ambitious mother. Bourke knew five years of miserable exile. It seemed impossible even to bring him home for the holidays. His loneliness decreased when an adored elder brother joined the college, but this boy died soon after, leaving his broken-hearted little brother with no comforts save French literature and his religion. Intensive education meant more to Mrs Cockran than her children's happiness.

On returning to Dublin at sixteen, Bourke asked to study for the Irish Bar. Thwarted, he sailed for America with £150 in his pocket. After this had run out he booked a passage home, but the ship's captain dissuaded him, pointing out that America held much more opportunity than Ireland. So Bourke remained in New York, teaching French, Latin and Greek until cousins provided funds to study for the American Bar. Equipped with an extra-ordinary intellect, he found the law an easy profession. As a promising barrister of twenty-two he married. His young wife died in childbirth a year later. Reckoning that his youth had been unfairly weighted with tragedy, Bourke took to heavy drinking—as emotional Irishmen of strong physique often do. He felt he was not the darling of the Fates. It was a dipsomaniac friend who stopped him. One day at lunch this man, a broken-down lawyer, suddenly looked at Bourke lifting a glass of brandy to his lips and said: 'You can choose between the gutter and the heights in a way that is given to few men.'

Bourke understood. He replaced the glass on the table and refrained from touching alcohol for thirty years. In that minute he mastered the impulses of his own passionate nature—a sensitive nature outraged by misfortune, angry against the world. When he left his law practice to enter the political arena, Bourke became America's greatest orator.

He had perhaps reached his apex in the summer when Moreton Frewen had heard him attacking the theory of silver money in Washington. As a Democrat standing for Sound Money in that debate which has been called 'the most important economic discussion that ever took place in the American Congress', Bourke Cockran made a speech which fully revealed his erudition and his grasp of philosophy. 'An overcrowded House listened spellbound in wonder and admiration', says a report. The history of coinage became the history of human beings. Bourke Cockran could hold 15,000 people entranced for an hour and twenty minutes on a stifling hot August day, and when he spoke in the enemy's camp an editorial wrote fairly, 'They might hate his cause, but they could not resist the spell of genius'. Bourke was the most emotional of men, but he developed perfect vocal technique. He was never swayed by the sound of his own voice—he trained his memory and he was never nervous. The quick wit came from command of his own emotion. When my grandmother visited New York, Bourke took her to hear him speak. She knew nothing of his subject but found herself so moved that tears poured down her cheeks. Bourke turned around as he finished to catch her eye and gave her the wickedest of winks. (Sarah Bernhardt made the same confession to her—there was never a moment when she could not wink at a stage hand.)

Not all great orators can be equally riveting at the dinner table, but Lord Ripon stated in an article about Bourke: 'When I was a young man we used to regard Carlyle as the greatest conversationalist of his time. Well, I heard Carlyle and Gladstone many times and I am quite convinced that in wit, wisdom and elegance of expression neither of them approached the American statesman Bourke Cockran.'

Jennie captured him for her dinner parties and then an amusing friendship sprang up between these two hot-blooded individuals. Bourke had recently lost his second wife and he was nursing a raw heart. He had come to Paris for a change of scene. Jennie on the rebound *was* a change of scene. The two of them could not but be mutually attracted, but their relationship entailed the clash of broadswords rather than the handing of bouquets. Two beings of violently tempestuous nature, they each complained about their 'romance' to Leonie. Bourke said that Jennie wore him out—she was so overcharged with energy, and Jennie said it was exhausting to be alone with Bourke, they quarrelled unless she had a table of guests where he could 'show off'. Jennie and Leonie never dominated the conversation, but they were past masters at the art of starting up subjects when men who could talk were at their disposal—an art not to be despised, though somewhat corresponding to that of ball boy at tennis.

Battered Jennie needed to be helped to her feet and here was the man to do it. Bourke needed diversion and here was the cleverest hostess in Europe. So the sun shone again and the blows of winter were forgotten. Clara just looked pretty and admired all the contestants. She was busy having a very discreet love affair with King Milan of Serbia. Jennie was horrid to her about it, and said that Milan didn't know how to use a knife and fork!

Unselfish Leonie, the quietest but also the wittiest of the sisters, immediately recognised the calibre of Bourke Cockran. He was a man after her own heart, so erudite, so humorous, with that prodigious memory for literary quotation. He could be as versatile in Greek as in French and English, but few dinner tables could appreciate this, and he dropped his knowledge sparingly. In a way Leonie fell in love with Bourke as she had with Charles Kinsky, but she left him to 'poor darling Jennie' who wanted to drive around in his open landau and do all those expensive things which Mr Cockran was well able to afford. After all, she was happily married and poor Jennie was 'unhappily unmarried'. The consolation must be hers. So the exuberant Jennie drove and flirted with Bourke Cockran and introduced him to *le beau monde* while Leonie became his confidante.

186

After the Grand Prix in mid-June everyone left Paris and Jennie moved to Aix-les-Bains (for her health!) She was there when Mrs Everest died and Winston wrote a letter choked with emotion. 'Everything that could be done—was done. . . . She was delighted to see me on Monday night and I think my coming made her die happy. Her last words were of Jack. I shall never know such a friend again.' She whom Jennie had only half-appreciated and the Duchess of Marlborough called 'horrid old Everest' had played her part and gone. The seed of kindness she had planted in a brave little boy's heart would live on. Three weeks after her funeral Winston visited Blenheim in mournful mood, writing to his mother:

23 July, 1895   Blenheim
All the trees in leaf and flowers everywhere. I went this morning to Bladon to look at Papa's grave. The service in the little church was going on and the voices of the children singing all added to the beauty and restfulness of the spot. The hot sun of the last few days has dried up the grass a little—but the rose bushes are in full bloom and make the churchyard very bright. I was so struck by the sense of quietness & peace as well as by the old world air of the place—that my sadness was not unmixed with solace. It is the spot of all others he would have chosen. I think it would make you happier to see it.

This mood continued to show in letters throughout the summer. He thought nostalgically of Connaught Place and the 'days when fortune still smiled'. 'My darling Mummy. I am longing for the day when you will be able to have a little house of your own and when I can really feel there is such a place as home.'

Jennie talked a great deal about Winston to Bourke Cockran who, having no son of his own, wistfully enjoyed helping the young to find their feet. It was not Bourke, however, who advised her to write suggesting 'Supply of Army Horses' as a suitable *special study*! 'No, my dearest Mamma—I think something more literary and less material would be the sort of mental medicine I need!' protested Winston.

When Bourke returned to America, he casually asked Jennie to send her son, should he ever visit New York, to stay in his apartment. If Winston was interested in politics he could give him a few tips.

he promised to keep the eventuality in mind, for indeed she did not want Winston to forget his American heritage.

She and Bourke Cockran parted none too soon. Their duet was that of two pairs of cymbals. But both had been stimulated and Jennie returned to England mightily pleased with a summer which had 'restored her health' and served Charles Kinsky right!

✣ 20

The occasion to pass on Bourke's invitation arrived extremely soon. Having bought a new house Jennie went to Scotland, whence she wrote to her sister Clara on October 3rd: '. . . I shall go to the Mintos for a few days & then to London to look after "35A *Greater Cumberland Place*" as the boys call it—I hope to get in to it the end of November; but you know how long it takes to do anything & I am going to have it all painted from top to toe, electric light, hot water, etc., I have got Leonie's man Wallace to see to the work. . . . How nice it will be when we are all together again in our own "owns"! The boys are so delighted at the thought of "ringing their own front door" they can think of nothing else—You poor dear Puss! You must not get low & blue—after all if yr health & spirits are good *c'est tout ce qui'l faut*—Remember the saying— that 3 things alone are necessary for happiness—if you choose to count them. "Health, Peace & Competency." I really think you can aspire to all 3—As for the bonheur du foyer who has it? I haven't for years as you know—but if I had to lead my own life over again with dear R. just as it was I would—in preference to anyone else— & so wd you with Moreton—So it is no use repining—Cheer up— you have lots of people who love you including your "I am boring" [King Milan of Serbia]!'

Winston had indeed been writing wistfully; 'Poor old Everest— how she would have loved to see us ensconced in a house once again . . .' but now he suddenly changed his tune. Jennie had to realise that he had become the busiest and most unexpected of lieutenants. On October 4th he announced:

My dearest Mamma,
I daresay you will find the contents of this letter somewhat startling. The fact is that I have decided to go with a great friend of mine, one of the subalterns in the regiment, to America & the W. Indies. . . . We shall go to New York & after a stay there move in a steamer to the W. Indies—to Havana where all the Government troops are collecting to go up country & suppress the revolt that is still simmering on, after that train by Jamaica and Hayti to New York & so home.

Jennie sought to throw cold water, she warned that the trip would cost much more than he estimated 'especially in New York; N.Y. is *fearfully* expensive and you will be bored to death there—all men are'.

But within a week her son, with permission from the Commander-in-Chief, had obtained maps from the Director of Military Intelligence who asked Winston and another officer Reggie Barnes to collect military information. 'This invests our mission with almost an official character & cannot fail to help one in the future', wrote the twenty-year-old, and made an arrangement with the *Daily Graphic* to publish his war letters.

Jennie relented and offered to pay his ticket as a birthday present. Naturally she handed on Mr Cockran's invitation.

So it was that two English officers arrived at 763 Fifth Avenue and the impressionable Winston made the first serious friend of his life. He had no idea what 'mother's friend' would be like. And Bourke could only have expected a callow young man, the son of a famous English parliamentarian and what probably interested him more—the grandson of old Leonard Jerome.

When the young men came down to dinner they found that Mr Cockran, who neither drank nor smoked himself, entertained in tremendous style. The food, the wines, the cigars were perfect. And Winston, straight from the barracks of Aldershot where horses were the chief topic of conversation, found himself enthralled by the rolling, thunderous cannonade of Bourke's stories. Perhaps wisely, Jennie had not briefed him on Mr Cockran so he was able to feel the full surprise impact.

My father, who knew Bourke well in later years—indeed he was married in his house—has written in a biographical introduction:

Bourke Cockran! The magical name, the silver tongue and the golden heart! in the thunderous United States, where the lightning generations flash and break across each other's tracks, and in the silent spaces of his native Ireland the name lives like a pealing memory for those who heard him, or even as the sound of far-forgotten wars beyond the mountains for those who read and followed his words.

But how to evoke the voice which has passed into the soundless land? How to reproduce Bourke's conversation 'which drowned all opponents and convulsed all listeners'?

No recordings of Cockran's voice exist, but an echo of his artistry, of his command of language and his sense of values will ripple on in audible history, for Winston was his rapt pupil! There at Bourke's candlelit dinner table the twenty-year-old red-head lapped up talk so good that in future years he would pay his host this tribute: 'I must record the strong impression which this remarkable man made upon my untutored mind. I have never seen his like, or in some respects his equal . . . his conversation, in point, in pith, in rotundity, in antithesis, and in comprehension, exceeded anything I have ever heard.'

Far from the boredom which Jennie had assured him awaited men in New York, Winston discovered excitements of every sort, for Bourke introduced him to the city's interesting personalities. He gave a large dinner for him, inviting the leading lawyers and judges, and he enabled him to attend an important murder trial. He had intended to take pains for Jennie's sake, but he found that he enjoyed the youth for himself. And Winston blossomed forth in the presence of this sympathetic, fascinating and mature mind.

Bourke had such warmth, he was a loving character with much to give—and he handed it out generously. Winston wrote to his mother on 10th November 1895.

763 Fifth Avenue

It is very pleasant staying here as the rooms are beautifully furnished and fitted with every convenience & also Mr Cockran is one of the most charming hosts and interesting men I have met. . . .

I have great discussions with Mr Cockran on every conceivable subject from Economics to yacht racing. He is a clever man and one from whose conversation much is to be learned.

There were also Jerome cousins to take him out: 'We are members of all the Clubs & one person seems to vie with another in trying to make our time pleasant. . . .' And in a long letter to Leonie he analysed his impressions: 'Altogether my dear Aunt Leonie, my mind is full of unreconcilable facts. The comfort of their cars & the disgraceful currency—the hospitality of American Society & the vulgarity of their Press—present to me a problem of great complexity.'

To Jack he wrote: 'I think, mind you, that vulgarity is a sign of strength. A great crude, strong, young people are the Americans—like a boisterous, healthy boy among enervated but wellbred ladies & gentlemen.'

For a week Winston viewed New York with Bourke Cockran. They even went out with the Fire Commissioner to practice alerts on fire stations. Within five and a half seconds of the bell the horses had been rushed into the shafts, the harness fell on them and they were galloping down the street. Great fun!

Travelling on with Reggie Barnes to Cuba, where a nationalist insurrection against Spain had turned into a full-sized war, Winston went straight to the front whence he wrote exciting despatches for the *Daily Graphic*. He spent his twenty-first birthday under fire and was given a Spanish military decoration.

Jennie may have sighed at Winston's longing for danger, but he wrote so happily on December 6th: 'The General, a very brave man—in a white and gold uniform on a grey horse—drew a great deal of fire onto us and I heard enough bullets whistle and hum past to satisfy me for some time to come. He rode right up to within 500 yards of the enemy and there we waited till the fire of the Spanish infantry drove them from their position. We had great luck in not losing more than we did—but as a rule the rebels shot very high. We stayed by the General all the time and so were in the most dangerous place in the field.'

Winston was back in England before March and much criticised in the Press. One paper commented: 'Spending a holiday in fighting other people's battles is rather an extraordinary proceeding even for a Churchill.' But Winston felt he had started to make a name for himself.

Having reported the war from the Spanish side he naturally appeared biased against the insurgents, and America favoured any anti-colonial revolt. Winston wrote to Bourke Cockran after his return: '29 February [1896] . . . I hope the United States will not force Spain to give up Cuba—unless you are prepared to accept responsibility for the results of such action. If the States cares to take Cuba—though this would be very hard on Spain—it would be the best and most expedient course for both the island and the world in general. But I hold it a monstrous thing if you are going to merely procure the establishment of another South American Republic—which however degraded and irresponsible is to be backed in its action by the American people—without their maintaining any sort of control over its behaviour.'

Winston had heard Bourke make one or two minor speeches and the rhythms of great oratory remained echoing in his mind.

Bourke maintained that eloquence springs from sincerity and that to speak well a man ought to be stung. But more than this is needed. The golden voice of Bourke Cockran, those vocal chords forged in western Ireland where some thousand years of beautiful speech has kept music in ordinary talk, could not be passed on, but his sense of drama and of timing a cutting shaft was possible to practise. His dicta sounded simple. 'What people really want to hear is the truth—it is the exciting thing—speak the simple truth.' Winston, talkative himself had listened spellbound while Bourke, relaxed in his library, read favourite speeches aloud—visualising the annihilation of opponents or the eulogy of a dead Tammany leader: 'Only in a republic like ours could this child of poor parents, of limited education in his early life and with no advantages, save those he made for himself, have risen to a position of eminence and power in the councils of the nation. . . . No sense of fear ever deterred him from denouncing the wicked and the venal and no sense of expediency ever led him to accept the support of a hand which was tarnished with political immorality. . . .' The grandeur of the phrases and the clarity of delivery were like wine to a young man who intended to learn to speak in public.

Bourke promised to post on his speeches . . . a sort of correspondence course in oratory! On April 26th, 1896, Bourke wrote:

'I was so profoundly impressed with the vigor of your language & the breadth of your views as I read your criticism of my speech that I conceived a very high opinion of your future career.'

They disputed Home Rule for Ireland. Here of course Cockran, who was an Irishman born and bred, held strong views on national freedom. Winston replied in his father's vein:

27 April 1896: Does Germany surrender Alsace and Lorraine? Does Austria give up Hungary? Does Turkey release Armenia? or Spain grant autonomy to Cuba? One more instance—should the United States accede to the demand for Confederate independence? And one more argument. You may approve of Home Rule on principle but I defy you to produce a workable measure of it.'

Winston meant of course that it was unworkable because of Protestant Ulster. Irishmen in America tended to forget the Black North.

In London Jennie was now installing herself in 35A Great Cumberland Place, a late Georgian house needing only six or seven servants to run and lying just outside Mayfair, so that she could commend herself for economy.

Among the several hundred letters written to her by the Prince of Wales, many are addressed to 35A Great Cumberland Place. He never dated a letter, but happily Jennie kept the envelopes with postmarks which clearly show not only the date but his and her whereabouts. Their junketings make a biographer's head spin. H.R.H. writes from Sandringham, Windsor, Easton Lodge, Nice, the yacht *Osborne*, Scotland and Germany, and the letters are addressed to Jennie on her tours of the big country houses of England. No member of Edwardian society seemed to stay a week in the same place. The early letters begin 'My dear Lady Randolph'; this changes in 1896 to '*Ma chère Amie*' and all are signed '*Tout à vous, Albert Edward*' (or '*A. E.*'). None of the letters are particularly interesting, though all are extremely human. Obviously they were very good friends indeed, obviously they discussed their own and other people's love affairs, but no note of tenderness enters the Prince's missives. There is plenty of chaff, numerous compliments and some stern advice, but one suspects those innumerable tête-à-tête meals were chiefly devoted to laughing at other people.

Hardly a week passes in 1896 and 1897 in which H.R.H. does not ask if he may call at five, or thank her for a charming dinner.

Sometimes he asks her to choose his *invités*—'you will make it a success'. There are countless private jokes and double meanings which exclamation marks imply were saucy, but the tone over ten years' correspondence never grows more than extremely friendly. On September 8th, 1895, the Prince wonders, when Jennie was much seen at Cowes in the company of handsome Hugh Warrender, 'where your next loved victim is . . . !' We wonder too. They evidently discussed betting and racing. The Prince is delighted she backs his Derby winner 'Persimmon' and he takes interest in her clothes and compliments her on her tact. How, one wonders, could the heir to the throne find time for such a profusion of little notes about dinners and race meetings and social flirtations?

When in the September of 1896 the 4th Hussars sailed for India the Prince writes: 'I hope I shall see Winston so as to wish him good-bye', and Jennie gives him constant news during her son's absence.

Jennie had indeed tried hard all this summer to obtain Winston another journalistic commitment. Kitchener was organising an expedition up the Nile and there was tribal unrest in Matabeleland, but Winston's efforts to see action were frustrated. In July he had tried to get attached to the 9th Lancers, departing to South Africa. 'I have applied to their colonel to take me should such a contingency arise—and Bill Beresford has wired to him on my behalf . . . my dear Mamma you cannot think how I would like to sail in a few days to scenes of adventure & excitement—to places where I could gain experience and derive advantage—rather than to the tedious land of India where I shall be equally out of the pleasures of peace & the chances of war. . . I cannot believe that with all the influence you possess and all those who would do something for my father's sake—that I could not be allowed to go—were those influences properly exerted . . . I put it down here—definitely on paper—that you really ought to leave no stone unturned to help me at such a period. Years may pass before such chances occur again.'

'Adventure and excitement'—these are words which make elderly generals frown and yet a young man must crave them. But all pleadings fell through and Winston had to sail with his own regiment. On September 23rd Jennie wrote to him: 'I am thinking of you in the Red Sea piping hot—here it is like December. I have thought of you so much darling boy since we parted at South-ampton. . . . I had a long talk with the Prince at Tulchan and he begged me to tell you that you ought not to race—only because it is not a good business in India—they are not square & the best of reputations get spoiled over it. *You* don't know but everyone else does that it is next to impossible to race in India & keep clean hands. It appears that Colonel Brab told the Prince that he wished you hadn't this pony. Sell it & buy polo ponies—I'm *sure* you will regret it if you don't. . . . Now my lecture is over. . . .'

Blandford's widow, the kindly 'Duchess Lily', had generously given Winston a £200 charger when he passed his examination into Sandhurst and now her new husband, Lord William Beresford, thought a 'racing pony' named Lily would be an appropriate gift to dispatch to Bombay.

Winston wrote back hotly defending his ability to keep clear of cheats: 'Of course I shall do what you wish in the matter & if you insist on my getting rid of the pony I will sell her—but . . . it would be a very great disappointment to me & rob my life out here of one strong interest . . . these sort of valuable ponies are not sold every day for £300 when they are untried & unknown . . . this pony was given to me by Bill Beresford, not in order that I might convert it into pounds & shillings but to keep & use.'

Jennie continued to repeat warnings while her son couldn't understand why she should distrust his 'ability to resist the temptation to resort to malpractice', adding 'let me beg you, my dear Mamma, to bear in mind that it is one thing for you to say "sell" & quite another for me to find anyone to buy. . . . ' She continues her warnings and on October 8th she writes: 'The Prince is coming to dine with me on Sunday & I have asked Lily & Bill.' And in November, while staying with the Prince of Wales, she gets back to the subject. 'How I should love to be with you my darling boy. . . . I don't want to enter a long dissertation on Racing in India, I am only telling you what the Prince & other people say . . . and that is that there is very little fair play in India & if you are honest you have very little chance of winning with the best horse. And remember one error of judgement will be counted against you.'

Many of Jennie's letters to her sons are written while staying with the Prince and Princess at Sandringham. She wrote to Winston: 'I came here on Monday . . . a very pleasant party although not wildly exciting . . . the Pembrokes, Marlboroughs, Cadogans, Cooch Behars, etc. I am going to stay over Sunday when the Salis-

burys, Arthur Balfour & the new Bishop of London are coming—
the latter used to be private tutor to your father—Moreton Frewen
has been rather foolish—went to America to help Bryan (on account
of financial propensities & has got himself disliked in consequence—
as if he hadn't better things to do.) Bless you. Take care of yourself—
I love your letters. When do you begin yr Hindustani? My love to
the Bungalow!' The Hindustani grammar remained unopened.
Winston was saving himself for other rostrums.

And then to Jack: '...I think you are right about staying another
term at Harrow—if it is not too hard for you. Of course I have
given in about Winston's pony—and I hope he will sell it after it has
won a race—if it ever does! It has been very pleasant here—lovely
weather until today—they killed 6000 head of game. Sunny and
Consuelo Marlborough were here also and Cooch Behars—but all
the people went yesterday and we have a new lot... Lord Salisbury,
Mr Balfour....'

It must have been curious for her, sitting at dinner with these
men who had worked so close to Randolph in the past, who had
raised themselves on his wit and slipped away uneasily when he
went too far.

While Jennie enjoyed the 'Prince's set', Winston enjoyed riding in
military races and he proudly wore his father's racing colours, pink
and chocolate. But when out of the saddle he found time dragged.
Conversation in the officers' mess struck him as puerile, but it ill-
behoved a new officer to pass judgement. He began to spend
evenings reading seriously or sending letters begging for news from
a wider-minded world. On 21st October, 1896, he wrote his mother:
'Bourke Cockran writes me a long letter—describing his campaign
against Bryan & is very pleased with himself indeed. He has had
great audiences and much enthusiasm. He has received the volume
I sent him and is delighted. I shall endeavour to lure him out here—
India to an American would be the most alluring experience possible
to a human being. . . . Do persuade people to write. Aunt Clara,
who writes such good letters or Aunt Leonie. Turn on the devoted
Warrender—stimulate Jack and above all write yourself. The
regiment is completely isolated. I find no one worth speaking to or
looking at—in the social circles of Bangalore. Miss Plowden was
here last week—but alas—I never met her in England so forbore
to call.' Two weeks later he achieved his object.

'*4 Nov.* I was introduced to Miss Pamela Plowden—who lives here. I must say she is the most beautiful girl I have ever seen—"Bar none" as the Duchess Lily says. We are going to try to do the City of Hyderabad together—on an elephant.'

On November 19th, as Winston's twenty-second birthday approached, his mother wrote from Lady Desborough's house, Panshanger. 'Darling. I wish I cd give you a good kiss—Meanwhile a cheque will be quite as acceptable £50. I know you are hard up, but so am I & I pray you to consider that it means a great deal to me & you must make it go as far as possible . . . an enormous party here . . . lots of people ask after you. . . . You must write to people if you want letters.'

She was a fine one to counsel economy but Jennie determined that her son should keep the family's reduced circumstances in mind.

From the first Winston took a dislike to Anglo-Indian society, and especially to the women he saw at the races. 'Nasty vulgar creatures all looking as though they thought themselves great beauties', and before he had spent two months at Bangalore he was writing to his mother: 'If I can only get hold of the right people my stay here might be of value. Had I come to India as an M.P.—however young & foolish, I could have had access to all who know & can convey. As a soldier my intelligent interests are supposed to stop short at Polo, racing & Orderly Officer. I vegetate—even reading is an effort & I am still in Gibbon.'

Winston's irritation at finding himself tied to a regiment in India grew. He begged his mother to get him a transfer. '*Please do your best* . . .' he begged. 'Two years in Europe—with a campaign thrown in—would I think qualify me to be allowed to beat my sword into a paper cutter & my sabre tache into an election address.' Winston writhed with jealousy at the thought of other young men getting into Parliament or winning medals in Eygpt. 'I meet none but soldiers & other people equally ignorant of the country & hear nothing talked but "shop" and racing. . . .'

Jennie did her best, but an importunate mother can madden the staff. On November 27th she wrote from Blenheim: 'I am going to wire to you today to write at once & apply to the War Office to be allowed to go to Egypt. . . . The chances of being taken are extremely remote as the competition is tremendous—but there is an outside chance of Sir H. Kitchener's personal influence being brought to bear & I am going to try it for you. Should it succeed you must know & remember that it means signing a paper to the effect that you will serve in the Egyptian Army for two years—& there will be no getting out of it if you don't like it—On the other hand should this fail you must not let it unsettle you & make you take a dislike to your work in India. Life is not always what one wants it to be, but to make the best of it as it is, is the only way of being happy—Of course the War Office will take no notice of yr application but as soon as you have applied I will write to Kitchener & if he asks for you you will probably be allowed to go. In my heart of hearts I have doubts as to whether it wd be the best thing for you—but Fate will decide.'

While waiting, she tried to keep his spirits up. 'I read interesting accounts of your polo matches in the Field which I send you. It must have been great fun & very exciting. Your last letter of 18 Nov. seems rather depressed. . . . I have been busy arranging things for Jack. . . . I am much against him going into the Army & I can't afford to put him in a smart cavalry regt., & in anything else he would be lost & unhappy. Besides at the best it is a poor career—I think he might do at the Bar. He has plenty of ability & common sense—a good presence & with perseverance & influence he ought to get on—The City he hates—He is going to leave Harrow this term. Spend a year or more in France & Germany. Then study Greek for a year with a tutor . . . & go to Oxford. . . .'

On December 17th [1896] she wrote from Wynyard Park: 'I am having a very pleasant week here although it is rather a boy & girl party. Both old Ld Crichton & Herbert Crichton are here—the latter asked a great deal after you & intends answering your letter— he looks very good-looking in his red evening coat. There is 7 or 8 degrees of frost & snow on the ground—so the hunters are in despair—I am beginning to wonder about going to St Moritz—it is so far & expensive and I want to go later to see that statue W.S. is making of yr Father—Old Jim Lowther is here & we have long talks about politics—he is in great admiration of Rosebery's Edinburgh speech. They say that Ld R. is going to marry Lady Dudley—I don't believe it—I don't think much of a woman whose children dislike her . . . I don't know how soon I may hear from the Sirdar but I will wire you if he takes you, you will have to square your Colonel . . . I am sending you by this mail 12 vols of Macaulay—8 history 4 essays.'

'Dec. 24, [1896] Blenheim.

'Here I am with Jack until next Monday & very pleasant it is although mostly family—12 degrees of frost, all hunting people cursing. I envy you your rose gardens & sun. If you don't go to Egypt (which I am beginning to think is more than doubtful as I am told Kitchener won't take anyone under 27) I will come & stay with you next year. . . . Sunny tells me that Ld Albemarle—who has just returned from Egypt gives a dreadful account of the cholera—However when the Sirdar has accepted you it will be time enough to worry. Darling Boy how I wish that you were with me & that we could have a good talk about everything. I am glad that you are beginning to like India & that it won't be distasteful to you to remain there if the Egyptian plot fails. There are drawbacks to everything of course. Meanwhile enjoy the intervals of polo & military work. I hope you will find time for reading. Think how you will regret the waste of time when you are in politics & will feel yr want of knowledge—I am looking forward to the time when we shall be together again & all my political ambitions shall be centred in you.'

Jennie induced Kitchener to put her son's name down on the special service list for Egypt, but there were no immediate vacancies.

Winston had to bide his time in India playing polo and reading Gibbon and Macaulay, and writing to Bourke Cockran. He took Jennie's admonition seriously—'Think how you will regret the waste of time when you are in politics & will feel yr want of knowledge.' Bourke Cockran sent him more speeches and when alone he could read them through, practising those intonations which lent fire and clarity to the sonorous sentence.

On November 3rd, when newly arrived and sensing boredom, Winston had written a very long letter to Bourke Cockran. It began with an assessment of the expenses of the recent American election and an argument that the American system of government cost far more than the English: 'You may rejoice that it is better to be free than wealthy. That is a question about which discussion is possible: but I assert that the English labourer enjoys an equal freedom with the American workman & in addition derives numerous advantages from those appurtenances of monarchy which make

200

government dignified and easy—& the intercourse with foreign states more cordial.

'I know what a stalwart democrat you are. But look at the question philosophically—cynically if you like. Calculate the profit and the loss—Consider the respect human beings instinctively and involuntarily feel for that which is invested with pomp and circumstance. As a legislator discard unbending principles & ethics and avail yourself of the weaknesses of humanity. Yours may be the government for the gods—ours at least is suitable to men.

'Your tour of political meetings must indeed have been interesting and I regret so much that I had not the opportunity of accompanying you and listening to your speeches. From what I have seen—I know that there are few more fascinating experiences than to watch a great mass of people under the wand of the magician. There is no gift so rare or so precious as the gift of oratory—so difficult to define or impossible to acquire.

'My Indian experiences have now lasted over a month. . . . This country would fascinate you. Indeed I imagine no more interesting experience than for an American to visit India. . . . I give you an open invitation to come. My house is large and there is ample room for visitors. . . . You must come out here if only for a flying visit.

'Yours very sincerely Winston S. Churchill.

'PS. I cannot tell you how much letters are appreciated out here—so do write. W. S. C.'

Lieutenant Churchill craved some one of intelligence to talk to but Bourke did not reach India and he had to work alone, modelling his literary style on Gibbon and Macaulay and his style in oratory on what he could remember of the music of Bourke's delivery.

When asked to make a speech he would be ready. But Winston was only reaching twenty-two and his brother officers expressed little appreciation of a first lieutenant scribbling away at an article (unpublished) entitled *The Scaffolding of Rhetoric* which began: 'The orator wields a power more durable than that of a great king. He is an independent force in the world. . . . Abandoned by his party, betrayed by his friends, stripped of his offices, whoever can command this power is still formidable. . . .' Mr Churchill had more than military races in view.

🙣 21

All through the spring of 1897 Jennie endeavoured to aid a son tormented by ambition. When some young officer received a medal for service in South Africa and command of a native police force Winston could not contain his envy: 'Compare that with the reward of those who conscientiously perform the routine duties you are always advocating.' Then he wanted to apply for three months' leave in England to pull strings for himself.

To Jack, who had left Harrow, she wrote:

Dearest Jack,

I enclose a letter from Winston . . . I also had one from Kinaird-Smith—nothing in particular but he rather hints that he thinks it would be a mistake for Winston to come home on such short leave, and it wd only unsettle him—and I think so too. If Egypt comes off he will naturally leave India. After all he has only been 6 months in India and has not seen anything of the country. I'm afraid he is very restless. . . .'

When Jack departed to France she implored him: 'As I said darling child remember this year is the only one of yr life you can give up entirely to French. Make the most of it. Do like Winston—talk incessantly.'

Never a great hand at finance herself, Jennie tried to impart a healthy respect for solvency into her sons: 'I cannot increase your allowance', she wrote to Winston. 'As for your wild talk of coming home for a month it is completely out of the question. Not only on

202

account of money but for the sake of your reputation. They will say, & with some reason, that you can't stick to anything. You have only been out 6 months & it is on the cards that you may be called to Egypt. There is plenty for you to do in India. I confess I am quite disheartened about you. You seem to have no real purpose in life & won't realise at the age of 22 that for a man life means work—& hard work—if you mean to succeed.' But the deep natural feeling between them remained and Winston continued to pour out his heart in unconstrained letters, and Jennie to sympathise: 'I can quite understand what you say of the Anglo-Indian society. It must be odious. . . . How little one hears of any of the generals in time of peace. There is really very little honour & glory to be got out of the Army. A moderate M.P. gets better known in the country & has more chance of success than a really clever man in the Army. . . .' She tried to share her own interests with him. 'We dined with Cecil Rhodes last night. I cannot say that I was very much impressed by him. He does not give one the idea of a clever man—a strong one if you like, determined & dogged but intellectually weak. He is going to appear before the House on Thursday which I think is too late in the day. No one wants it.'

The transformation from lazy schoolboy into aspiring politician seemed to have occurred in a flash. Winston's letters to his mother now burgeoned with political views and even here she did not hesitate to administer rebuke: 'I hope you have changed yr mind about Crete—subsequent events must show you that the Concert of Europe were *obliged* to act as they did. . . .'

Winston enjoyed his correspondence. He was beginning to savour words; Lord Salisbury, who had broken his father, he described as 'an able & obstinate man, who joins the brain of a statesman to the delicate susceptibilities of a mule'. The delegated duties of Brigade Major delighted: 'I am becoming my dear Mamma a very "correct" soldier. Full of zeal etc. Even in homeopathic doses—Responsibility is an exhilarating drink. . . .' This was at about the time that owing to a misunderstanding one of his cheques bounced and Jennie flew into a temper; writing on March 5th: 'I was glad to get your nice letter telling me of yr work as Brigade Major. What an extraordinary boy you are as regards yr business affairs. You never say a word about them & then spring things on one. If you only told me when you were hard up—& why—perhaps

I shd not be so angry. But I don't believe you ever know how you stand with your account at the Bank. I marvel at their allowing you to overdraw as you do. Neither the Westminster or the National Bank will let me overdraw £5 without telling me at once. Dearest this is the only subject on which we ever fall out. I do wish you wd try & reform. If you only realise how little I have & how impossible it is for me to get any more. I have raised all I can & assure you unless something extraordinary turns up I see ruin staring me in the face. Out of £2,700 a year £800 of it goes to you two boys, £710 for house rent & stables, which leaves me £1,500 for everything —Taxes, stables, food, dress, travelling & now I have to pay interest on money borrowed. I really fear for the future. I am telling you all this darling in order that you may see how impossible it is for me to help you—& how you *must* in future depend on yourself.'

In their long correspondence she affectionately scolds him for almost everything, for extravagance, for ignorance, for being pompous, for not brushing his teeth, for buying polo ponies and for not buying polo ponies. On March 11th [1897] she enquires: 'I hope you have received the books I sent & are duly grateful. . . .' Still trying to dissuade Winston from returning to England she wrote; 'I really think there is a good chance of yr getting to Egypt & in any case you are gaining much military experience in India & showing that you can work & do something. Darling I lay awake nights thinking about you & how much I want to help you—if only I had some money I *wd* do it. I am so proud of all your great & endearing qualities. I feel sure that if you live you will make a name for yourself but I know that to do it you have to be made of stern stuff & not mind sacrifice & self denial. I feel I am reading you a lecture & you will think my letter a bore. . . .'

Unamused by the officers' mess, the fidgety lieutenant was only too anxious to exhibit 'stern stuff' to his dearest Mamma, but the little wars kept blowing up so far from the 4th Hussars.

As her income diminished Jennie grew increasingly testy about money. Clara Frewen had through her husband (now known as *Mortal Ruin*) involved both her sisters in a financial mess. A trickster called Mr Cruikshank had defrauded them of several thousand much-needed pounds. This preyed on Jennie's mind until she felt it incumbent to travel to Monte Carlo, hoping that Fortune might treat her more fairly at the gaming tables. Having installed Jack at

Versailles she wrote to Winston on April 2nd: 'I was rather lucky at the table and made enough to pay my expenses. . . .The Prince came over from Nice & dined with me. I told him of your wish to come home & he begged me to tell you that he was very much against it & thought you ought to take the opportunity you had to go to the frontier & see something of the country.'

She arranged for the Marquis de Brèteuil and for Bourke Cockran to give Jack occasional meals and on her return to Great Cumberland Place she deluged him with maternal advice: 'Bourke gave an account of your breakfast—I am not reading you a lecture darling boy but you don't write as fully as you might about all you do & people you see. I have had a long letter from Winston who has of course a wild scheme to go as war correspondent with the Greeks. Luckily the war will be over by then . . . I hope you are working hard. Of course I like you to enjoy yrself but I am not certain that you don't go too often to Paris. Jack darling the temptations of a big town are strong I know—and you are very young but you are sensible beyond your years, and a great dear—and I am sure that my confidence in you won't be misplaced. Keep to good society & the friends I have introduced you to—and you won't come to harm and above all *work*.'

Despite the cautions of his mother Winston asked for leave and returned to England in May 1897. He had hoped to look in on the Turkish-Greek war as a correspondent but annoyingly for him it ended just as he reached Brindisi. In London he found his mother out of mourning and the life and soul of the 'Prince of Wales's set'. She obtained invitations for both her sons to the Duchess of Devonshire's famous fancy dress ball. Winston improvised a soldierly costume and Jack went as a sixteenth-century French courtier. Mrs Everest would have enjoyed a hand in this—And what would her ladyship have thought up? There were several Napoleons glaring at each other on the great staircase of Devonshire House but Jennie and Leonie had no rivals in their choice of costume. Wearing a great Byzantine head-dress, and carrying a golden orb in one hand and a huge lily in the other, Jennie represented the Empress Theodora while Leonie had chosen her favourite Wagnerian character, Brünnhilde. Helmeted, and with sword and shield, Leonie could not venture on to the dance floor, nor could Jennie or many another lady robed for coronation or beheading. Some carried eagles with outspread wings, some harps, goblets or sceptres. There were eight duchesses present, the richest of whom chose to come comfortably as Charlotte Corday in a mob cap. The host and hostess, attired as Queen Zenobia of Palmyra and the Emperor Charles V, greeted their guests at the top of their marble staircase. The Prince of Wales strutted as a magnificent Grand Prior and the Princess as Marguerite de Valois. Many people had copied portraits of their ancestors and several brought relatives in their retinues. Lady Tweedmouth as Queen Elizabeth had eight huge Yeomen of the Guard in attendance and Daisy, Princess of Pless, attired as Cleopatra in a 'gorgeous dress of blue silk covered with diamonds and turquoises', surrounded herself with gaudily-costumed negro slaves among whom was her brother, the handsome young George Cornwallis-West. Finding himself unappreciated with a blackened face he went home early, cursing the theatrical designer who had clad him in 'a multicoloured bed-quilt'. So it was that Jennie first set eyes on her future husband.

Jennie was much amused at two statuesque sisters dressed as *The Furies,* who kept their hair in place with hair nets. One costume she had seen many years before at her father's fancy dress party in New York. The fascinating Mrs Ronalds, who had then won the palm dressed as *Music* with a coronet of crochets in her hair lit by gas, wore the same outfit—only the head-dress was now lit by electricity. Leonard Jerome had been in love with her. Now the musical Duke of Edinburgh was her admirer. The bars of music on her Brompton cemetery tombstone with 'Forever thine' would guard her heart's secret.

Towards the end of the evening Jack Churchill, somewhat overplaying his part, challenged a Crusader with a double-handed sword to a duel. Winston acted as second and the Empress Theodora was none too pleased when her seventeen-year-old son had to be sent home with a cut on the leg and his pink silk stockings in shreds.

So the warm weeks of the Diamond Jubilee Season rolled by and the cool winds of impending South African trouble blew but lightly into dinner table conversation. How even was the tenor of that existence. Only the insufferable Winston kept pestering generals for adventure or Tory organisers for a chance to speak.

Three weeks after the Devonshire House Ball, when many of the grandees were re-trying their costumes at country house parties, Winston mounted a political platform for the first time. He had

206

learned that the Tories needed speakers at country meetings and bazaars. 'I surveyed this prospect', he wrote in *My Early Life*, 'with the eye of an urchin looking through a pastrycook's window.' His speech, carefully prepared and delivered with the rhythms of Cockran's mighty voice in his memory, was a great success. Seldom did a Primrose League Rally receive a minutely-rehearsed, fiery oration. The newspapers noted Winston's aspiration to enter Parliament. He had slipped in the thin end of the wedge.

A week later, while staying at Deepdene with the Duchess Lily (now Lady Bill Beresford) for Goodwood Races, Winston heard that Pathan tribesmen had revolted on the Indian frontier. He hurried away from the race-course to telegraph Sir Bindon Blood, who had promised him a job in the event of a flare-up, and took the first train towards Brindisi to catch a ship back to India. Duchess Lily, who had introduced Sir Bindon to Winston at Deepdene a year previously, was somewhat dazed. One moment Winston was contented on the lawn. An hour later he had vanished in a cloud of dust. Jennie thought the departure precipitate. From Aden she received a letter asking her to perform numerous chores. He had forgotten not only his polo sticks but his little dog 'in the hurry & bustle of getting off'.

All through August she received despondent letters, for Sir Bindon Blood did not immediately reply: 'I cannot think he would willingly disappoint me & can only conclude that someone at Headquarters has put a spoke in my wheel.'

Eventually Sir Bindon wrote that he had no vacancies on his staff but if Winston could come to the Frontier as a war correspondent he would 'do a little jobbery'. Winston obtained a month's leave from his regiment and having telegraphed Jennie to get him employment with a big newspaper immediately he started the five-day train journey. 'To go as correspondent it is necessary to have a special pass & this is in some cases refused if the paper is not of sufficient importance. I hope most strongly I shall not arrive at Nowshera to find you have taken no steps. . . . Dearest Mamma before this letter reaches you I shall probably have had several experiences some of which will contain the element of danger. I view every possibility with composure. It might not have been worth my while, who am really no soldier, to risk so many fair chances on a war which can only help me directly in a profession

I mean to discard. But I have considered everything & I feel that the fact of having seen service with British troops while still a young man must give me more weight politically—must add to my claims to be listened to & may perhaps improve my prospects of gaining popularity with the country.'

Jennie did her stuff with the newspapers. After a rebuff from *The Times* she succeeded in getting Winston accredited to the *Daily Telegraph*.

Winston wrote from Malakand Camp:

5 September [1897]

My dearest Mamma,

Your telegram received. Herewith 2 letters for the D.T. I do not know what terms you made with them—but it should certainly not be less than £10 per letter. Having read please forward—and decide whether they should be signed or not. I am myself very much in favour of signing—as otherwise I get no credit for the letters. It may help me politically to come before the public in this way. . . . I live with Sir Bindon Blood—who is very kind to me. I am at present correspondent of the *Pioneer* to which I have to telegraph 300 words a day. At the first opportunity I am to be put on the strength of this force—which will give me a medal if I come through. As to fighting—we march tomorrow, and before a week is out, there will be a battle—probably the biggest yet fought on the frontier this year. By the time this reaches you everything will be over so that I do not mind writing about it. I have faith in my star—that is that I am intending to do something in this world. If I am mistaken—what does it matter? My life has been a pleasant one. . . .

Jennie wrote him on 9th September.

'My darling Winston, Again I write only a line for I feel you cannot receive this for at least 5 or 6 weeks. . . . Old Lawson [owner of *Daily Telegraph*] answered a letter I wrote him by telegram saying "Tell him to post picturesque forcible letters".'

And on September 21st she wrote from Scotland: 'I am surprised not to have had a wire from you from Nowshera—I try to think that no news is good news, but I confess I wish I could hear from you. . . . There are so many things I want to talk to you about but I am so in the dark as to yr whereabouts or knowledge as to where

208

this is likely to reach you. . . . How you managed to get round your colonel is a mystery to me. Well! Darling I can only hope for the best and pray that all will come out well. . . . I believe in yr Lucky Star as I do in mine.'

Fifteen of Winston's letters were printed, under the signature of 'A Young Officer'. Jennie had explained this:

Alloa House, Alloa

7th October 1897

Darling Winston. . . . You may imagine with what interest I received yr letters and to know that you are safe. I suppose you will have seen some of the fighting and by the time you receive this will be thinking of returning to Bangalore. . . . I read your letters for the D.T. to Lord Minto who thought them excellent but begged me not to sign yr name. He said it was very unusual & might get you into trouble. The first one appeared yesterday headed "Indian Frontier by a young officer". The Editor wired to say they wd give £5 a column. . . . I'm afraid it's not as much as you had hoped, yr first letter was just one column. . . . I wrote to the Prince and told him to look out for your letters. Also to lots of people. You will get plenty of quodos/kudos (can't spell it). I will see that you do darling boy. . . .

Winston was incensed by the anonymity imposed on his letters. 'I had written them with the design of bringing my personality before the electorate. I had hoped that some political advantage might have accrued.' Jennie reeled under the impact of his wrath. The advice of Lord Minto was 'worthless'. She had 'not for the first time decided on a negative course'. If he was to avoid doing 'unusual things' it was difficult to see what chance he had of being more than an average person. 'I was proud of the letters & anxious to stake my reputation on them.' Winston even upbraided her for not correcting the proofs properly and allowing one letter to be cut to fit a column. Jennie could have wept. She had tried so hard. She was also ordered to get more than £5 a letter. 'Will you kindly ask Moreton Frewen if he will go & see the Editor & point out that such a sum is ridiculous.'

Mr Frewen could carry weight here for he had sent young Rudyard Kipling's verse to the *Daily Telegraph* and the paper had refused it as 'not up to our standard' about one year before Kipling soared to fame.

Jennie had rapped Winston on the knuckles for the last time. Suddenly he reversed the role. She was to fag for him with publishers and generals. She *ought* to read and correct his proofs but if she could not then a proper reader must be found. If anything went wrong it would be her fault. She took his fulminations philosophically, writing to Jack: 'Winston writes from Bangalore rather disgusted at the D.T. giving so little—but I think the Prince who is here—will give old Lawson a hint—he says he will. Poor Winny he thinks his letters are not a success—but they *are*!'

Winston's personal accounts from the North West Frontier in September and October 1897 are so graphic that it is hard to imagine a mother's feelings on reading them. These long, vivid, pencil-written letters marked 'Private' accompanied the carefully composed letters intended for the *Daily Telegraph* and gave hair-raising accounts of his own adventures near the fighting. 'I started with the Cavalry & saw the first shot fired. After half an hour's skirmishing I rode forward with the 35th Sikhs until firing got so hot that my grey pony was unsafe. I proceeded on foot. When the retirement began I remained until the last & here I was perhaps very near my end. If you read between the lines of my letter you will see that this retirement was an awful rout in which the wounded were left to be cut up horribly by these wild beasts. I was close to both officers when they were hit almost simultaneously and fired my revolver at a man at 30 yards who tried to cut up poor Hugh's body. . . . It was a horrible business for there was no help for the man that went down. I felt no excitement & very little fear. All the excitement went out when things became really deadly. . . . I do not look ahead more than a day—or further than the hills that surround the valley. . . . Europe is infinitely remote—England infinitely small—Bangalore a speck on the map of India—but here everything is life size & flesh colour.'

Did Jennie receive these letters at her house in Great Cumberland Place or in some country house? 'October 2. . . . My dearest Mamma, Since I last wrote to you we have had another severe action. . . . I was under fire for five hours but did not get into the hottest corners.'

It was, he thought, imperative to draw attention to himself and with an innocent frankness he wrote to his mother after returning to the 4th Hussars: '. . . I am very gratified to hear that my follies have not been altogether unnoticed. To ride a grey pony along a skirmish line is not a common experience. But I had to play for high stakes & have been lucky to win.'

With joy he learnt that he had been mentioned in dispatches: 'Lieutenant Churchill had made himself useful at a critical moment', said the official report. He wrote to his mother on December 2 [1897] '. . . I cannot tell you with what feeling of hope and satisfaction I receive your information that I have been mentioned in dispatches by Sir Bindon Blood. . . . I am more ambitious for a reputation for personal courage than anything else in the world. A young man should worship a young man's ideals.'

Even more sensitively he expressed these feelings to his brother: 'I never imagined such a thing possible. I had no military command and only rode about trying to attract attention when things looked a little dangerous. Perhaps my good grey pony caught the speaker's eye. I hope it is true. Being in many ways a coward—particularly at school—there is no ambition I cherish as keenly as to gain a reputation of personal courage. . . .

'I am glad your sojourn in France is over. You will find it of the greatest service in life to speak French. I wish I did. . . .

'When you get to the University—you should I think study history and economics—two of the most valuable and interesting branches of human enquiry. . . . A good knowledge of history is a quiver full of arrows in debate. . . .

'I hope too as time goes on—if money matters do not obstruct us—you will be able to travel and see something of this great Empire of ours—to the maintainance of which I shall devote my life.'

These letters crossed one from Jennie describing a big house party at Lambton Castle—the Prince, Duchess of Manchester, Lord and Lady Pembroke, etc. To all of these she spoke of Winston's doings and she could truthfully tell him what interest his letters had aroused in high places: 'Write to the Prince he will like it—I will tell him'.

By the end of the year Winston's first book *The Story of the Malakand Field Forces* had been posted to her and she was hard at work trying to find the right publisher.

She spent Christmas at Blenheim with 'Sunny' Marlborough and his American bride Consuelo Vanderbilt who has described her mother-in-law Lady Blandford and Randolph's sister Lady Sarah Wilson somewhat ungraciously in her book *The Glitter and the Gold*. But for Jennie she had only praise: 'Lady Randolph

Churchill was a beautiful woman with gaiety that made her the life and soul of any party. She was still, in middle age, the mistress of many hearts, and the Prince of Wales was known to delight in her company. Her grey eyes sparkled with the joy of living and when, as was often the case, her anecdotes were risqué it was in her eyes, as well as in her words, that one could read her implications. She was an accomplished pianist, and intelligent and informed reader and an enthusiastic advocate of any novelty. Her constant friendship and loyalty were to be precious to me in adversity!' When Consuelo visited the old Duchess in Grosvenor Square she received standing orders: 'Your first duty is to have a son, because it would be intolerable to have that little upstart Winston become Duke. . . .'

By 20th January 1898 Jennie had, through Arthur Balfour, obtained a contract with Longmans to publish *The Story of the Malakand Field Force*. Winston wrote wild with excitement: 'By its reception I shall measure the chances of my possible success in the world.'

As well as keeping an eye on vacancies in the House of Commons and attending to proof-reading, Jennie must redouble her efforts with Kitchener, whose army was about to move up the Nile. '10th January. . . . Oh how I wish I could work you up over Egypt! I know you could do it with all your influence & all the people you know. It is a pushing age & we must shove with the best.'

Winston was determined to go to Egypt. So was Jennie, but for a very different reason. On January 28th there came a few words on finance. Jennie had to read a very clear-cut letter from her twenty-three-year-old who was not pleased to learn that she had run through a quarter of her capital and had borrowed on her and his life insurances without consulting him.

'. . . Speaking quite frankly on the subject there is no doubt that we are both, you & I, equally thoughtless, spendthrift & extravagant. We both know what is good—and we both like to have it. Arrangements for paying are left to the future. My extravagances are on a smaller scale than yours. I take no credit to myself in this matter as you have kept up the house & have had to maintain a position in London. At the same time we shall vy soon come to the end of our tether. . . . I sympathise with all your extravagances—even more than you do with mine—it seems just as suicidal to me when you spend £200 on a ball dress as it does to you when I purchase a new polo pony for £100. And yet I feel that you ought to have the dress & I the polo pony. The pinch of the whole matter is that we are damned poor. . . .'

He wrote as if they were of the same age—and in a way they always would be—of the age that cannot resist a pretty dress or an outstanding horse.

In February, entrusting the proof-reading of Winston's book to Moreton Frewen, Jennie left for Egypt. Her son thought she had gone entirely on his account.

'16th Feb 1898. . . . Your telegram reached me on Saturday and I can assure you I feel vy grateful indeed to you for going to Egypt. It is an action which—if ever I have a biographer—will certainly be admired by others. I hope you may be successful. I feel almost certain you will. Your wit & tact & beauty should overcome all obstacles. . . .'

Jennie never ceased trying to help Winston but she had other fish to fry. Since Kinsky's marriage Jennie had glanced around England for good-looking young men to escort her to parties. Swains flocked to her bidding, for her looks could still silence a room. Among the officers of the Seaforth Highlanders battalion which had been advancing up the Nile was one Major Caryl Ramsden—nicknamed 'Beauty Ramsden' for the obvious reason. After a boring year in Malta, Ramsden had the luck to rejoin his regiment for Kitchener's advance. Jennie did not keep his letters. It was not as a scribbler that he excelled but as a soldier with an unfair share of good looks.

Jennie stayed at the Continental Hotel and found Cairo gay. She saw the Pyramids and wrote the appropriate things home about the Sphinx. Occasionally she sent messages to the unbending Kitchener concerning Winston kicking his heels in India. She had hardly unpacked when the first letter arrived from him: '. . . Meanwhile I hope you are making all things smooth in Egypt. As I have been attached to a Field Force I am entitled to three months' leave on full pay and shall proceed to Egypt—subject to the approval of Providence—the last week in June. You should make certain of my being employed there.'

Several letters from the Prince of Wales addressed to Jennie at the Continental survive, but she kept no diary of her peregrinations, which have only been recorded by casual letters to her sisters. After sightseeing and going to many parties she travelled up the Nile to meet Major Ramsden. Egypt is very wonderful in the early spring, scented with orange blossom and lit by a moon that grows till it makes the sky seem small. There were blissful days and nights on a *dahabeyah*—the river boat which replaced her hotel. It was all very romantic until the tearful parting when Major Ramsden received orders to rejoin his unit at Wadi Halfa. Jennie returned sadly to Port Said, only to find her ship had been delayed for several days, so she raced back up the Nile in case Ramsden had not yet departed.

He hadn't. Jennie burst into his room without knocking and found him embracing Lady Maxwell, wife of the Army Commander. A khamseen was blowing and Jennie had a temper in the best of weathers. On this occasion her outburst was overheard. Within a few hours a humorous account had been written to the Prince of Wales who was holidaying at Cannes. He thought Jennie's discomfiture a great joke.

Two letters from His Royal Highness which reached Jennie in Rome survive. In one of them he teased her: 'You had better have stuck to your old friends than gone on your Expedition of the Nile! Old friends are Best!'

She did not appreciate chaff at this juncture, and during her journey back to London she thought out a suitable reply. When Leonie hurried around to Great Cumberland Place to welcome her darling sister home she found Jennie, still in travelling clothes, scribbling away at her desk. 'Listen' and having recounted the story Jennie read out the Prince's letter and her reply: '*So* grateful for your sympathy—as your Royal Highness knows exactly *how* it feels, after being jilted by Lady Dudley!' Tactful Leonie agreed that she had compiled a masterly answer and offered to post it. She took it home and told Jennie next day that it was always wise to sleep on such missives. But Jennie composed what she considered an even wittier version and insisted on the satisfaction of slipping it into the box herself. It is unlikely that this letter has been preserved in Windsor Castle's archives, but the Prince's gentlemanly reply lies before me along with all the other letters and their precious dated envelopes: The post mark is 8th April, 1898: 'Grand Hotel, Cannes: *Ma chère Amie*, Many thanks for your two letters of 5th and 6th—I must ask your pardon if my letter pained. I had no idea "*que c'était une affaire si serieuse!*" . . .'

214

By April 15th all was forgiven. He asks her to arrange a dinner at Great Cumberland Place and compliments fly as usual: 'I must write to thank you for your charming dinner of last night. . . . I thought your party was exceptionally successful.' And, more important still: 'I am delighted with Winston's book—admirably written & most interesting.'

Jennie's pride had been scratched, but not her heart. That operation lay ahead.

22

The Prince of Wales might find *The Story of the Malakand Field Force* admirably written, but its author was rending his garments, for Uncle Moreton Frewen had made a fine hash of correcting the proofs. Not only had he failed to notice errors but he had altered the punctuation and in some cases the sense of the book which Winston had hoped would bring him immediate fame.

Jennie was not up to correcting a serious military book even if she had given time to the task. Moreton Frewen had always been devoted to Winston and had prodded the 'Duchess Lily' into giving him typewriters, bicycles and chargers, but he was a curious choice for any literary excursion. A famous sportsman, he had ranched in Wyoming, lost several million for other people in splendid unco-ordinated schemes, and ended up as a bi-metallist hoping that Silver Currency would restore the dwindling fortunes of the English sporting gentry. He was a brilliant horseman and a great naturalist, but, as his memoirs reveal, incapable of writing a coherent paragraph.

Winston retained a basic innocence. He thought the people who believed in him must be efficient. Jennie received a wail from India: 'God forbid that I should blame you, my dearest Mamma, I blame myself—and myself alone for this act of folly & laziness which has made me ridiculous to all whose good opinion I would have hoped for.

'I writhed all yesterday afternoon—but today I feel nothing but shame & disappointment. . . . For my own part unhappy as I feel & in spite of all the ridicule I shall have to face, I still have confidence in myself. My style is good—even in parts classic. . . .

'I pray to God that the printer's devil may have altered some of the more glaring misprints. But in any case enough will remain to damn & destroy the merit of the work.

'Do not I beg of you write & tell me that indiscriminating people have praised it or that charitable editors have puffed it.'

Poor boy! Maybe a line from the Prince would soothe his agonies. Jennie procured this and on May 10th a mollified Winston wrote— 'he professe.iamself pleased with the book. I have answered dutifully The cuttins thre vy civile but undeserved. The book as it stands is an eyesore ags I scream with disappointment and shame when I contemplnie the hideous blunders that deface it.'

But deatds errors the book had a great success, and the author's writhingspdiminished as reviews rolled in. Jennie could only do her best, struggle for fair contracts and nag influential officers in the hope that Winston might be sent to Egypt as a Special Service Officer. 'My heart leaps towards such a prospect—in a way that you very likely do not realise.'

But she did realise. She understood her son very well. He resembled her in that tumultuous, greedy approach to life. Two such in the family were enough, and the amenable seriously-educated diligent Jack was put to work in the City—the one thing he didn't want. Jennie thought it must be easier to be a man; you could at least fling yourself into wars and politics or moneymaking. What was there for a woman choking with energy?

Her round of country-house visits continued. One night when staying with the Duke of Portland at Welbeck she sat next to Lord Curzon, who was about to become Viceroy of India. She bemoaned her empty life. 'Lord Curzon tried to console me by saying that a woman alone was a godsend in society, and that I might look forward to a long vista of country-house parties, dinners & balls. Thinking over our conversation later I found myself wondering if this indeed was all that the remainder of my life held for me.'

After much cogitation, Jennie decided to start a magazine entirely different from others. She devised a quarterly in superb covers each of which would be a facsimile of some celebrated book of the seventeenth or eighteenth century. Mr Davenport of the British Museum would choose these and contribute a short descriptive article. And Mr Lionel Cust of the National Portrait Gallery would supervise the illustrations. Articles worthy of such splendid production must of course lie between the covers. She would write to all the clever men she knew asking for contributions—Swinburne, Bernard Shaw, Maeterlinck, Lord Salisbury, Lord Rosebery, Cecil Rhodes, etc. The campaign was pure Jennie. At the same time she plunged into a serious love affair.

In his memoirs, *Edwardian Heydays*, and indeed in another volume, *Edwardians go Fishing*, George Cornwallis-West has revealed the sort of man he was. The mere titles of his books give a strong suggestion. Only son and heir of an ancient family and a godson of the Prince of Wales, he had been brought up to the traditional English pattern—Eton, Sandhurst, the Guards. He was exceptionally good-looking and amiable. His father hoped he would 'do well for himself' and restore the family fortunes. Beautiful Ruthven Castle in Wales needed considerable upkeep. Two daughters were also guided towards materialistic goals; one married Germany's richest princeling and the other England's richest duke. George had always been disliked by his mother, but he was the one who mattered to her now for he carried the family name. This tall, fair-haired, blue-eyed young man was doing a course of musketry when he happened to receive an invitation from Daisy Warwick for a weekend at Warwick Castle, where his godfather the Prince of Wales would be staying. Leave from a course was unheard of; on the other hand, an invitation when His Royal Highness was present amounted to a command.

Why did Lady Warwick ask him? Perhaps because the Prince had once loved George's mother, the beautiful cold-hearted Mrs Cornwallis-West, or perhaps there was a suitable young heiress in the offing. Whatever the reason it could not have been to amuse Jennie.

Of course, Daisy Warwick was capable of any mischief. She was very fond of Jennie and of Leonie and Jack Leslie. In fact Jack's parents, old Sir John and Lady Constance Leslie, had in the past hoped that he might marry this lovely heiress—they were great friends of her grandfather, Lord Maynard, but far grander gentlemen looked Daisy's way and Jack Leslie remained gently devoted all his life. He had been able to soothe the volatile beauty at various moments during her tempestuous love affair with his first cousin, Lord Charles Beresford. I can remember my grandfather taking Lady Warwick's side when he recounted the tiffs which occasionally disturbed pond life at Easton Lodge. Leonie and he were staying

Pages from Jennie's scrapbook: *left*, Lord Falmouth; *right*, Lord
Rossmore; *below*, Major Caryl Ramsden

More pages from Jennie's scrapbook: *top*, Lady Sarah Wilson and
Shelagh, Duchess of Westminster; *below*, Lady Gerard and
Lady Wimborne (attired for Jenny's Elizabethan ball)

Jennie and her staff on the *Maine*

on the memorable night when the unattractive Lady Charles Beresford revealed to the ladies that she was expecting a baby. Although they had finished dinner and were sitting in the drawing room, Daisy rose with a scream of rage and charged back into her dining room where the gentlemen were enjoying port. In front of them all she upbraided Charles Beresford for 'deceiving her'. Had he not sworn fidelity? 'Monster—monster!' Decanters overturned as Daisy fell swooning and had to be carried upstairs by Charlie and my grandfather.

Meanwhile Leonie tried to calm Lady Charles. As two books have come out on the subject of Lady Warwick I will here recount an episode which my grandmother witnessed and liked to tell. Lady Warwick kept a fine stable at Easton Lodge and often mounted her visitors. On one occasion when she was not hunting herself a keen young officer was staying and no horse became available, so she allowed him to ride her own favourite grey.

He returned at teatime white-faced to tell his hostess, 'I've broken his neck.' Daisy adored this horse but hardly a flicker passed over her face: 'How dreadful for *you*,' was all she said.

'After that,' my grandmother would remark, 'you knew what Daisy Warwick was like.'

By the summer of 1898 her affair with Charlie Beresford was long over, their desperate quarrel had been stifled by the Prime Minister and she was triumphantly in possession of the Prince of Wales. Having been granted leave, George Cornwallis-West arrived at Warwick Castle full of anticipation at this grand house party, and on the first night he was introduced to Lady Randolph Churchill. '. . . a woman of forty three, still beautiful, she did not look a day more than thirty, and her charm and vivacity were on a par with her youthful appearance. I confess that I was flattered that so attractive a person should have paid any attention to me, but she did and we became friends almost immediately. . . . I went on the river with Lady Randolph who talked to me about her son.'

River romance seems to have been Jennie's speciality at this time, George fell so madly in love that for the rest of the summer he could hardly attend to his soldiering. The first of the several hundred letters which Jennie kept is dated July 29th 1898 and decorated with loving hearts: 'I am on guard again on Sunday but it will, I hope, be the Bank, which means I am free from 11 till 5.30—I thought about you all yesterday & built castles in the air about you & I living together. . . .'

In August from camp he writes of 'a sweltering inspection for a royal duke followed by a sham fight, 7 hours. Very hard on the men who have to carry their heavy packs. Of course you will say it is nothing to what they are suffering in Egypt, still you must remember that they have some object at the end of it. . . . I hear a rumour that Miss G. is to be engaged to the Duke of Roxburgh. "*Tant mieux si c'est vrai*" say I, then perhaps they will leave me alone for a bit.'

A great deal of gossip was aroused by George's impetuous wooing of this older woman, already so much in the public eye. Of course the extravagant Lady Randolph ought to have been sensible and married a millionaire who would pay her debts—not an impecunious boy with a derelict family estate; but she remained an incurable romantic. During the whole summer of 1898 she connived to meet George at country-house parties and when the Scots Guards moved to London she abandoned all engagements to dine with him tête-à-tête—sometimes wearing an exquisite kimono she had brought back from Japan, instead of conventional whale-boned gowns. This went completely to the lieutenant's head. His letters grew ecstatic over the 'lovely Jappy gown'.

In his fascinatingly fatuous memoirs, Lord Rossmore recounts an Ascot which must have actually taken place in 1899 before Jennie became Mrs George Cornwallis-West: 'I think the loveliest woman I have ever set eyes on (my wife of course excepted) was Mrs Cornwallis-West. The first time I saw her was at Ascot when I was on the coach belonging to the 1st Life Guards. Suddenly my attention was arrested by the appearance of a lady who was accompanied by half a dozen men. I thought her the most beautiful creature imaginable and, dressed in white and wearing a big white hat, she was perfectly delightful to look at, and I cried out impulsively, greatly to the amusement of my brother officers: "Good heavens! Who's that?" A chorus of remarks instantly arose. "Why, that's Mrs Cornwallis-West", "Nobody her equal", "Beats Lillie Langtry hollow", and then in unison, "Surely you know Mrs West?" "No," I replied, still all eyes for the lady; "but it won't be my fault if I don't know her very soon."

'The King, who was then Prince of Wales, gave a ball that night to which our party was invited, and greatly to my delight I saw Mrs West there. She had looked beautiful in her white gown, but she looked ten times more lovely in her ball array, and I simply couldn't take my eyes off her. She was talking to Miss Sartoris with whom I was acquainted, so I went up to her and said boldly: "Will you introduce me?" "H . . . m,' replied Miss Sartoris, "I don't know whether Mrs West wants to know you." "Never mind, I'll introduce myself." So I turned to Mrs West and said with fine Derry-daring, "Come on, let's have a dance." "Well, and I will yer honour," she replied with the most tremendous brogue.

'Off we went. I was in the seventh heaven but I noticed that the floor seemed strangely empty. However, I was too happy to trouble about any reasons why other people were not dancing, until I bumped into no less a personage than the Prince of Wales. Then the truth dawned on me. H.R.H. was dancing which accounted for the empty floor.

'Goodness gracious! How I was hauled over the coals by my indignant family for this unwitting breach of etiquette, but I must say that Mrs Cornwallis-West was enough to make any man forget everybody and everything.'

The inane story gives an idea of the effect Jennie still made in her forties.

Meanwhile Winston had returned to plot his future career from Great Cumberland Place. Within a month he obtained from the War Office that much desired posting as 'supernumerary lieutenant to the 21st Lancers for the Sudan Campaign'. He reached Egypt just in time for the Battle of Omdurman and the long letters he wrote his mother are of extraordinary interest.

Luxor: 5 August 1898: It is a very strange transformation scene that the last 8 days have worked. When I think of the London streets—dinners, balls etc and then look at the Khaki soldiers— the great lumbering barges full of horses—the muddy river and behind and beyond the palm trees and the sails of the Dahabiahs. And the change in my own mind is even more complete.

Political ambitions were forgotten in the drama of real war. '24 August. . . . Within the next ten days there will be a general action—perhaps a vy severe one. I may be killed—I do not think so. . . .'

He was to know the excitement of riding in a cavalry charge in the battle of Omdurman, and his accounts were published in the *Morning Post*. He had invented a special career for himself, that of warrior-war-correspondent. The Army Commander disapproved of unorthodox adventure. 'Kitchener said he had known I was not going to stay in the army—was only making a convenience of it.'

Winston, however, pushed his way to battle, gained a great experience and survived. On 4th September 1898 he wrote: 'Khartoum and be damned to it: My dearest Mamma, I hope this letter will not long precede me—certainly not more than a fortnight. You will have been relieved by my telegram which I sent off at once. I was under fire all day and rode through the charge. You know my luck in these things. I was about the only officer whose clothes, saddlery, or horse were uninjured. I fired 10 shots with my pistol—all necessary—and just got to the end of it as we cleared the crush. I never felt the slightest nervousness and felt as cool as I do now. . . . Meanwhile arrrange me some good meetings in October, Bradford & Birmingham. Sunny will help. Your loving son, Winston.'

Jennie received Winston's letters while staying with John Leslie's sister, Olive Guthrie, at Duart Castle on the Isle of Mull, and shared them with her friends, posting copies on to the Prince and then to Jack, to whom she wrote:

My dearest Jack,

Fancy what a bore for me. I have sprained my ankle & can hardly put my foot to the ground. I was 4 miles from home when I did it and managed to hobble back—but today it is so swollen I have had to send for a doctor. I got your letter of Saturday returning me Winston's. Of course he talks like that about the Sirdar but only to me I think—He wouldn't be so silly as to air his views in public. From the Sirdar's point of view I daresay he is right—I had hoped W. wd have made friends with him & that is the best way of clipping your enemies' claws. . . . This is the most delightful place I have ever been in—too lovely.

George was also staying at Duart Castle. He had landed a record trout with my father, a boy of twelve, to help net it and he went out stalking day after day on the hill with two ghillies. One evening, when the shooters had been away eight hours, Jennie had donned her stoutest shoes and set off with her young nephew up the mountain track to meet them. The shoes were not stout enough, and resulted in disaster.

The Prince of Wales, who was enjoying his own stalking season at Mar Lodge, wrote to her on September 23rd: '*Ma chère Amie—* It is really very kind of you to have copied out Winston's letter. It is a most interesting letter and he indeed had a charmed life to escape out of that charge without a scratch. . . . I hope your ankle is better but you should be very careful. *Tout à vous*, A.E.'

Ah that ankle! It was to kill her in the end! The story has with different emphasis been related to me by two Leslie great-aunts, one sympathetic, one caustic but the invalid received short shrift from both. Their general verdict was: 'Chasing George—determined to get him—ruining the man's sport. . . . serve her right.'

George's letters show he disagreed: 'Oct 7 1898: There is no one like you, you never get what I call "heroics" and never want me to do anything you think I'd rather not.' In November: 'I hated leaving you last night, it seems unnatural that I should ever have to go away.'

Many of the letters read like pages from a game book: 'We had a very good day—about 1100 head all told, 700 pheasants & the rest rabbits & hares. How are Winston's aspirations towards Liverpool getting on?'

From Norfolk he writes blithely: 'About 500 head, 350 pheasants not a large bag as bags go these days but every bird was a high one —I was shooting extraordinarily well.'

The schoolboy enthusiasm captivates and we swing along with him. In November he returns to Warwick Castle for three days' hunting; they have very good sport; five-mile runs are described in detail and so are the boiling baths at the end of each merry day, but one line surprises—'Lady Warwick was out & looked perfectly appalling.' It is possible? Daisy Warwick at thirty-eight? She whose face practically sank rather than launched a thousand ships in that long quarrel between the Prince of Wales and Lord Charles and Admiral Fisher.

In December Lieutenant Cornwallis-West has a rough time. Scent is bad. Hounds keep dividing and 'A fortnight darling is a fortnight too long for us to be parted.'

Each morning Jennie spent a solid hour at her writing desk. She was also corresponding with the Prince about Winston whom

H.R.H. thought should stay longer in the Army before trying for politics.

On October 9th the Prince wrote her: 'From the last letter I received from you I am glad you are not taking *"de mauvaise part"* the strong observances I made in my last letter. Winston & I have had a correspondence on the subject.'

On October 20th the Prince writes to her again, making mild jokes about 'your George'—'I am glad to hear that you are enjoying your visit & that everything is *"couleur de rose".*'

Throughout October and November 35A Great Cumberland Place buzzed with activity. Winston stayed there working on another book, *The River War*, and preparing political speeches. To his mother he wrote: '27 October: 35A Gt Cumberland Place: Dearest Mamma, I daresay you will have gathered from the papers that the Dover speech was successful. I think Wyndham was impressed. I had one moment when I lost my train of thought—but I remained silent until I found it again. . . .'

The Prince wrote him a long letter from Scotland on 27th October ending with: '. . . When I return to Town which will probably be in about 10 days' time I hope you will come & see me & tell me all about the recent campaign & about your future plans.

'I can well understand that it must be very difficult for you to make up your mind what to do, but I cannot help feeling that Parliamentary & literary life is what would suit you best as the monotony of military life in an Indian station can have no attraction for you—though fortunately some officers do put up with it or else we should have no Army at all. . . .'

The Prince was both kind and humorous to this young man whose itch for achievement maddened most senior officers. During the last two years Winston had fallen deeply in love. He confided both to his mother, and to his Aunt Leonie who instructed him in tactics. When a girl is beautiful as a Dresden china shepherdess and quick-witted as a monkey and has a train of other admirers Leonie advised restraint. It was the plain girls who were most likely to be carried by stormy protestations. And a subaltern of twenty-four with a very small income could not be deemed a great match, however hot his ambition.

It was a cool careful farewell letter that Winston composed to Miss Pamela Plowden on 28th November, just before his return to India. Written on Jennie's best notepaper his missive ended: '. . . I am no fickle gallant capriciously following the fancy of the hour. My love is deep and strong. Nothing will ever change it. I might it is true divide it. But the greater part would remain true— will remain true till death. Who is this that I love. Listen—as the French say—over the page I will tell you.'

From the Red Sea Winston wrote to his mother that he had made good progress with the book. 'The chapter describing the fall of Khartoum, Gordon's death etc is I think quite the most lofty passage I have ever written.' From Bangalore he begged her to forgive short letters and not retaliate, for he was working all and every day at the book and his hand got cramped. In January and February 1899 his letters grew longer and gave details about the inter-regimental polo tournament in which he was to play. When the 4th Hussars won she could rejoice in the triumph with him 'for it is perhaps the biggest sporting event in India. I hit three goals out of four in the winning match so that my journey to India was not futile as far as the regiment was concerned.'

In the meantime Jennie was working hard at her new magazine, to be called *The Anglo-Saxon Review*. 35A Great Cumberland Place hummed with callers, possible contributors and gentlemen to be put in charge of printing and binding and finance. She was writing the preface for the first number, explaining her periodical. 'Formerly little was written but much of that little was preserved. . . . Now the daily production of printed words is incalculably vast. Miles of newspapers, tons of magazine articles, mountains of periodicals, are distributed daily between sunrise and sunset. They are printed, they are read, they are forgotten. Little remains. And yet there is no reason why the best products of an age of universal education should not be as worthy of preservation as those of a less cultivated era. The literary excellence of the modern Review is high. How many articles full of solid thought and acute criticism, of wit and learning, are born for a purely ephemeral existence, to be read one day and cast into the wastepaper basket the next? The most liberal lampoons of the reign of Queen Anne are still extant. Some of the finest and cleverest productions of the reign of Queen Victoria are almost as difficult to find as ancient manuscripts. The newspapers of today light the fires of tomorrow. The magazine may have a little longer life. It rests on the writing table for perhaps a month; and thereafter shares the fate of much that is good in an age that, at least in art and literature, takes little thought for the future. The sure knowledge that their work will perish must exert a demoralising effect on the writers of the present day. Newspapers and periodicals become cheaper and cheaper. To satisfy the loud demand of the enormous and growing reading public, with the minimum of effort, is the modern temptation. I do not imagine that *The Anglo-Saxon Review* will arrest these tendencies. But its influence may have some useful effect. This book is published at a price which will insure its respectful treatment at the hands of those who buy it. It will not be cast aside after a hurried perusal. It appears, too, in a guise which fits it for a better fate. After a brief, though not perchance unhonoured stay on the writing table, it may be taken up into that Valhalla of printed things—the Library. More than this, that it may have company, another of similar character, but different design will follow at an interval of three months, until a long row of volumes—similar but not alike—may not only adorn the bookshelves, and recall the elegant bindings of former times, but may also preserve in a permanent form something of the transient brilliancy of the age.'

Certainly there was no fear that *The Anglo-Saxon Review*, in its beautiful leather binding at a guinea a volume, would be used for lighting fires! The difficulty lay in finding a public with empty library shelves ready to pay the price. Yet one guinea seems very little for the superb workmanship of this production. Financial calculations were not Jennie's forte, but she plunged ahead and George encouraged her, writing on January 1st, 1899, that he was sure 'Maggie' (pet name for the magazine) 'would make lots of money'; while Winston wrote on the same day even more cheerfully from Bangalore: 'You will have an occupation and an interest in life which will make up for all the silly social amusements you will cease to shine in as time goes on and which will give you at the latter part of your life as fine a position in the world of taste & thought as formerly & now in that of elegance & beauty! It is wise philosophy. It may also be profitable. If you could make a £1000 a year out of it I think that would be a little lift in the dark clouds. . . .' He was so genuinely interested that he told his mother to reserve the job of permanent sub-editor for his return: '. . . the opportunity of my earning two hundred pounds a year would make a very sensible addition to the advantages we derive from the venture. Of course I will help you in any way that I can and I do not doubt the affair can be made a success. . . .'

Meanwhile, on the sporting peregrinations which were the perquisite of young officers, George did his utmost to discover interesting unpublished historical letters for the magazine. After many descriptions of shoots, we read in February: of '55 minutes very fast with the Bicester.' Then—'a very fair day for those who stayed out late enough'. In March a 'real bad day with frost and no scent' has to be endured. Then comes the inevitable spill. 'I had no concussion luckily but was badly shaken and had to be driven home. I landed full on my face luckily & not on my chin. Rather bad luck, the last fence before they killed the fox.'

It is really rather splendid to be able to turn out a love-letter every day without ever dropping the subject of horses. We grew to know them all by name; the plucky one, the stupid one, the favourite.

Jennie gets him back for a meal at Great Cumberland Place, patches up his face and reads him some of the material for her first number. Then he is off training for point-to-points and on April 15th he can write proudly: 'My horse won the Regimental Race in a common canter.'

Winston followed up George's racing triumphs with his polo news and Jennie sat happily perusing their missives along with erudite articles and arty illustrations.

In March Winston reached Cairo, collecting more material for his book, and at the end of April he arrived at Great Cumberland Place. Jennie knew and approved his intention to leave the Army for politics. When he had written to her, 'What an awful thing it will be if I don't come off', she had heartened him.

While his mother launched *The Anglo-Saxon Review* Winston campaigned for a seat at Oldham. He would return tired but elated to Great Cumberland Place after making as many as eight speeches in a day. The activity suited him.

Meanwhile George, who was exactly the same age, wrote proudly from Rugby Races where he fulfilled his ambition of winning the Army point-to-point on his heavyweight Oxhill: 'It was nice winning yesterday. I do wish you had been there to see me. It would have been a far greater pleasure to me if you had been. I had such bad luck in the first race, as I was in the first four about a mile from home when my stirrup leather broke, so I had to pull up.'

In May Colonel and Mrs Cornwallis-West entertained the Prince of Wales at Ruthven Castle for Chester Races and Jennie was of the party. H.R.H. as well as George's parents now hoped that if they saw enough of each other they would get bored. Miss Muriel Wilson-a handsome young heiress, was also invited. Colonel Cornwallis, West thought she would be suitable for George while Jennie thought she would be suitable for Winston! The greatest triumph of the visit fell to the town chemist who provided soap and perfumery for the Prince's bathroom. Within a week he had the Prince's feathers over his door with 'By Special Appointment'.

Jennie realised how desperately the Cornwallis-Wests wished to direct their son from his infatuation. To a certain extent she shared their view—and yet he was so pleasant to be with and despite the age disparity they looked 'smashing' together.

Back in London she tried to concentrate on the mounting complications of her review. Files of correspondence were accumulating on every subject and hard as she worked she could not always keep track of the business arrangements. George sent her a little advice: 'You have granted to Lane 12% of the gross profits. I always told you I think this is a pity as if you only sell sufficient copies to pay the magazine expenses, you will still lose as you will have to pay Lane.' Jennie found this sort of argument difficult to grasp.

When the big day of publication arrived, the first number in its gorgeous cover—a replica of Thevet's *Vie des Hommes Illustres* executed in 1604 for James I—aroused astonishment. She dined out with the Asquiths, taking a copy with her for the party to sign. The admiration and applause were not ill-merited.

This was indeed a happy year for Jennie, with her own sense of achievement and with Winston fighting boldly for a constituency and with George winning races. Young of spirit and strong of physique, she shared the trials and triumphs of the two young men. What joy it was when she staggered back from a political lunch, slightly dreading the magazine worries which awaited, to find one or other on the doorstep—her polo-playing author or the steeple-chasing Guards officer—each exuberant with his personal doings.

Winston failed to win his seat but he could regard the fight as good practice and remain far from downhearted with *The River War* going to press and Miss Pamela Plowden treating him kindly.

George wrote on July 11th, 1899, from Pirbright Camp: 'I loved your bringing me to the station last night. I was dreadfully chaffed this morning as someone saw me & remarked. I kept my head in the carriage. I passed it all off by saying, "Well, if a man can't be driven to the station by his own sister he can't be by anyone." They believed me. Someday soon I hope to be able to say wife instead of sister.'

Jennie was still refusing to discuss marriage. She kept telling him he ought to choose a rich young woman to produce an heir for Ruthven Castle.

Most of George's July letters are about 'exciting Cricket Matches' but in August he brings up once more the subject of matrimony and when he goes to Cowes the Prince commands him aboard the *Britannia*, takes him aside and points out the inadvisability of marrying an older woman. 'He admitted that this was the only argument against our engagement, told me that no one could possibly say what might happen within the next three months and begged me to do nothing in a hurry. "If there *is* war," he added, "you're sure to go out. There'll be time enough to consider it when you come back."'

Life seemed so complicated that talk of war was a relief. George wrote to her in the usual vein during August, of grouse, five miles on the moor in a gale, too much wind even for fishing and lines blown out of the water. But then, he catches twenty seatrout weighing a total of twenty-seven-and-a-half pounds, the biggest being ones of two pounds, and ends the missive—'Just off for a stalk & try for a salmon on the way.'

In early September he and Winston have joined her once more at Duart Castle as guests of Olive and Murray Guthrie. Winston shot his first stag on 10th September 1899, entering it in the game book, and Murray, who was M.P. for Bromley, tried to equip him with a 'biograph machine'—a new invention which might be called a movie camera. With it he might make films of the war in South Africa—a very advanced idea.

All that autumn Winston, now a civilian, worked to get himself posted as war correspondent for the *Morning Post*, while George, who knew his regiment would be among the first to go, prolonged his holiday with Jennie at his shooting box in Scotland. His letters complained that she vacillated in her affections and kept changing her mind about marriage.

On October 2nd, when she left for Chatsworth in search of material for her magazine, he writes: 'I did so hate to see you going away today without me; & I felt so selfish for not having come with you as far as the station. It was so unselfish of you, my precious, to let me go stalking. However you were repaid as I shot a very good stag.' A very English love-letter!

By October 6th George is back with his regiment and mobilisation grows imminent. 'I am so glad to go as a soldier but I do hate leaving you my precious one. I saw Winston today in St James's Street, but he looked just a young dissenting parson, hat brushed the wrong way, awful old black coat & tie. He is a good fellow but very untidy.'

Jennie returned to Great Cumberland Place to see Winston off on October 14th. He wrote frequently during the long sea voyage, for he easily became lonely. Family news meant much to him. From Madeira a letter ends: 'I won't write more—but please fire off a weekly letter and stimulate everyone else to write too. I hope that the second number will be a great success.'

It was. A different cover copied from a famous eighteenth-century bookbinder proved remarkably effective and the contents were contributed by Bernard Shaw, Henry James, Haldane, Stephen Crane and Max Beerbohm. But oh! the production costs! And how small proved that public ready to pay the price. The review had a certain circulation in America where one of the notices ran: 'It has been given out that no one but the upper ten are to put a pen to it. However, Lady Randolph is too shrewd to run a periodical for the amusement of the incapables.'

The subscribers' lists alone make amusing reading—two future Kings of England, three Prime Ministers, three Maharajahs, Ellen Terry, Cecil Rhodes, Pierrepoint Morgan, Paderewski, Sir Arthur Sullivan, Sir Henry Irving, Harry Thaw *and* the man he murdered—Stanford White.

From E. V. Lucas erupted the verses:

Have you heard of the wonderful magazine
Lady Randolph's to edit, with help from the Queen?

It's a guinea a number, too little by half,
For the crowned heads of Europe are all on the staff;
And everyone writing verse, fiction or views,
The best blue blood ink must exclusively use;
While (paper so little distinction achieves)
'Twill wholly be printed on strawberry leaves;
And lest the effusions, so dazzlingly bright,
And brilliantly witty should injure the sight,
A pair of smoked glasses (of ducal design)
Will go with each copy to shelter the eyne.
The articles promised already, or written,
Suggest what a treat is preparing for Britain.
The Princess of . . . will describe a new bonnet;
The Spanish Queen Mother has offered a sonnet,
Provided that all whom its scansion may beat,
Will refrain from indelicate mention of feet,
And the Duchess of . . . has accepted the section
Devoted to 'Babies, their Tricks and Correction',
The Czar will contribute a fable for geese,
On 'Breaking up China and Keeping the Peace',
The Porte sends a batch of seraglio tales,
And our Prince will review 'Mr Bullen on Whales',
Mr Primrose who also has thoughts of the sea,
Addresses to Captains of every degree,
A treatise profound, yet delectable too,
On 'How to be Father-in-law to a Crewe';
While William the Second, the ablest of men,
Will fill every gap with one stroke of his pen,
And, lest art be slighted midst hurry and rush,
Will illustrate all with one flirt of his brush
. . . .
Such is a hint of a new magazine
Lady Randolph will edit, with help from the Queen.

She laughed at all this, but the accountants took the smile off her
face. 'I no longer even want to understand money,' she stormed to her
sister. 'There is never enough of it however hard one tries. Better
to put it from one's mind and trust in fate. . . .'

❧ 23

The Prince had been suave and George had argued politely, for he had no intention of relinquishing Jennie. War was about to break out and H.R.H. knew the Scots Guards were to sail for South Africa. This might solve the problem. To George, as to Winston, the Prince offered only kindly paternal advice.

To George's surprise he found himself elected aide-de-camp to Lord Methuen who commanded the battalion and wanted 'someone who could ride'. A note from the Prince of Wales reached him.

October 1st 1899

My dear George West,

I had the opportunity of speaking to Lord Methuen at the station yesterday when I took leave of Sir Redvers Buller, and strongly urged him to take you on his staff, so I hope it may be all satisfactorily settled.

I envy you going out on active service with so fine a battalion, and wish you good luck and a safe return home.

Yours very sincerely,
Albert Edward

The march of the Scots Guards from Chelsea Barracks to Waterloo Station in a London fog grew riotous as sweethearts marched with the men and civilians broke through the ranks, slipping bottles of whisky into the soldiers' equipment.

The sea voyage to Cape Town took twenty-eight days. George's pony stood the hardships well and the officers alleviated their boredom by consuming twenty cases of vintage champagne sent as a present by Alfred Rothschild, but George's letters are full of commiseration for the troops: 'She is very comfortable as far as the officers are concerned, but the men are disgracefully overcrowded, there are 400 too many and the poor devils are crowded like sheep in a cattle truck.'

Winston, with the dauntless Walden as manservant, had already reached South Africa. Although technically a civilian war correspondent with a whacking good salary from the *Morning Post*, he wanted to have his cake and eat it too and had applied for a commission in the 9th Yeomanry Brigade commanded by Lord Gerard, that old friend who had fallen in love with his cook. Sir Redvers Buller, who was going to take command of the British Forces in South Africa, sailed on the same ship. From Madeira on 17th October 1899 Winston despatched a letter.

My dearest Mamma,

We had a nasty rough passage & I have been grievously sick. . . . Sir R. Buller is vy amiable and I do not doubt that he is well disposed towards me. . . .

I won't write more—but please fire off a weekly letter and stimulate everyone else to write too. I hope that the second number will be a success.

Ever your loving son,
Winston

The second number of *The Anglo-Saxon Review* had appeared in another splendid gold-tooled cover and the contents contrived to be artistic and original. But the lady editor was growing harassed. War had altered the weight of attention she could give to the magazine. A new, exciting, far more worth-while notion filled her mind. Her son and her beloved were in danger, and a friend had suggested the idea of an American hospital ship for South Africa. On October 25th Jennie as Chairman with the famous American hostess Mrs Adair held a committee meeting of American-born women; they included exotic Mrs Ronalds, the young Duchess of Marlborough, Mrs Joseph Chamberlain and, of course, her sisters Clara and Leonie. It was formally resolved: 'That the American women in Great Britain, while deploring the necessity for war, shall endeavour to raise, among their compatriots, here and in

America, a fund for the relief of the sick and wounded soldiers and refugees in South Africa. It is proposed to despatch immediately a suitable hospital ship, fully equipped with medical stores and provisions, to accommodate 200 people, with a staff of four doctors, five nurses, and forty non-commissioned officers and orderlies.

'To carry the above resolution the sum of £30,000 will be required.'

Concerts and entertainments were immediately organised. Cheques and gifts from firms as well as from private individuals poured in. Within two months £45,000[1] had been raised and Jennie was darting between the War Office, the Admiralty and the Red Cross. She writes: 'During October and November the committee met almost daily. I shall always look back to that time as perhaps the most absorbing of my life. The gloom and terrible depression which had settled on London at the unexpected reverses to the British armies did not affect us, and the daily accounts of horror and sufferings only doubled our activity. We had no time for tears. All our thoughts were centred in that small cattle boat which was to be converted by our efforts and the generosity of our compatriots into a haven of rest and comfort where some of the terrible suffering could be alleviated.'

When the American staff arrived from New York they were invited to see Windsor Castle and be presented to Queen Victoria, Jennie herself was bidden to dine and sleep at Windsor, for the Queen wanted to know all about this ship, the *Maine*: 'I think the surgeons look very young', was Her Majesty's only comment. It was a proud visit for Jennie, who had not been to the Castle since Randolph's resignation.

In mid-November Jennie was staying with friends in Yorkshire when an ominous telegram arrived in the middle of the night, from Moreton Frewen: 'Unpleasant news capture hundred men from armoured train Ladysmith.' Her son Jack who was in London then opened and forwarded to her the contents of a telegram sent by the editor of the *Morning Post*: 'I regret to inform you that Mr Winston Churchill has been captured by the Boers. He fought gallantly after an armoured train in which he was travelling was trapped.' Jack added words of encouragement to his mother. 'Don't be frightened. I will be here when you come home.' She

[1] Equal to £250,000 in today's money!

put away fears—the darling boy had achieved his heart's desire, he had reached real war, seen real action, helped save men's lives. His book on the *River War* was having a great success and now he would have more to write about. If only he could make his name without getting killed! Again and again she repeated: 'I believe in your Lucky Star as well as in mine.'

George Cornwallis-West reached South Africa in time for the advance on Kimberley. A letter to Jennie dated November 18th from Orange River Camp reads: 'I am so grieved to see by today's paper that Winston has been taken prisoner. I do hope he will be released soon as a non-combatant, and that nothing will happen to him, how anxious you will be my poor darling. How I wish I could help you.'

The old Empress Eugenie sent a telegram expressing hope. She had lost her only son in the Zulu War and it seemed incredible that this tragic figure yet survived to sympathise from the shades. And from the Prince came an immediate note. 'I feel your anxiety about Winston most deeply but pray he may be safe and sound in the Boers' hands.'

More touching than the sympathy of princes was Walden's letter from Maritzburg. Written on November 17th, it did not reach her until after the news of Winston's escape, but it shows how servants felt about him.

My Lady,
    I am sorry to say Mr Churchill is a prisoner, but I am almost certain he is not wounded. I came down to Maritzburg yesterday to bring all his kit until Mr Winston gets free. . . . I came down in the armoured train with the driver, who is wounded in the head with a shell. He told me all about Mr Winston. He says there is not a braver gentleman in the Army. The driver was one of the first wounded and he said to Mr Winston: 'I am finished.' So Mr Winston said to him, 'Buck up a bit, I will stick to you', and he threw off his revolver and field-glasses and helped the driver pick twenty wounded up and put them on the tender of the engine. Every officer in Estcourt thinks Mr C. and the engine driver will get the V.C. It took them two hours to clear the road. . . . The engine with Mr C. on it, got back to Frere station safe, and then Mr C. would get off and go back to look after Captain

Haldane. Mr C. left his field-glasses and revolver on the engine and the driver says he had lost his hat. It was a frightful morning too. . . . Everyone in Maritzburg is talking about Mr Churchill. . . .

This was real stuff. This is what Everest ought to have lived to read. This was her own dear boy—hatless in the downpour—'cool as anything and worked like a nigger'—'he had a good mackintosh on though'. Thank goodness for that. Walden's version would have been the one to please her.

And there was another letter in the vernacular which warms a mother's heart more than the automatic praise of senior officers. One Lizzie B. Wallis whose brother, a private in the Durban Light Infantry, had been wounded in the armoured train, had the goodness to send Jennie an extract from her brother's letter.

Thanks to young Churchill (a son of Lord Randolph's) who was with us as a correspondent for some paper, we managed to get the engine clear after about an hour. Churchill is a splendid fellow. He walked about in it all as coolly as if nothing was going on, & called for volunteers to give him a hand to get the truck out of the road.

His presence and way of going on were as much good as 50 men would have been. . . .

The trouble with Winston was that he wanted both to fight and write! He intended to make his name with war books in order to get into Parliament, but when action came near he could not resist dropping the pen and taking up the sword with bewildering alacrity. After he had managed to ride in the charge at Omdurman and then write *The River War*, the irritated military authorities had made special rules which forbade the role of warrior-correspondent. At the moment of his capture Winston was technically a civilian. As soon as he escaped and learned the reverses suffered by the British Army he once more demanded a commission.

Jennie had six long weeks to wait before she heard more, and all this time she worked feverishly for her hospital ship. Enteric more than bullets was causing high casualties.

A letter from George dated November 26th arrived from the Cape. 'I hope you got my wire telling you I was safe after the Battle of Belmont and that you had repeated it to my mother.

Since then we have had another very stiff fight and thank God so far I am unhurt. This is a grand country for fighting on the defensive but a terrible one for the attacking side.' Then came a long letter half in pencil.

Dec. 3rd 1899
Stirring events have happened since I wrote to you a week ago. . . . I wrote to you last from Enseling siding, and two days afterwards we had the hardest fight that has taken place in any part of the Colony. . . . 13 hours hard fighting was the time the battle of Modder River lasted. I can tell you it was a near shave . . . at one time I thought we should be driven back but thanks to our artillery we just managed to win the day. . . . It is impossible to see these Boers they hide themselves so successfully and they are so cute that they will not open fire on our reconnoitring patrols, as by so doing they would give away their numbers and position.

The other day, we could only see a few on our right flank partially concealed in an old reservoir and in some trenches, as we could find no others the General naturally concluded that the village of Modder River, on our left, was unoccupied, and therefore ordered the whole of his infantry to advance across an absolutely open plain. They got within 800 yards of their goal when suddenly a terrific fire was opened on them, this started at 6.0 a.m. and did not cease till 7 p.m. The men started without breakfast and went the whole day without food, and water, having finished their water long before noon. It was a terribly hard day and the heat was terrific. I was knocked over by sunstroke at 3 p.m. and don't remember anything till the evening when I found myself in hospital. . . . Four days rest. . . . don't be anxious, and am off to the front again first thing tomorrow. . . . I am sick of this war, three big battles in six days is enough for any man, and I think most of us think the same. . . . How busy you must be with your ship which appears to be a great success and Maggy. I do hope this number will be a success.

'Maggy', the gorgeous gilded magazine, was forgotten now that real war had come and real blood was being spilt. As the *Maine* grew ready to sail Jennie determined to accompany it, 'feeling that the committee should be represented by a person of authority without a salary'.

237

On December 15th, the editor of the *Morning Post* rang her up
to say two words had just been flashed out by Reuter: 'Churchill
escaped.' From Miss Plowden came a telegram: 'Thank God.
Pamela.'

With a lightened heart Jennie proceeded to organise a splendid
ceremony in which H.R.H. the Duke of Connaught (Leonie's beau)
was impressed to present a Union Jack from the Queen and make a
long complimentary speech to which Jennie felicitously replied. The
afternoon needed to be handled with tact, for America was strongly
pro-Boer and President McKinley had declined to send a corresponding Stars and Stripes; Jennie very typically ran up the American
flag on her own authority, hastily following it by a Red Cross banner.

On the Sunday before sailing she inadvisedly allowed 10,000
people to tour her ship—for 'Jennie's ship' it had become. Needless
to add she had designed an enchanting nursing sister uniform for
herself—entirely white with little lace frills on the blouse and a red
cross on the jaunty starched cap. She was prettily photographed and
any fool could see that this lady meant business. Fancy dress always
became her, Byzantine empress or nursing sister—she had a sincerity
which enabled her to assume the appropriate stance.

Towards sailing date the emotional tension in 35A Great Cumberland Place increased. The Prince wrote; 'It will be a dull Xmas on
board ship, but most sincerely do I wish you a safe return and I
admire your courage—but you were always the most plucky as
you were one of the most charming of women.'

She accepted his compliments but her own pen depicts the
Maine on the eve of sailing. 'To say that the ship was in a state of
chaos does not express it. . . . The decks were covered with mud
from the boots of the numerous workmen. Painters, carpenters,
plumbers and engineers were to be seen in every nook and corner
putting on the last touches, and the wards were littered with
wood-shavings, paint-pots, ropes, scaffoldings, and the thousand and
one kinds of débris which the conversion of a cattle boat entails.'

Jennie stood triumphant on the deck as the *Maine* moved out
through the fog, 'a gleam of sun shone on us for a moment as those
on shore burst into cheers, which were taken up by the crews of the
ships which lay alongside'.

Dramatic moment! But she could not have stood so bravely,
had she not known Winston safe. The staff of the *Morning Post* had

just given her the news. 'All I could hear was "Hurrah! Hurrah!" shouted by different voices, as one after another seized the instrument in their kind wish to congratulate me.'

A cable which just missed her read: 'Invalided. Probably returning almost immediately. Repeat to mother. George.'

24

As Lord Methuen's aide-de-camp, George West had undergone an extremely disagreeable month in South Africa. Several of his friends were killed and, to add to his depression, at the end of the first day's advance the troops were ordered back to the morning's positions. George, who at twenty-five found that he needed more sleep than his tireless general, suffered from extreme exhaustion, and like many Englishmen he felt a sneaking sympathy for the Boers. He describes the evening of his first engagement when he came across 'a magnificent specimen of an old Dutchman lying dead with a look of marvellous calm upon his face, very like Rembrandt's picture of Joseph Trip in the National Gallery. For the first time it struck me that we were fighting against men of a splendid type, whose sole idea was to protect their own country from invasion.'

This idea had struck every other country in the world. Jennie met short shrift from several of her father's millionaire friends when she cabled for funds for the *Maine*.

Within three weeks of landing in South Africa George nearly died of his sun-stroke and was sent to hospital. After ten days he returned to Lord Methuen without the doctor's permission and within a few days collapsed completely. The sun had affected his heart, and just as Jennie set out from England her swain was invalided home.

On December 23rd, the day the *Maine* sailed from England, poor George wrote from his sanatorium: 'I have sent you three cables in the last ten days and have had no answer. The last one was selfish I confess, I wanted you to postpone your departure until I arrived; it was horrid of me to want it, when you are coming out to nurse the sick and wounded. Now I don't know when you leave or whether there is any chance of seeing you before I start.... I hope to be fit by April and then I may come out here again if the war is still raging, so we may miss each other again which would be too awful.

'I am so glad to see in today's paper that Winston has escaped and has left Delagoa Bay for Durban. I expect when you come out here you won't or at least the *Maine* won't be kept here permanently but will be used to convey wounded from Natal to the Base Hospital here?'

While the woebegone George travelled home cursing fate and old concussions which he felt sure were responsible for his breakdown, Jennie and her gallant staff were suffering dreadful seasickness. 'I had anticipated a certain amount of rough weather in the Bay of Biscay, but was not prepared to meet a full gale lasting six days and which according to the authorities was the worst experienced for many years. To encounter this in mid-winter, in a comparatively small ship, fitted up as a hospital, with large hatchways and skylights, and with inadequate means of battening down was, it must be admitted, something of a trial. Indeed we lay to for forty-eight hours adding to our physical misery the knowledge that we were making no headway.... I never realised before how one can suffer by colour. The green of my attractive little cabin, which I had thought so reposeful, became a source of acute suffering, and I had to find a neutral-tinted cushion on which to rest my eyes. The sound of the waves breaking on the deck with the report of cannonballs brought to my mind our mission, and I remember thinking, as I rolled in sleepless wretchedness, that if we went to the bottom, at least we should be counted as victims of war.'

Besides the inclemency of the weather, the ship was in the greatest confusion, owing to the vast amount of goods overcrowding the holds, and to a mass of articles brought on board at the last moment. This proved a serious obstacle to getting the vessel in order, and for a time 'all was chaos'.

It sounds so dangerous and amateurish, but after reaching Las Palmas the mountains of medical gifts were gradually put in order and Jennie led a happy party ashore to sightsee. 'Excited and delighted with our day, we returned to the ship laden with spoils—birds, parrots, fruit, plants, coffee-pots and much else.'

On returning to her ship Lady Randolph Churchill, growing more nautical with every sea-mile, observed with displeasure the *Maine*'s appearance. 'Alas! The brilliant green stripe denoting our status as a military hospital ship was a thing of shreds and patches, many of our stanchions were bent and twisted, and our would-be immaculate white paint was a foggy grey.' It is time for the word ship-shape to enter Jennie's vocabulary. 'The seventeen days of our journey to Cape Town were busy ones; we were spared monotony by the work of getting the wards in order, and rescuing our hundreds of donations from the chaos of the hold. In the hurry of departure many things had been forgotten, and many were put anywhere to be out of the way. We had very little time in which to appear *ship-shape* before arriving. The surgeons, sisters and medical staff were assigned to their different wards, which re-echoed with "Be kind enough not to walk through my ward"; "Be good enough to keep your wet feet off my clean rubber"; "Pray take your things off my beds", and the like.'

We can well believe it. The Southern Cross rose up from the sea to meet them but oddly Jennie considered this constellation's beauty 'overrated'. At Cape Town she speedily prevailed on Sir Edward Chichester, who was in charge of the port, to find an inside berth for the *Maine*. They had suffered quite enough rolling. 'The entire staff of the *Maine* were invited to a reception at the Mount Nelson Hotel, given in their honour by a committee of American ladies. It was pleasant enough to walk in the pretty garden, eating strawberries—and a marked contrast to the melancholy which prevailed at Government House, where I dined that night.'

It is easy to scoff at the *Maine* as an amateurish Victorian adventure, but within three months of raising the idea Jennie also raised the money and found the staff and reached the scene of action. Lord Roberts 'inspected' her ship in Cape Town, and there are period-piece photographs of her showing him around, wearing a sun hat and a long skirt which she lifts when stepping through a hatchway—a sergeant-major in high-heeled white shoes! 'Wards, mess rooms, dispensary, operating room, everything was visited and much approved of. The only thing wanting to prove our efficiency was beds filled with the wounded.' She had a couple more rounds to fight, because the authorities wished the *Maine* to return immediately with wounded to England. This was not the purpose of the ship, and Jennie remonstrated firmly, pointing out that if the ship were treated as a mere transport for convalescents 'the international value of the gift would certainly suffer, and the large, expensive and efficient medical staff on board would have nothing to do and would be greatly disappointed as interesting serious cases would not be likely to be sent us'. The Senior Medical Officer said the *Maine* had better move on to Durban and take orders from Sir Redvers Buller.

On January 27th the ship left Cape Town. By good luck Jennie was able to give a lift to her son Jack, who had arrived in Cape Town a few days previously. Less welcome guests were eight army reserve sisters who insisted on bringing their own maids! Jennie commented: 'I did not envy the hospitals which were to benefit by their services.'

After another sea-bashing and a terrifying hailstorm they reached Durban on January 30th, and were ordered to remain outside the harbour. Thirsting for news, however, Jack, who had come to join the South African Light Horse in Natal, made for shore in a small boat. This was intercepted by a naval tug with a message from the commandant to say that Winston was in Durban, having obtained two days leave to see his mother.

Pending the arrival of patients, Jennie gave herself two days off to enjoy her sons' company. There are certain interludes in every human life which remain apart. The atmosphere of tenseness, of affection, of nearness in spirit becomes so strong that one short day or even one short hour remains unforgettable. Such was Jennie's visit to Natal's Government House with her sons. They felt the winds of destiny had blown them together. Each of them was completely free. Here in the Drakonsberg Mountains Jennie had the boys entirely to herself and they had her. It was a precious twenty— four hours. The battles to relieve Ladysmith were pending and next day her sons had to depart. Both were now lieutenants in the South African Light Horse. After his escape Winston had enjoyed a great ovation from the Durban crowds and General Red- vers Buller had written to Lady Londonderry: 'I must say I admire him greatly. I wish he was leading regular troops instead of writing for a rotten paper.'

And so it was that, despite a rule to the contrary, Winston was given a commission without requiring him to abandon his status as a war correspondent. General Buller must have realised that rules are made for ordinary people, not Churchills.

When her boys went off to battle, Jennie busied herself inspecting the military hospitals of Pietermaritzburg until a telegram from Durban announced that wounded were expected. Hurrying back to the *Maine* she found the ship's staff 'in a pleasurable state of excitement at the prospect of the work before them'. No sooner had she reached the ship than wounded started to pour in and the surgeons, nursing sisters and orderlies set to work. Jennie, a starchy-white Queen-Bee, hummed encouragement, sent reports to the London committee and cheered the wounded. 'They delighted in giving their histories and experiences, and particularly the crowning one of how they received their wounds, which with the slightest encouragement they would show with great pride, as well as the extracted bullet if they had one.'

Those who were too sick to write dictated letters, or tried to, for the aptitude does not come easily and after the usual formal opening would often come 'a great scratching of heads and biting of fingers'. 'Won't you send your love to anyone?' Jennie would ask. 'Not out of the family', would be her answer, with a reproving look, but 'One very gallant Tommy, who lay with a patch over his eye, an inflamed cheek and a broken arm, asked me to add to his letter, "The sister which is a-writing of this is very nice".'

Among the first officers sent to the *Maine* limped the twenty-year-old Jack with a leg wound. He carried a letter from Winston telling of the engagement in which they had both endured a hail of bullets. Winston remained sanguine about his own safety, writing to Miss Plowden: 'I have a good belief that I am to be of some use and therefore to be spared.' And he liked the tone of a letter from Captain Scott, commander of the cruiser *Terrible* which was landing seven-inch guns for the defence of Ladysmith. 'I feel certain that I shall someday shake hands with you as the Prime Minister of England; you possess the two necessary qualifications genius and plod.'

But concerning his young brother Winston felt a very human nervousness. To dearest Mamma he wrote of feelings which many must have suffered but few could so accurately express: '. . . He

244

is unhappy at being taken off the board so early in the game and of course it is a great nuisance, but you may be glad with me that he is out of harm's way for a month. There will be a great battle in a few days and his presence—though I would not lift a finger to prevent him—adds much to my anxiety when there is fighting. . . .'

Jennie knew that her hospital ship with its excellent nursing and cool sea air was proving a heaven for two hundred wounded men. Now she determined to go to the front inspecting various hospitals on the way. Having obtained a military pass from the General in charge and the loan of his personal railway carriage from the Governor of Natal, she proceeded. 'Provided with food, armed with Kodaks and field-glasses, not to mention a brown holland dress (my substitute for khaki) in case we should meet the enemy and wish to remain invisible, we started on our journey—Miss Warrender, Colonel Heusman, the commanding officer of the *Maine* and myself, and, last but not least, the coxswain of the *Terrible*.' She never did things by halves: a camouflage-gown and binoculars would be Jennie's idea of a suitable outfit.

She was asleep when the train reached Frere at 5 a.m. A tap on the window awoke her. "Lady Randolph Churchill, are you there?" "Yes, very much so," I answered, as I dropped the shutter and put my head out, finding an officer of the Seaforth Highlanders on the platform. "I knew you were coming up, and thought you would like a cup of coffee," he said, "if you will accept the hospitality of my tin hut fifty yards from here," adding: "You won't get anything more for a long time." '

She was about to jump down when he remarked on her lack of shoes and hat! 'As I walked to the hut, dawn was just breaking—long orange-red streaks outlined the distant brown hills; through the haze of dust showing on the skyline trains of mule-carts were crawling along, and in the plain little groups of soldiers and horsemen were moving about emerging from their tents.'

Twenty miles further along the line she saw the wrecked armoured train from which Winston had been taken prisoner and the graves of those killed. At Chieveley she was escorted over the camp by an aide-de-camp and shown the naval gun which had been dragged there from H.M.S. *Terrible* with its name 'Lady Randolph Churchill' painted in big white letters. 'The weatherbeaten and in many cases haggard men, with soiled, worn uniforms hanging on their spare figures, the horses picketed in lines or singly, covered with canvas torn in strips to keep the flies off, the khaki-painted guns, the ambulance wagons with their train of mules, and above all the dull booming of "Long Tom" made us realise that here was war!' In 1900 it was a rare, a strange, an almost unbelievable realisation.

On the return journey she spent two sympathetic hours at the Remount Depot 'where about 2,000 horses were at that moment resting before being sent to the front, hundreds of them having just arrived from South America. What a fate! To be penned up for weeks on a rolling ship, then crammed into an open truck under a blazing sun, to be taken out, stiff and sore and dazed, given two days' rest, and then sent up to the front only to be food for Boer bullets. Poor things—so understanding—such good friends—the hardships they suffered and the lingering death many had to undergo was one of the most hideous features of the war.'

On returning to the *Maine*, Jennie received a telegram from her sister-in-law Lady Sarah Wilson, who had been caught in Mafeking, saying that rations were strict but sufficient, news scanty, health fairly good.

'Life on board became a round of daily duties, varied only by excitement in regard to war news. It was interesting to distribute newspapers to the soldiers. They were so keen and eager in discussing every point. Even those who were bedridden and too ill to read would clutch you as you passed. "Any news? Ladysmith? Nothing? What, back again, Chieveley Camp? That Buller's unlucky; better try another; and we wants to get to them poor chaps." I argued on the principle that perhaps the general hoped in effect to *reculer pour mieux sauter*, but the heads would wag sagely.'

When eventually H.M.S. *Terrible* heliographed the news of Ladysmith to all ships in harbour 'the band played itself out, the men sang themselves hoarse and at last after a bouquet of fireworks we went to bed'.

Now a flood of sick and wounded poured into Natal. To relieve the pressure all hospital ships, including the *Maine*, were ordered back to England with convalescents. Before departing Jennie obtained a pass allowing her to travel to Ladysmith. With Miss Warrender and Winston she viewed the devastation, and kept her new toy—a Kodak—much in action. 'One must see it all to realise the stupendous difficulties; the harsh impossible ground to get over, the gaining of it inch by inch, the smallest mistake costing hundreds of lives. . . . . Blinding dust up to one's ankles, scorching sun, shut-up empty houses, an expression of resigned martyrdom on every-one's face—Such was my first impression of Ladysmith. Sitting on the top of our gripsacks on a Scotch cart drawn by mules, we drove through the town, presenting as we thought a strange appearance; but no one noticed us.' They dined with General Buller who provided beds but *no sheets*. Next morning Jennie visited the Tin Camp turned into a hospital and noted realistically that it seemed a very difficult place 'to get well in'.

Lord Dundonald, who commanded the South Africa Light Horse, lent them a horse which had never been in harness before. Driven by an intrepid sergeant, Jennie suffered a four-mile charge over rocks to her sons' camp. There she was restored by tea in a tin mug. 'By this time I was too tired to take in any more, and the hazardous drive back in the semi-darkness quite finished me. Making a hasty and apologetic toilet we dined with the general in a tent commanding a fine view of the town. The dinner was good and the company better.' Her memoirs artlessly describe the war scenes of long ago when each victory was celebrated with fireworks, when nursing sisters travelled with personal maids and apologies were due for a hasty toilet when dining with a general at the front.

In March she bade goodbye to Jack and Winston and the *Maine* sailed from Durban, cheered by every ship in harbour. Although she hated leaving her sons and the drama of war work suited her temperament, she felt the emotional tug towards England. George Cornwallis-West's heart was said to be 'permanently damaged'. A letter written from his father's home in February proves that sick leave was proving extremely irksome: 'I have just received your wire re-directed—saying you are going to remain at Durban a month—I thought and hoped that once you had arrived at Durban and got things started on board the *Maine* you would think of returning. . . . I am alone with my father who never misses an oppor-tunity of dropping hints about financial difficulties and how easily they could be overcome if I married an heiress. . . .'

It would, of course, be sensible if George did marry money and she married one of the numerous rich men who would have been honoured by a beauty of high repute, but Jennie remained a romantic. One of George's sisters had married the Prince of Pless and sported the biggest emeralds and pearls outside the Russian court, and the younger sister was to be guided into the arms of the Duke of Westminster. *They* would be rich, why shouldn't she and George live in artistic penury?

She made one last effort to intercede with Lord Roberts concerning Winston, who now wished to join the forces pushing through the Orange Free State, but Lord Roberts proved sticky, for Lord Kitchener—outraged by young Churchill's criticisms in *The River War*—had just become his Chief of Staff.

Kitchener's annoyance was understandable, but it seems unbelievable that Winston's enemies should have resented articles appealing for a generous policy towards the conquered Boers: yet Jack wrote to his mother on 3rd April from Ladysmith. '. . . Winston is being severely criticised about his peaceful telegrams. . . . They say that even if you are going to treat these Boers well after their surrender, this is not the time to say so.' The *Morning Post*, his own paper wrote editorials disapproving of leniency towards valiant subjugated rebels.

It was 11th April when Field Marshal Roberts finally sent an ungracious note to the effect that Winston would be allowed to accompany his force as a war correspondent *for his father's sake*!

Winston did one good turn to Roberts who was being mocked for the number of Dukes on his staff. He relieved him of cousin Marlborough, who joined him on the march to Johannesburg. In the meantime Winston heard that he had been invited to stand for parliament by two constituencies and he spent what he must have felt were his last months of active service courting hairbreadth escapes. 'I do not think I have ever been so near destruction', he wrote his mother after one episode. But faith in her son's Star kept Jennie tranquil. She enjoyed the voyage home and Mrs Ronalds the Treasurer, showed a good account of the budget while Lord Lansdowne, Secretary for War, wrote a most gratifying letter. She had hardly reached London when Winston issued orders in the usual vein: 'Make sure that I get two thousand pounds on account of the royalties.' He thought, and rightly, that the fame of his exploits amidst bullets and shells ought to increase the value of his next book.

Jennie's hospital phase was over. Eleanor Warrender dedicated her entire life to nursing henceforth, but George Cornwallis-West laid claim to Lady Randolph. Through May and June she hesitated while friends begged her to consider the discrepancy in age. George's family tried their utmost to dissuade him, but he disliked his mother who had treated him cruelly as a little boy, and he thought his old father stuffy. George sought happiness rather than fortune. He was considered the best looking man in England and Jennie the most beautiful woman of her generation. Surely they could forget that tiresome twenty years.

The Boer war went on, interminably it seemed, and Jennie could not wait to get her sons home. Winston's yen for danger she understood. She fussed in a different way about Jack. He was still being adjured to spell correctly, and to keep *au fait* of things political as well as to boil his drinking water. She was not quite so sure of *his* Star!

May 26th 1900

35A Great Cumberland Place.
My darling Jack,
  I have at last had a letter from you, the second since the 17th of March when I left Durban but I know how hard it is to write in your case. I have written every mail to Winston, I confess they were scraps, but I have been so very busy. I told him to forward them to you and hope he has done so. Of course I have been following Buller's advance and have had some bad moments thinking of you but have trusted for the best and think you are as capable of looking after your skin as well as most. I am glad to think the end is approaching and that the war must soon be over now. I am also glad that you are moving, anything is better then stagnation in an unhealthy camp. How fit you must be as riding suits you I know. I am much more frightened of fever than of bullets so don't be rash as regards water etc. I have a long letter from Winston today from Bloemfontain dated March 1st. He seems to have had a narrow escape at Dewetsdorp from falling into the Boers' hands, as an advance party met the enemy Winston's saddle turned and I understand his horse galloped away but luckily his own people turned back for him. He did not give me the account himself. I suppose I shall see it in the papers, meanwhile Pamela heard it from someone and told me. I am sure that you

like him are heartily sick of the whole thing, everyone is and all longing for peace and home. . . .

Harassed by the financial predicament of *The Anglo-Saxon Review*, as well as by acrid comment on her personal life, Jennie turned for comfort to her sisters who soothed rather than advised. In adversity the Jerome sisters closed ranks.

In late May she was writing to George apologising for being 'snappy and tired'. To Winston, after an outburst while 'trying to cope with bills and bores' she mentioned a possibility of accompanying the *Maine* on its third voyage. 'But all my plans are vague. Sometimes I think I may marry G.W. . . .' She went on affectionately: 'You know what you are to me and how you can now and always count on me—I am intensely proud of you and apart from this my heart goes out to you and I understand you as no woman ever will—Pamela is devoted to you and if yr love has grown as hers I have no doubt it is only a question of time for you 2 to marry —what a comfort it will be to you to settle down in comparative comfort—I am sure you are sick of the war and its horrors. You will be able to make a decent living out of your writings, and your political career will lead you to big things. Probably if you married an heiress you would not work half so well.'

In the meantime George's angry father wrote to Leonie whom he suspected of encouraging the match:

> Ruthven Castle
>
> I am aware that you have assisted Lady Randolph Churchill in her insane infatuation for my son—because a telegram signed by you fell into my hand in which you invited him to meet the hospital ship 'Maine' on its arrival at Southampton.
>
> I wish seriously to ask you if you consider this marriage can possibly lead to the happiness of either? . . . The life of a couple so ill-assorted is doomed, is painful to think of—and the marvel to me is that a woman as talented and experienced as your sister could coolly contemplate it as nothing out of the common.
>
> I can only add that if this marriage takes place it will estrange the whole of my family from my son and so I have told him.
>
> I am, yours truly,
> W. Cornwallis-West

Leonie may have shown this letter to Jennie. If so, the effect it had was to produce an announcement of the engagement in *The Times* during Ascot Races, when it caused the maximum amount of talk.

Jennie wrote blissfully to Jack.

35A Great Cumberland Place
June 23rd 1900

My dearest Jack,

I hope this will find you with yr face more or less turned towards home. . . . My darling boy I wonder if you will have had the cable I sent you telling you that I was going to marry George? I also wrote a long letter to Winston on the subject telling him to forward it to you. I can't think what he is about—I hear he has not written to Pamela for 8 weeks—Now as regards my marriage I should like to tell you all my plans for you and myself—but it must be in a very concise form as time presses—& I have *such* a lot to do—the Review, my book, my marriage! . . .

And again on June 30th, for the 'darling boys' must be reconciled to the idea of a very young stepfather:

June 30th 1900

My darling Jack,

I do hope soon to hear something of you. It is *such* ages since I had a line. . . . I had a cable from Winston to say he starts for home on the 4th of July. I wish you were coming too darling boy. You won't stay out much longer? You will find Cassel ready to receive you—and your 'Momma' with open arms. Winston will be here in time for my wedding if all goes well—It will be very quiet—no breakfast except for the family—but I won't do it in a 'hole and corner' fashion as tho' I was ashamed of it. I pray from the bottom of my heart that it won't make you unhappy—you know how dearly I love you both and the thought that it may hurt you—is the one cloud in my happiness—You won't grudge me the latter? Nothing could exceed George's goodness and devotion and I think we shall be very happy. Everything I can do for you I will. Meanwhile my real friends are most kind and have given me charming presents and they all like him so much that they are reconciled. . . . Leonie has had a

251

boy—Lionel. I do so long to hear from you and how you both are—you must be rather short of clothing.

Best love,
Your loving mother,
J.R.C.

George Cornwallis-West in his memoirs describes the effect the engagement produced on his commanding officer, who told him he would have to leave the Scots Guards if he married Jennie. 'Considering that she had a host of friends including himself, and was liked by everybody, and that there was no rule in the regiment against subalterns marrying, I considered such an ultimatum outrageous and saw red. If I had had any doubts as to the wisdom of what I was about to do they were blown to the four winds by what I considered nothing less than an unwarrantable piece of interference, etc., etc.'

George dashed off in a hansom to the Adjutant-General who reassured him. No officer could be asked to leave a regiment because he married a woman older than himself. Three days later the regimental commander sent for him in a towering rage and castigated the Adjutant-General, 'the enemy of the Brigade of Guards'. Meanwhile congratulatory telegrams were pouring in from brother officers in South Africa. George, outraged, asked for an interview with the Prince of Wales who gently suggested that he should go on half-pay until the dust settled. H.R.H. also wrote Jennie a letter of admonition. He had from the start deplored the idea of her marrying a man so much younger than herself. 'But I want him,' said Jennie to Leonie—and that was that. In a temper she tore up the Prince's letter of remonstrance and let fly in her uncontrolled way. The Prince's reply she kept, and it shows what a forbearing friend he could be.

My dear Lady Randolph Churchill,

It has been my privilege to enjoy your friendship for upwards of a quarter of a century—therefore why do you think it necessary to write me a rude letter—simply because I have expressed my regret at the marriage you are about to make? I have said nothing behind your back that I have not said to your face—You know the world so well that I presume you are the best judge of your own happiness—but at the same time you should think twice before you abuse your friends and well-wishers for not congratulating you on the serious step you are going to make! I can only hope that we shall all be mistaken.

Believe me,
Sincerely yrs,
A.E.

On receiving this, the Lady Randolph Churchill promptly married her Lieutenant. The ceremony in St Paul's, Knightsbridge, was attended by Marlborough and most of the Churchill family. On her wedding morn she composed a careful letter:

35A Great Cumberland Place
July 28th 1900

My darling Jack,

I am more than distressed to think that my letters with the exception of one have not reached you. You must guess that your 'Momma' would not forget you—I wired you and Winston that I was going to marry George—and here I am actually at the day—I would give much if you were here and I could give you a big fat kiss. I could assure you with my own lips what you already know—and that is that I love you and Winston dearly & that no one can ever come in between us. I shall always remain your *best* friend & do everything in the world for you. You both can count on me—I am glad to think you know and like George— He has behaved like a brick. By next mail I will write and tell you all about the wedding. Sunny is giving me away and I am well supported by the Churchill family. People have been wonderfully kind and given us heaps of presents. I want you to come home as soon as you decently can. Both Winston and I hate to have you away. I have all sorts of plans for you and want to make your life as pleasant as possible. God bless you my darling boy.

Ever your loving Mother,
J.R.C.

Jennie may have been selfish but even on her wedding morning she could find time to write such a letter.

❧ 25

George Cornwallis-West humorously, but not ungallantly, described the tenor of his honeymoon to my father. Jennie was in the throes of issuing numbers six and seven of the *The Anglo-Saxon Review*. She had kept up the magnificent covers and was collecting erudite articles which even today make a readable anthology. But the huge monetary loss was fussing her. She travelled with a hamper of correspondence concerning contributions and illustrations, copyrights and translations. Some of the letters were articles in themselves on subjects ranging from Catullus to Waterloo.

She also travelled with a smaller hamper of unpaid bills, which she went through at intervals. It made her feel virtuous to set them in order, almost as if she had paid them off. 'Fancy having to take bills on a honeymoon,' said Jennie with a slightly martyred expression. 'But one must be businesslike.' And she would look helplessly at her new husband. 'Of course I was eager to put her affairs in order', George told my father, 'but I found it a bit thick when expected to pay for Lord Randolph Churchill's barouche purchased in the 'eighties.'

On the whole, however, he agreed with his wife. Bills were unfair. They depressed the spirits and spoiled the day devoted to their perusal. George and Jennie were birds of a feather, birds of paradise made to charm and to adorn, not to cope with vulgar business.

But George was a great trier, and having paid up large sums for his lady and persuaded her to let 35A Great Cumberland Place

254

occasionally and economise by staying at the Ritz, he came firmly to terms with the situation, resigned from the Army and determined to earn a living. He made splendid endeavours but such men were neither bred nor trained to understand money.

His letters of September 1900 after two months of marriage carry sensible advice as well as sporting news. 'Beloved Wife. . . . Get rid of Lane [her business editor for the *Review*]. . . . Only a minute to write before dinner. I got a stag but again got fearfully wet.'

Jennie had left George for a few days during the General Election to help Winston who was standing for Oldham. He had written very firmly, 'My dear Mamma, I write again to impress you how very useful your presence will be down here. . . .' By October 1st he was a Member of Parliament and proving himself a star turn on any platform. Since March, Jennie had been working on his behalf in regard to lecture tours which could make a few much needed thousands, and now she was ordered to find out from Joseph Chamberlain and Arthur Balfour if it might weaken his political position to appear as a paid lecturer on public platforms. She obtained encouraging answers from his father's old friends and after a remunerative English tour Winston left for America, whence his letters to her are full of dissatisfaction. Pro-Boer feeling remained very strong and his agent very grasping. However he again stayed with Bourke Cockran in New York and there met Mark Twain and Theodore Roosevelt.

Meanwhile George, possessing no genius but much goodwill, met Sir Ernest Cassel, the Prince of Wales's financial adviser, who had always admired Jennie and was putting Jack into the City. 'It was he who broached the subject and asked me what I thought of doing with myself. I told him the administrative side of an electrical engineering concern rather appealed to me. "Not the city?" he asked. I replied that the prospect of going on a half-commission basis to a firm of stockbrokers and touting for orders from my friends had no allurements for me. He thought a moment and said, "There are many young men who should never go east of Temple Bar. Perhaps you are one of them."'

Shortly after this, Cassel sent him as a sort of unpaid apprentice to an electrical firm supplying the Glasgow Corporation power station. George found Glasgow a hideous place in which to live.

He writes: 'Looking back, I am convinced that Cassel's idea of sending me there was to find out whether I really meant to take up a business career seriously or not.'

George learned what he could on the technical side and became a director of various companies. 'Up to now, the only men with whom I had come in contact in subordinate positions had been those who had served under me as private soldiers or N.C.O.s and who, when given an order, executed it as a matter of course. I was now to come in contact with employees of the companies that I directed, and although many of them were old soldiers, it did not in the least follow that they executed orders with the same alacrity as they had in the Army.' Having digested this fact, George got on well. He himself kept to military punctuality when attending board meetings; on one occasion when his motor car broke down he even chartered a special train so as not to be late, although this cost him 25 per cent of the year's fees.

Whatever George Cornwallis-West gave up to marry Jennie he enjoyed her extraordinarily varied circle of friends. 'Through her', he writes, 'I became an Edwardian, in the sense that I was a member of that particular set in society with which King Edward associated himself, a set with which a young officer in the Guards, or the son of a country gentleman living in the country was not likely, in the ordinary course of events, to become particularly intimate.'

In fact he liked Jennie's older friends better than his own vintage. Among the oldest and wisest and richest of these was the frail Scottish father of Mrs Ronnie Greville (who entertained the Prince lavishly on his millions.) 'I liked the old man immensely, and often used to go walks with him. One day I was explaining to him that my sole motive for having gone into business, apart from having something to do, was to endeavour to make sufficient money to pay off the mortgages on my family estates. He stopped in his walk and looked at me with his head on one side, and, in the Scottish accent which was natural to him, he said: "A most praiseworthy object, young man. I hope ye'll succeed, but I doot ye will." "Why?" I asked. "Some men are born to make money, it just comes natural to them; others never will. Maybe ye're one of the latter." I felt rather crestfallen. "I've worked hard all my life," he went on, "but it's been an easy thing for me to become rich, I just couldna help it; and the only pleasure it gives me is the thought that I'm able to give pleasure to others. But money doesn't necessarily come from hard work." I thought of Cassel's remark about men who should never go east of Temple Bar, and thought how strange it was that two millionaires should have said practically the same thing. I realise now that for a man to make money he must have a natural flair for it.'

Amidst George's ambling pages of pleasant anecdote, endearingly interspersed with irrelevant underexposed photographs of 'A typical English trout stream' and 'A typical Scottish salmon river', there is one concerning an evening when Jennie was for once thrown out of her conversational stride. Seated next to the Japanese ambassador she held forth on her impressions of his land and led him to speak of Japanese literature and proverbs. 'What,' she asked, 'would be your equivalent of "A penny wise and pound foolish"? His Excellency thought solemnly before answering: 'The man who goes to bed early to save candles gets twins.' Silence at the dinner table!

Lord Randolph's sisters, Lady Wimborne, Lady Tweedsmouth and Lady Sarah Wilson had, over the years, become Jennie's true friends and she often took her new husband to Blenheim where the young Duke entertained happily enough it seemed, after his American marriage. Winston frequently came also and brought his brilliant friend, F. E. Smith.

The Prince of Wales soon forgave Jennie for ignoring his advice and losing her temper. The Cornwallis-Wests were invited to all the great country houses set on entertaining H.R.H. As Jennie was as well liked by the Princess of Wales as by Mrs Keppel, she became in a way the very centre of the Prince's set, which many criticised but all longed to get into.

When the old Queen died, society went into mourning for six months, but black clothes made no difference to the discreet, highly stylised revels of Edward's set. Through Jennie, Winston was invited to stalk at Balmoral, an unusual privilege for a young politician. A letter to his mother records: 'I have been vy kindly treated here by the King, who has gone out of his way to be nice to me.'

George Cornwallis-West described a large weekend party given by the Grand Duke Michael of Russia (exiled to England after a morganatic marriage). On the return journey they travelled back to

London with the King on a special train—it was a long, hot journey and the effort to constantly amuse became gruelling. To his trepidation, George was made to join a rubber of bridge and won thirty pounds from His Majesty, who produced an enormous bank roll of notes from his pocket with which to pay. This impressed George deeply. Had the roles been reversed he could not have done the same! The highlight of the journey occurred when a lady wiped her face with the novel *papiers poudrés*. The King insisted on trying two on his nose and there were screams of laughter from dutiful courtiers and a general clean-up before reaching London.

But at long last the King held power and could use his intelligence freely. Old friends flocked around him and he loved them, but only Mrs Keppel had access to state documents and advised.

When George's sister, Shelagh, became engaged to the Duke of Westminster, Jennie had written to Leonie (Christmas Day 1900):

> Blenheim
>
> Quite a nice lot of wedding presents I have had, the Prince a Fabergé monster and the Princess a brooch. I hope Seymour got a little Fabergé frog I sent him, promised by Tiffany's. Winston seems to have done well! Shelagh and Bend'Or are to be married in February; people feel very spiteful about them, she certainly is not popular but they will cringe to her when she is a Duchess. . . .

Jennie and this young sister-in-law remained great friends. Jennie and George enjoyed their visits to Eaton Hall and to the magnificent receptions held in old Grosvenor House. A famous collection of paintings lined the staircase, which must have been one of the great sights of that era. George could not help feeling proud of his tall, blonde sister blazing with diamonds in the ballroom. But how angry she became when, at the end of a ball for the Crown Prince of Germany, His Imperial Highness completely disappeared. George, who had remained after the last guests to talk it over with his sister, set off with the equerry to search Grosvenor House. There were many rooms and long corridors. They did not wish to alarm the servants so they tiptoed around calling softly. Eventually the Crown Prince was located—locked in one of the best bedrooms with a certain peeress.

Jennie and Shelagh held an indignant conference. What does one do now? 'Better go to bed and leave them. The Equerry can wait outside the door,' Jennie solemnly advised. George thought it funny, the ladies were outraged, the detectives embarrassed. Only the lady emerged unruffled and drove home, tiara and all, apparently well pleased with herself. The Kaiser heard of the incident and the repercussions of this party lasted quite a while.

On February 14th, 1901, Winston took his seat in the House of Commons and that evening he sent to Jennie the most touching compliment that a son could devise. 'I enclose a cheque for £300. In a certain sense it belongs to you; for I could never have earned it had you not transmitted to me the wit and energy which are necessary.' Four days later she had the inexpressibly moving experience of sitting in the Ladies Gallery, where so often in the past she had trembled for Randolph, to hear her son make his first speech. During these early months in the House he pleaded forcefully for generous treatment to the Boers and Jennie wrote to Leonie: 'Winston has just returned and has been reading to me a speech he intends delivering in the House next week—very good and just expresses my views on the South African War.'

In the late spring Mr Broderick, Minister for War, launched a scheme for Army Reform which Winston considered expensive and unnecessary. He prepared a speech criticising 'Mr Broderick's Army' which he delivered near to midnight on May 13th, 1901. Jennie heard him refer splendidly to his father who had resigned on a like issue and she was glad that he dared to post his speech to the *Morning Post* before it was delivered, just as Randolph used to do. 'I took six weeks to prepare this speech, and learnt it so thoroughly off by heart, that it hardly mattered where I began it or how I turned it,' he admitted.

There is hardly a year in which some scandal does not crop up in the Army and there had been extraordinary questions asked about the Guards, as Jennie's undated letter to Leonie shows:

35A Gt. Cumberland Place

I met the King at dinner last night—most affable about you. I had sent him one of your letters which he thought most amusing and well-written. I shall miss the opening of Parliament.

Winston and a very large faction are tooth and nail against the War Office and Broderick. The country is taking it up immensely and especially the matter of the Flogging Scandal in the Guards Act! At a first night recently two young guardsmen who were late were shouted at by the Pit to 'sit down'—whereupon a wag called out 'They can't! They're in the Guards!'

Goodbye darling Leonie and enjoy yourself and make the most of those Shining Hours.

Jennie was now on perfect terms with the King as another letter to Leonie shows:

(February 14 1902)

The King came over yesterday for a deer drive and got a stag. The day before I went to Balmoral and spent two hours with him: we walked all over the house and the place. He talked about you. Also of the Duke of Connaught but not very kindly— I suppose really that he and the Duke are not on the best of terms. (The royal brothers had various disagreements, chiefly over the Duke of Connaught's military employments.)

When King Edward's coronation took place in August 1902 Jennie and Leonie were naturally in the King's box, which he packed with lady friends who could not enter the Abbey as peeresses. Jennie sat between Countess Torby (the Grand Duke Michael's wife) and Daisy of Pless who wore her famous diamond and turquoise crown, all her European orders and a train of cloth of gold. Jennie and Leonie and Mrs Keppel and George's mother (who was a *very* old friend of King Edward) wore splendid diamond tiaras 'begged, borrowed or stolen', and a certain amount of amused comment arose. 'What that lot doesn't know about King Edward . . . !' purred Monsieur de Soveral, the Portuguese ambassador, intimate of the King and wittiest of the diplomatic corps.

So the first years of Jennie's inauspicious second marriage rolled by in a serenity which amazed all gloomy prognosticators. They were right in the end, of course, but it proved a long wait before the crack in her happiness appeared.

For one thing, both George and Jennie were extremely busy. He was darting around England seeking to earn a living and with all her extravagance Jennie was a hard worker. When *The Anglo-Saxon Review* had to close down for financial reasons she gritted her teeth and sat down to make money by writing memoirs. To Jack she described the usual author's moodiness: 'I am writing my book. My feelings fluctuate about it—sometimes I think it is going to be splendid—and then again I am most depressed.' *The Reminiscences of Lady Randolph Churchill* proved a best-seller in America as well as England. George had encouraged her with 'You *know* you can do anything you set your hand to', and the only person to be thoroughly annoyed by these charming, if not always accurate, memoirs was Clara, the meekest of sisters, who flared up in honest fury at discovering that Jennie had taken all *her* stories concerning the Second Empire Court and pretended they had happened to her. Jennie even attributed to herself some of King Milan of Serbia's letters! 'But, darling, I have to make money and thought it would improve the book,' she argued when Clara travelled up from Brede especially to scold. 'And what if *I* want to write a book?' Even Leonie said it was 'too naughty'.

Leonie's letters, written when she accompanied the Duke and Duchess of Connaught to India for the Durbar, unfold a forgotten historical episode. Jennie kept almost every letter ever written to her and certainly these descriptions are more entertaining than the delightful George's accounts of how again and again he shoots pheasants, hooks fish, loses fish, goes hunting, has a wonderful run, has a dreadful run, finds a hot bath or finds a tepid bath, and at intervals cracks his pate.

The path of love had not run smooth for Winston, and it was good for him to have a change of scene that autumn. When the Duke and Duchess of Connaught, with Leonie and Jack Leslie in their party, travelled to Luxor to lay the last stone of the Aswan Dam, Sir Ernest Cassel, who had financed the enterprise, took his yacht up the Nile and invited Winston to join the party which included Lord Randolph's Fourth Party colleagues, Hicks Beach and Gorst, as well as Mrs Keppel. Winston found himself in older company all *au courant* of current politics but he had no young partner with whom to sightsee or watch the Nile by moonlight. When the royal party sailed for India Leonie wrote long daily descriptions to Jennie, who had longed to come but thought it wiser not to leave George.

18 December 1902
H.M.S. Renown

In the Red Sea
Dearest Jennie,

    I sent George a few Cairo cigarettes as an Xmas card. . . . So far we have had no contretemps among so few, and we are now busily reading up books on India. . . . Winston will tell you all about Aswan. He looked better the last day I saw him on a donkey at Luxor! But he had been seedy. This climate agrees with the Duke who looks ten years younger, is full of energy and too kind and amiable for words. The Duchess and I read a good deal together. . . . I thought of you when I saw the Sphynx—because you had been impressed by it—it *does* give one a strange weird feeling. General Murray of Seaforth Highlanders sat next to me at luncheon and said his wife *liked* you—all that was long ago! Goodbye my dearest Black Jane. Be happy with that Darling of a George—and don't forget me—*Do* write to Duke of C's camp.

Leonie

Viceroy's Camp,   New Year's Day
Delhi   1903
Dearest,

The papers will give you a full account of all today's proceedings—It was certainly a glorious pageant—I wished a dozen times you had been here to enjoy it. . . . Mary Curzon looked extremely well and was simple and did her part with great sang-froid—the crowds coming back were like a glorified Derby Day crowd. . . . The Camp is a marvel of comfort and everyone seems to be enjoying themselves. . . . The Curzons meeting trains at the station and all mounting their elephants there and proceeding through the town. . . . The life is very pleasant but the cold at night is *intense* and one takes one's bath in the morning practically out of doors! . . . There seems great enthusiasm wherever the 'King Emperor's' name is mentioned. They make a kind of religion of their loyalty—We ride in the mornings and see the native camps—the mass of retinue is something marvellous—the lower classes are hardly human beings—they are so numerous—live on nothing—move about silently—and timidly. . . . There has been a good deal of buying of jewels but I don't think Indian jewelry very attractive . . . and I never want to see a turquoise again! Ld Kitchener is entertaining in great style and is very affable—Everyone asks after you—I had a long talk with Mary Curzon who said she admired you for not coming out—although it was her loss. Her beauty is the kind that does the best for these functions. She really looks very beautiful and has marvellous clothes—It is all such a jumble of London ladies and Indian princes . . . gold cloth and barbaric jewels. . . . We saw the 'Purdah' ladies yesterday—every man was sent miles away —and they were very quaint in their dress and their ways— They had to be consulted whether a Maharajah aged 2 cd be brought in to their presence! The back view of the elephants at the procession reminded me of Mme Hirsh! Forgive disjointed letter. Love from yr devoted L.

Durbar Jan 23rd
Western Frontiers—We are seeing the Khyber Pass and travelling over the ground Winston wrote about in his *Malakand F.F.* The scenery was all so wild and beautiful. . . . Here we are in the heart of Central India—miles away from any town—camp pitched in the middle of the jungle. . . . We each have a tent and then dine in the Duke's big tent—the luggage arrived by elephant five hours after us. . . . We are to remain here 10 days. . . . We start out about 10 in the morning and drive 10 miles. Then mount elephants and go through thick jungle to little stands made in the trees. . . .

Leonie loved the jungle 'beautiful in the evening light—weird trees with huge leaves and orchids hanging from the branches— no sound except elephants' heavy tread on crackling dead leaves', and described a dead tiger carried on a litter made of branches as 'like the swan in Parsival'!

Meanwhile Winston was trying to forget his private woe in a mass of work at his flat at 105 Mount Street. After years of romantic hope he had that spring been forced to realise that the lovely Miss Plowden enjoyed skating on thin ice. In August 1901 George Cornwallis-West had written to Jennie: 'Jack dined with me last night and opened his heart about Pamela ——; he says she is the same to three other men as she is to Winston . . . I am sorry for Winston as I do not think he would be happy with her.' Yet only a year before Winston had so confidently written: 'I think a great deal of Pamela, she loves me very dearly.'

One very ominous letter falls from this bundle. It is in Clara's handwriting and must be to her husband: 'Tell me about Winston. Jennie tells me in a letter that he is *not* going to marry but that is entirely *entre nous*. Leonie says Jennie seems so happy and contented so I do hope George's little flirt with Mrs Pat Campbell means nothing. But Winston is more serious. Oh how I hope he won't marry Pamela. She is not the wife for him although she is so pretty and attractive.'

There had been a distressing morning which my grandmother recounted to me thirty years later. Winston had burst into her room looking ill and distraught. 'Aunt Leonie—Do you know I haven't slept one wink last night? I've paced my room the whole night through— till dawn came—without lying down.' He had discovered that two other young gentlemen also regarded themselves as secretly engaged to Pamela. She was so beautiful and sought-after and kind that saying yes had seemed the easiest way to keep them all happy. My grandmother, always slightly indignant as she recalled this episode, said that she had driven straight off to Miss Plowden and said: 'You *can't* do this to my nephew.' Forced to make a decision, Pamela chose a handsome young Liberal, the Earl of Lytton. He was a friend of Winston and they often spoke on the same Free Trade platforms. Pamela asked Winston to be their 'best friend', which did not lessen the hurt. The marriage took place on April 3rd, 1902. And that was that.

❧ 26

George Cornwallis-West had a weakness for beautiful elder women, and the fact that he was regarded as the 'best-looking man in England' made it easier for his unguarded admirations to start forest fires. Much of the time he was immersed in sport and in business affairs, but not *all* the time. Jennie could never relax—lovely clothes and quick repartee kept her the most enchanting of hostesses, the most desirable of guests. She had to guard against getting fat. Her figure had never been her best point; she was strongly, stockily built. This had been less noticeable in the days of tight waists, huge skirts, frills and flounces. Now that she was forty-five and fashion was showing elongated lines, she ought to have dieted. But the starvation craze came two generations later and as she felt well she ate well. The wonderful eyes, the flash of her glance, remained, but she no longer rode and the golf played to accompany George did not keep her slim. She kept to certain styles which she knew becoming—white lace jabots and colossal velvet hats. She had such taste, such knowledge, such zest for life, but money and accounting remained a nightmare.

There is a chapter in George's memoirs entitled 'Unsuccessful Enterprises' which the sympathetic reader skips. We can see how hard he tried and how excellent his ideas were. As well as working for the British Electric Traction Company, he patented an automatic rifle, concerning which, after long deliberations, the War Office refused, saying it 'would encourage the waste of ammunition by the soldier'. Then he nearly made a fortune with a man who had

265

discovered a method of opening oysters to start off artificial pearls, but the thoughtless fellow died, leaving his secret scribbled incomprehensibly on a sheet of paper in the bank. Then a dishonest solicitor rooked him of £10,000.

With relief we turn to subsequent chapters beginning with 'The first brown trout I ever caught was at the age of nine . . .', or 'My first recollection of firing a gun', or 'For a man who is fit, able to walk, climb and sometimes even to run, there is no finer sport than deer-stalking.' Then the reader grows happy. We know where we are.

Sporting George was among the first Englishmen to own a petrol-driven motor-car. His letters from 1902 onwards are full of triumphant 100-mile runs 'without even a puncture'. During the summer of that year, in a vein he tries to keep modest, he describes breathtaking speeds. 'Five hours for 110 miles. Not bad considering I had a puncture and the last forty miles pitch dark.'

In August 1903, while Jennie stayed at Blenheim, George went racing at Goodwood and then home to Wales where he shot over his father's land and the letters are full of snipe, grouse, golden plover, teal and how much it rains. From Tranby Croft, the scene of the famous card-game scandal involving the Prince of Wales, George writes merrily that he is playing golf and adds: 'I am glad you are working at your play. Stick to it.'

Winter comes and he writes: 'My beloved. I feel a beast going off but I get so little hunting.' George went stalking with his brother-in-law the Duke of Westminster while Jennie visited Chatsworth. Her worries concerning Mrs Pat Campbell were parried by fatherly advice: 'Don't flirt too much with either Hugo or George. I trust neither. They both have temperaments and get carried away. Squeezer got a glorious 13 pointer today weighing 18 stone. Seymour Fortescue and I had blank days but it is all nonsense about our host taking the best beats. He is most fair and generous.' George wrote this without knowing that Bend'or Westminster was gallantly slipping a cheque for £8,000 to Winston to pass on anonymously with a word of sympathy for Jennie.

If left alone in London, Jennie dined out every night. Her vehement wit was always in demand at the enormous dinners which took place throughout May and June. She gave luncheon parties but few dinners, for her house was considered too small—the dining table only seated twelve. But this inability to entertain on

266

the grand scale did not matter, for the Edwardians considered any 'cutlet for cutlet idea' boring and middle class. Jennie was invited out for what she contributed, not for the meals she could return. When the Prince wished to have lunch with her he preferred to be alone, when he asked her to arrange a dinner he left it to her 'excellent taste' to choose guests to amuse him. For years she employed Rosa Lewis to cook on these occasions, thus saving her own kitchen staff from hysterics at the responsibility.

George worked hard while leading his social life. Jennie kept engagements for both husband and son. No Edwardian ever forgot an engagement. They were always giving each other jewelled pencils, little ivory tablets and leather memorandum books to jog the memory. Although Jennie and Leonie would know the views of any politician they met and could tease or flatter him about his last speech, they needed constant written reminders concerning trivial matters: when shopping both regularly left their purchases in hansom cabs and were weekly visitors at Scotland Yard's Lost Property Office.

Jennie was a tempestuous employer but her devoted servants remained for years and understood that quick temper. On one occasion, soon after marrying George, she had the annoyance of finding an extremely expensive hat to be unbecoming, so she gave it to her maid who did not like it either or else forgot to take it when leaving the bedroom. On her return a pack of hounds appeared to have torn the hat to pieces—velvet bows and feathers lay all over the floor. Her ladyship was looking slightly guilty but what a lot she had got out of her system!

The evening ritual of dressing for dinner inevitably caused tantrums and, according to Seymour—a frequent eyewitness—hairbrushes, etc., would fly through the air. Clara, Jennie and Leonie all threw; they never spoke the spiteful or sarcastic word, but teacups and even jam-pots were known to hurtle past offenders' ears. Then their eyes would fill with tears and they quickly asked forgiveness. Heaven knows how they inherited this trait. Leonard Jerome was a self-controlled and mannerly fellow. Mrs Jerome may have smashed china in secret but she kept it off the record. Happily the three sisters were poor shots and their immediate contrition aroused sympathy as much as indignation.

At the end of the London season in July the mighty departed for their country homes or to Cowes. For several years Jennie rented a villa called Egypt on the sea-front which lay near to the Villa Rosetta of happy memories where Randolph had proposed. Clara with her son Hugh would join them for a 'little yachting' and a great many parties. After Cowes week George might take Jennie to stay with his sister Daisy at Fürstenstein before he hurried back to Scotland for his stalking. The Princess had always loved Jennie, whom she found 'gay, courageous and kind', but she disliked Winston, said so frankly and indeed wrote in her memoirs published between the world wars: 'Despite the disparity in ages we were all pleased with the marriage and hoped it would bring lasting happiness to them both. It made Winston Churchill a connection of ours, a prospect we viewed with somewhat mixed feelings. I cannot honestly say I ever cared for him much, but at any rate, like his friend, Lord Birkenhead, he is immensely alive and individual, and in this age of stereotyped personalities that is something.'

In Daisy's memoir-diary, a treasure trove for rambling historians of the period, there are occasional revealing paragraphs concerning her efforts as an Englishwoman married to a German to discourage her countrymen from criticising everything German. A page from her diary in January 1903 when she was in London shows genuine concern: 'On Tuesday night I dined in London with Consuelo Manchester [Duchess of] to meet the King. He told me I was *trés en beauté*. I always feel rather shy when he talks like that. . . . During dinner he spoke very freely (too freely) about Germany, America, Venezuela, and so on. The Duchess and her sister Lady Lister Kaye are American and so is Adele Essex who was also there, being the only ladies apart from Mrs George Keppel. On several occasions they turned apologetically to me, but the King said: "Oh Daisy doesn't mind; being married to a German does not make her change her national feelings." I thought, neither does it make one insensible, so I let them go on arguing and talking about everything, and when they had finished I *had* my say at them, and then dropped my fan and someone coming to pick it up caused a change in the conversation.

'The next day I lunched with George and his wife. Winston her son was there, Mrs Keppel, Soveral and others, and an American senator, a famous orator and traveller, whose name I have forgotten. They again began poking fun at Germany, criticising her policy towards America, how little it mattered one way or another what Germany thought or did, and similar rudenesses. At last I turned with a bright red face to the Senator and said, "Now tell me what you think. My husband is a German, but please ignore that, only tell them a few positive facts." Then he reduced them all to silence; even Soveral had not a word to say.'

The friction between his sister and his stepson, Winston, often embarrassed George, who was peaceful by nature, and in August 1903 between race meetings and shooting parties he wrote to Jennie: 'I can't make out what Winston meant when he said he did not wish to be invited to Fürstenstein—when he wrote and asked me to ask Daisy to ask him. I did so and she foolishly began to talk about her dislike of his politics. I said I thought she was very narrow-minded and finally she said she would put him up. Of course I didn't tell Winston all this so don't you. She is silly and so is he for making out he never intended to go.'

Old Colonel Cornwallis-West remained a very trying father-in-law, but Jennie learnt philosophy. There is a revealing paragraph in a letter Winston wrote her on 22nd August, 1904: 'I thought a good deal over all you said to me about yourself & I feel sure you are right to concentrate on and take pains with the few people you really care about. But I have no doubt that when papa W. is at length gathered to Abraham you will be able to renew your youth like the eagle.' Mrs Cornwallis-West liked Jennie, but her attitude to her son would cause George in after years to say: 'Whatever happens don't bury me anywhere near my mother.'

In 1905 Jennie moved out of town. George considered this an economy, and she needed a place where Winston could invite political friends, for all his contemporaries and critics seemed to have large country houses at their disposal. After viewing several places Jennie lost her heart to Salisbury Hall near St Albans, a seventeenth-century manor house, surrounded by a thirteenth-century moat. Warwick the Kingmaker had built a castle here and the old fortifications remained in part, as well as the Elizabethan hall embellished with unique stone-carved plaques. The carved wood staircase was, they were told, enlivened by the ghost of Nell Gwynn or rather more pleasantly by the echo of her silvery laugh. If not very practical, Salisbury Hall was exceedingly beautiful and full of historic curiosities.

Jennie never loved a place so well. It had everything: magnificent fireplaces, panelled rooms, a first-class pheasant shoot for George and an old lime tree with forked branches where Winston could construct a tree house for the composition of those acrid speeches which were making him so many enemies in the House. Jennie complained that if he dropped his notes the grass around that tree would be scorched. Jack, the 'practical one', delighted in this country home where he could relax from the onerous task of trying to make money in the City. He advised on bathrooms and wandered around peacefully watching his mother in a sun hat directing the planting of 'shrubs to keep the moat firm' and lines of 'flowers for cutting'. Jennie loved large floral arrangements, which were a novelty in those days. It was the first patch of earth that had ever been her own. 'I'm tired of looking at other people's big gardens—I'd rather have my own small one,' she said. At that time it was possible to hunt and shoot only seventeen miles from Westminster, and friends could drive down to Salisbury Hall in less than an hour. This meant that she did not always have to put them up and was able to do London entertaining in a fascinating country setting. Here, in fact, Jennie invented the 'weekend' in lieu of long country house visits.

Although the Jacobean manor could only sleep about eight there was a labyrinthine servants' wing and several cottages, so that a staff of fifteen could be accommodated. Walden who understood aristocratic living and had had to take some hard knocks during his voyages, approved completely. Mrs Walden delighted in the large kitchen—from which her dishes had to be transported by minions to the stone-floored dining hall, and George, who had learned all about wiring with the Glasgow Corporation, supervised the installation of electric light. Since the wicked Duke of Marlborough had died he was probably the only gentleman in England who could actually change a fuse without lethal results. And when Seymour Leslie came to stay, George steered him towards engineering as a career: 'All the future lies in electricity.' He was right, of course, but as the old Scotsman had said: 'Some men are born to make money, it just comes natural to them. Others never will.'

Jennie's efforts to entertain brilliantly but economically were well repaid, for, as Daisy Warwick wrote in *Afterthoughts*: 'One never thought of giving a party without her. She was as delightful to women as to men'.

Country house politics still played an important part in the English scene and pleasant surroundings for 'good talk' were considered a necessity for the ruling class 'to help them think'. Jennie had not got the sharp mind of Margot Asquith, the Prime Minister's wife, or of Violet, his daughter, but she could invite Winston's friends down, say something funny and leave them alight with their own wit. Seymour can remember Winston standing in front of the enormous Tudor fireplace holding forth on Free Trade. When the arguments grew too hot Jennie might lift an eyebrow and the ladies could drift out to punt gingerly around the moat. Yes, she thought, there was everything here for those she loved—the best people, the best pheasants, the best tree!

Sunshine? Was there always sunshine? So it seems in Seymour's memory—always a hot summer day with Winston in the rustling foliage of the old lime, or a golden autumn evening with George and his gun dogs exuberant after sport. Always sunshine. Always Walden beneficently carrying the silver tea-service, and the crackle of a wood fire. Always peace in a world where wise monarchs ruled and gentlemanly Prime Ministers conferred. England had no quarrel with the world.

27

On May 31st, 1904, Winston left the Tory Party to become a Free Trade Liberal. He crossed the floor dramatically to occupy the seat on the Opposition bench which had been his father's. Memories bitter and sweet flooded back to Jennie. Not by nature a political creature, her nerves had been nailed to the House of Commons for thirty years now. Late on the night that Winston changed party, Seymour Leslie found her storming up and down her library. She glared at her nephew. 'Haven't you heard? The moment Winston crossed the floor to the Liberal benches and rose to speak, that detestable Arthur Balfour and his entire party got up and walked out of the House! What an insult from a Prime Minister. . . . I'll never speak to him again!'

Balfour had done all he could to help young Winston, so his annoyance is understandable. He had loved Randolph and suffered to see him sicken, but Jennie always felt that he and Lord Salisbury had ridden to fame on Randolph's brilliance and then been hasty to shed him.

She would have been intrigued had she been able to read a page in the diary of Wilfred Scawen Blunt at this time. After lunching with Pamela and Victor Lytton, where Winston was present, Blunt wrote: 'In opposition I expect to see Winston playing precisely his father's game, and I should not be surprised if he had his father's success. He has a power of writing Randolph never had, who was a schoolboy with his pen, and he has education and a political tradition.'

When they were not racing together or staying with Leonie in London or visiting the great country houses frequented by the Prince, the Cornwallis-Wests entertained a mixture of people ranging from Eleanor Duse to Paderewski. Jennie had met the great Polish pianist when he was unknown, and she had played duets with him until one day she looked up at him and said: 'Stop. You are too good for me!'

In the election of January 1906 Jennie (who was in favour of women's votes) accompanied Winston to Manchester to fight for his seat. In the happy vein reminiscent of the days when Randolph was electioneering she wrote to Leonie:

Manchester,
January 6, 1906

The election is most exciting—they say it will be a close thing. The female suffrage women are too odious. Every night they make a disturbance and shriek and rant. They damage their own cause hopelessly. Mr Marsh is here, very pleasant. . . .

Winston's chief case in this election turned on Free Trade. On January 14th he achieved a great victory in the polling. Jennie describes the scene to her sister:

Winston is at Wolverhampton tonight but I shall probably be seeing him tomorrow. Manchester was wonderful! I have been to lots of elections but I never saw such excitement. We were all at the Town Hall during the counting of votes and afterwards to the Reform Club where the scene was indescribable. Winston told me two days before that he thought there would be a clean sweep and the passing of Arthur (Balfour) complete. *Quelle débâcle* all round! You see every (Tory) minister is out with the exception of Foster. This month has been very portentous for Winston. His book, high office, now Manchester! He is quite calm. I am very busy with his house in Bolton Street. It will be charming.

Leonie, married into a staunch Tory family, was uneffusive. Jennie, nettled, wrote her on January 28th:

I am amused by what you say about turncoats—I suppose that is a dig at Winston for going to the other side. There is no doubt it takes a big man to change his mind. You might have quoted Dizzy, Gladstone and last but not least, Chamberlain. As for Arthur Balfour, his mind is never made up so he has none to change. Winston is very well but he will be happier when he gets his little house.

The whole rhythm of that rich rustling Edwardian life trembled as the voice of misery rose from the industrial areas. Edward had been the first Prince of Wales to visit slums incognito and to express horror at what he saw. Now society wondered how the politicians could relieve the hungry herds of workless human beings in every city. Eddie Marsh has described this electioneering visit to the slums of Manchester and how Winston looked around with pity at the small foul streets where no beauty was to be seen or worse still nothing *clever* was ever said. It was a new drab world to him and his heart was touched,

This was just before the Vienna Academy of Fine Arts decided to reject the drawings of an eighteen-year-old Austrian who, unable to study as the great artist he believed himself, turned his ambition to becoming architect of a new world instead. For five years he would starve and sleep on park benches, hawk his postcards to small cafés and mesmerise people when he talked. So Hitler learned to become an orator. His tutor was Hate, and Reason never held his hand.

The hundreds of letters which George wrote between 1900 and 1911 were carefully kept by Jennie. She must have had cupboards full. Some letters (before he got into serious financial trouble) suggest investments for Winston's book money. A typical example, dated April 16th, 1906, from Ruthven Castle, his home in Wales, boasts gently of his new sport—'runs' are now in a motor-car not after foxes:

Darling Old Puss Cat,

I have just got in from fishing but did no good as like everywhere they are suffering from a drought here and there is no water in the river! We motored this morning to fish in a lake near here but they wouldn't rise. . . .

Had a lovely run yesterday. I averaged 31 miles an hour the whole way. It was a glorious day and the roads were lovely. . . .

Ever your loving Husband

In the spring of 1907 Jennie, flustered by George's financial troubles, let Salisbury Hall and visited Daisy of Pless in the South of France. On the way there she stayed in the Ritz in Paris and wrote proudly to Jack of her economies. 'My bill for a week £15 as I am lunched and dined out every day.' The Princess of Pless published subsequently her diary:

'*April 14th*, Villa Espalmador: We are all going on a motor trip—Jennie, my sister-in-law—who married George and still loves him immensely poor dear; she is uncommonly nice and still very handsome, but of course the difference in age is a sad and terrible drawback (no babies possible); well, she is coming with us. The Duke of Marlborough, her cousin by marriage . . . also comes; then Adele Essex . . . etc.'

'*April 15th*, Avignon. We left Beaulieu at ten-thirty, stopping an hour at Nice for lunch and about forty minutes at Aix in torrents of rain and a thunderstorm. . . . Jennie and Marlborough arrived only at nine, they ran out of *essence* or whatever the stuff is called that makes the motor go. I think *essence* is a most inappropriate name for a substance that smells so horribly. . . . After dinner we wanted to have the table moved so the Duke pushed it and down the whole thing went. Dessert, wine, butter, olives, dates, plates; the corner of the room into which everything fell looked like a pigsty . . . it really was rather funny as nothing was left on the table but the cloth. The Duke was miserable; by the way he looked at the debris one might have thought he was peering at his own life, which at the present moment is in much the same state.'

Lord Randolph's nephew, the hapless boy 'Sunny', brought up in the emotional cataclysm of the Aylesford scandal, was now learning on his own account the miseries that marital state can create.

Jennie, who from a ringside seat had watched the battle of the Duke's mother and father, was sympathetic with him, but she herself did not always feel secure.

A letter from George at about this time, referring to an evening out together, shows a penitent tone: 'I'm awfully worried as I find you thought I chased you away. You know I didn't and that I'd sooner see you than all the others.' But on the whole every letter starts: 'My Beloved—Tell me what we are going to do this week', etc. The marriage held because George and Jennie still had so much in common and he admired her spirit.

Apart from the trivialities of George's life, torn between business and sport, Jennie never ceased to work for her elder son. Jack, whom she loved equally, worked away in the City under Cassel's guidance, but it was the demanding, the tyrannical fascinating Winston who kept her on the go.

Since 1901, when he had delivered a speech which took six weeks to prepare and learn by heart, a speech appealing for a smaller Army and bigger Navy delivered in a style comparable with that of his vintage years, Winston had not ceased to enthral or enrage the House of Commons. For a woman who had suffered as Jennie had over her husband, this phenomenon of a son was a joyous excitement. Sometimes he must have reminded her of Randolph. But Lady Violet Bonham-Carter has written that when she asked her father, the Liberal Prime Minister Asquith, who had known Randolph well, which of the two rated higher he replied; 'You can't compare them. Randolph was irresistible. He had incomparably more charm, more wit. But—Winston is by far the better fellow of the two.'

In 1905 Winston's *Life of Lord Randolph Churchill* had appeared to take its place among the great biographies of the English language, and throughout 1906, as Under-Secretary to the Colonies, he kept his name on every tongue. When Winston needed a Private Secretary it was Leonie who clinched the selection of Edward Marsh, that 'obscure clerk in the Colonial Office' whom she considered the most delightful and erudite of men. In his memoirs, Marsh has described meeting Winston at a party purposely arranged for this encounter: 'A little later I saw him on a sofa with Mrs Leslie . . . looking in my direction and as it seemed discussing me; but I thought no more about it.'

Next day Marsh called on Pamela Lytton, who had also 'boosted' him at the party, and then dined with Winston at Mount Street. The letter he wrote to my grandmother lies still among her papers at Castle Leslie.

13 December 1905

Dear Mrs Leslie

Such an excitement. I *must* tell you. Your nephew has asked me to be his private secretary for 6 months or so. It will be the

276

most interesting thing I've ever done but I'm most terribly afraid of not being the right person and turning out a failure. I'm sure it's your doing. When you come back in May I'll tell you whether I bless you or curse you! You'll find me a grey-haired skeleton in either case as he means to work me to death. It's funny that just after we were discussing the problem of what I should do to age myself this easy solution should have dashed forth.

No more luncheons or dinner parties for me for six months! but I don't mind as you will not be in London.

Yours sincerely
E. Marsh

I've just dined alone with Winston. He was most perfectly charming to me but made it quite clear what he would expect in the way of help and I almost *know* I can't do it—it's awful!

But he did it for thirty years—until his retirement—and the friendship continued until his death.

Leonie was now more deeply embedded in London society than Jennie and she loved pulling strings. Her own son Shane also needed cossetting at this epoch. He did not want to go into the Army like his father, or into politics like his grandfather or into the City like his cousins. To her consternation (bravely dissimulated) he had determined to become a poet! A small book of Irish ballads and other not over-remunerative verses had already appeared between covers and she could not help feeling a little proud. One afternoon when out driving with Lady Falmouth (the rather stuffy wife of Jennie's admirer 'Star') she happened to mention that her eldest son had just published a book of poetry. Lady Falmouth stared in shocked amazement. 'What odd things people do nowadays,' she remarked coldly.

There is a slightly envious note in some of Jennie's letters to her sought-after sister at this time, such as this from Salisbury Hall: 'I feel I was cross and unreasonable the other day when I saw you. I am sorry. The fact is when I go to London, there are only two people I ever try to see, one is Winston, the other you. Both are aforesaid disappointments. One is on account of work, the other on account of pleasure. I may go away feeling sore at heart. I snatch a few minutes of Winston's society by driving him to the Colonial Office, and the most you can afford are a few words uncomfortably (for me) on the telephone . . . You know I love you and that when you want me I am to be found.'

George had to be so often away. Despite her weekend entertaining Jennie needed more people in her life, grandchildren maybe, but so far there seemed no likelihood.

In September 1906, while touring Italy with several friends, including the heiress Muriel Wilson, Winston had written to his mother: 'Nothing could exceed the tranquil *banalité* of my relations with M. but I am very glad I came. . . .' Nothing came of whatever tentative approaches Winston made to Miss Wilson and Jennie began to wonder if her sons would ever marry, but during the next twelve months she saw them capture the most beautiful and original of wives.

In October 1907 Winston (with Eddie Marsh doing fourteen hours' work a day on board ship for him) set forth on an official tour of African colonies, and Jennie received long vivid letters from the Red Sea. When Winston returned in January 1907 his mother was still trying to save money; she chose to pig it at the London Ritz this time. Winston wrote to Jack: '. . . please ask Mamma to engage me a bedroom, a bathroom & a comfortable sitting room, & to make the vy best terms she can with the Manager. She should tell them that if they make me comfortable & do not charge me too much I will in all probability stay a month, but if they overcharge me I will clear out at once & tell everyone what robbers they are. . . .' This missive might have been penned by his parsimonious grand-mother Mrs Jerome.

In April 1908, just before Winston got the Board of Trade and entered the cabinet (necessitating a by-election), Jennie returned to Salisbury Hall and recommenced her entertaining. A great happiness had come her way: Jack was engaged to the Earl of Abingdon's daughter, Lady Gwendoline Bertie, a fey creature, not pretty in the kittenish Edwardian fashion, but translucent as if made of amber and opals, relaxed and quiet-voiced. Lord David Cecil has written of her 'subtle twilight beauty'. She had no money—a factor per-petually discussed in Edwardian society—but as Jennie had written to Jack at the time of her own marriage: 'You know I am not materialistic for you or myself—more's the pity!'

Now she hoped fervently that Winston would find the right mate. He was so brilliant but so hard to suit. His mate must be different from other women as he was different from other men, a creature of fire to capture his imagination but willing to forgo her fire for his. It is rather interesting that Jennie, whom people called worldly, should have been so pleased when a penniless girl, the daughter of her old friend Lady Blanche Hozier, had once caught Winston's eye at a ball. But having asked his mother to introduce him Winston did not ask for a dance, he just stared! Clementine Hozier did not appreciate this and four years passed before she met him again. This happened to be at dinner in March 1908 when he was Under-Secretary for the Colonies, and on this occasion Winston paid a great deal of attention to the twenty-four-year-old girl. Jennie swiftly followed it up. Within the month she had invited Lady Blanche to bring her daughter for a Sunday to Salisbury Hall. Blanche was quite a character, and her gay peregrinations to France had blended with those of the Jerome sisters over more than thirty years. Estranged from her husband, Sir Henry Hozier, this daughter of a Scottish Earl had indeed brought up her children to know what it meant to be 'penniless'. By the time that Clementine was produced at Salisbury Hall for Winston to 'talk to' she had taken a fair battering in Edwardian society. Not only was she forced to go out in hats she had made herself (some feat, considering the fashions of the time), but to earn pocket money by giving French lessons. Jennie instinctively felt how perfect Clementine would be for Winston and hoped against hope that she would be the one he chose. All went well. Suddenly and quite naturally Winston who had no small talk, found himself attracted by this girl. Lady Crichton, who was spending that weekend at Salisbury Hall, related to her daughter (who told me) that she had noticed Jennie appeared in a jubilant mood and she attributed this to Jack's approaching wedding. On Sunday night the other guests departed and on the following morning Lady Crichton and Jennie drove up to London together. Then Jennie could no longer restrain herself and taking Mary Crichton's hand she revealed the 'secret'—Winston had told her that he was going to ask Clementine to marry him. 'And she will be the perfect wife for him. You see my Winston is not *easy*; he is very difficult indeed and she is just right.'

Clementine had to leave for a tour of the Continent with her mother, but after that auspicious Sunday at Salisbury Hall Winston found it natural to keep up an animated correspondence. Having just entered the cabinet as President of the Board of Trade he had to face an immediate by-election, and to his chagrin he lost his Manchester seat. He was then offered a safe one at Dundee. '. . . still I don't pretend not to be vexed. Defeat however consoled, explained or discounted is odious.' All this made lively reading for Miss Hozier as she travelled with her Mama.

She must have known that Winston was in love with her, but she did not know that he was unburdening his agitated feelings to his friend F. E. Smith (Lord Birkenhead). According to Miss Ethel Royden, a family friend who was staying with the Smiths, Winston wondered: 'Is it fair to ask this lovely creature to marry so ambitious a man as myself?'

Miss Royden never forgot the day that Winston brought Miss Hozier to tea. She sat there beautiful but timid while Winston looked half triumphant, half shy!

Meanwhile Jennie encouraged with tact. Jack's wedding was gay but somewhat complicated, because Lady Gwendoline was a Catholic, which necessitated one day spent signing the registry and sightseeing in Abingdon and a second day of church service. However, as Winston noted: 'Both were entirely composed & the business was despatched with a celerity & ease that was almost appalling!'

Clementine received a full description.

8 August (1908)
My dear,
I have just come back from throwing an old slipper into Jack's departing motor-car. It was a very pretty wedding. No swarms of London fly-catchers. No one came who did not really care, and the only spectators were tenants and country folk.

I was very glad to get your telegram this morning that you will come to Blenheim on Monday. There will be no one at all except my mother and the Smiths and Mr Clarke, my secretary of the Board of Trade, and the duke and his little son—

Here at Nuneham we have the debris of the wedding party and also of Burley-on-the-Hill. . . . Among the former—Leonie —who brings me news from Cowes—of a young lady who made a great impression at a dance four nights ago on all beholders. I wonder who it *could have* been!

Clementine hesitated about going to Blenheim. She must have guessed that Winston would propose. He was never one to hide his feelings. She was down to one last cotton frock and the struggle to dress in the manner expected of a young lady in Edwardian society daunted her. In the end she went, maidless and a little crumpled, but perhaps her dryad beauty, her glowing red hair and huge blue eyes were off-set by not being over-ironed.

Winston proposed in an ornamental summer house and was accepted. The joyous news echoed through the palace where Winston had been born and Jennie could be first to kiss the girl she had hoped her son would capture. To mundane Edwardian society a maiden without a penny to her name did not appear a 'great catch'. The letters which poured in after the engagement tended to stress the fact that Clemmie was very 'lucky'. Appalled perhaps by so much *luck*, she began to hesitate, but vacillation was firmly stepped on by a brisk nineteen-year-old brother.

The moment Winston had been accepted he wrote to Pamela Lytton: 'I am to marry Clementine & I say to you as you said to me when you married Victor—you must always be our best friend.'

Was this the returning of a barb?

Jennie spent hectic hours at her desk writing the news personally to close acquaintances and, of course, to the Prince and Princess and the royal Dukes before the announcement appeared on August 15th.

Lady Blanche Hozier was delighted. She wrote on August 13th to Wilfred Scawen Blunt:

> Blenheim
>
> . . . Yesterday he came to London to ask my consent, and we all came on here. Winston and I spoke of you and of your great friendship with his father. He is so like Lord Randolph, he has some of his faults, and all his qualities. He is gentle and tender, and affectionate to those he loves, much hated by those who have not come under his personal charm. . . .

While Jennie dealt with royal telegrams, Winston forwarded bundles of letters of congratulations to his 'dearest and most truly beloved'. To his brother and new sister-in-law he wrote:

Jack and Goonie,

It is done and done forever.

I am to marry Clementine almost at once.

I hope we shall be happy like you are, and always all four of us bound together by the most perfect faith and comradeship.

Yours ever

W.

Miss Muriel Wilson, the heiress whom many in Edwardian society had thought Winston ought to marry, wrote a delightful note saying she had watched him with Clemmie and that she was so extraordinarily beautiful she felt he could not help falling in love with her.

Within a month the marriage took place, a smart affair at St Margaret's, Westminster, with famous names inside the church and costermongers in pearly suits lining the streets outside. The latter loved Winston because he had restored some of their old trading rights. Jennie, Leonie and Clara (whose daughter Clare Frewen was a bridesmaid) were in full array. Leonie related to us that when the bride walked out of the church on Winston's arm a gallant Cockney shout went up, 'She's got a lovely face. God bless her!' 'It seems only the other day I was late at her christening,' said her godfather John Leslie, as Clemmie walked up the aisle holding the white prayerbook he had given her. There was a vast reception at the house of Clementine's great-aunt, Lady St Helier, in Portland Place where the 'pearly' kings and queens danced in the road. Winston was popular in the Board of Trade. Then the young couple drove away and Jennie returned triumphant to Leonie's home to 'lie down and talk it over'.

Everyone felt curiously pleased at this wedding, but it was Jennie, earthy Jennie, who knew by instinct that her son had found the right woman. No money—she brushed that aside—Winston was an earner. No, it was something else which made her rejoice, the sure sense that behind this gentle loveliness lay qualities of steel—absolute integrity and fortitude that would not snap if things went ill for Winston.

✳ 28

During his honeymoon which started at Blenheim Winston wrote a letter of feeling to his mother ending:

> . . . Best of love my dearest Mama. You were a great comfort and support to me at a critical period in my emotional development. We have never been so near together so often in a short time. God bless you.
>   What a relief to have got that ceremony over! and so happily.
>   Your loving son,
>   **W.**

> PS. I open this letter to tell you that George said he could wish me no better wife or happier days than he had found in you.

A week later he wrote again from Venice:

> We have been happy here and Clemmie is very well. . . . We have only loitered and loved—a good and serious occupation for which the histories furnish respectable precedents.
>   Do try and find a rich bachelor.

This curious command stemmed from Winston's hope of obtaining a good price for 12 Bolton Street. The house was too small for a married man and Jennie was left in charge of the lease disposal. Winston thought a rich bachelor might pay handsomely.

Jennie never shirked onerous duties for her son but she did throw cold water on Winston's unrealistic valuations: she wrote factually:

283

29 September

My dearest Winston,

I am writing from Bolton Street where I have been working to get your house straight—no easy matter I can tell you! but I hope you will like it. . . .

I never heard from your solicitor about the house and I am still trying to place it for you—Trollope has sent me lists of very suitable houses quite cheap, large and under £300! . . . But first get rid of this—you will *never* get a large premium for it—better make up your mind.

A PS. added: 'Sarah tells me the King was very much touched to see that you had used his walking sticks on your wedding day! perhaps you didn't?'

By the time her sons returned from their honeymoons and were installed in suitable married quarters Jennie was toying with the idea of an American lecture tour. She wanted to make money but hated public speaking. Finally, after a publisher's dinner at which she had to make a speech, she decided to abandon the idea. There were too many joys at home.

During the next year a grandson and a granddaughter arrived, and Winston became a youthful Home Secretary. Jennie's cup of happiness brimmed. Not only was her son successful but he held a ministry where his compassionate nature could expand. Leonie forwarded a letter written to her by John Galsworthy about Winston's prison reforms: 'I have always admired his pluck and his capacity, I now perceive him to have a heart and to be very warm.' Jennie liked this, and Mrs Everest would have liked it too—she had not prayed that her darling boy should become famous but good.

Jennie found members of the younger generation interesting and treated them as equals. When Leonie's eldest son Shane, now deep in Irish politics, wrote his opinion of her memoirs she replied from Salisbury Hall:

(November 14 1908)

I was delighted to get your letter and to hear that you liked my book. Everyone does not think the same alas! for I received a letter the other day from an irate Irish man calling me an 'antique alien' because I had said that 'Paddies and Biddies' mustered strong on St Patrick's Day in New York. . . . You must come to little Salisbury Hall and we will try to have some interesting people to meet you. Two Sundays ago Lord Crewe, Mr Lloyd George, Mr Birrell and Winston came down. . . . quite a Cabinet Council! In fact they did hold an informal one on the Irish Question. I wish you had been there.

And a few days later when lending him books she mentions the author son of her cousin Kitty Mott:

Lawrence Mott's stories are full of 'atmosphere'. What a pity he has taken to drink. He can't put pen to paper much less have thoughts! The *War in the Air* H. G. Wells is prophetic. I think of what may happen if these aeronauts advance as they will. Bless you. . . . In a hurry as usual.

Yr Affec^{ate}
Aunt Jennie

Leonie's sons were growing up. Poet Shane was twenty-three and soldier Norman twenty-two. During the spring of 1910 Leonie's house in Great Cumberland Place became the scene of much secret confabulation. Her son Norman, a lieutenant in the Rifle Brigade, had, while in Cairo, become romantically entangled with the pretty wife of Ysoury Pasha. Love-letters were intercepted by the palace servants and brought to the notice of the Pasha and of Norman's chief, Sir John Maxwell (whose wife had annoyed Jennie in Egypt long ago).

When Ysoury Pasha issued a challenge to a duel Norman had to choose between fighting a duel against Army regulations or discrediting the Army by refusing. His commanding officer sent him back to England, where H.R.H. the Duke of Connaught, Lord Cromer, Sir Ernest Cassel and his great-uncle, Lord Charles Beresford, could discuss the problem in Leonie's drawing room. With Leonie handing out tea and Norman the cucumber sandwiches, they came to the whispered conclusion that the challenge must be accepted, but in secrecy, for the Prince Consort had made duelling a cashiering offence.

So secretive did Leonie become that not even Seymour, practising electrics on the top floor, knew what was going on and twice fused the lights during these conclaves, thus adding to the atmosphere of drama. Norman, a great polo-player but little schooled in swordsmanship, had to practice fencing with his father behind locked doors. When Sir Ernest Cassel discovered the best master in Paris he departed for an intensive course—all day and every day he practised the defensive positions which this tutor insisted could alone save his life.

During all this Leonie, by nature discreet, devised such security precautions that the very smoke-screen aroused attention. Kitty Mott (married to a charming American socialite millionaire) could not keep away. Seymour, hearing his mother grumble at 'tiresome Kitty nosing about', wondered what on earth was up. Code words were used for people and places. Paris was referred to as 'Brighton' and Ysoury as 'Mr Jones'. Jennie scented a crisis but was never over-curious concerning other people's affairs and when she found her sister disinclined to talk she flounced out of the house grumbling: 'How tiresome you are with all your mysteries.'

The duel was fought in Paris. For over an hour Norman managed to parry Ysoury's thrusts, then he received a slight wound and knew honour was satisfied. He hurried back to London where his advisers appeared content. No rumour ever reached the press concerning this, the last duel fought by a British Army officer. Four years later a German bullet would reach the heart that Ysoury's sharp foil left gladly beating.

Despite George's wandering eye, Jennie felt her marriage secure in that she and George were basically congenial and shared the same every-day humour. Salisbury Hall gave what each desired, easy entertaining and first-class shooting. They came to London often and danced happily together at all the big balls.

Among the people who came to Salisbury Hall on one of Jennie's famous Sundays was Eleanora Duse, but this visit could not have been more of a flop. It was just after Duse's parting from D'Annunzio and the great actress drove across the moat in tears. Jennie led her into the panelled drawing room where she spent the day in seclusion, receiving only the lady visitors with comforting words, handkerchiefs and Mrs Walden's special calming *tissane*.

Sir Ernest Cassel loved Salisbury Hall and he did his best—without much success—to instil financial flair into George and Jack. Certainly he issued no warning, as did Nell Gwyn's ghost shortly before George's family solicitor absconded with that £10,000! George recounts the story in a chapter entitled 'Things Spooky and

Practical Jokes'. As it was getting dark he came down the carved-wood staircase (where present owners say the loveliest silvery laugh is still heard occasionally when the house is empty) and there in the old stone-flagged hall he saw a beautiful young woman in blue velvet pass through a doorway. On following her he found the passage inexplicably empty. She had looked exceptionally like a pretty former nursemaid nicknamed 'Old Girlie', and still employed in his home, and when told of the incident Jack suggested telephoning his mother to ask if anything had happened to this woman. The answer came that she was well and about to marry a quartermaster in the Artillery. It was a few weeks later than Daisy of Pless came to stay, and while looking at George's collection of prints of Nell Gwyn she remarked: 'I never realised before the truth of what people used to say about "Old Girlie"—Don't you remember they said she was exactly like the pictures of Nell Gwyn?'

After this George sent a letter describing his experience to a medium who reported that he had seen 'an apparition of Mistress Eleanor Gwyn, come to warn him against an impending danger'. Within a month the family solicitor made off with £10,000.

King Edward was charmed by Salisbury Hall and paid many short informal visits. Only once did he actually come to stay, and many a brainstorm and tantrum went into the preparations for this. Jennie had not the resources of the great houses which His Majesty regularly visited—she had not the long secluded wings, the 'royal bedroom', the squads of perfectly trained servants. As the King was getting very heavy and found it hard to walk up stairs, she created a downstairs suite. The panelled drawing room was hung with green silk to make it resemble a bedroom and the 'gentleman's cloakroom' with its mahogany fixtures and marble wash-basins was transformed into a private bathroom. This left Jennie with only the beautiful Tudor hall, the oldest part of the house, and the billiard room the newest excrescence, in which to entertain. But Walden rose to the occasion and huge, cunningly complicated repasts appeared on the gleaming refectory table. The maids, minions, and gardeners were drilled to scurry around, and Mrs Walden survived the ordeal of cooking for the King. To Jennie's relief the visit was private—no county had to be entertained.

All those members of the Churchill family who had once resented Jennie had come to love her. 'Fannie' Tweedmouth, Randolph's

287

sister whom she and Clara had been so horrid to when all were girls, had grown into a dear friend. Now she was dying of cancer and George describes the evening he brought Jennie home from Fannie's last dinner party. As they drove away Jennie in tears said that Fannie had just been told not to expect more than a few weeks. 'She had been the life and soul of the evening, and nobody would have guessed that this terrible sentence was hanging over her.' So ended a friendship grown from a prickly beginning.

George Cornwallis-West has published what he thought of his wife. 'Jennie was a very remarkable woman. She dressed beautifully and her taste not only in clothes but in everything was of the best. She had a marvellous flair for decorating houses and there are many houses in London which, thanks to her, have a cachet of their own, and which bear to this day the unmistakable proofs of her artistic talent. Like many well-bred American women, she had the will and the power to adapt herself to her immediate surroundings. She was equally at home having a serious conversation with a distinguished statesman as playing on a golf course. A great reader, she remembered much of what she had read, and that made her a brilliant conversationalist, but although gifted with extreme intelligence, she was not brilliant in the deepest sense of the word. She was not a genius.

'Possessed of great driving force in matters which interested her, she was a good organiser, as was proved by the success she made of the *Maine* hospital ship. Her greatest undertaking was the "Shakespeare's England" exhibition at Earls Court. (This originated for raising funds for a National Theatre.) As is so often the fate of schemes of this kind, artistically it was a success, financially a ghastly failure. . . . In money matters she was without any sense of proportion. The value of money meant nothing to her; what counted with her were the things she got for money, not the amount she had to pay for them. If something of beauty attracted her, she just had to have it; it never entered her head to stop and think how she was going to pay for it. During all the years we lived together the only serious misunderstandings which ever took place between us were over money matters. Her extravagance was her only fault, and with her nature, the most understandable and therefore the most forgivable.'

The bewitching, velvet-voiced Mrs Patrick Campbell, greatest

288

actress of her time and 'brilliant in the deepest sense of the word', had not yet dug her claws deep into Mr Cornwallis-West. He first met her through Jennie when they rented Mrs Asquith's house in Cavendish Square. Stella, who liked handsome men as much as Jennie did, pounced on him as a companion to read parts aloud to, but the real trouble ensued, ironically enough, through Jennie's efforts to make money by writing a play. Her carefully compiled memoirs had proved a best-seller in America as well as England and George had encouraged her to try her hand as a playwright—it looked so easy. It was also George who suggested that Mrs Pat should produce the play.

Jennie wrote a totally unsuspecting letter to Leonie on June 27th, 1909: 'Darling Sniffy. . . . The rehearsals are getting on and this week there are to be two daily. Mrs Pat has really been an angel and the Play would not exist without her. . . . I can't understand why I feel so calmly about the Play. Bernstein tells me he's *dans les trances* for weeks before hand. Perhaps I do not know the horrors before me! I gave a supper party at the Ritz last Friday, too successful for words. . . . Kitty, Anne, Consuelo, Juliet, Violet Rutland, Mrs Pat, Stella (her daughter), Muriel Wilson, Henry Ainley, Yeats, Hugh Cecil, Bernstein, Marthe Bibesco, Maurice Baring, Milwood (my leading gentleman), Clare [Frewen], Winston and Jack etc., We kept it up till 2.30 a.m. 100 wild dances and fandangoes . . . everyone taking the floor. . . .'

But three weeks later the atmosphere at the Haymarket Theatre in July 1909 when *Borrowed Plumes* was produced for a fortnight as a 'try-out' must have been over-electric, even for electrician George. He scurried from author to director, whose intense dislike of each other began to increase hourly. The only written account of the proceedings is that in Mrs Patrick Campbell's memoirs. In this she says of the play: 'It had certain points of cleverness and I considered that, with ingenious production and good actors, it could be pulled together, and perhaps made into a success. . . .

'An exaggerated importance gradually grew around the production, owing to Royalty and many distinguished people being interested in it. . . .

'Jennie, I fancy, imagined producing her play would be of social advantage to all of us: I was intolerant of what I thought nonsense, and showed it quickly.

'At the first performance everybody who was anybody, and who could procure a seat, was present. The critics enjoyed themselves, the applause was of the heartiest, the play was looked upon as clever.

'Mr Walker in *The Times* was nice about me and funny about hats—In fact Mr Walker wrote columns about the audience at the first special matinée as well as the play! "These are the occasions that reconcile one to the theatre. For a sudden feminine glory invades it and transfigures it, so that it becomes an exhibition of beauty and elegance: the very latest dialogue on the stage is accompanied by a *frou-frou* of the very latest Paris fashions in the stalls. An especially pleasing detail is the air of sweet resignation—is it the firm composure of the martyr or the serene smile of the seraph?—with which the ladies remove the wide-brimmed and very high-crowned hats of the present fashion from their heads and pose them on their knees. It is with an effort you divert your gaze from this fascinating spectacle to the proceedings on the stage. But this is only to exchange one pleasure for another of the same sort. For on the stage you have a bevy of ladies supporting—beautiful caryatids that they are!—the same remarkable hats, with the privilege of not having to remove them. . . .

' "And yet, by a sort of paradox, what was perhaps the most beautiful thing, certainly the most suave and distinguished thing in the Hick's theatre yesterday afternoon—we mean of course Mrs Patrick Campbell—wore no hat."

'Then in the unexpected way things sometimes happen in this world, George Cornwallis-West was seriously attracted to me. . . . I believed his life was unhappy, and warmly gave him my friendship and affection.

'This caused gossip, mis-judgment and pain. . . .'

Mrs Pat put it mildly. Her 'friendship and affection' were of an intensity which drove stonier men than George out of their wits.

Poor Jennie's play at which she had laboured with such hope received bad reviews and lost money even while she press-ganged relatives and royalty to fill the stalls. It also lost her a husband. But not immediately.

For some time yet Mrs Patrick Campbell contented herself with inviting George to 'go over plays' in her charming little house in Kensington Square. Visitors began to note that George seemed always to be there when they arrived and remained behind after they left. Then she frequently suggested he should take her up the river to spend 'a quiet day' reading some part. This was more ominous, but for a time at least she remembered her own adage, 'It doesn't matter what you do as long as you don't do it in the streets and frighten the horses.'

✿ 29

In May 1910 the sudden death of King Edward saddened England. The kind, pleasure-loving king died in fact from the surfeit of rich food produced by his adoring subjects! Years of gargantuan meals and large cigars must have over-taxed lungs and digestive organs, but every hostess vied to place ever vaster and more exotic dishes before His Majesty. He had been a warm-hearted friend and he was sorely missed. Queen Alexandra's letters to Jennie show how fond she had become of this American dynamo, whose good spirits had enlivened many Sandringham parties. She would not be invited there again. The cosy Edwardian heyday was over and a virtuous cool breeze blew through the court as the sailor king and stately Queen Mary mounted England's throne.

King Edward's death left Asquith stuck at a crucial stage with the Parliament Bill. The Prime Minister had been sure that if the Lords did refuse to accept the Bill curtailing their powers King Edward would create new peers to see it through. Lloyd George had spearheaded the attack with his famous remark: 'The House of Lords is not the watchdog of the Constitution; it is Mr Balfour's poodle.'

During the next six months society remained in mourning and the Liberal Party 'went easy' to allow the new monarch to catch his breath. In November came a General Election and Winston used unsuitable mocking language about Balfour who was now Leader of the Opposition. Margot Asquith as well as Jennie sought to restrain him.

In the following spring mourning was put aside, banners decked

292

the streets for the Coronation and Jennie's second grandson arrived. He was named Randolph and 'Clemmie' enjoyed the favour of watching the Coronation from the King's box *because she was a nursing mother.* The lovely ladies who had been granted this honour at the previous Coronation had to try for other places in the Abbey.

It was during this unusually hot summer of 1911 that the possibility of war with Germany suddenly hit the cabinet. Notes of extraordinary bluntness were read by the ambassadors of each country when the truculent Kaiser sent a gunboat to argue with France over a Moroccan port. No one could believe that anything as uncivilised as real war could break out, but Europe was alerted.

In the unprecedented July heat England vibrated with indignation. Prime Minister Asquith remained firmly at the helm, pacifist Lloyd George changed his tune, and Winston, abandoning talk of economy, with extraordinary prescience wrote a memorandum for the Army and Navy in case hostilities started. He was still Home Secretary, but in those days members of the cabinet pooled their ideas.

In late September Asquith grew restive. Feeling the importance of a galvanising leader in the Admiralty, he invited Winston to Scotland and suddenly asked if he would become First Lord. Winston unhesitatingly accepted. He had always believed that the British Empire depended on her Navy more than on any Army she could put into the field.

No sooner had Winston moved into the Admiralty than he started a tussle with the Chancellor of the Exchequer for money to build more battleships.

Jennie related with amusement her maid's reaction to Winston's promotion. The faithful Gentry revelled in titles and when told the good news she merely exclaimed, 'How wonderful! And now perhaps Mr Winston will be made a Sir!' Jennie remonstrated, 'But he wouldn't accept it. *That* isn't what he wants.' But Gentry was the truer prophet!

Troubled as the cabinet was no one could quite believe war possible. On March 22nd, 1912, Arthur Balfour wrote to Winston: '. . . A war entered upon for no other object than to restore the Germanic Empire of Charlemagne in a modern form appears to me at once so wicked and stupid as to be almost incredible. And yet it is almost impossible to make sense of modern German policy without crediting it with this intention.' The idea seemed mad. Why should Germany want to fight? The shadow passed as a cloud can pass over the sun and yet leave the atmosphere chilled.

Jennie remained immersed in her own activities. She had for years been trying to raise interest in a National Theatre. It was an age of great acting and pretentious production. With Granville Barker, the playwright, and William Archer, the critic, she headed appeals for a London theatre which, not being dependent on ordinary box office, could set a standard. They issued a broadside: 'The National Theatre. A Scheme and Estimate', and merged with another movement to form the Shakespeare Memorial Theatre. Jennie had taken the chair at the first meetings, which were held in Leonie's house, and her enthusiasm infected a number of progressive spirits who longed for a live theatre.

The Liberal Government, keen on popular culture, talked sympathetically but the basic idea proved unrealistic. The 'Committee' was to provide the 'bricks and mortar', after which the authorities *might* endow it. King Edward, deeply interested in educating the masses, gave his support and a number of rich people contributed enormous donations. Jennie persuaded Mr Carl Meyer to give £70,000 'anonymously' (but not too anonymously for he received a baronetcy soon after).

When the Committee had collected £100,000 a site was purchased opposite the Victoria and Albert Museum, and a foundation stone solemnly laid (the most mobile rock since the Stone of Scone, it has travelled from place to place during the last sixty years until it finally rests on the South Bank).

Today's National Theatre has come into being in a reverse sequence to the original plan, the acting company has set to work before the actual theatre is completed. But built it must be, for the funds raised by Jennie's Committee have been carefully husbanded and merged into today's £7,000,000 government scheme.

Jennie's first great venture to raise money was imaginative. In those days Earls Court, with sideshows and restaurants around the large open stadium, was an amusing place in which to spend a hot evening. Jennie had the idea of staging a magnificent exhibition there called 'Shakespeare's England'. All the facilities were to be used, the restaurants disguised as Elizabethan taverns and the sideshows intriguingly dressed up. George called this her greatest undertaking, but sadly added: 'As is so often the fate of schemes of this kind, artistically it was a success, financially a ghastly failure.' She began by coaxing £40,000 from Cox's Bank and George hurried off to Paris, where he obtained another £10,000 from Mrs W. B. Leeds, the widow of an American millionaire who greatly admired him. Before the month was out rumours went around London that George was in fact eloping with Mrs Leeds, but Jennie put a stop to that. She got George back plus the £10,000 for her 'charity'.

Jennie planned and held meetings with C. B. Cochran, an enterprising boxing promoter (who would become the foremost impresario of the age) as her secretary, for six months. Under the impetus of her enthusiasm money disappeared, but she had much to show for it. The models of the old Tudor houses, the Globe Theatre, the Mermaid Tavern and other Elizabethan dwellings were exquisitely designed by the great architect Sir Edward Lutyens. On the last occasion that I saw Sir C. B. Cochran (in June 1945) we sat in war-smashed London talking about Jennie and he said: 'Her ideas were wonderful. It was money that perplexed her. She threw it around like water.'

Under her energetic direction the show ought to have captured public imagination and earned vast sums, but it was really too sophisticated for popular taste of that time. There was nothing vulgar or incorrect so only the intelligentsia bought tickets. And a wet summer did not help. It must have been heartbreaking to produce the most fascinating exhibition of the century only to find the turn-stiles turned less than for an ordinary circus.

'The Mermaid Tavern in the gardens was run as a club, and Jennie had roped in all her friends and her friends' friends to become members; it contained a very good restaurant and a room where one could read the papers and write.' Yet even this lost money. George relates Jennie's opening lunch there. 'She drew upon her friends from all classes of society; the "idle rich", the Corps Diplomatique, the Bar and the Stage were all represented.'

There were comic incidents such as when a famous actor wrote asking if he might bring a lady friend. Not realising, or perhaps not caring, as to whether he brought his wife or his known mistress, Jennie answered in the affirmative. He arrived in her crowded reception room, swept up to his hostess with a theatrical bow and declaimed, 'May I be allowed to present to you the mother of my children!' De Soveral, the Portuguese ambassador, turned to George and said, '*Tiens! Ca c'est magnifique!*'

The end of the exhibition was to be celebrated by a medieval Tourney[1] in the huge hall. Under Jennie's and Lutyens' direction it was laid out as the courtyard of a medieval castle and a handsome slice of young peers was required to tilt with papier-mâché lances! The combatants wore magnificent suits of armour each costing £100. Arms were emblazoned on breast-plates, and every detail had to be correct according to the sixteenth-century 'Statutes of Arms':

'How many waies the prize is won
How many waies the prize fhall be lost
How broken fpeares fhall be allowed
How fpeares fhall be difallowed.'

There were pages to learn by heart, what to do and what not to do.

'Whofo beareth a man down out of the faddle, or putteth him to the earth, horfe and man, fhall have the prize before him that ftriketh cournail to cournail three times.'
But 'Hee that ftriketh cournail to cournail two times, fhall have the prize before him that ftriketh the fight three times'.

And so on and so on.

Jennie had a fine time issuing directions. 'All gripes, chokes, and foule play forbidden.'

The name of pieces of tilting armour and harness had to be learned by heart and superb programmes in fake vellum with coats of arms in colour and prints from the British Museum were prepared. Weeks of painstaking organisation and enthusiastic rehearsal were required. Each participant could choose his own cortège and the Mermaid Tavern dealt out much refreshment to exhausted squires and argumentative heralds. Queen Alexandra and three of the princesses promised to attend, and all the wives, sisters, children,

---

[1] This was to be the only medieval tournament since the ill-fated Eglinton Tournament in the early nineteenth century when it rained each day. There has been none since.

cousins, nannies and butlers of the gallant knights bought expensive tickets, but as the great day approached it became horribly clear that dukes and earls have far smaller popular followings than music-hall comedians. There are various descriptions of the Tournament but none so pricks the mind's eye as a perusal of one of the superbly produced vellum illustrated programmes. What they alone must have cost!

The 'Triumph' began with trumpeters and pursuivants. Then came the Parade of the Knight Marshall of the Lists and of the Judges. The names of people already in this story grow noticeable. John Leslie and Lord Granby ride by. The Lords Shrewsbury and Essex and Hugh Warrender (one of Jennie's lesser devoted admirers through a quarter of a century) bear banners. Lord Lonsdale acts as Knight Marshal of the Lists and then comes the Parade of the Queen of Beauty. The Viscountess Curzon is carried in under a canopy attended by 'Wayting Ladyes' whose names include Englands' great beauty Lady Diana Manners (Duff Cooper), Victoria Sackville-West (author and wife of Harold Nicolson), Countess Zia Torby (Lady Zia Wernher, winner of the 1966 Derby) and Jennie's niece Clare Frewen who would become famous as Clare Sheridan, traveller and sculptress.

Then comes the Parade of the Princess Errant who is no other than George's sister Daisy of Pless, attended by 'an immense train supposed to be representative of the strange countries of the East' —Prince Christopher of Greece 'extraordinarily handsome in a richly brocaded Cossack costume and cap shimmering with jewels and trimmed with sable' and the Prince Bentheim in cloth of gold, the Hereditary Grand Duke of Mecklenburg-Strelitz, the Spanish Duke of Alba and—can we believe our eyes—a prancing white horse carries His Highness, Prince Charles Kinsky who has succeeded to the family estates and is free to wander once more!

The Parade of the Knights who are to joust at the tilt is headed by the Duke of Marlborough in black armour attended by his esquire bearing a banner—his cousin John Spencer-Churchill. It was rather a family affair but Winston wouldn't play and F. E. Smith, who had promised to ride boldly as a yeoman with George, sent instead his brother who had seldom mounted a horse and 'groaned loudly when sent forth on a palfry clad in hot, heavy armour'.

A leaflet accompanying each programme explained in simple

language the Rules for Jousting at the Tilt and when the six brave knights, each wearing plumes of a different colour, set to with vehemence their audience held its breath. The Duke of Marlborough the Earl of Craven, the Earl Compton, the Viscount Crichton and Baron Tweedmouth tilted with visors down, and Marlborough, a light and brilliant horseman, proved the *pièce de résistance*: 'he rode as if at polo and could not be shaken in the saddle'—however, Jennie had decreed that someone *must* be unhorsed or the combats would look too easy. Cousin Lord Tweedmouth was selected for this role and took it like a man.

After the tilting came a Ballet de Chevaux. George's younger sister the Duchess of Westminster, Lady Sarah Wilson, Lady Juliet Duff and thirty other carefully picked persons gave a display. 'All the ladies in the Ballet were first-rate horse-women, all lovely and mostly tall. It really was interesting to see how well some people looked in their Elizabethan clothes. . . . They said Lord Curzon's suit was presented to an ancestor by the King of Spain in 1500 and was valued at six thousand pounds. . . . The horses all belonged to the Life Guards and therefore were accustomed to music and noise and behaved beautifully.' The Princess of Pless adds artlessly: 'The newspapers and the public liked me because I rode the enormous piebald horse belonging to the Drum-major of the Life Guards which has since been immortalised on canvas by Munnings. We galloped twice around the arena and it was great fun.'

But expensive fun. In the din of the Tourney the Herald and the Pursuivants shouted, according to custom, 'Fight on, brave Knights, man dies but Glory lives; fight on, Death is better than defeat, fight on, brave Knights, for bright eyes behold your deeds.' At last the Knight Marshal of the Lists had to cry 'Hold! Enough! Holà! Holà!' And the Herald ended proceedings with '*A l'hoftell Ployez les Banniers!* To lodging! To lodging.'

Then Queen Alexandra departed, the thankful knights were pulled out of their armour, the ladies shed their 'sheeny damask gowns' and all retreated to the Mermaid Tavern, ready for cups of tea and stronger.

Ten days later they were at it again, dancing in velvet and cloth of gold at Jennie's Elizabethan Ball at the Albert Hall. Worldwide publicity attended the venture. An American paper slightly (but only slightly) exaggerated when it wrote:

George Cornwallis-West

Above The first number of *The Anglo-American*

Opposite above Clare Sheridan
Opposite below Jennie with her grandson, Peregrine Churchill

Jennie in 1920

Mrs Cornwallis-West's leadership is aided by eleven duchesses and forty of the smartest ladies of the day. The executive ability, the dynamic personality and the vital energy of the American are the forces which have wrought her full brilliant career. She weathered ridicule following a marriage with a mere youth, and it is true that the vagaries of 'Winsome Winnie' Churchill have estranged her from powerful Tory influence—yet in this gala season the dark-haired handsome New Yorker bobs up as 'the woman of the moment' and has been chosen as the leader of the enterprise to raise $50,000 in one night.

Gallantly Jennie tried to marshal her friends. She made them get up lavish parades, but many began to feel stingy about more ruffles and farthingales, also they feared it would be difficult to dance in Elizabethan brocades. Mrs Hwfa Williams, possessor of a store of exquisite Greek costumes, added a new note with her All-Pink Parade, she herself being towed in by chains of real roses pulled by an assembly of titled gentlemen in togas. Among the names of her satin-clad retainers is that of Prince Youssoupoff, who a few years later was to help murder Rasputin in scenes more blood-red than rosy pink. Very little money resulted from this fantastic effort, but Jennie soldiered on, and her National Theatre committee eventually raised and invested a quarter of a million pounds.

George Cornwallis-West recounts in his memoirs that Mrs Leeds never reproached him for losing her £10,000. He does not add that she got a husband out of the Tournament and became a Royal Highness when she married Prince Christopher of Greece who had played his part among the splendid Eastern knights! Her money was not lost in vain. Cox's Bank felt differently.

The winter of 1912 became a sad one for Jennie. She recovered from the financial disappointment over these ventures; they had been so successful from every other point of view. But she saw less and less of George, and eventually he wistfully asked for a divorce. The plea he made, that his family desperately desired an heir, was understandable. Jennie could not pit herself against him. Although horrified by the word 'divorce', and heartbroken to lose him, she agreed. She spent a miserable Christmas for George sent her the evidence on a date that hurt.

December 24th 1912

Dearest George,

I am glad that I was prepared for your letter—the blow falls hard enough as it is—But if this thing is to take place it can't be done too quickly now—and we shall both be happier when it is over—Thank God I have physical and mental strength and courage enough to fight my own battle in life.

George suffered painfully from his dilemma. Apparently he did not really wish to be given up. He wrote back:

January 2nd [1913]

Dearest Jennie,

Thanks for your nice letter. I have been on the verge of ringing you up once or twice but honestly don't think I could bear the sound of your dear old voice just now. . . .'

In the following July Jennie's case went through the Law Courts. Nine months later, just before the decree became absolute, she learned to her indignation that it was George's intention to remarry immediately and his choice was not the young girl she had visualised as her successor, nor even a millionairess who could restore Ruthven Castle, but her arch-enemy Mrs Patrick Campbell—twelve years older than George and in yet more precarious financial straits. The blow stunned. She felt her sacrifice had been for nothing. Moreton Frewen wrote angrily to Clara: 'So that beauty George West is to be married on Tuesday to Mrs Pat Campbell—the decree absolute is Monday. Full fathom five they dive to a joint folly', and George's two sisters burst into furious telegrams. Those sent by the Princess of Pless remain in the Chartwell archives—the tone red-hot on crumbling Post Office paper forms. 'Wired you twice. Don't make decree absolute.'

But with aching heart Jennie decided that at this stage it was right to go through with it. George, who was at his wits' end trying to keep Mrs Pat calm for her approaching role as Eliza in Bernard Shaw's new play, *Pygmalion*, received assurance that he could marry his great actress before her first night.

April 4th 1914

My dear George,

Mr Wheeler brought me your message. The d.n. will be made absolute on Monday and I understand that you are going to be married on Tues. You need not fear what I may say for I shall not willingly speak of you. And we are not likely ever to meet. This is the *real* parting of the ways. But for the sake of some of the happy days we had together—should you ever be in trouble and wanted to knock at my door it would not be shut to you. I am returning you my engagement and wedding rings—I say goodbye—a long, long goodbye.

Jennie

This was the generosity of true love. A heartbroken Jennie could not cap the triumphant wit of Mrs Patrick Campbell who commented: 'Ah the peace of the double bed after the hurly-burly of the *chaise longue.*'

❧ 30

The years were chasing her but Jennie fought a spirited rearguard action. On her sixtieth birthday she came in after a dinner party and sat on Leonie's bed. 'I shall never get used to not being the most beautiful woman in the room,' she said. 'It was an intoxication to sweep in and know every man had turned his head. It kept me in form.' Leonie, who had never been pretty, would tell this story, adding: 'It sounds like sour grapes but I learned that sympathy and understanding can hold men longer.'

While awaiting the bitter moment of release from George, Jennie travelled to Italy to attend the marriage of her nephew Hugh Frewen to the daughter of the Duke of Mignano, and to buy antiques for her new house at 74 Brook Street. A few days before the wedding Jennie attended a ball at the Grand Hotel where Hugh introduced her to a great friend of his also serving in the Colonial Service in Nigeria. Montagu Porch was dark, handsome and intelligent with a slight well-built figure and prematurely white hair. He had a good deal of what George Cornwallis-West had always warned her against in men—temperament. Years later he would tell a newspaper reporter: 'I can remember still the first moment I saw her. . . . She wore a green gown and looked very beautiful.' When he asked her to dance she refused, saying: 'I think you had better go and dance with some of the younger girls.' He thought this a rebuff, but as Winston and his secretary Edward Marsh had been instrumental in procuring him his job of Administrator in Northern Rhodesia he had a subject on which to converse, and he

302

did not leave her. She had an 'eerie feeling for ancient Egypt' and Porch had made a collection of stone implements when excavating the Valley of the Kings. Also she liked him chiefly because he had left Oxford to fight in the Boer War.

A mixed marriage was a rarity in Italy and when, a few days later, Hugh Frewen the Protestant groom had to sit indignantly listening to a service which the Roman priest delivered more as scolding than blessing, Mr Porch's humorous black eyes met Jennie's in amusement.

For a week or so afterwards she enjoyed showing him the sights of Rome which she knew so well. Montagu Porch finished his leave and returned to Nigeria very deeply in love despite the twenty-three years between them.

Jennie put in time visiting Bend' Or the Duke of Westminster who had now parted from George's sister Shelagh. From his hunting box near Pau she wrote to Leonie:

December 30 1913

I have never seen Bendor before without Shelagh and the difference is great. Far more intelligent than he ever appeared in her company . . . the best of hosts, genial and thoughtful.

Winston and he get on capitally. . . . We lead the simple life and don't indulge in politics. Winston does a good deal of work and messengers arrive with pouches. . . . I've had a few nice Xmas presents. From the Queen (Alexandra) an ivory box with miniatures, Cartier clock from Charles (Kinsky), ultramarine pendant from Bendor etc., I hear Goonie was godmother to Shane's baby Anita [the author]. She writes from Blenheim that she is taking her 'responsibilities most seriously'. . . . Bendor is going to Eaton on the 9th and he tells me that Iris is to be there. I hope that *cette fine mouche* won't undermine me with him.

On the whole Jennie did not seem to be doing too badly, but back in London she had one of her rare fits of the blues. Ringing up Leonie she said: 'I've met a young man I shall probably marry. I'm getting tired of going to the theatre with my maid.' This dire news rallied Jennie's friends. Was it possible that night after night the poor dear could find nothing better to do? It turned out that in actual fact Jennie had during the last ten years *twice* gone to the theatre with Gentry in attendance because a lady could not go out unaccompanied. Reticence concerning her moods was not in Jennie's nature. If she felt sorry for herself the world must know it. But in some ways she had grown pleasantly philosophical. Her drawing rooms were always overcrowded with knick-knacks accumulated through the years, and when a burglar removed most of these she laughed away her loss, telling Seymour: 'That burglar relieved me of an obsession! I had been taking large houses I could not afford just to hold all my belongings.'

This winter was the most restless and unrewarding of Jennie's life. My grandmother Leonie told me of an afternoon in that bleak spring of 1914. She was resting prior to a ball she had much looked forward to when Jennie, in a very agitated state, had herself announced. Everything was going wrong. She had lost her husband, no one was paying her any attention, bills were accumulating, she didn't know where to turn, friends had forgotten her, a lonely life in penury lay ahead. Having poured it all out and received her sister's sympathy she tragically swept out. 'Darling I must leave you to your nap.'

But my grandmother, the most compassionate of mortals, could not rest. She wept for poor Jennie and, deciding it would be too heartless to attend a ball when her sister was in such straits, took to her bed and turned out the light.

Next morning the telephone began to ring. One friend after another asked why she had missed such a wonderful evening, adding, 'Jennie was there looking wonderful—the life and soul of the party— never seen her in better form.'

Even twenty years later Leonie would grow indignant when she recalled that event. 'But it was a lesson. You must never let people off-load their troubles on to you. They just chew you into a piece of limp string and go off revived.'

Of course Jennie was selfish, not unkind, not ungenerous, but utterly self-centred. Her relationship with her sons had always been warm. She loved and hugged them as babies, she forgot about them as schoolboys, she rallied to their side as young men and slaved during their early years of endeavour. Winston she completely understood. Hot-headed ambition, the thirst for fame, that galli-vanting in the cannon's mouth, the bullying of publishers, the nagging of generals—all that lay in Jennie's province. Despite her admiration for Clementine and Gwendoline, the role of mother-in-law suited her not at all. She could never quite adjust herself to the idea that the two sons with whom she had long been on terms of equality should really give priority of thought to their wives. She expected Winston and Jack to remain her devoted servitors. Of course she adored 'Clemmie' and 'Goonie', but she did not treat them as grown-up women as important as herself. Whenever Jennie went to Paris to replenish her wardrobe at Worth she would buy them each a hat. Not a hat like her own, magnificent, beribboned concoctions, but nice cheap little hats from the *Bon Marché*, suitable she said for the young—a sartorial distinction they felt keenly.

The months after the decree absolute were hard ones for Jennie. She could not even divert herself at the theatre, for the best play of the season was *Pygmalion* with Mrs Patrick Campbell scoring a triumph as Eliza. So she tried to keep out of London and to concentrate on her grandchildren and on Winston. This was more trying than ever for Clementine. Because Winston was often too busy to see her Jennie began complaining about what *she* had once endured from *her* mother-in-law: 'Every day like it or not Randolph had to drive to Grosvenor Square to have tea with the Duchess.' This was utter nonsense and even the most dutiful daughter-in-law was apt to say so quite loud.

It was, of course, a fair diversion to have that son storming around as First Lord of the Admiralty. His four years in this post, fighting for more dreadnoughts and creating a naval air force, were probably the most satisfying of Winston's life. He felt himself so completely part of England's Navy. The personal inspections were joy to him. Visits to the Fleet filled him with delight and acted like champagne on his admirals. Every spring the First Lord went on a cruise on the 3,800-ton Admiralty yacht *Enchantress,* and in May 1913, when Jennie was feeling at a low ebb pending the divorce, he had asked her to come too. The party included Clementine, Asquith, his wife Margot and his daughter Violet, Admiral Beatty and the ever-delightful Edward Marsh. Lady Violet Bonham Carter gives graphic accounts of these cruises. In this instance her diary of the time describes Margot and Jennie as 'two rather explosive elements both singly and—still more—conjointly'. It was perhaps unfortunate that Jennie at this sore point of her career should have to travel in the confines of the glorious yacht with a woman as talkative as herself. Margot loathed the sea and had only embarked because she hated to be 'out of it!' She and Jennie did not 'click'. They both wanted to tell stories of the past, had different versions and contradicted one another. Winston was courteous and patient as ever, but he must have been thankful to escape ashore and see the Adriatic islands. At the Parthenon he wished he could use British sailors with pulleys to right the fallen columns. This was considered very prosaic. But it has been done since to the world's applause.

How fulfilled he was in command of fighting men and fighting ships! He did not weigh the hatred aroused by the punch of his wit. The whole of Tory England loathed him for the energy with which he had defended Asquith's social reforms. 'Treachery to his class' was how the Tories regarded Winston's attack on the House of Lords, and indeed he had used naughty language, about the angry Dukes in particular. 'These unfortunate individuals who ought to lead quiet, delicate, sheltered lives, far from the madding crowd's ignoble strife, have been dragged into the football scrimmage, and they have got roughly mauled in the process. . . . Do not let us be too hard on them. It is poor sport—almost like teasing goldfish.' It ill-behoved Mr Churchill to use such terms when, if his cousin Sunny had died, he would have been Duke of Marlborough himself—and a pretty kettle of fish that would have been! Marlborough took no part in the Peers versus People debates but the Duke of Beaufort stated he would like to see Winston Churchill and Lloyd George 'in the middle of twenty couple of dog-hounds'.

The intense feelings engendered by party politics during the early part of the century can be illustrated by an incident related to me by the present Duchess of Abercorn. It was a hot summer day in 1913 and she was a small girl accompanying her mother, Lady Crichton, on a shopping expedition in South Audley Street. As they paused on the steps of Goodes china shop an open electric car drove slowly by containing a solitary lady 'in a ravishing dress of zebra dark-blue and white stripes and a large hat'. She waved to Lady Crichton who greeted her gaily and then turning to her nine-year-old daughter explained: 'That was Mrs Winston Churchill. Poor Clemmie, so few people will speak to her these days.' The child felt astonished that anyone so pretty should not be spoken to. This was at the time when Winston was fighting to build up the fleet and to discourage over-optimism regarding German intentions.

All his enemies could remember was his advocacy of pensions, Free Trade and, most hated of all, Irish Home Rule. Seymour recalls an argumentative family lunch during the Ulster Crisis at this time, when Leonie and Jack came over from their Irish home which lay within the realm of dispute. Leslie, a Protestant landowner whose family had sat beside their lake for 300 years, could not visualise being governed by Roman Catholics from Dublin and felt like Lord Randolph Churchill that 'Ulster would fight and Ulster would be right'. Jennie led off with a tirade against the Ulstermen's open defiance of Asquith's Home Rule Bill, while Leonie weakly protested. Jack Leslie was slightly deaf and when Jennie, whose turn of phrase could be vivid enough, snapped, 'Well if you stand with Carson you'll roll *in your own blood*,' he asked, hand to ear, 'What does Jennie say?' 'She says that she and Winston are going to roll us in our own blood.' 'Goodness gracious me! What ever for?' Seymour, who was present, shook with laughter and struggled to change the conversation.

But the sisters seldom let politics irritate them. On March 29th, 1914, Jennie wrote to Dearest Sniffy: 'I have been living at the House of Commons, most exciting. It is curious (as Winston said to me the other night after his speech) the discrepancy between the feeling in the House and the lurid headlines and virulent abuse of the Tory Opposition Press. . . .'

In one of her fits of the blues she again wrote Leonie:

London
July 24, 1914

I wish we could see more of each other. Life is so short and we both so down the wrong side of the ladder! The fact is that we are both 'Marthas' instead of 'Marys' and allow things which do not really count to take up our time and keep us apart. We pander to the world which is callous and it only wants you if you can smile and be hypocritical. One is forever throwing away substance for shadows. To live for others sounds all right—you do, darling! ! but what is the result? You are a very unhappy woman all round! As for me every effort I make to get out of my natural selfishness meets with a rebuff. My sons love me from afar, and give me no companionship even when it comes their way. The fault is undoubtedly with me. Every day I become more solitary and prone to introspection which is fatal.

Bless you and take care of your health—You say you haven't time but nature will force you to in a disagreeable manner.

Seymour says his mother commented indignantly: 'I'm *not* an unhappy woman!'

The Irish Home Rule Bill was due to go through in August 1914. Right up to the outbreak of war the Tories could only think of impeding its passage. Jennie had written to Leonie:

April 13, 1914. Lord Robert Cecil said at a demonstration in the Park that Winston 'in his dark and tortuous mind' had prepared everything to force a conflict between the Orangemen and Nationalists and 'wished and hoped that blood would flow like water'. I asked Winston if he had read this speech, he only laughed.

Blood was about to flow like water, like torrents in fact, but not over the issue Lord Robert spoke of. On July 29th, 1914, Jennie wrote again to her sister and still the main issue seems to be party warfare over Home Rule.

July 28, 1914. As I am writing the fate of the Government is hanging in the balance. . . . I saw Winston for a second yesterday; he seemed to think the worst of the European situation and thought war inevitable. As regards Ireland, he thought there was bound to be fighting. Altogether for once he was in a pessimistic frame of mind, but not in respect of the Government. . . .
Later. I lunched with Winston at the Admiralty today, only Lord Morley who said that he has never in his life known the leader of a Great Party use the language that Bonar Law, Tory Opposition leader, has used towards the Government and the Prime Minister (Asquith). . . .
Winston is really so 'big'! Speaking of a possible solution of the vexed question, I said, 'If that happens you will have the other side saying they have won the day.' 'What would that matter,' answered Winston, 'if good came of it.'

On August 1st, 1914, she wrote again:

Darling Sniffy,
Only a line to tell you that Winston tells us Poincaré has written an impassioned letter to the King imploring his aid. The fleet will be mobilised today probably. . . . Money is getting

fearfully tight here and one cannot get a cheque cashed and the Banks will give no gold. But Winston says the financial situation will be easier as they are going to issue at once paper pound notes. . . .

This 'extraordinary possibility' had long been envisaged by Moreton Frewen, but in less drastic circumstances, and he had always insisted that paper currency would necessitate wheelbarrows to carry it!

During the ten days before war broke out Winston was, according to the Prime Minister 'very bellicose, demanding instant mobilisation'. Yet basically this man, who was to prove England's greatest war leader, hated bloodshed. He had written his wife in 1909 when watching the German Army manœuvres: 'Much as war attracts me and fascinates my mind with its tremendous situations. . . . I feel more deeply every year & can measure the feeling here in the midst of arms what vile & wicked folly & barbarism it all is. . . .'

Lord Beaverbrook has described the evening of August 1st when with F. E. Smith he dined with Churchill at Admiralty House. A dispatch box was brought in which Winston opened with his skeleton key. It contained a single sheet of paper on which was written: 'Germany has declared war against Russia.'

Winston rang for a servant, changed his dinner jacket for a lounge coat and left the room without speaking a word. He was not depressed, he was not elated; he was not surprised. . . . He went straight out like a man going to a well-accustomed job. In fact he had foreseen everything that was going to happen so far that his temperament was in no way upset by the realisation of his forecast. We have suffered at times from Mr Churchill's bellicosity. But what profit the nation derived at that crucial moment from the capacity of the First Lord of the Admiralty for grasping and dealing with the war situation.

Now Jennie could hardly ever steal a minute from her son; she could but pray like any other mother, but it was never for Winston's safety. That she took for granted even when he insisted on flying over the fleet with his newly formed Royal Naval Air Service, even when his instructor was killed and F. E. Smith voiced the feelings of half England when he asked him to cease being so foolish. It was in Winston's nature to court danger, and in this case he considered the risk necessary.

Jennie's immediate reaction to war was to write to the papers saying that all male servants ought to be allowed, even encouraged, to join the Army. Every man must do his duty and the grandees of England (whose sons were being mown down in bloody swathes) simply must learn to do without footmen. The splendid Walden had inspired her to this. Although much over age he had determined to join up and begged Mr Winston to pull strings! Hugh Frewen was surprised and delighted to find him as an N.C.O. at the War Office 'looking immaculate in military uniform as he escorted officers to various departments'. In his place Jennie engaged two parlourmaids—the first ever seen in Mayfair. She clad these Amazons in Tudor costume (left over perhaps from the Elizabethan ball) and they were much photographed for the Press. Later on she had the footmen's livery recut for female form and astounded American visitors record how smart they looked! Women to serve at table were a nine-day wonder.

Winston now lived like a meteor, tearing around the ports and visiting his ships. Bonar Law had already started to plot his downfall, but when the terrible days of the Dardanelles were over Kitchener would be able to say to that brash young man of whom he had once disapproved: 'There is one thing they cannot take away from you. The fleet was ready.'

31

The war brought to a sudden end the most ill-natured phase of political life since the Irish Home Rule debates of the 'eighties. Winston laid by the problem of conciliating Protestant Ulster to concentrate on the clean-cut task of fighting the Germans—the fierce old Saxon enemy who had given Britain such a battering in the long ago. As First Lord of the Admiralty, he continued to frighten his friends and disconcert his colleagues by continually putting himself in danger. He enjoyed flying, and he wanted to gain his pilot's certificate. Having founded the Naval Air Service and written in a minute that: 'Terms and conditions must be devised to make aviation for war purposes the most honourable, as it is the most dangerous, profession a young Englishman can adopt', he took full advantage of every opportunity to inspect his fleet from the air and he particularly wanted to find out what could be seen of submarines at various depths from an aeroplane. In this vision he was really one war ahead; he had invented what would one day be called the Fleet Air Arm. When war broke out in 1914 he had thirty-nine aeroplanes, fifty-two seaplanes, a few small airships and about 120 trained pilots whose enthusiasm equalled his own. It was hard on his wife to know her husband was perpetually flying in planes when the casualty rate was still one death for every 5,000 flights, and it was as a gift to her that he relinquished this activity soon after his instructor had been killed. Jennie never fretted; she seemed impervious to danger for herself and others.

Soon after war broke out, Kitchener, fearing Zeppelin raids, asked Winston to undertake the aerial defence of Britain. Winston immediately moved his little bunch of planes to France, where they set up bases near to the enemy lines. In their unbelievable machines, apparently constructed of bamboo and string, his heroic pilots destroyed six Zeppelins in their hangars. Yet successful as it was, Winston's unconventional activity aroused criticism. Why should the First Lord of the Admiralty always be leaving his desk in Whitehall? Why was he so restless? Why must he attract attention?

Meanwhile, the vital gift of Irish Home Rule having been postponed for the duration, the Irish Nationalists raged at this 'cheat'. On the day that Asquith put the Home Rule Bill 'on the statute book with suspended operation', Jennie, who had sat out thirty years of this controversy, wrote to Leonie.

[September 15th 1914]   74 Brook Street
Dearest Sniffy,

I suppose you will have been following the Home Rule debate in the House. I can't see that putting the two Bills on the Statute Book is going to make any difference if they are not in operation until after the war—and then only after an Amending Bill and a General Election. I had Winston for a moment yesterday and asked him what he thought about it. All he said was that Bonar Law's speech made him 'sick' and that *they* [meaning the Opposition] were 'so stupid it was incredible'.

Meanwhile a fierce battle is raging and up to last night 1,500 casualties but he knew no names. . . . A lot of Americans leaving for New York but oh that Ritz Hotel! . . . Shelagh [Westminster] and Sarah [Lord Randolph's sister] both with their hospitals not able to get over, and the wounded are very badly looked after in France.

Kitchener asked Winston if a brigade of Marines could be sent to Dunkirk to demonstrate that British as well as French troops were fighting in the area. Winston dispatched the brigade and requisitioned fifty London omnibuses to drive them to Ypres, Lille and Tournai.

England reeled with horror as the casualty lists rolled in. Columns of small type in each day's paper recorded the names. By Christmas nearly every one of Jennie's friends had lost a son and she had to turn comforter to the sister who had so often comforted her.

Leonie's delightful twenty-seven-year-old Norman was killed by a German sniper. Mrs Pat Campbell's only son was also killed.

Jack Churchill and Clara's son Hugh Frewen were front-line officers, Oswald Frewen a lieutenant on a destroyer. Their letters from trench and shell-hole and battleship were shown to Winston. He liked this unofficial reporting from his cousins who were, as he put it: 'the men at the tip of those arrows on the war maps'. Before he was killed Norman Leslie had written to his mother why he thought it worth dying for England's sake: 'Remember we are writing a new page of History.' Many thousands of idealistic Englishmen perished in the trenches with that thought in their minds. Jennie wrote comfortingly to Leonie: 'I hear there is a good photo of Norman in *The Tablet* of this week . . . also that extracts of his letters are shown on a screen in the Cinemas.'

Eager for 'warwork', Jennie and Leonie applied to the War Office, but their talents seemed useless. Hoping that exquisite French might enable them to translate for generals, they offered full-time service, but ladies were not wanted except to wash dishes in the soldiers' canteen at Victoria Station! Jennie recoiled: 'I would do it so badly!' She joined Lady Maud Warrender, a first-class soprano, who went around singing to the wounded. Burning with emotion, Jennie pounded the piano at barracks and hospitals and eventually helped to run the convalescent home of her sister-in-law, Lady Sarah Wilson, in the country. All this was tame compared to her work in that other war, which seemed so remote and light-hearted compared to the present holocaust. But in 1914 the authorities were not inclined to allow society ladies to point out the unnecessary miseries of the wounded. A new, astonishing role was discovered for the 'debutante daughters', who trained to be nurses at the V.A.D. Hospital in Charles Street; but Jennie found no real fulfilment. She could only work well if she was Queen Bee.

It was Leonie who learned to alleviate the pain of her own loss by working as a kitchen scullion in the Y.M.C.A. canteen at Victoria Station. Here in a dim-lit nook she endlessly handed out cups of tea and washed up. At least she felt close to the men who were just leaving for the blood-soaked mud of Flanders, and this atoned for filthy sinks and clogged drainpipes. Her jokes might be the last they heard on earth, her smile the last a woman gave. 'This was the real thing. The back-breaking work helped me,' she said. 'Grim

313

Victoria Station with the trains whistling out into the dark with singing soldiers and rolling back with silent bandaged figures—that was the nearest I could get to the war. I was so glad they rationed sugar. I loved sugar in my tea and I almost enjoyed not having it. . . .'

But claws could show through Leonie's sweetness. One night a wistful Major loomed up out of the gloom, and she recognised George Cornwallis-West, now anything but happy with Mrs Pat. Hoping for sympathy he told her: 'The day of my divorce was the saddest of my life.' 'Perhaps the happiest in my sister's,' snapped Leonie, splashing cups in the dirty water.

We get a glimpse of Jennie during that first winter of war from an American cousin, young Mrs Sherman Haight, who lunched with her several times a week and accompanied her on visits to soldiers' families in the Limehouse slums. Jennie was always liked by working people and tactful when trying to help in family troubles.

Anne Haight thought the house economies excellent: 'The silver had been put away and the food was served from cooking pots of copper lined with silver to keep hot. Winston often came to lunch and one day I arrived from riding to see quite a number of people outside the door. King George and Queen Mary had that morning sent word that they would be pleased to lunch!' Anne struggled into a suitable gown, and found herself sitting next to His Majesty, who endeavoured to amuse her with anecdotes while Winston talked passionately about the war. He could not make conversation; he either sat sunk in thought, oblivious to others, or he held forth.

Occasionally Jennie, wearing a toque of violets which she knew to be particularly becoming to her silver-streaked hair, would walk her cousin across the Park to see Winston at the Admiralty and Anne Haight got the impression that he drew on his mother's vitality. She was down-to-earth and instinctive. People of all sorts turned to her in stress.

On Easter Sunday the Haights arrived at Jennie's house for lunch and realised they were rather too early. So apparently were the two young men sitting on the doorstep in the sunshine. The Prince of Wales and the Duke of York stood up to explain that Jennie had promised them some American jazz records, but the whole household was still at church. Jennie and Winston then appeared walking arm in arm, and the young Princes were given their jazz.

Meanwhile Daisy of Pless hung miserably around as an English wife in Germany, while Prince Charles Kinsky, now a major in a regiment of Hungarian Hussars, was elegantly reading *The Times* which he somehow got through the censors. His young cousin, Prince de Clary, visiting the headquarters of the Austrian 1st Army during the offensive into Russia, remembers seeing him there. 'I found him on a bench reading an old *Times*. His first remark to me—in English of course—was "How odd—old X—is taking a strong line against racing during the war".' Yes, it was better while the great guns smashed the life they knew, to read the racing news—rather than compare the columns of English and Austrian friends killed.

Another story of the middle-aged Charles Kinsky exists. As the Russians retreated they left Cossack detachments in civilian clothes to hide in the great forests, doing sabotage and taking what prisoners they could. 'As there were no roads for mechanical vehicles and telephones could not be put up, all orders had to be carried on horseback by the A.D.C.s, who usually took strong escorts. I remember once seeing Charles Kinsky arrive quite alone,' writes his cousin, 'and when the General asked him why on earth he had not taken an escort he answered, "I really could not be bothered with a guard. Should I run into Cossacks I'll remember enough Russian from my Petrograd days to deal with them!" On his way back he did indeed meet two Cossacks in uniform. Pulling out a revolver he bellowed at them to say they could consider themselves his prisoners. The Cossacks were bewildered at this torrent of Russian from an angry officer and allowed themselves to ride back as prisoners.'

Jennie always felt a nostalgic pang as she walked past Charles's flat in Clarges Street, and one day the English butler who remained there tending his master's possessions met her in the street. Letters could occasionally pass the censorship of both countries and in the far off Russian forests Prince Kinsky received one from his faithful servant. 'Yesterday I saw Lady R.C. She told me to let you know that I saw her and that she is well.'

As far as I know this was the final communication, but a few years after the war Prince de Clary visited Charles Kinsky's heir at the family shooting box in Bohemia. 'He took me to his uncle's room and asked me whether I knew the lady whose portrait was hanging over the writing-desk.' It was Jennie! She had been his only love though she never knew it for sure.

Meanwhile the war rolled cruelly on and Winston worked out methods to prevent the German trenches encircling his air bases. In January 1915 the Director of the Air Division received a letter from Mr Churchill which began: 'I wish the following experiment made at once:

> Two ordinary steam-rollers are to be fastened together side by side, by very strong steel connections, so that they are to all intents and purposes one roller covering a breadth of at least twelve to fourteen feet. . . .'

The Landships Committee of the Admiralty produced two designs, one of which was the blue-print for the world's first tanks.

As Winston would someday write: 'The air was the first cause that took us to Dunkirk. The armoured car was the child of the air, and the tank its grandchild.'

In September 1914 Winston had gone personally to Antwerp and tried to talk the authorities out of capitulating. Leonie sat with Jennie in London muttering, 'You ought to have *made* him learn French properly.' Within the week Prime Minister Asquith was astonished to receive a message from Mr Churchill asking if, being certain he could save the city, he could be relieved of the Admiralty to take over military command of Antwerp. The cabinet gasped at such temerity but Kitchener said: 'I will make him a major-general if you will give him the command.' Asquith did not dare, and Antwerp fell after five days' hard fighting. According to the British official history those five days of incalculable value were entirely due to Winston, but the House of Commons found it hard to stomach the theatrical touch. The First Lord returned to London in a strange mood, and called immediately on the Prime Minister to ask if he could be relieved from the Admiralty. Asquith's diary reveals: 'His mouth waters at the thought of Kitchener's Armies. Are these glittering commands to be entrusted to dug-out trash, bred on the obsolete tactics of twenty-five years ago, mediocrities who have led a sheltered life, mouldering in military routine?

'For about an hour he poured forth a ceaseless invective and appeal and I much regretted that there was no shorthand writer

316

within hearing as some of his premeditated phrases were quite priceless. He was, however, three parts serious and declared that a political career was nothing to him in comparison with military glory.'

But he remained First Lord into the spring, when the greatest chance of the war arrived at the Dardanelles. Even now, fifty years later, the facts make bitter, painful reading. The war might have been ended with one great blow, but Winston, who saw this so clearly, could not prevail on old Admiral Fisher to believe in the project, or definitely to order the 'Admiral on the spot' to proceed to take the narrow straits. The 'Admiral on the spot' had no blind eye, he waited and wondered, his successor waited and wondered. Alas for England, her big man, Roger Keyes, held only a junior command; he performed valiant deeds and begged for action, but he could not override his seniors. The great opportunity of ending the war by taking Constantinople by surprise was lost. Then in April 1915 came the bloody heartbreak of the troop-landings, the horrors of the ill-organised Gallipoli campaign with divisions standing idle in Egypt when they could so easily have been helping. The ghastly military procrastination resulted in a blood-bath.

Instead of reinforcing the Mediterranean fleet, Admiral Fisher said he had always been against the Dardanelles and insisted on withdrawing ships. Winston remained quite sure of the proper battlefield—it was Turkey not the Western Front. Admiral Fisher created confusion by resigning and the Tory Opposition, led by Bonar Law, who hated Winston, seized the opportunity of telling the Prime Minister that they would not support his government unless Mr Churchill left the Admiralty. The Tories seemed to hate Winston more than the Germans.

Asquith and Lloyd George had to break the news to him and Bonar Law ignored Winston's letter of protest: 'Many Sea Lords have come and gone, but during all these four years (nearly) I have been according to my patent "solely responsible to Crown and Parliament" and have borne the blame for every failure: and now I present to you an absolutely secure Naval position; a Fleet constantly and rapidly growing in strength, and abundantly supplied with munitions of every kind, an organisation working with perfect smoothness and efficiency, and the seas upon which no enemy's flag is flown. Therefore I ask to be judged justly, deliberately and with knowledge.'

Poor Winston. It never entered his head that a small-minded, gloomy man like Bonar Law could detest him. He detested nobody. He could only think about winning the war. Now he brooded in anguish, and no one could comfort him. E. Ashmead Bartlett, the only war correspondent allowed by Kitchener to report from Gallipoli, returned to London for a few days in June, and in his diary gives a graphic description of an unhappy evening at Jennie's house at this time.

June 10 1915. This evening I dined with Lady Randolph Churchill to meet Winston. The Lulu Harcourts and Duchess of Marlborough were also present but I forget who else. I am much surprised at the change in Winston Churchill. He looks years older, his face is pale, he seems very depressed and he feels keenly his retirement from the Admiralty. But even if he be the creator of the Dardanelles Expedition, he is in no wise responsible for the manner in which it is being carried out. He has no one but himself to blame for his misfortunes. He held the most important post in the Cabinet at the outbreak of the war, and he had only to curb his impetuosity and direct its labours, guided by his advisers, and he would still be First Lord. But his nature rebelled at the prospect of sitting in an arm-chair directing naval strategy when others were actually fighting. He was torn between conflicting emotions, the demands of his great office, and his paramount desire to take an active part in the war itself. . . .

At dinner the conversation was more or less general, nothing was said about the Dardanelles, and Winston was very quiet. It was only towards the very end that he suddenly burst forth into a tremendous discourse on the Expedition and what might have been, addressed directly across the table in the form a lecture to his mother, who listened most attentively. Winston seemed unconscious of the limited number of his audience, and continued quite heedless of those around him. He insisted over and over again that the battle of March 18th had never been fought to a finish and, had it been, the Fleet must have got through the Narrows, This is the great obsession of his mind and will ever remain so.

318

Bartlett was correct here. When many years after another war I asked Clementine Churchill what had been the most terrible strain Winston had ever endured she answered without hesitation: 'Oh, the Dardanelles. I thought it would break his heart.'

Ashmead Bartlett goes on to describe how after dinner he walked back with Winston to the Admiralty which Balfour, the new First Lord, had begged him not to vacate in haste.

> The ornate rooms and official papers seemed to mock him; the deserted hall so lately full of sycophants, admirers and place seekers now only re-echoed the sound of his own voice. He presented the perfect picture of a fallen Minister. Once again he cried out in the silent night: 'They never fought it out to a finish. They never gave my schemes a fair trial.'

The pain was augmented by the continued slaughter on the Gallipoli Peninsula, where every military chance for intelligent co-ordination was missed. The earlier naval missed chances would grow even more apparent in history. There is one more entry in Bartlett's diary before returning to the scenes of disaster. He wanted to say goodbye.

> June 12th. Winston was spending his last day at the Admiralty, as he was about to leave for the country. He looked ill and worn, but was calm. Having picked out a few books, he passed out into the street, saying goodbye to the office he loved so well— probably for ever.

Here Bartlett surmised incorrectly: but twenty-five years were to pass.

A single comic interlude enlivened these heart-searing months. The Jerome sisters' cousin Kitty was married to Mr Mott, that amiable millionaire whose moderate ambition in life had been realised when he had been elected to one of London's exclusive clubs. Meanwhile his wife, the greatest snob in Euro-American history, enjoyed entertaining royalty in general and the Kaiser in particular. An invitation to his Imperial Majesty's yacht in the summer of 1913 had filled her with somewhat inordinate enthusiasm for Queen Victoria's mixed-up kid of a grandson. When war broke out the Motts wisely retreated from Europe to the Ritz Hotel in New York, and during the first ghastly massacres of the war this well-meaning but unprescient lady dispatched a fulsome cable to Kaiser Wilhelm which was picked up by a British warship and handed to the Press with Mrs Mott's address changed from Ritz Hotel to Rats Hotel. Moreton Frewen wrote to Jennie's nephew, Shane Leslie. 'It appears that that appalling woman not only sent that treacherous cable to the Kaiser but another to King George! Stamfordham intercepted that of course and supposed it was a crank, but within a few minutes he saw the Kaiser's in the evening papers and showed both of them all round the royal circle to the accompaniment of much merriment. A terror—she hunted titles from a baronet to an Emperor as you and I would stalk stags! . . . That is a lady I always had the most supreme contempt for as a sublimated snob. Aunt Jennie is cabling tonight I believe to ask if she may deny it on authority. If Kitty did send the cable, and it sounds like her terminology, she can never set foot in England again.'

Cousin Kitty was proved guilty, and Jennie cabled 'forbidding' her the ports and nice Jordan Mott, who had no idea his wife was buttering up the Kaiser, had to write his London clubs offering to resign!

After Winston left the Admiralty, Asquith only dared to offer him the sinecure of the Duchy of Lancaster. This at least kept him a member of the War Council although it carried no departmental work. 'It was a cruel and unjust degradation', wrote Lloyd George. 'It was quite unnecessary in order to propitiate them, to fling him from the masthead whence he had been directing the fire, down to the lower deck to polish the brass.'

To Lord Riddell, who tried to comfort him, Winston bitterly rejoined that he was finished in respect of all he cared for, 'the waging of war: the defeat of the Germans. I have had a high place offered to me—a position which has been occupied by many distinguished men and which carries with it a high salary. But all that goes for nothing. This is what I live for.'

His wife and mother fretted for him through the terrible summer, Clementine fiercely protesting to the Prime Minister that Winston had 'the supreme quality which I venture to say very few of your present or future Cabinet possess—the power, the imagination and the deadliness to fight Germany'. He was lucky to have such a wife in those dark days. Her belief must have kept him alive.

Jennie remained indignant and optimistic; she could not imagine that any Government could be so stupid as not to make use of Winston's genius. To sister Clara at Brede Place in Sussex Jennie wrote:

July 4th 1915
I'm afraid Winston is very sad at having nothing to do. When you have had your hand at the helm for four years it seems stagnation to take a back place and for why? No fault can be found with his work at the Admiralty and they give him the sack whereas a gigantic mistake is made at the War Office [Kitchener's late effort in Gallipoli] and the man responsible for it is screened and given the Garter. It makes my blood boil. However the truth will out and we shall see a mighty fall. What do you hear of Wilfred?

Wilfred Sheridan, who had married Jennie's only niece, Clare Frewen, was about to be killed in France.

On September 11th, 1915, Jennie wrote: 'It was too sad my missing seeing the Zeps considering one passed over the house and all the maids saw it and the shrapnel bursting around it. . . . Winston and Clemmie have gone to the farm. Lovely day but I am feeling sad mostly about Winston.'

And to Leonie she raged:

[October 12th 1915] This slow and supine Government are now beginning to realise what Winston has preached for the last six months. If they had made the Dardanelles policy a certainty, which they could have done in the beginning, Constantinople would have been in our hands ages ago. *In confidence*, it is astounding how Winston foresaw it all. There is a minute of his, written the beginning of June, in which he warned the Government that Germany will not bring back troops from Russia to the West, but will lose them to march through Serbia, having reduced Bulgaria. But nothing will make them listen—Winston is on the war-path!

Any mother might have written this letter about her son but history rages with her. '. . . Nothing would make them listen. . . .' Winston was on the war-path alone.

Certain that Turkey was the key to victory, he continued to

press in favour of the Gallipoli campaign but the Germans had now had time to reinforce the defences and losses on the beaches grew increasingly terrible. In early November, just when the top of Vimy Ridge had been reached, it was decided to evacuate the forces and resume the endless blood-bath of the Western Front.

Hugh Frewen managed to survive six months on the Gallipoli beaches, and he wrote an eyewitness account of the carnage to Winston, who answered him.

[Frewen Papers]

16.10.15
19 Abingdon Street
Westminster

My dear Hugh,

I was so glad to get yr most interesting letter, but the news of the death of my poor friend Kenneth is sad reading. I had a splendid letter from him only a few days before. He was a gallant man.

I hope you realise how much we who stay at home feel we owe you all: and with wonder & admiration we watch your feats of arms & endurance. Everyone is so brave & daring nowadays that these qualities are scarcely noticed at the front; but at home we feel in a real sense your debtors.

You have been having gt experiences and I rejoice you have so far come safely through them.

My hope is that in the end the usefulness of the sacrifices made will be apparent. But war is a cruel game.

You have done well indeed and we often in the circle here think of you and wish you luck.

Poor Wilfred has gone but Clare has her little son to live for.

It is a terrible time and the world can never be the same again after the storm has passed.

My confidence in our ultimate complete victory is undimmed.

With every good wish,
Yours affectionately,
Winston

Winston suffered deeply at the loss of friends as well as at the, to him futile, methods used to fight the war. Jennie said he craved danger to ease his own pain. Lord Melville's son, the Hon. Kenneth Dundas, to whom Winston refers in this letter, was Hugh's company

322

commander in the Anson Battalion. As a District Commissioner in Kenya he had entertained Winston during his tour of inspection in the past. Winston came in sadly to Jennie after he had heard the details of Kenneth's death from Hugh and told her: 'He slipped out of the Colonial Office and obtained a commission in the Royal Naval Division before they realised he'd gone. He was a man of such honour.' Winston sighed and spoke of a far away evening in Africa when Dundas complained that after he had given certain undertakings to the local chief the Administration had refused to honour them. 'What did you do?' asked Winston. 'Sent in my resignation,' replied Dundas. 'You should not have done that, they might have accepted it. You should have said that unless your action met with the support you had the right to expect you would not accept responsibility for the consequences!' Winston was a fighter but also wary; resignation offering was not his method with superiors— 'the devils might accept!'

Jack, the ever cheerful, gallant Jack also came home full of experiences from Gallipoli, and Jennie was able to see something of him and Goonie while they lived at 10 Talbot Square, a few minutes' walk away. Jack's verses concerning his sector of the peninsula were printed in an Army broadsheet:

> 'Y Beach, the Scottish Borderer cried,
> While panting up the steep hillside,
> Y Beach.

> To call this thing a beach is stiff,
> It's nothing but a bloody cliff.
> Why beach?'

When Asquith formed his new War Committee, to Winston's bitter disappointment it did not include him. While Clemmie comforted, Jennie was incredulous. How could they discard their one fighting leader? Unable to bear 'well-paid inactivity' Winston set about obtaining a commission in the Oxfordshire Yeomanry. Jennie wrote to Leonie who was running a Belgian refugee camp in Ireland.

[November 12th 1915] I want you to know before you see it in the Press that Winston has resigned and is going to join his regiment at the Front next week. When the War Council was finally appointed the other day his usefulness in the Cabinet came to an end. If he stays in the Government he is responsible indirectly for the conduct of the war.

Later. You will be grieved about Winston, poor fellow, he is only concerned about not finishing his job of the Dardanelles, but when we are in Constantinople, they will not be able to withhold the praise which will be his due. Arthur Balfour is the best person to follow him at the Admiralty as he knows the truth.

A few days later Beaverbrook called on the Churchills in Cromwell Road, 'The whole household was upside down while the soldier-statesman was buckling on his sword. Downstairs Mr "Eddie" Marsh, his faithful secretary, was in tears. . . . Upstairs, Lady Randolph was in a state of despair at the thought of her brilliant son being relegated to the trenches. Mrs Churchill seemed to be the only person who remained calm, collected and efficient.'

The delicate, fragile-looking 'Clemmie' was showing nerves of iron. She never needed them more than during this heart-rending first year of war, for the near-miss of the Dardanelles nearly broke Winston's spirit.

The war might have ended in 1915 and millions of lives been saved but Winston could not force Kitchener and Fisher to plunge. No Nelson had arisen among his admirals, and none remembered Nelson's words, 'In war *something* has to be left to chance.'

32

At least he could find occupational therapy in the trenches. Winston turned hungrily to the 'honourable course'; physical danger proved lick to his wounds. His mother wrote to Leonie:

[December 20th 1915]
You can imagine how jumpy we are all feeling with Winston in the trenches. I see that the Dardanelles is being evacuated. It is sad to think of all the lives lost for nothing, quite apart from the terrible loss of prestige.

The supineness of the Government will be shown up at the end of the war when the papers are published and the public will realise how easy it would have been to get to Constantinople had men only been sent when they were asked for.

I am afraid Winston will feel very sad, although of course if the Government won't go in for an active policy out there, there is nothing to do but come away. Meanwhile Winston has been offered a battalion which will be in the fighting line. It is quite true that his orderly was killed near him the other day. A shell exploded in the trench. It appears that Winston wrote such a good paper on trench warfare that it has been circulated to all the officers at the front.

While Englishmen fought Winston had to fight with them. Having asked for a month's training in trench warfare before commanding the brigade offered him by General French, he was attached to one of the Grenadier battalions about to move into the line and met a somewhat chilly reception. 'I was infinitely amused at the elaborate pains they took to put me in my place and to make me realise that nothing counted at the front except military rank and behaviour. It took about forty-eight hours to wear through their natural prejudice against politicians of all kinds, but particularly of the non-Conservative brand.'

Mud and shellfire were balm in his present mood and again, as in the Boer War, he seemed fascinated by danger. The orderly to whom Jennie referred had been killed during Winston's brief absence from his dug-out. His 'Star' in the form of a chance invitation to visit a general had led him away just before the shell landed. The unfortunate thing for Winston was that his panache, which so appealed to the ordinary Englishman, enraged the Tories. They distrusted him for being sorry for the poor, for wanting old-age pensions, for trying to win the war with a quick decisive blow on the soft underbelly. Whatever he did was called 'climbing on the band-wagon'—even when he had made the wagon himself and beat his own lonely drum.

Now the House of Commons meanly demanded that the former First Lord of the Admiralty should not have 'preferential treatment' in the Army. General French, who had offered a brigade, had to reduce this to a battalion. Beaverbrook wrote succinctly: 'A Premier may have to throw a colleague overboard to save the ship, but surely he should not jerk from under him the hen-coop on which the victim is trying to sustain himself on the stormy ocean.'

Lieutenant-Colonel Churchill plunged into his job with enthusiasm and humour. The Scots Fusiliers greeted their new commanding officer coldly, but he won them over in a day by calling a solemn conclave to announce: 'War is declared, gentlemen, on the lice.' The men as well as the officers grew intrigued by this extraordinary character. He gave them something to write home about. A Captain Gibbs, who was present, wrote in a little book, *With Churchill at the Front*: 'Apparently he was a man entirely devoid of fear. "War is a game to be played with a smiling face", he often announced, and to Winston the smiles seemed to come naturally.'

All through the winter he commanded his battalion with zest in the icy, muddy trenches, but then he started to hunger once more for the opportunity to exert influence on those events he felt were being terribly mishandled. He knew himself to be a great leader and could not resist returning to the rostrum of Westminster. In March he gave a long speech on naval policy, and then, when his battalion was amalgamated with another, leaving him without a command, he asked to be released from the Army. Even this evoked criticism, but Winston was so intent on winning the war he never noticed the resentment that his different efforts aroused. 'He cared for the Empire profoundly,' wrote Beaverbrook, 'and was honestly convinced that only by his advice and methods could it be saved. His ambition was in essence disinterested. He suffered when he thought that lesser men were mismanaging the business.'

While Clementine remained heroically calm, Jennie raged. But she gave all she could of herself to ease her son's torment. On June 8th, 1914, she wrote to Leonie.

Admiralty House
Devonport
Nancy Astor is here, not staying in the house; she is madder than ever. I gather the authorities do not appreciate her, she is so erratic. How beastly the papers are about Winston. I can't understand it when one thinks of what he did in the war. There wasn't any mistake made at the Admiralty. Well, I dare say it will all come right in time but it is very sickening.'

'Thank God for his Jerome resilience,' replied Leonie.

The malice felt by the English upper classes against the 'upstart' Winston and his American mother is revealed in Lady Cynthia Asquith's *Diaries* (published 1968). On August 8th, 1916, she recounts a rumour that Sir John Cowans, the Adjutant General, had given a commission to a private soldier whom Lady Randolph fancied and that she had then insisted he be reduced to the ranks because he did not please her! The episode is hardly worth relating, for, as Lady Cynthia adds: 'Cowans, poor man, has the reputation of jobbery owing to his susceptibilities to the "ladies" but this story sounds incredible.' It certainly does, but it shows up the venom circulating in wartime London which could drive such an unlikely tale into circulation.

Of course, Jennie was perfectly capable of thinking she had spotted a Field Marshal's baton in some handsome soldier's knapsack, but the true story was very different. It concerns George

327

Cornwallis-West's mother, who had indeed taken up, and then dropped for reasons best known to herself, a young Irish soldier, who then complained to the Irish Members of the House of Commons that she had, through pique, managed to prevent him being given a commission. The matter was taken up in the House of Commons and did cause some trouble to Cowans, who remained a superb general until the end of the war. It was typical of London society to twist the story around Jennie and to alter it unattractively in the process.

During that terrible summer of 1916, when Haig was unimaginatively hurling waves of English bodies against the German fortifications, Winston wrote to Asquith: 'It is a fair general conclusion that the deadlock in the West will continue for some time and the side which risks most to pierce the lines of the other will put itself at a disadvantage.'

And again he fretted: 'Leaving *personnel* and coming to ground gained, we have not conquered in a month's fighting as much ground as we were expected to gain in the first few hours. . . . From every point of view, therefore, the British offensive *per se* has been a great failure.' He was sure the war ought not to be fought out in France against prepared positions but by attacking through the Balkans. This question of fighting in the East or the West dominated the next year. The West, with its terrible casualties for both sides, remained the main front.

While eating his heart out, Winston made a discovery which he has most beautifully described in his book: *Painting as a Pastime*.

When I left the Admiralty at the end of May 1915 I still remained a member of the War Cabinet and the War Council. In this position I knew everything and could do nothing. . . . I had long hours of utterly unwanted leisure in which to contemplate the frightful unfolding of war. At a moment when every fibre of my being was inflamed to action, I was forced to remain a spectator of the tragedy placed cruelly in a front seat. And then it was that the muse of painting came to my rescue—out of charity and out of chivalry, because after all she had nothing to do with me—and said 'Are these toys any good to you? They amuse some people'.

Lady Violet Bonham Carter in *Winston Churchill as I Knew Him*

describes an extraordinary weekend which she spent at Hurstmon-
ceaux Castle in June 1916 as the guest of Claude Lowther who had
restored the fifteenth-century brick walls. The only other guests at
dinner were Jennie and Winston and Clemmie and a large ram
'with muddy hooves and clotted pelt, roaming at large among the
priceless furniture and *objets d'art*'. Jennie uttered a scream when
nearly knocked down, while Mr Lowther explained that this
animal was the mascot of 'Lowther's Lambs', his Territorial battalion. But neither ram nor his eccentric host, who appeared dressed
as for a court ball, nor his mother's bright chatter, could bring a
smile to Winston's face. His gloom did not disperse until next
morning in the garden where Lady Violet saw the ignored war
leader forget his woe:

> His coming was heralded by a procession of gardeners bearing an
> easel, a large canvas, a chair, a box of paints and a bristling
> bundle of brushes . . . his tensions relaxed, his frustrations evapora-
> ted . . . Watching him paint on that June morning I became sud-
> denly aware it was the only occupation I had ever seen him practise
> in silence. . . . The spell was only broken once that day by the
> dull distant thunder of the cannonade in France. He broke off then,
> laid down his brush and spoke with bitterness of his position;
> of the unfair attacks upon him for the failure in Gallipoli, of his
> desire for a public enquiry in which he could have the chance of
> vindicating himself. . . .

Jennie could not help her son. She could but torment herself.
On August 27th, 1916, she wrote to Leonie: 'Winston and Clemmie
are at Blenheim. His last paintings are very good. Lavery says that
if Winston cared to take painting up as a profession he could, but
of course he uses it as an opiate.'

The atmosphere of London remained hectically, horribly gay.
It was really macabre to offer such jollity to soldiers on leave from
that 'Mud-Massage'. Unbelievable casualty lists continued, and
after 1916 there descended an apathy and eventually a despair
etched with cynicism as one disastrous offensive followed another
on the Western Front. A semi-blackout caused gloom rather than
inconvenience. Civilians ate their hearts out behind blinds and an
unhappy guilt corroded all efforts at pleasure. When Seymour saw a
little of Jennie he said she played Debussy and cried easily. Hating

329

evenings alone, she would drive out through the darkened streets to Sir Thomas Beecham's opera at the Aldwych or to the new Sunday stage clubs which tried out highbrow foreign plays. Occasionally she attended a dinner party. One of these is recorded in a letter from Seymour to his mother:

[March 22nd, 1916]
Such an amusing dinner at Mrs Charles Hunter's last night after Beecham's Russian Concert. George Moore, the Ian Hamiltons, Jennie and others. George Moore was funny; laboured and brought forth several bon mots: '*Un confrère est un faux frère*'— 'A literary movement consists of three people who live in the same town and detest each other' (a perfect description of his days in Dublin). We sat till nearly 11 and had a free-for-all fight over Free Trade. Jennie became very cross and scolding, unable to get a word in— '*Well*, if you *won't* let me speak—I was going to tell you about what the Germans said to a friend of mine only last week about Free Trade. . . .'
George Moore: '*Ce n'est pas une question de morale, vous savez.*'
Jennie: 'Let *me* speak!'
Mrs Hunter: 'As a business woman let *me* get a word in!'
Ian Hamilton: 'Why—ah—in Gallipoli, the splendidly developed Turkish. . . .'
Jennie: 'I just tell you people *that* (etc. etc.)'
The uproar, all talking at once! I trace it to the economy champagne we had drunk. Tomorrow Jennie and I go to hear chamber music.

Work for servicemen, and hospital concerts, were Jennie's only solace. The air raids became too frequent to amuse. In September 1917 she wrote to Leonie: 'The raids have been very disturbing. It was strange to sit still at the opera after the galleries had been evacuated by the police. Beecham unmoved conducting better than ever. Margot [Asquith] and Pamela Lytton disappeared but no one else. The guns were crashing all around. Bombs fell near Talbot Square [where Goonie was expecting a child] but all was well.

'Meanwhile the children are rightly to be kept in the country until the raids are over. It is fair today so we shall probably have them tonight.'

Two months later from Wimborne she wrote a long letter to

nephew Shane: '[November 4th, 1917] I have come here to see my old sister-in-law Lady Wimborne—not to avoid London raids—although having been in them all up to now I have had quite enough of them. I daresay Seymour has given you ample descriptions. I was at the opera one night when the guns overpowered the orchestra and the bombs fell quite close. But no one moved and the music and singers went on calmly. What stirring and unpleasant things are happening! Russia and Italy and Ireland! But the latter is not as bad as appears on paper and the Catholics are going to play the right game I think. Sinn Feinism will give Home Rule to Ireland.'

All during 1917 Jennie became steadily more dejected over Winston's lack of office. How could England cast aside her natural leader? When Seymour dined with her she kept bursting into tears and made him play piano duets with her when he was tired from working in Vickers armament factory. 'No husband, no lover. She has become a trial', was his unsympathetic verdict.

But then a ray of sunshine appeared. An officer rang her doorbell —not the unhappy George, but Mr Montagu Porch stood on the doorstep. He had arrived on leave to profess his attachment. Jennie continued to laugh him off. 'It is too ridiculous. You are three years younger than Winston.' But he cheerfully persisted in stating his affections and she began to wonder.

When Asquith fell and dynamic Lloyd George became Prime Minister, Winston believed that he must once more be given office but the Conservative Opposition remained adamant. They would *not* agree to a Coalition unless he was kept out. On January 1st, 1917, Jennie wrote to her sister: 'I know nothing of Winston as to the Air Ministry. He may or may not get it. I think he has been so cruelly and unjustly treated and I don't think I can ever forgive Asquith's disloyalty to him. I hear that at a big luncheon at Maud Cunard's the other day, the Asquiths and several ex-ministers talked loudly in Winston's praise and said how "wonderful" he was. Much use saying it now.'

Another tragedy had nibbled Winston's nerves. He had for years been riveted by the idea of tanks. Unfortunately Haig insisted on experimenting with a few. Winston begged the Prime Minister to hold them back until large numbers could be made available but Haig was allowed to attack with fifty, thus ruining all element of surprise.

As Prime Minister, Lloyd George did what he could for Winston. He released the Report of the Dardanelles Royal Commission and in July 1917, against much opposition, gave him the Ministry of Munitions. Lloyd George described the resultant outburst. 'It was interesting to observe in a concentrated form every phase of the distrust and trepidation with which mediocrity views genius at close quarters. Unfortunately genius always provides its critics with material for censure—it always has and always will. Churchill is certainly no exception to this rule.'

Winston's new job did not include a seat in the War Cabinet. 'Not allowed to make the plans,' he wrote, 'I was set to make the weapons.' Once more the idea of a huge tank attack dominated his mind. Haig still could not grasp the importance of this new weapon but on November 20th, 1917, the first great tank attack in history took place and was a colossal success. Five hundred tanks penetrated the German lines to a depth of six miles, two hundred guns and ten thousand Germans were captured. No reserves existed or the war might have ended a year earlier. All Winston could do now was to increase tank output, but it was too late for a decisive surprise battle. Jennie wrote to Leonie:

> Do you see how successful Winston's 'caterpillars' have been and how disgusting the *Daily Mail* is today? Winston worked at those things, scratching the money for them and working like a nigger to get the idea accepted *two years ago*. Two years ago he went to France to 'boom' them and Haig sent for him when he was at the Admiralty to explain them. Of course Winston did not invent them but they would not exist today any more than the Monitors would, had it not been for his foresight and push, and now they want to take away from him the credit for them. It makes my blood boil—the injustice and meanness with which he is treated.

In early 1918 she wrote slightly assuaged:

> I saw Winston at the Ministry of Munitions yesterday. Very pleased with a telegram he had had from Haig, saying that their victories were owed to Winston and his munitions!
>
> Seymour dined with me last night, both tired, and I'm afraid I was grumpy and of poor company. Goodnight and bless you.

Winston was responsible not only for guns and shells and steel-plates for ships, but for aircraft production. Lloyd George records:

Owing to the energy which Mr Winston Churchill threw into the production of munitions between 1st March and 1st April the strength of the Tank Corps increased by twenty-seven per cent, and that of the Machine Gun Corps by forty-one per cent, while the number of aeroplanes in France rose by forty per cent.

The Ministry of Munitions also undertook to supply the American army with all its medium artillery.

This was really better than commanding a brigade in the trenches —especially for Winston who disapproved of trench warfare! As it was he managed to fly over to France most afternoons and could eventually write: 'I managed to be present at nearly every important battle during the rest of the war.'

In March 1918, when the Germans opened that last terrible forty-day offensive which cost the British 300,000 casualties, Winston was sent to visit Clemenceau personally. Foch gave them a brilliant exposition of the battle, assured them the Germans were nearly beaten, and kissed Clemenceau on both cheeks in the French fashion. Winston and Clemenceau then set out to visit Army and Corps Commanders. They insisted on driving as far forward as possible. The whine of shells overhead seemed to assuage these two excitable tigers in their car decorated with satin tricolors.

Meanwhile Montagu Porch obtained three weeks' leave and Jennie asked if he would care to visit Leonie in Ireland. With Seymour as a kind of chaperone, they drove to gloomy Euston and caught the Irish Mail. Arriving at Dublin next morning Seymour procured seats in a brand new breakfast car where to their surprise and delight they could tuck into a proper Irish breakfast—bacon and eggs and porridge and cream! Arriving at Castle Leslie in the depths of Monaghan forests, Jennie looked so radiant that Irish neighbours (who had little else to talk about) commented and gossiped. A horse-drawn brougham transported them from the tiny sham-Gothic station through large sham-Gothic gates, and Leonie, leading her sister to the best bedroom overlooking a silent, silvery lake, re-marked: 'Jennie—you look happy and settled.' The Irish maids scampered about, the cook produced her best dishes and the creaky old butler carved and served. Fresh from English rationing, Jennie exclaimed at the unwonted spectacle of legs of lamb every day for lunch, and rabbit pie every night for dinner.

How deceptively quiet Ireland seemed in those days, waiting in anger after the 'swindle' of the postponed Home Rule Bill and the repression of the 1916 Easter Rising. While the Western Front roared in its last hateful churn-up of human flesh, the woods here contained a primeval peace. Leonie seemed sad in the big house which Norman would never return to, but she drove her guests around the county and encouraged Jennie to accept Montagu Porch if she wished. 'Well, you know I couldn't marry a man of my own age so what am I to do?' reasoned Jennie.

With Seymour and eight old gardeners they marched out to see Mr Porch plant a 'Holy Thorn' brought from his own country home at Glastonbury. This visit, dated 28th March to April 15th, 1918, in the visitors' book, sealed the curious romance.

They travelled back to England technically engaged and London gossiped unkindly. Lady Cynthia Asquith records the sour witticisms of George Moore who had often been a guest in Jennie's house and adds: 'Porch has been in love with her for five years. She *said* she was not in love with him but suffers very much from loneliness and wishes for a companion. She says: "He has a future and I have a past so we should be all right." '

On June 1st, 1918, Winston and her two daughters-in-law were witnesses at Jennie's third marriage. Winston could only snatch an hour off to attend at Paddington registry office. Clementine and Gwendoline arrived first and found a charlady scrubbing the steps. 'And which of you two is the bride?' she asked quizzically. The daughters-in-law looked at each other in confusion. 'Neither— *we* are married to the bride's sons.'

But Jennie in a pale grey suit with a green velvet hat made a splendid entrance. She looked unbelievably youthful and before he hurried back to Munitions Winston shook Montagu Porch's hand and in his artless way exclaimed, 'I know you'll never be sorry you married her!'

33

Peace came in November 1918 finding Jennie happily married, Winston a moderately appeased Minister for Munitions and Jack a field officer wearied by danger and discomfort. Jennie had moved house for the last time. She was now in 8 Westbourne Street near Kensington Gardens, and here she took part in the first tentative efforts to re-establish a life in that London where the clip-clop of horses' hooves had been entirely replaced by the hum of car engines.

Many of the old aristocrats never reappeared: they remained in their country estates grieving over lost sons or they disliked the new mixed society. The three Edwardian figures who found they could accept the emergent pattern were Jennie, Leonie and Margot Asquith. Instead of sighing for past splendours Jennie delighted in the new moods and new freedoms. Her nature was uncensorious and full of curiosity. She even thought the unrestrained dances which were emanating from America were fun, and she amazed one of her luncheon parties who were arguing the point by jumping up crying; 'But you *must* all learn the Boston Trot—watch me!' And she proceeded to give a spirited demonstration.

Leonie could never recover entirely from the loss of her son Norman, but with her gaiety and grace of spirit it was impossible that she should not emerge from the Irish mists and draw original minds to her dinner table. Like Jennie she tended to discard people of her own age as 'tedious'. She had so much to give to the young— wisdom, advice, humour, philosophy. She said: 'It is important to create an atmosphere in which people revive. You must never

335

think of yourself. You must learn to help people to manage their own thoughts—you must make yourself have happy thoughts— don't dare be depressed. It's against the rules.'

Perhaps with this in mind Jennie decorated the interior of 8 Westbourne Street. It was full of her 'inventions'. The drawing room she papered with artificial wood-panelling: 'Such a clever idea—you can sponge it after pea-soup fogs', and the curtains were of golden brocade. Her daughter-in-law Goonie was bidden to guess the secret of the net curtains glimmering throughout the house—'They are dyed yellow to give an impression of sunshine! We've all been through hell and now we must cheer up. Of course we know the sun isn't always shining but we must pretend it is!' The electric-lamp bulbs were also tinted and everyone looked rosy— 'But you can't see to read,' complained her sons. Beautiful objects filled every corner. Some of the furniture carried memories of Connaught Place in the days when Randolph led the Fourth Party— the big bookcase had seen him meet Parnell and heard him prac- tising the terse, fiery speeches which were so surely leading him to the Premiership. But Jennie's individual and ever-evolving taste made each of her houses quite different. Since Salisbury Hall, Jennie had banned tablecloths. Now her long marble dining table carried mats for each place and although people were wont to criticise her 'theatrical taste' they were copying her. The two Amazonian parlourmaids, now wearing long black skirts and elegantly tailored striped jackets, remained as an economy, but they added an exotic touch by burning incense in large iron spoons before announcing the meal.

Seymour attended one of her first luncheon parties. It was for Goonie, the Portuguese ambassador de Soveral, and Lady Cynthia Asquith. He reported that talk was all of the embassies going into top gear after four years' gloom, of the declared independence of young girls and of Lady Sarah Wilson's 'pluck' in travelling abroad without a lady's maid.

On another occasion Jennie amused Lord Acton by contradicting the phrase, 'The woman who hesitates is lost.' 'That's nonsense,' she said. 'The woman who does *not* hesitate is lost.' Every type of person attended these luncheons. One May day she invited Sir Sefton Brancker, a leading light in the new Ministry of Civil Aviation. Talk turned to the possibility of air travel becoming

336

quite usual. 'I must see what flying is like,' insisted Jennie, and Brancker drove her and Seymour to Hendon where he flew them in a small D.H.4—'An extraordinary experience', wrote Jennie. 'Right above the clouds in a little coupé'.

Covent Garden Opera House, long used as a furniture store, was cleared and dusted. Melba, whom Jennie had known for many years, returned to sing, and the excitement of Diaghilev's ballets and of new trends in painting created a small renaissance for those who could care. Jennie's interest in the theatre and music had never faded. Megan Foster, the Welsh singer, told me that she made her début at some musical soirée just after the war and was trembling with nerves when 'an older woman with extraordinary eyes' came up without introduction and started to converse about the ordeal of performing in public so naturally that her fear melted. 'I learnt afterwards this was Winston Churchill's mother and a few months later I saw her again. She recognised me instantly and I have never forgotten the impact she made on a terrified girl.' Jennie could lend vitality, but only to intellectuals and artists and children. It was no good coming to her with a tale of woe.

In January 1919 Lady Sarah Wilson broke the ice by giving a Victory Ball. Seymour described this to his mother:

> A really fine ball, carpet and awning out, 50 Rolls-Royces, lines of cars down the street in two rows. Archie Clark-Kerr (furious because not asked) complains that at 4 a.m. he was awakened by fearful pre-war shouts of 'Mrs Astor's car'. Champagne supper downstairs, and small tables, front room for Mrs Keppel and bridge, dancing upstairs, emergency buffet in the cedar room. Randolph Wilson 'presented' (What *has* happened to him??) Rows of Churchills; Lord Furness, Goonie, Maud Cunard, Jennie dancing. The Furness cotillion is tomorrow. Jennie tells me Prince Bibesco is engaged to Elizabeth Asquith. Hope expressed she will wash for the wedding. However, intelligence which she has, is preferable to cleanliness! One could make a wife *soignée* by chaff or force but who shall make a stupid wife endurable?

It was early 1919 but the feel of the 'twenties had begun. While the social scene changed, while Jennie met Ravel, Joseph Conrad, Arnold Bennett, Stravinsky, Picasso and Delius, while she 'ate quails' and played mah-jong at Melba's parties, Winston called in vain for generosity to the defeated foe. If Germany was kicked down in the gutter she would rise again in wrath. If generously treated she might become England's friend. As after the Boer War, these pleas for magnanimity only caused resentment, and when in April 1919 Winston attacked the mass atrocities of revolutionary Russia he was mocked for his ducal blood. His words were violent but exact:

> The miseries of the Russian people under the Bolsheviks far surpass anything they suffered under the Czar. The atrocities of Lenin and Trotsky are incomparably more hideous, on a larger scale and more numerous than any for which the Kaiser is responsible.

His voice and that of Maynard Keynes criticising the economic consequences of Versailles went unheeded.

For a time Jennie and Monty Porch went out to 'every lighted candle', but although they were perfectly happy *à deux*, and the young did not care about the difference in their sixty-four and forty-one years, he felt sensitive to the scathing comments of older people. 'Better the mosquitoes of Africa than the pricks of London drawing rooms,' Porch was heard to remark, and at intervals he returned to business in Nigeria.

'But we look so well together,' Jennie would insist. 'So lucky your hair went white when you were young—it's really much whiter than mine.'

Lady Asquith recounts, and this story rings very true, for Porch was a small well-made man, and Jennie had become plump: 'She asked her sister Leonie if she thought they looked absurd together and Leonie's reply was: "Oh you look as if you might over-lay him at any moment."'

Whatever the cracks, Jennie was serene at last. To a letter from George Cornwallis-West she could reply magnanimously:

8 Westbourne Street
Hyde Park

17.6.19.

My dear George,

I heard all about you from Clare therefore was not surprised at your letter—I am glad you wrote . . . and in your heart of

338

hearts you must know that I never could have any but kindly feelings towards you.

I never think of you but to remember all those happy days we spent together . . . I have forgotten everything else. I do wish you all that is best. . . . Peace is an essential of life and if you have that you are on the fair way to happiness. Life is frightfully hard. One's only chance is within oneself—I shall hope to see you again soon. Bless you. . . .

Always your best friend,
Jennie

Years later Ethel Smyth, the composer, whom Jennie and Kinsky had together helped to emerge from her sheltered social background to take on a professional musical career, wrote to Shane Leslie about Jennie's third marriage: 'No one else but she would have dared Fate to do its damnedest in such a way once more! I don't believe anyone in the world would have had the courage. . . . But I wish she had married Kinsky! He was so delightful. . . .'

In September 1919 Jennie agreed to act as co-hostess with an American friend in a large country house party at the Château de Villegenis, ten miles south of Paris. She picked out the personalities of the day, summoned them and gave them ideas. Lady Colefax was to create the best literary salon of the decade and Lady Cunard would become a famous figure in her way, presiding at Covent Garden Opera with George Moore and Sir Thomas Beecham as her obedient pets for many a year. Stephen McKenna, the novelist, and Sir Walter Raleigh, the scholar, enlivened the mornings, while every afternoon Jennie could drive into Paris to see old friends like Bernard Berenson.

Jennie's houses overflowed with treasures. She loved antiques and could never resist an exciting 'find'. I can dimly remember going to 8 Westbourne Street with my mother and being shown the doorhandles. They appeared to be of silver, Aladdin-treasure knobs delicious to the touch. 'I have them made out of the backs of old watches,' Jennie was saying. 'Isn't it a good idea—they feel so nice.' 'You like the best of everything, don't you,' my mother laughed. And I wandered from knob to knob stroking each with grubby paws.

Looking back I can see how suitable this particularly exotic touch was to Jennie. Some people slam doors in your face, Aunt Jennie opened them. She might give you a rough time when she was in a temper but she always showed you something exciting. A visit to 8 Westbourne Street slightly resembled Alice's trip with the White Rabbit. The rooms had a feeling of the unexpected.

And amidst the plethora of valuable bric-à-brac, the yellow brocades and new ideas, Aunt Jennie was the one grown-up who never chided when one touched the ornaments, slid down the stairs or tasted the red ink, Her eyes twinkled with amusement; we knew she thought us funny or even rather sweet and this unusual opinion made us adore her. A woman charms children in much the same way she charms men. We who were four, five, six years old at the time felt her magic.

Peregrine Churchill, Jack's youngest son, has given me his memory of a grown-up luncheon party in this house when he was about five. Seated beside his mother he endured as much as he could of adult conversation and then slipped away to bang on the piano next door. His mother hurried angrily after him, but Jennie told her to return to the other ladies and sat down beside her naughty grandson. 'Look,' she said, 'you have been banging only the black notes. Now I am going to play you a tune and tell you its story.' She related the story of Siegfried, playing the themes and then picking out the warning song of the bird. 'Of course, it isn't really a bird singing in the cardboard tree—it is a great big fat soprano like this,' and she puffed out her cheeks and designated voluptuous contours. 'If she really got into the tree all the branches would break so she stands on a box behind the scenes—but it doesn't matter—her voice is so lovely—you mustn't mind singers being fat —you just listen and use your imagination.'

Jennie was oblivious to her luncheon party; intent on the rapturous upturned face of the little boy she continued the legend until her slightly indignant guests called that coffee was getting cold. But Peregrine never forgot. A new world had been opened to him, and in later years whenever he heard the bird music in *Siegfried* the memory of his grandmother would come surging back—acting the story all for his benefit, picking out the easy chords, casting her spell. Peregrine never banged a piano again; he learnt what to do with the black notes.

34

In December 1919 Jennie and her husband re-visited Leonie in Ireland. We children were there at Castle Leslie and I can remember sitting by the fire in my mother's bedroom while Aunt Jennie talked about 'happiness'. Probably they did not realise I was listening, for I caught and repeated some phrase which shocked my grandmother. The nursery brigade had taken a fancy to the gentleman we were instructed to call 'Porchy' and with the innocence of five years I lisped my liking in adult terms. How I used the word 'lover' I do not know, but a chilly silence reigned among the grown-ups, and I was sent back to the nursery on the top floor—out of sight and out of hearing. Looking at Jennie's signature in the Castle Leslie guest book, December 22nd, 1919, to January 15th, 1920, reminds me of this infantile indiscretion.

In February Seymour accompanied Jennie to the wedding of 'Sunny' Marlborough's son Lord Blandford, and wrote a description to his mother. Consuelo Vanderbilt had parted from her Duke so the guests wondered who would receive them in the bleak Marlborough town house in Portman Square. As they lined up on the stairs they were amazed to see the gleaming figure of Queen Mary standing in front of the bride and groom, herself receiving the startled guests, who dropped into sudden curtseys and bows.

Jennie was able to point out interesting pre-war figures to Seymour. There was one well-known figure there, a venerable but aspiring Don Juan whom she labelled memorably, 'They say he is more buzz than bizz'.

341

During the spring and summer of 1920 Jennie devoted a great deal of attention to her niece, that tempestuous 'Frewen gal' who resembled her in many ways. Clare Sheridan, now a war widow with two small children, was trying to earn her living as a sculptress. Lord Wilton had tried to marry her but although she made use of this eligible young man when she had 'flu she craved a free artistic life. During the last icy winter of the war Jennie had written to Leonie after Simon Wilton took Clare to convalesce at Bournemouth: 'He went there and got her rooms. I wish they could get married soon. He is very obstinate and headstrong but very devoted, but I think she tries him highly. He has been nursing her night and day; fills her hot water bottle and sticks it in the bed; gives her medicine and poultices etc. There is neither romance nor vanity on her part. Personally I could not bear it, but Clare never likes to do anything like anyone else. I hear that on coming of age his fortune will really be between 90 and 100 thousand a year!'

But Clare threw him over to become a penniless sculptress studying her art under John Tweed. Her first serious effort was a gigantic war memorial so unconventional in emotional impact that no committee would purchase it. Her first London exhibition was dominated by this huge helmeted figure, entitled 'Victory', wearing an expression of utter exhaustion while a sword fell from the nerveless hand. This realism was not how the smug side of England wished to commemorate the brave dead boys.

Clare's husband, Wilfred Sheridan, had disappeared in 1915 while leading a hand-grenade attack in the same week that Clare's son was born. Though seen to fall, his body was never recovered. The violent loss triggered off in his young widow a desire to live violently, to travel, to create, to write. She had many good friends, of whom the greatest was her cousin Winston—now Minister for War (a safe post in peacetime!) and F. E. Smith—now Lord Birkenhead, Chancellor of the Exchequer. They were the world's best company and both men sympathised with lively, artistic Clare and encouraged her career. They *thought* they understood her. While Clare modelled a bust of Winston he sketched her—which made her cross, for she took her work seriously, but he could always tease her out of the stormy tears to which she was prone. When 'F.E.' invited Clare for cruises on his private yacht, Winston came too. 'Don't worry,' he wrote to Jennie. 'I am her cousin and can hold the candle and be chaperone too.' He was very fond of this tempestuous relation. Neither he nor Lord Birkenhead realised how resentfully she smouldered. Clare enjoyed the drama of trying to earn a living but she did not enjoy existing on a small widow's pension in between exhibitions. Jennie, who felt very close to her, wrote warningly to Leonie about bubbling Jerome blood—'the spark has lain dormant in Clara but come out in Clare'. She did all she could to help, praising her talent and urging important people to visit Clare's little studio. 'Don't scorn titles—they bring commissions.' Marble busts of English princesses began to appear among Clare's imaginative bird fountains. She lived in a curious aristocratic Bohemia of her own devising; famous men and royal ladies flocked to her little candle-lit dinners in the studio where there was never quite enough to eat but conversation had to be brilliant. Winston and F.E. continued to spoil this amusing argumentative woman and she talked much about the joy of getting her hands into the clay.

In September 1920 she landed them a jolt. Lloyd George had been anxious to reopen trade relations with Soviet Russia and the first members of a delegation, Kamenev and Zinoviev, arrived in London. They were socially shunned until by chance they met Clare Sheridan. Knowing her important political connections they poured out compliments, and the flattery worked. Clare agreed to do their busts for a substantial fee and during the sittings they hinted that if she returned to Russia with them she could sculpt the men of the moment—Lenin and Trotsky. Like a naughty schoolgirl playing a prank, Clare did not say a word to Winston or to F.E. with whom she spent her last weekend in England. At the end of August she lunched with her aunt and talked happily about her busts of Princess Patricia of Connaught and the Crown Princess of Sweden. Although Jennie's eagle eye noticed an unusual animation, there was no mention of an imminent journey to Moscow in the middle of a terrible civil war.

Only Clare's cousin, Shane Leslie, received her confidences. Having promised secrecy he escorted her to the station and on September 16th, 1920, he wrote to Clare's brother Oswald.

I am very uneasy about the girl. She reached Stockholm with Kamenev and this morning's papers report his arrival with his 'wife'! (His real wife is in Moscow. . . .) However she can take

343

good care of herself and I had such a long serious talk with her the night before she went that I am certain she will not make any liaison, even Platonic, with any of these red harbingers of new Russia. She will go and act as an artist only but Heaven knows when she will be able to get back. . . .

We must keep the matter a dead secret as long as possible. Francis Meynell is here and tells me that there are Govt. spies in the Bolshevist H.Q. so that Winston may learn of her escapade any moment. The old birds will have fits but I can reassure them I think to a certain extent. . . . Anyway keep the matter a dead secret and send me to Talbot Square any letter for the girl, as I have a way of sending her letters by hand.

Yours distractedly,
Shane

The 'old birds', Clare's parents, reacted sharply. Moreton Frewen wrote furious letters to Shane, accusing him of complicity in the plot. 'Now a word about your indiscreet oath to give her a week's start. Is an oath of that kind binding? . . . and after a scene with Winston you divulge at dinner to the three worst women gossips in town that she had not started for Stockholm to sculpt the Crown Princess but with Kamenev to see Lenin in Moscow. . . . Depend upon it that is why Winston is so angry with you. Had you said to him privately, "I am released from my oath. You by a cypher message through the F.O. can have her stopped in Stockholm", then we had saved a daughter and he a scandal.'

Poor Clara, trying to make Sussex neighbours believe that her daughter was off to sculpt the Crown Prince of Sweden, wrote piteously to Leonie. 'Moreton, Oswald and I thought best to keep Clare's doing to ourselves but Jennie writes me that rumours are going about London—we think we must tell *you* and Jennie what is happening—no one else. She *has* gone to Sweden to execute some orders and now writes that she *may* go on to Russia—perhaps to Moscow but we are not to worry about her at all. We three poor things here at Brede are anxious and miserable for if she does go into Russia, Heaven only knows how she will ever get back. She writes me she is just off to see the Crown Prince Gustaf which seems comforting to me. Oswald and I are trying to quiet down Moreton who is frantic!'

Jennie wondered how newspaper reports that Clare had abandoned the Swedish court for the Kremlin could be considered comforting! She trotted around London saying nothing but listening to other people expostulating—that Winston's cousin should run off into Red Russia! Even if the expedition remained impeccably virtuous it was certainly dangerous. Lord Birkenhead was even angrier than Winston. Clare had been going around with them looking so starry-eyed and innocent, playing at being the helpless widow—how could they have dreamed she had this trip in mind? Jennie could not at first believe that Clare, who always confided in her, had quit the company of witty Birkenhead and Winston to tag along with that dismal Russian trade delegation. She had seen Kamenev and Zinoviev in Clare's studio and a less attractive couple of males she could not imagine. To her sister Clara wrote (September 19th, 1920): 'Where *is* Clare? I'm told the rumour in London is that she has gone off with——Kamenev! ! ! ! Ha! Ha! Honestly I was told this seriously. People don't know what to talk about do they?'

Within a week the cat was out of the bag and Jennie and Leonie were devising the best way of twisting the news into less disreputable shape.

Leonie sent tactful letters to her Leslie in-laws. To Olive Guthrie: 'I expect you have heard of Clare's mad escapade of going off to Russia to do Lenin's bust? I hoped it would not be known and have sat here biting my nails and marking time but Jennie writes there are rumours. I had a few lines from Clare on her way, radiant at the prospect, begging me to explain to Moreton and Clara. Clara writes me so quietly. Making every allowance for Clare's love of adventure I do admire her for it. I know you will be a good friend to us all and make light of it. When we meet we can both damn her to our hearts' content.'

Shane enjoyed the uproar and evaded the barrage of reproach, writing to Clare's mother (September 24th, 1920):

. . . It was impossible to dissuade her and as she was armed with a passport from a high friend in the Foreign Office and accompanied by the Secret Service I imagined Winston would have had her turned back at Stockholm. I asked Lord Buckmaster. He said she was perfectly in the law and within her rights in going to Russia and that I could have done nothing. Aunt Jennie says I should have called a policeman but I could only have invoked a White Slave Regulation and I preferred at least to chaperone her departure in a way that made it obviously not an elopement. Besides in respect of the higher law she assured me that there was no intrigue and she is less likely to be made up to in Moscow than in some of the stately homes of England. She goes as an artist. I dissuaded her from wearing jewellery and I hold all her jewels and Wilfred's in my bank in trust for her children.

Opinions hummed between the Jerome sisters in Ireland, London and Sussex. Leonie wrote to Clara on September 24th:

I beg of you not to worry unduly. These things seem so much more terrible at the moment. . . . Her love of adventure and artistic aspirations lead her into rather dangerous experiments but I'm sure she will come out of it all right—particularly if we all keep calm and minimise the whole escapade. I had a few letters from Stockholm and wrote to Jennie as Clare sent her her love— also asked me to comfort the 'old birds'.

But the old birds took no comfort. Oswald replied to Leonie:

Ma and Pa have taken Puss's journey desperately much to heart. One would think there was one woman only in the world and that all eyes were riveted on her. Of course you and I agree that it is unfortunate that she has gone. We also, knowing her, realise that once she meant to go no one could stop her. She left without a passport as it was. Ma talks about 'shutting her up in a room'. I gather Shane is the miscreant who omitted to do this!! In vain I talk of *Habeas Corpus*—what does Ma care for the Magna Carta or the Police? As it is, her friends know. Lady Lavery alone is as good as a gramophone on a house top.

My Government invited Kamenev here, my Prime Minister shook hands with him. So did I. He is the most greengrocerish little bourgeois I ever did it with.

That was what Jennie could not get over—Kamenev and Zinoviev were so unattractive! And the horrors of the Civil War were well known. Clara, fussing herself into a fever when she could no longer conceal the facts, received soothing letters from her sister.

346

She has done nothing dishonourable. She is misguided but it is not for *Family* to turn against her. Darling, if I *may* advise you— say *nothing* or just as little as you can. Put on a brave face and act just as if everything was all right *and* very likely things *will* turn out all right. Clare is a dear, impulsive, illogical artist. They are different beings from the ordinary run of people, and must be judged differently. Besides *why* judge? We are none of us so faultless.

Winston had a forgiving nature, but Clare had put him in the ridiculous position of appearing to send his relations on artistic missions to the Kremlin while he inveighed against the atrocities of the Russian regime. Shane thought fit to warn her of this and wrote to Moscow on November 10th:

I am negotiating privately with *The Times* to take your story which with a little literary camouflage should be the best story out. We are sick of Mrs Asquith. . . . I am afraid it would be difficult to give your busts of the Red Leaders a good exhibition unless you loaned or sold them to Mme Tussauds. You say you wish the common people and not Society to see them. Madame Tussauds is the only place where you could exhibit them profitably and safely today. Agnews decided not to exhibit Kamenev and Krassin in Bond Street. . . . Do stick to Art and Literature and leave politics. . . . And say nothing about poor Winston. Lloyd George chaffs him terribly in the Cabinet about you and he has threatened to put you into quarantine when you return. So tread delicately and print nothing that has not been passed over my typewriter. PS. If you take my advice I may recover caste with the family! There are only three people who will never forgive you. 1. Your father. 2. The Lord Chancellor [Lord Birkenhead] 3. Eddie Marsh [Winston's secretary].

In the bundle of letters concerning Clare's escapade several from her in Moscow to Shane Leslie in London survive. October 11th, 1920:

Not one word of news, either by letter or telegram since I left a month ago today. Yesterday Kamenev sent a wire to you for me —asking for news of the children. . . . This week I did Lenin, spent eight hours in his office. It *was* interesting. I told him about you—he thinks we are funny sort of cousins for Winston to have! . . . I have done Dirjinski, the President of the Extraordinary Commission, and Zinoviev, President of the Petrograd Soviet, and I'm waiting for Trotsky to get back from the front. . . . Am also going to do a typical soldier of the Red Army, and a peasant. . . . H. G. Wells has just been, but everyone agreed that in his lightning trip he can have learnt nothing, and has absorbed none of the atmosphere. The courage and the calm grim determination written on the faces of the people in the street is beyond everything inspiring. . . .

A week later another note creeps in. 'If one were not so conscious of the titanic sub-stratum efforts and work that are emanating from this great centre one would mistake the apparent calm for supreme dullness.'

The boredom and discomfort of 'life at the top' in the Kremlin soon wore down Clare's revolutionary ardour. She walked alone around the bleak streets of Moscow and homesickness crept on her. She scorned England but how she wanted to get back there! Then she wrote:

My two dresses, which are all I brought, are beginning to be shabby. My coat is stained, and my shoes getting worn down. The weather is increasingly cold, and on the coldest days I wrap my travelling rug around my shoulders, so I am now beginning to look more like other people in the street! . . . Tomorrow I am to be given a fur coat from the Government Store, it is a great excitement, and then I shall look respectable again which is perhaps a pity.

When she had finished the busts of Lenin and Trotsky, Clare returned to Stockholm wearing a superb sable coat! She was somewhat hurt that the Crown Prince Gustaf Adolf did not receive her, and back in London social rebuffs were frequent despite the fact that Shane had placed her letters on Bolshevik Russia in *The Times* and launched her on a picaresque career as an international journalist-sculptor.

The Communist leaders did not seem to have filled her pockets with gold and soon after getting home she felt the necessity to sell the sable coat. Somewhat naturally, Winston did not attempt

348

to aid this transaction, but Jennie asked my mother to bring a rich American friend to inspect the coat in her house. I trotted around from Talbot Square with my mother and curiously enough I can remember most of the conversation concerning that coat, even the moral character of the American who bought it. It was typical of Jennie to be ready to help her niece when she was ostracised by London society. In Aunt Jennie's drawing room I saw Clare Sheridan for the first time. She looked wonderful, and I wondered why kings and queens should grow angry because a lady wore a Cossack hat and a red shirt!

35

She was sixty-seven in January 1921, but her *joie de vivre* remained and her life with Montagu Porch, against all prognosis, remained completely happy. When he departed on a trip to Nigeria in the early spring she wrote a letter which he treasured for forty-three years:

March 8, 1921

My darling,

Bless you and *au revoir* and I love you better than anything in the world and shall try and do all those things you want me to in your absence.

Your loving wife,

J.

PS. Love me and think of me.

During Montagu's absence Jennie travelled to Italy to stay with various friends and look for antiques. The Italian spring filled her with delight and she wrote rapturously to Leonie from Florence. Leonie's handwriting has pencilled the first sheet: 'Nearly her last letter to me, so happy, Bless her.'

April 20 1921

I shall come home as good and sweet-tempered as a cherubim. How wonderful is this place! and what fun I am having! It seems positively selfish to be having such a good time and you in Ireland amidst a civil war.

Winston, Clementine and I stayed with the Laverys at Cap

d'Ail and he painted some delightful pictures. Vittoria [Duchess of Sermoneta] met me in her car and I found Rome very gay, races, dances, *antiquaires*. Her *palazzo* charming but not grand like the Colonna palace where I lunched—such magnificence!

They all play bridge *madly* and for very high stakes. I had to stop, you know how badly I play and the Romans are rapacious to a degree!

Fancy my misfortune to meet a 'White' Russian at whose sequestered house Clare stayed in Moscow. She had read Clare's diary of her Russian journey in *The Times* and was very bitter, accusing Clare of having been given her furs by one of the commissars! I still see her scornful furious face. . . .

I have bought some lovely things at the *antiquaires* and there has been a fight between the Fascists and the Communists.

The Duchess of Sermoneta, one of Jennie's oldest friends, took her shopping in Rome and introduced her to a particularly good shoemaker. Jennie had always taken pride in her pretty American feet and ankles—'at least they don't age and the new short skirts are a blessing to us Jeromes'. She bought a pair with very high heels and many years later the Duchess told me that she had a curious foreboding and actually warned Jennie about the height of heel.

Six weeks later, back in England, Jennie went to stay with Lady Horner, the great intellectual hostess who had been worshipped and painted by Burne-Jones in her youth. Now she was living in Mells Manor, a panelled Elizabethan mansion where for three centuries the oak floors and staircase had been wax-polished. Jennie chose an Italian brocade dress for the first night at dinner and her buckled high-heeled Italian shoes. The gong rang before she was ready and she grew fussed with her maid. Edwardian-trained, she was never late for dinner; the time-consuming cocktail did not exist. As she hurried down the slippery staircase she tripped and fell—the ankle, which had given trouble ever since that sprain in Mull so many years ago, snapped and she lay in agony for two hours, begging not to be moved.

Next morning a dreamy country doctor diagnosed multiple fractures and an ambulance drove her back to Westbourne Street. There she lay in the magic house crammed with beautiful things.

351

The piano—unique among Bechsteins in that children were allowed to play it—now was silent. The high-heeled slippers were put away and never worn again. Dr Hartigan, our family doctor, called daily to see her and then came on to my mother, who was awaiting a Caesarian operation at her house in Talbot Square, to regale her with details in a droning chant. Aged seven, I heard all this with horror. Yet more nightmarish was the evening when my mother came back from visiting Aunt Jennie to recount *her* version—'Jennie's leg has turned green and black—I am sure it's gangrene—why can't the doctors see?'

Dear Aunt Jennie—how we hated this lurid picture. And then came worse news. Her leg had been cut off. The servants talked of it unceasingly. She had been a frequent visitor at our house and their versions remain in my mind still. Our governess, a sadistic, religious maniac, trailed us around the park loudly whispering scandal to other custodians of the young. 'A lady ought to wear low heels and long skirts,' she said. 'Her fall resulted from the sin of vanity.'

All this took place in June 1921, a month of blazing heat, a month I hated with forlorn fury. I can remember what the kitchen maid, the housemaid and the nursery maid said about Aunt Jennie. They had no pity! Even at this late hour of her life they luxuriated in the disaster—was it because she had been so beautiful? Twice a day we were marched to the Park past her house but never allowed to go in. Our grandmother arrived from Ireland and hardly left her sister's bedside: 'because nurses were still scarce.'

The terrible, hot, unhappy days rolled by. Our mother—grown unaccountably less attractive to us—seldom called us to her room. We heard that she no longer went to see Jennie because she was awaiting some ordeal of her own. If only one could help these tear-stained grown-ups! But they did not take us into their confidence. The nursery smouldered with half-understood drama.

And through this impenetrable jungle of unhappy grown-ups one kind person stands out—Bourke Cockran! He had come to London with his pretty third wife, Anne, who was my mother's sister. While awaiting the Caesarian operation deemed necessary they had taken Leonie's house, and then as Jennie's condition began to cause anxiety they had to send for her to return from Ireland. Even Uncle Bourke looked distracted, and did not show his usual interest in us, which we resented.

352

Then one morning, the 29th June to be precise, the voice-tube from the basement to our top-floor nursery whistled and a servant's voice said: 'A little brother for you'; half an hour later it rang to say that Lady Randolph Churchill had died. We were taken to the Park 'for air' which we sorely needed. When we saw our grandmother entering Jennie's house we were forbidden to run to her. When a man came out, head bowed, and stepped into a car we were grabbed firmly. 'That's Mr Winston Churchill,' said our gaoler.

From that moment on, no one wanted us anywhere! Certainly not asking questions. Later on an exact account of Jennie's last afternoon on earth would be found in the diary of her nephew, Oswald Frewen, who had come up from Brede on his motor-bicycle.

Tuesday June 28th—Brought up a nice bunch of yellow lilies for Aunt Jane [Jennie] and took them around in the afternoon. The butler said she was getting on well and was, indeed, seeing people, so I sent up to ask if she would see me and she *did*! Aunt Leonie there. She looked her old self, asked after every individual member of my family, even Romey, and was very sweet but kept grimacing with pain. She said she had never realised in her hospital what the men were suffering, and said 'The more it hurts the more those devils of doctors like it: they say it's healing.' Leonie said quite low, 'You mustn't stop too long', and Jennie overheard her and said, 'Oh no, I like to hear you two pussies talking.' However I left soon after.

On the following morning Jennie awoke in good spirits. She awaited with interest the result of our mother's Caesarian and when the nurse brought her breakfast tray she said: 'What's the time? Half past eight! Mrs Leslie is having the operation. I wonder what it will be?' Then she pushed away her tray, cried, 'Nurse, Nurse, I am feeling faint', closed her eyes and never opened them again. An artery had given way and she was in a coma before Winston and Jack could arrive. Leonie had to be notified in the hospital waiting room where she had just learnt of my brother Desmond's birth. My father and Bourke Cockran and his wife, our Aunt Anne, were there with her—all distraught. It was Bourke who drove Leonie to 8 Westbourne Street, where her sister was still breathing. Jennie had not expected to die that day. Leonie felt she was still there wanting to know about the next generation. By noon the news of her death had reached the Press and her sister Clara, travelling from Sussex, learnt of it from the street posters. Oswald returned to the house and recorded:

I had never seen her before without puckers round her mouth, and powder on her nose and flashing eyes full of vivacity. Here the mouth had set, not in a Cupid's bow but in a crescent, corners drooping, grim as a warrior chief and nose emerged aquiline, the wax-like complexion was sallow, the brow noble. It might have been the body of a Roman Emperor or a Redskin Chief. . . .

Winston and Jack stood side by side in the poignant moment when their mother was carried down in her coffin. Clemmie would tell me years later that it was the last weeks of undaunted courage that made her really love Jennie.

On the following day Winston wrote to H.R.H. the Duke of Connaught, the surviving brother of Jennie's 'Prince of Wales'.

2 Sussex Square
June 30, 1921

Sir:

Your Royal Highness's most affectionate letter about my dear Mother has profoundly touched my heart, and I thank you Sir, most earnestly for it, and even more for the lifelong friendship of wh. it is the expression.

It was a cruel disappointment & blow to have this fatal event, just as we were entitled to believe that the immediate danger was surmounted. But since it was to be, I am thankful that her sufferings are at an end and that she sleeps after her life of sunshine and storms.

She looked beautiful yesterday in her coffin. Since the pangs of the morning thirty years had rolled from her brow and one saw again her old splendour of features and expression, without a wrinkle or a trace of pain or weariness she lay as if carved out of marble in the heyday of her beauty.

Poor Leonie had a fearful day yesterday with this intense grief and also her own anxieties. She showed all her greatest qualities.

354

Once more I thank you Sir for all the kindness you have shown to me and mine.

And remain Your Royal Highness's devoted servant,

Winston S. Churchill

Our grandmother was indeed under strain, but she had a kind word for us children and showed us the telegrams from famous people. A few survive; one from Queen Alexandria shows her personal feelings on that long friendship:

No words of mine can express my grief at your beloved sister's too sad and unexpected collapse just when we thought she was getting over her terrible trial please express my most heartfelt sympathy to all her dear ones.

Alexandria

The funeral train left from Paddington Station at 9.45 on the morning of July 2nd. On it travelled Jennie's sons and their wives, her sisters and her nephews Shane and Seymour Leslie and Oswald Frewen, also the ever faithful Walden, Lord Blandford, Eleanor Warrender and a few close friends. Oswald's diary gives an account of Winston fussing over poor Clara and of his pleasure when, on reaching Oxford, he and his mother were led by Winston into the leading motor to drive the last ten miles, 'and we headed the procession to our glee; Ma's because she was getting the honour due to the older sister, mine because the Leslies and Churchills were eating our dust instead of we theirs'. His version describes a 'little quiet gentle country church, a sympathetic parson, boys' and women's voices in choir, the grave lined with white roses and pale mauve orchids'.

Another nephew, Shane Leslie, wrote a different description in a letter to Clare Sheridan two days later.

July 4, 1921

... Your father was too ill to attend but the rest of us went down to Bladon on a stifling hot day—your mother bowed down with grief and supported by Oswald. The sisters gave a large heart worked in roses and we all brought wonderful flowers. Lavery painted the chapelle ardente which I arranged with lights from the Rosary Church. But it was a sad sad business and the service seemed very inadequate to her gifts and character—Either there should have been a Requiem Mass or else a nicely chosen service arranged for the occasion with hymns from the Greek anthology and lessons from Swinburne. But Second Corinthians is inappropriate. However Goonie and I arranged for a Mass to be said the next day and went ourselves. I think she would have liked it much more. The feeling shewn was very considerable and even George West sent a wreath—for auld lang syne. Jack and Winston were like widowers while the poor Porch returns from the end of the world in Nigeria. To Asia, America and Africa it was necessary to cable to reach her relations. Almost to the minute that she died Marjorie had a baby—a son born by Caesarean operation—and both are doing well—*mors januna vitae*—from

Your affec
Shane

On this hot summer day while Jennie was laid beside Randolph in the unknown little graveyard at Bladon, Bourke Cockran took me and my brother Jack to choose what gifts we wished in Harrods toy department. No governess accompanied us, so we had the pleasure of this dear uncle to ourselves, but he seemed absentminded. He allowed me to pick a big tricycle and my brother, ignoring all persuasion to the contrary, chose an enormous drum which he seldom ceased to bang—appropriately but not soothingly—during the next weeks. Money meant nothing to 'Uncle Bourke' and we always chose huge toys when he took us out to buy presents.

In the evening Bourke drove us to see our mother and the little brother Desmond. We knew no more of the facts of life than the facts of death—perhaps less. Great Aunt Jennie had gone away in a big box and baby brother had arrived in a little box—there it was in the corridor outside our mother's room filled with flowers. We stared unenthusiastically into a cot and wondered how so repulsive an object could have issued from such nice tissue paper.

On the following day we saw our weeping grandmother pulling the black band off my father's arm before he went to visit our mother, 'so as not to upset her'. Back and forth daily to the Park we walked, past Jennie's house. We never entered it again. We realised as accurately as the grown-ups what had happened—a live person, a very live person, had departed too soon.

ENVOIE

Jennie said she would live to ninety.

She should have. This would have taken her to 1944—the turn of the tide. With a courage that endeared her to all, she was facing her mutilation with a joke, when unexpectedly the scythe swept.

Many of the characters in this history lived on for years, some through the Second World War, a few to watch Winston's gun-carriage drawn through a silent London to St Paul's. Leonie survived until 1943 and up to the day of her death England's great war leader was exchanging affectionate telegrams with his favourite aunt. Bourke Cockran visited us every summer until he died. George Cornwallis-West finally found happiness with a young wife. Montagu Porch lived until this book was begun in 1965. Jennie's nephews, Hugh Frewen, Shane Leslie and Seymour Leslie, have given their own versions of their unusual aunt. Shane, my father, penned this sketch of her: 'The thin wispy clouds veiling and un-veiling the moon in a high wind remind me of Jennie being dressed and undressed by weeping Lady's maids before a stormy departure to a party.'

Jennie's leather-bound music books still lie beside the piano at Castle Leslie. The music of her personality lasted long after she had been laid away. There were discords of course; she was easy to criticise, but she was human and the warmth of her spirit emanates even now from the letters in her clear open handwriting. I have liked to touch the things that were hers, the letters and objects, the book of memoirs inscribed to 'The best and dearest of sisters'.

Sometimes I feel Jennie might have fared better in a more heroic epoch. There was not really enough for a woman of her calibre to to do in Victorian England. Recently she has been harshly exposed for sending Winston to a dreadful private school—but she did not choose that school and she took him away when she realised its beastliness. *The other parents left their sons.*

For ten years of her young life Jennie took it for granted that her husband must be Prime Minister. For twenty years she was sure her son would lead his country. She had to live on expectation. Jennie's faults help to make her amusing. She can't be whitewashed —she never sits still! But no malice and no envy mar her story. She loved and lost and wept and loved again. Hers is the tale of a proud head that never bowed to misfortune.

𝕏 INDEX

369